T0385676

THE LIVES OF LATIN TEXTS

THE LIVES OF LATIN TEXTS

PAPERS PRESENTED TO
RICHARD J. TARRANT

EDITED BY

LAUREN CURTIS

AND

IRENE PEIRANO GARRISON

Department of the Classics, Harvard University
Cambridge, Massachusetts
Distributed by Harvard University Press
2020

The Lives of Latin Texts: Papers Presented to Richard J. Tarrant
Loeb Classical Monographs 19
Copyright © 2020, President and Fellows of Harvard College. All Rights Reserved.
Published by The Department of the Classics, Harvard University
Distributed by Harvard University Press, Cambridge, Massachusetts, and
    London, England
Editors: Lauren Curtis and Irene Peirano Garrison
Compositor: Ivy Livingston
Cover designer: Joni Godlove
Printed by Sheridan Books, Inc., Ann Arbor, MI

Library of Congress Cataloging-in-Publication Data

Names: Tarrant, R. J. (Richard John), 1945- | Curtis, Lauren, 1984- editor. |
    Peirano, Irene, 1979- editor.
Title: The lives of Latin texts : papers presented to Richard J. Tarrant / edited
    by Lauren Curtis and Irene Peirano Garrison.
Other titles: Loeb classical monographs ; 19.
Description: Cambridge : Department of the Classics, Harvard University, 2021. |
    Series: Loeb classical monographs ; 19 | Includes bibliographical references. |
    Summary: "The papers in this volume are based on a 2018 conference in
    the Department of the Classics at Harvard University in honor of Richard
    Tarrant, Pope Professor of the Latin Language and Literature, on the
    occasion of his retirement. The breadth of authors, genres, periods, and
    topics addressed in The Lives of Latin Texts is testament to Richard Tarrant's
    wide-ranging influence on the fields of Latin literary studies and textual
    criticism. Contributions on stylistic, dramatic, metapoetic, and philosophical
    issues in Latin literature (including authors from Virgil, Horace and Seneca
    to Ovid, Terence, Statius, Caesar and Martial) sit alongside contributions on
    the history of textual transmission and textual editing. Other chapters treat
    the musical reception of Latin literature. Taken together, the volume reflects
    on the impact of Richard Tarrant's scholarship by addressing the expressive
    scope and the long history of the Latin language"-- Provided by publisher.
Identifiers: LCCN 2021015052 | ISBN 9780674260481 (hardcover)
Subjects: LCSH: Latin literature--History and criticism--Congresses.
Classification: LCC PA6011 .L58 2021 | DDC 870.9--dc23
LC record available at https://lccn.loc.gov/2021015052

CONTENTS

PART III. MUSIC

EDITORS' PREFACE

THIS VOLUME, which we present with gratitude, admiration, and affection to Richard J. Tarrant on the occasion of his retirement, results from a conference held in Richard's honor at the Department of the Classics at Harvard University on 21–22 September 2018. It has been augmented by several papers by friends, students, and colleagues who could not be present at the original conference but who wanted to be part of this more permanent and equally heartfelt celebration in print.

The wide range of authors, genres, periods, and topics addressed by the contributors are testament to Richard's tremendous and lasting influence on the fields of Latin literary studies and textual criticism. The authors to whom Richard has devoted, and indeed continues to devote, much of his career—Seneca, Virgil, Horace, and Ovid—are all represented. So are Latin authors from Terence and Caesar to Martial and Statius. A sizeable number of the contributors have, fittingly, chosen to honor Richard in essays on textual editing and the history of textual transmission; others focus on interpretive issues, whether stylistic, dramatic, metapoetic, or philosophical. Still others were inspired by Richard's love of music, and address the musical reception of Latin literature from Giuseppe Verdi to Bob Dylan and Anaïs Mitchell. Taken together, these essays consider the manifold ways in which the Latin language and its literary traditions were and continue to be woven into people's lives—from the medieval schoolroom to the Roman Republican stage, and from ancient graffiti to modern musical theater. As such, they speak to Richard's contributions not just as a leading scholar of Latin poetry, but also as a teacher who has inspired generations of graduate and undergraduate students to appreciate and grapple with the expressive scope and the long history of the Latin language.

We would like to extend our warmest thanks to the Department of the Classics at Harvard University, and especially to Kathleen Coleman, Chair of the Department, for their generous support of the conference and of this ensuing volume. Thanks to Sarah Eisen, Alyson Lynch, and Teresa Wu for their magnificent work in organizing the conference, to Jarrett Welsh who co-organized it with us, and to the many students, colleagues, and friends of Richard who are not represented in these pages but who chaired sessions, participated in discussion, and helped make it such a memorable occasion. In putting together the volume, we thank Annika Fisher for copyediting, Claire Saint-Amour for help in preparing the manuscript for publication, and Ivy Livingston for ushering it through production. Kathleen Coleman compiled the bibliography of Richard's work, for which we are very grateful.

Our final and most important words of thanks must go to Richard himself, teacher, mentor, and friend to both of us.

LAUREN CURTIS, BARD COLLEGE
IRENE PEIRANO GARRISON, YALE UNIVERSITY

RICHARD TARRANT

SCHOLAR, TEACHER, AND COLLEAGUE

Kathleen M. Coleman

Richard Tarrant (R. J. Tarrant, as he is registered in library catalogues) is a scholar of ancient literature, especially but not exclusively literature in Latin. He is interested in the history and influence of these texts through the entire extent of their transmission, and takes their subsequent readers seriously, rather than regarding them as intellectually inferior to the ancient authors themselves. As well as a literary historian, he is an expert in textual transmission and criticism, viewing ancient texts against their contemporary background and illuminating their linguistic and literary qualities, both in detail and on a broader canvas.

In this brief and selective appraisal, I shall do no more than gesture at some of the highlights, beginning with a genre very illuminating of a scholar's qualities: the book review. Clearly, an editor and commentator who constituted an entirely new text of Seneca's *Agamemnon* would be an obvious candidate to review a study of meter in Latin comedy. Richard's review of *Die Cantica des Plautus* by Ludwig Braun appeared in the same year in which he submitted the manuscript of *Agamemnon* to Cambridge University Press.[1] Given that journals do not print submissions right away, Richard evidently took on this review while finishing his own book, surely an act of selflessness, given the extremely technical nature of the topic and the even more technical nature of Braun's treatment. Richard's review, like the rest of his output in this genre,

---

This appraisal is based upon the opening remarks delivered at the colloquium in honor of Richard Tarrant on September 21, 2018, held by the Department of the Classics, Harvard University.

[1] Tarrant 1974a.

is a model of lucidity and learning, delivered without self-regard or posturing. Notably and typically, it conceals an acute conjecture in the *Truculentus* in a polite remark querying the palaeographical rationale for Braun's own more drastic conjecture at the same place in the text.[2]

As with Braun's book on the *cantica* of Plautus, Richard was an obvious person to review Frank Goodyear's Cambridge "Orange" commentary on Tacitus, *Annals* I, not least because of Goodyear's focus on textual issues. This review, too, appeared in 1974, the year in which Richard submitted his own "Orange" edition of *Agamemnon* to Cambridge University Press.[3] It is a stern review, but fair; quite apart from Richard's wise and knowledgeable assessment of many of the difficulties in Tacitus's text, and the singularity of the style, he has clearly thought harder about the needs of the users of a commentary than Frank Goodyear did. But he is generous, too, in acknowledging the excellence of Goodyear's earlier work on Tacitus. Richard's own profound thinking about the transmission of the *Annals* and the *Histories*—which hangs by some of the most fragile threads in the history of textual transmission—subsequently reaches fruition in his entries in the canonical *Texts and Transmission*, to which he was a major contributor.[4]

Richard's commentaries on the *Agamemnon* and *Thyestes* of Seneca have proven to be landmarks in helping us understand the nature of Seneca's tragedies, as well as the intricate difficulties of those particular plays. They also offer guidance on broader issues, such as the fraught decisions about spelling that confront all editors of Latin texts: Richard's appendix on orthography in his commentary on *Agamemnon* sets forth editorial principles concerning such dilemmas as whether to contract *-ii-* or assimilate prefixes; every fledgling editor could read it with profit, along with the addendum in his edition of *Thyestes* about euphony as a guiding principle in choosing between accusative plurals in *-is* and *-es*

---

[2] Tarrant (1974a:142) proposes to emend *cruciantque* at *Truc.* 450 to *crucianturque* instead of Braun's *quam cruciamur.*
[3] Tarrant 1974b.
[4] Tarrant 1983. Richard, one of six main contributors, also composed the entries on six major poets (Catullus, Propertius, Horace, Ovid, Lucan, and Juvenal), two dramatists (Plautus and Seneca [tragedies only]), and the *Anthologia Latina.*

in i-stem nouns and adjectives of the third declension.[5] Similarly, his appendices on colometry in both commentaries—especially his treatment of polymetric *cantica*—provide templates for editors of metrically challenging texts.[6]

Richard's *Thyestes*, published in 1985, goes even further than his *Agamemnon* in enabling modern readers to understand the richness of Seneca's language and, in Richard's words, his "complex stylistic repertory."[7] Whereas *Agamemnon* is aimed at scholars, *Thyestes*, published in a textbook series, is explicitly directed toward students, and offers a limpid introduction to all the fundamentals, including a succinct three pages on the transmission and reception of Seneca's tragedies.[8] If students are to read only one piece of scholarship on Seneca the tragedian, it should surely be these four dozen pages. Many of us— not only students—are probably baffled by the difficulty of imagining the plays on the Roman stage. Richard's compact treatment of the conundrum of performance helps us to grasp that reading was itself a form of performance in the Roman context and that the distinction between "reading" and "performing" a play is something of a chimaera in a world in which oratory, declamation, and reading aloud were the cultural norm. Most compelling of all, he issues a clarion call for the relevance of this text to his contemporary audience: "The vision of the *Thyestes* may even seem appallingly prophetic in an age when, as never before in history, paranoiac suspicion and the unbounded drive for power can literally consume the world."[9]

Richard's interest in writing commentaries is confined neither to his earlier career nor to Seneca. His deeply sensitive commentary on *Aeneid* XII has justly been awarded the Goodwin Award from the Society for Classical Studies *and* the Premio Virgilio from the Accademia Nazionale Virgiliana, the latter a measure of the international stature

---

[5]   Tarrant 1976a:363–368; 1985a:38.
[6]   Tarrant 1976a:369–381; 1985a:245–249. For a basic introduction to Senecan meter, see Tarrant 1985a:27–33.
[7]   Tarrant 1985:25.
[8]   Tarrant 1985a:1–48.
[9]   Tarrant 1985a:48.

of his work.[10] This commentary is a particular _tour de force_, partly because of the constraints of the Cambridge "Green and Yellow" series in which it appeared. Although working within a strictly enforced word limit, Richard's treatment never feels rushed. The balance that he achieves in the introduction could only be the result of long years spent thinking about the text, its Latinity, and its place in the Roman literary tradition. The conundrum of the final scene of ruthless killing has generated many explanations and defies them all. Richard guides us to think about it in terms of a tension that has to be held in equilibrium, but he simultaneously admits that no human response can sustain such ambivalence at any given moment. In drawing out the nuance and profundity that Virgil displays in every phrase, he never loses sight of the contemporary reader—in itself an example of equilibrium that is very hard to achieve in that most scholarly of endeavors, the philological commentary.

If a commentary holds up a mirror to the text, it also reflects the commentator, and three sections of the introduction to _Aeneid_ XII are perfect distillations of some of Richard's special interests. The section on "Sequels and Continuations" begins with Ovid and reaches a climax with the _Supplementum_ (also known as Book 13) published by Maffeo Vegio in 1428. This section contains, incidentally, a delicious example of Richard's occasional use of a colloquial phrase that nails the text as no formal pedantry could, when he explains the Anna Perenna episode in _Fasti_ 3 as follows: "In this account A[eneas]'s marriage to Lavinia becomes a sort of posthumous revenge for Dido; having abandoned one frenzied and vengeful woman, A. is now saddled with another."[11] The section on "Afterlife"—just three pages—is a cameo product of Richard's very considerable knowledge of European art and music, and the modestly entitled section, "Some Aspects of Virgil's Metre," combines the technicalities that students need to know with an evocative discussion of some of the emotional effects that Virgil conveys

---

[10] Tarrant 2012a. For the citation for the Goodwin Award in 2013, see https://classicalstudies.org/awards-and-fellowships/goodwin-citation-richard-tarrant. For the citation for the Premio Virgilio in 2015, see http://www.accademianazionalevirgiliana.org/images/virgilio14/premiati15.pdf.

[11] Tarrant 2012a:30.

by his disposition of dactyls and spondees or the presence or absence of elision. And Richard conveys it all with a Virgilian combination of economy and grace.

In his introduction, Richard quotes John Sparrow's remark about the necessarily tralatician quality of modern commentaries on Virgil, and then refutes this judgment, but he is explicit about his debt to commentators from the 17th-century Jesuit to the "alliterative triumvirate" (as he puts it) of Hardie, Harrison, and Horsfall.[12] Yet, on every page he brings us fresh insight into Virgil's text or makes us sit up and think with a novel comment about Roman habits of thought, as when, in conjunction with Turnus's prayer to Faunus and Terra (777–779), he remarks that one might expect ancient suppliants addressing a god to contrast their piety with the lack of respect shown by others, as Turnus does here. But Richard disarmingly—and thought-provokingly— confesses that the only parallel he can find is the prayer of the Pharisee in the Gospel according to Saint Luke.[13] His comments on Latin usage, too, can suddenly open our eyes, as with his remark on the penultimate line of the *Aeneid*, which begins with the adjective *feruidus*—a strong enjambement from the previous line, describing Aeneas plunging his sword into Turnus's body—and then continues with the phrase *ast illi*, suddenly shifting the focus to Turnus himself, as a chill descends on his limbs and his lifeforce escapes with a groan to the shades: Turnus's ally Juno, Richard reminds us, uses the combination *ast ego* in her two most prominent appearances, in *Aeneid* I and VII. Every reader of Richard's commentaries will have a favorite "Aha!" moment, when one of his notes shows them something breathtaking that they have never seen in a familiar text before.

We all have our dreams of discovering a lost manuscript or (less charitably) finding a new piece of a fragmentary inscription that will prove all of Theodor Mommsen's supplements to the original piece wrong—as Arthur Gordon actually managed to do in 1950, when he pieced together two fragments of the *Laudatio Turiae* and found that

---

[12] Tarrant 2012a:42, quoting Sparrow 1931:138–139.
[13] Luke 18:11–12.

out of eight lines, Mommsen had supplemented only one correctly.[14]
But dreams of serendipity are, of course, the refuge of the lazy and the
ignorant. It is sheer learning and hard work that achieve most of the
breakthroughs in classical scholarship—and piecing together those two
fragments of the *Laudatio Turiae* took someone with the breathtaking
epigraphic knowledge and expertise of Gordon. No lesser expertise lies
behind Richard's spectacular redating of the *Copa*, a 38-line poem in
the *Appendix Vergiliana* about a Roman country tavern. By scrupulous
analysis of its language, he has managed to shift its date by nearly a
century from a period just after Propertius to the time of Statius and
Martial, thereby removing the problem of its un-Augustan treatment of
the elegiac couplet and other difficulties besides.[15]

Sustained attention to an author's entire oeuvre by the most alert
and open-minded scholars can sometimes refute a prejudice so long
held that it has become a canonical judgment repeated in every handbook and introduction. The Elder Seneca is ultimately responsible for
the patronizing verdict that Ovid allowed his rhetorical training to get
the better of his literary taste. No, Richard contends, Ovid throughout
his oeuvre employs the tropes of persuasive rhetoric to expose its ultimate failure to persuade, the exception being the *Fasti*, where speeches
of persuasion are notably absent. In making this argument, Richard
takes the reader chronologically through Ovid's works, demonstrating
how each time a mouthpiece—either the authorial persona or a character in the narrative—delivers a *suasoria*, it fails, either immediately or
subsequently, and Ovid conveys the failure with increasing subtlety in
his successive works, always with ironic intent.[16]

Not only does this article offer an alternative explanation for a
feature whose interpretation has hardly been questioned for two thousand years; composed to celebrate the 75th birthday of Donald Russell,
it also belies the commonplace that Festschriften are the ultimate
repository for odds and ends that their authors dredge up in response
to invitations to contribute to honorific miscellanies (the present

---

[14] Gordon 1950.
[15] Tarrant 1992.
[16] Tarrant 1995d.

volume, naturally, excepted). Richard's contribution fits precisely at the intersection between ethics and rhetoric that is embodied in the title of the collection. It flows seamlessly, building the argument paragraph by paragraph, uncluttered by superfluous quotation, and relegating to lively and pertinent footnotes a discriminating selection of annotations. Richard is readable, as few scholars truly are.

A scholar is not known to future generations only by what he or she writes—at least, not any more. If the preservation of digital media keeps up with technological advances, students of Latin textual criticism who have not had the privilege of being present in Richard's classroom will be able to watch a series of short videos on the website of the Digital Latin Library to learn how he identifies and explains the particular form of textual corruption represented by interpolation.[17] With consummate clarity, Richard delivers an account of a type of scribal intervention in a text whose identification is in many ways one of the most distinctive features of his editorial practice. The scholarly world gasped at the skill—as well as the audacity—with which he excluded more lines of the *Metamorphoses* from his Oxford Classical Text than anyone of comparable sanity had ever done before.[18] And, characteristically, Richard seeks reasons for interpolation other than the assumption that the interpolator was motivated by a malevolent desire to steal the author's identity and claim it for his work—in other words, forgery. Instead, Richard identifies a particular type of interpolation that he calls "collaborative," where the interpolator has expanded upon the author's thought and expression. This he traces to the ancient practice of *imitatio* and skill in verse composition, cultural practices at odds with our notion of the sanctity of the authorial original. These ideas are developed in *Texts, Editors, and Readers*, Richard's superb contribution to the influential series from Cambridge University Press, *Roman Literature and its Contexts*. Richard's concept of "collaborative interpolation" is set out in a prior essay entitled "The Soldier in the Garden and Other Intruders in Ovid's *Metamorphoses*,"

---

[17] https://digitallatin.org/digital-latin-library/video-library/tarrant.
[18] Tarrant 2004a. The treatment of interpolation is singled out for detailed evaluation and praise by Possanza 2005.

a typically witty title that alludes in this instance to a line in Ovid's account of the attempted seduction of Pomona in her garden by the shape-shifting god, Vertumnus.[19] But hearing these theories and examples expounded on video in Richard's incomparable voice, rather than reading them on the printed page, may well have more immediate impact on generations brought up in front of a screen.

Video is performance, and like any good performer, Richard makes maximum use of facial expression and hand gestures in his videos on interpolation that were commissioned by the Digital Latin Library. Near the beginning of the first one, the gesture with which he illustrates a "confusion of letters" in a manuscript is unforgettably vivid. Even if readers do not know that he is a singer, they can guess it from the beautiful resonance of his speaking voice, to which I have already alluded, and they can hear his musician's ear behind the cadences of his writing. His lecture course "The Rome of Augustus" was a staple of the Core Curriculum at Harvard College for many years, and subsequently of the Program in General Education. One can only imagine what it must have been like to sit with seven hundred other students in Sanders Theater and hear Richard, together with Paulette Curtis, a graduate student from Anthropology, sing a duet from Purcell's *Dido and Aeneas* in the year in which Tom Jenkins, an accomplished pianist (and the author of an article in this volume), was the Head Teaching Fellow in the course. The students were enchanted. The contribution that Richard made to the dissemination of knowledge about the ancient world among generation after generation of undergraduates via "The Rome of Augustus" is an aspect of his service to the profession for which his colleagues feel special gratitude; teaching large numbers of non-specialists through the medium of translation is no easy task, and it requires a special act of empathy. Richard's capacity to interpret classical antiquity in an idiom familiar to these students might surprise people who would not imagine him describing Catullus and Licinius Calvus in Poem 50 sharing a "jam session."

If all teaching is performance, it should not be assumed that Richard's thespian career is confined to a place behind the lectern. In

[19] Tarrant 2016a; 2000.

2003 he starred in the role of the *Senex* in the *Menaechmi* of Plautus in a production to mark the resurrection of the hitherto moribund Harvard Classical Club. His performance was unforgettable. The investment of time and effort in learning all those lines and attending all those rehearsals is something to be remembered and appreciated when the time comes to evaluate the legacy of a scholar who might understandably have preferred to dedicate those many hours to the *limae labor* of scholarship, rather than contributing to the outreach value of an undergraduate venture.

Contributions to teaching beyond the classroom are not confined to the performative; alongside the videos that I hope will survive the vicissitudes of technological progress to enlighten future generations about interpolation, we should also count Richard's recent entry in the digital series *Oxford Bibliographies* on "Transmission of Greek and Latin Literature." As anyone who has contributed an Oxford Bibliography knows full well, these undertakings are fenced around by rules: each section *must* have an introductory paragraph that *must not* be more than four hundred words long; no section may be subdivided further than sub-subsections; no section, subsection, or sub-subsection may comprise more than ten entries; no entry may include a description longer than 70 words. We should rightly be impressed that one of Richard's sections has 14 entries; it is a brave scholar who defies the editor of *Oxford Bibliographies*. But his bibliography is not simply an example of selfless labor to the profession. It also demonstrates his far-reaching expertise in the transmission of Greek texts, as well as Latin, and the almost miraculous economy of his descriptions; only one entry comes anywhere close to the permitted word limit, and yet every entry is comprehensible and stylishly expressed. A further characteristic of Richard's scholarship, which is visible throughout his work, is also vividly on display here: the depth and breadth of his scholarly reading. His references in all his work are a judicious distillation of the scholarship on any particular topic, never a superficial "presentist" parade of the most recent publications, but also never neglectful of new work, while drawing attention to the value of the pioneers who have gone before—even centuries before.

Philologists sometimes have the reputation of being dry and pedantic, the epitome of Yeats's scholars bleaching the passion out of Catullus: "Old, learned, respectable bald heads / Edit and annotate the lines ... All shuffle there, all cough in ink; / All wear the carpet with their shoes."[20] But not all philologists fit the stereotype. Richard's writing, in particular, has the same lively sense of humor—an impish delight in absurdity, incongruity, and verbal wit—that many of his colleagues have observed on occasions as intrinsically unfunny as faculty meetings. His trailblazing article on parenthesis in Latin (and Greek) poetry has the delicious title, "Parenthetically Speaking (in Virgil and Other Poets)."[21] It is in this regard, as well as for their intrinsic value, that his indexes repay close attention: who else, compiling an index for *Aeneid* XII, would assemble under the letter *G* the following sequence: "gaze, Gellius, genitive, *Georgics*, Giordano, gladiatorial language or motifs, golf clubs"? This last entry is adduced not once but twice, first as Conway's example of the difficulty of carrying two of them in one hand, like Aeneas balancing his spears *bina manu lato crispans hastilia ferro* (*Aen.* 12.165), and then to argue the point about Turnus's "betrayal" by his sword (*perfidus ensis*, 731), which others, notably David West, have felt implausible;[22] Richard claims that an experienced warrior knows his weapon as intimately as a golfer knows his clubs.

In another genre, that of the encyclopedia entry, Richard's work is perpetually illuminated by a sympathy with subsequent readers of an ancient text. His entry for Mozart in the *Virgil Encyclopedia* ends by speculating why Mozart did not succumb to the contemporary craze fueled by Metastasio's libretto *Didone Abbandonata* and compose an opera based on the *Aeneid*. The reason, he thinks, is to be found among Mozart's settings of individual *scene* from various of Metastasio's libretti. These scenes include Dido's desperate and conflicted aria "Basta, vincesti ... Ah, non lasciarmi" (Enough, you have won ... Ah, do not leave me). Richard says simply, "Perhaps, having captured this microcosm of Dido's tragedy in music, Mozart saw no need for a

---

[20] William Butler Yeats, "The Scholars," lines 2–8.
[21] Tarrant 1998. Its title is the inspiration for Cynthia Damon's essay in this volume.
[22] West 1974:28–29.

full-scale treatment."[23] Richard has the knack of making us think with him. Even in a slender entry in an encyclopedia, he succeeds in doing that.

Indeed, in all of his writings, Richard's human sympathy is evident and never more so than in his acute appraisal of Charles Segal as a scholar and a colleague in the editorial tribute in the issue of *Materiali e Discussioni* published in Professor Segal's memory two years after his death.[24] The economy and personal feeling with which Richard composed that tribute make Charlie Segal come alive in the memory of those of us who knew him. Powers of observation and depth of personal feeling are necessary to write something so evocative. And it bears pointing out that the task fell to Richard because among his many liturgies for the profession, he is a member of the editorial board of *Materiali e Discussioni*, as he is of the Cambridge "Orange" series and Toronto Medieval Latin Texts. The unwavering standards of those publications undoubtedly owe much to his dedication.

It is hard to imagine the Latin curriculum at Harvard without Richard's signature courses on love elegy or the *Metamorphoses* or Neronian literature; his graduate seminars on the Augustan poets or Latin palaeography; or the many other contributions that he has made to the school's menu of offerings, including the doctoral supervision that has shaped the scholarship of many of the contributors to this book. But in retirement he is continuing to work with graduate students, and we expect the release from regular teaching to increase his output of scholarship, already so prolific. He has just completed a book on the *Odes* of Horace for the series *Oxford Approaches to Classical Literature*. It is fitting that this series was originally conceived by Charles Segal, about whom Richard wrote the moving tribute previously mentioned. It is truly admirable that Richard, a scholar who has so deeply absorbed the range, constraints, character, and behavior of the Latin language, agreed to write a book explicitly aimed at new readers encountering the *Odes* for the first time—and in translation. One might think it impossible to convey the tautness, grace, and

---

[23] Tarrant 2013:855.
[24] Tarrant 2002a.

sophistication of those poems to people unable to read them in Latin, but a prepublication view of the typescript shows Richard employing his characteristic sensitivity and discrimination to guide his readers to an appreciation of the artistry and sensibility that inform these poems. It is an act of dual sympathy: a deep sympathy for Horace and a comparable sympathy for the needs of the modern reader.

It may be relevant to Richard's acceptance of the commission for *Oxford Approaches to Classical Literature* that his very first book—a "pamphlet," according to the series title, but a substantial one of 62 pages—was a bibliographical guide to Greek and Latin lyric poetry in translation.[25] The series is a print predecessor of the *Oxford Bibliographies* mentioned above, comprising introductory paragraphs on individual poets, followed by succinct but substantial appraisal of translations of their works. Richard's treatment shows the same incisive evaluation, occasional delicious colloquialism, and generosity of spirit that characterize the rest of his writing. For instance, on the translation of Catullus by Celia and Louis Zukofsky that aims to reproduce the sound of Catullus and something approximating his sense, Richard's succinct judgment, "Little thought is needed to see that the plan is quite mad," is followed by a generous demonstration that at the phrasal level some of the translations are little short of inspired.[26]

Beyond Richard's new book on the *Odes* lies his forthcoming Oxford Classical Text of the entire oeuvre of Horace. The judgment of Mark Possanza sums up the achievement of his OCT of Ovid's *Metamorphoses*: it is "one of those rare critical editions which effects a permanent improvement of the text and sets a very high standard against which future editions of the poem will be measured."[27] Richard's next OCT will surely be a comparable advance in the editing of Horace, and will stand alongside his *Metamorphoses* as a milestone in the textual history of the Augustan poets. To anyone who knows Richard, it is immediately evident why these two poets—the one the embodiment of wit, the other of refinement—have occupied so much of his attention

---

[25] Tarrant 1972a.
[26] Zukofsky and Zukofsky 1969: see Tarrant 1972a:36–37.
[27] Possanza 2005.

throughout his career. Horace, Ovid, Seneca, and all the other Latin authors on whom he has written, together with the scribes who copied their manuscripts down the centuries, have found in Richard Tarrant an acute and eloquent interpreter, and generations of scholars, students, and readers—past, present, and yet to come—a judicious and inspiring guide.

HARVARD UNIVERSITY

WORKS CITED

Gordon, A. E. 1950. "A New Fragment of the *Laudatio Turiae*." *AJA* 54 (3):223–226.

Possanza, M. 2005. Review of *P. Ouidi Nasonis Metamorphoses*, by R. Tarrant. *BMCR*, June 27, 2005.

Sparrow, J. H. A. 1931. *Half-Lines and Repetitions in Virgil*. Oxford.

West, D. 1974. "The Deaths of Hector and Turnus." *G&R* 21 (1):21–31.

Zukofsky, C., and L. Zukofsky, trans. 1969. *Catullus*. London.

PUBLICATIONS BY R. J. TARRANT

1972a. *Greek and Latin Lyric Poetry in Translation: A Bibliographical Guide.* American Philological Association pamphlets 1. Urbana, IL.

1972b. Review of *Die Gesprächsverdichtung in den Tragödien Senecas*, by Bernd Seidensticker. *Phoenix* 26 (2):194–199.

1973. Review of *Latin Textual Criticism*, by James Willis; and *Textual Criticism and Editorial Technique*, by Martin L. West. *Phoenix* 27 (3):295–300.

1974a. Review of *Die Cantica des Plautus*, by Ludwig Braun. *CP* 69:140–146.

1974b. Review of *The Annals of Tacitus*, vol. 1, by F. R. D. Goodyear. *Phoenix* 28 (3):375–379.

1976a. *Seneca. Agamemnon.* Edited with a commentary. Cambridge Classical Texts and Commentaries 18. Cambridge.

1976b. Review of *Changing Forms*, by Otto Steen Due, and *Ovid's Metamorphoses*, by G. Karl Galinsky. *Phoenix* 30 (3):297–303.

1978a. "Senecan Drama and its Antecedents." *HSCP* 82:213–263.

1978b. "The Addressee of Virgil's Eighth Eclogue." *HSCP* 82:197–199.

1978c. Review of *Aurélius Victor. Livre des Césars*, ed. and trans. Pierre Dufraigne. *Gnomon* 50 (4):355–362.

1979. Review of *Der Thyestes des Lucius Varius Rufus*, by Eckard Lefèvre. *CR* 29 (1):149–150.

1981. "The Authenticity of the Letter of Sappho to Phaon (*Heroides* XV)." *HSCP* 85:133–153.

1982a. "Aeneas and the Gates of Sleep." *CP* 77 (1):51–55.

1982b. "Editing Ovid's *Metamorphoses*: Problems and Possibilities." Review of *P. Ovidi Nasonis Metamorphoses*, by W. S. Anderson. *CP* 77 (4):342–360.

1983. Entries in *Texts and Transmission: A Guide to the Latin Classics* (coauthored with P. K. Marshall, M. D. Reeve, L. D. Reynolds [general editor], R. H. Rouse, and M. Winterbottom): "*Anthologia Latina*," "Catullus," "Horace," "Juvenal," "Lucan," "Ovid,"

"Plautus," "Propertius," "Seneca (*Tragedies*)," "Tacitus (*Annals and Histories*)." Oxford.

1985a. *Seneca's Thyestes*. Edited with introduction and commentary. American Philological Association Textbook Series 11. Atlanta, GA.

1985b. Review of *Seneca's Drama*, by Norman Pratt. *CR* 35 (2):287–289.

1986. "Sophocles, *Philoctetes* 676–729: Directions and Indirections." In *Greek Tragedy and its Legacy: Essays Presented to D. J. Conacher*, ed. Martin Cropp, Elaine Fantham, and S. E. Scully, 121–134. Calgary.

1987. "Toward a Typology of Interpolation in Latin Poetry." *TAPA* 117:281–298.

1989a. "The Reader as Author: Collaborative Interpolation in Latin Poetry." In *Editing Greek and Latin Texts: Papers Given at the Twenty-Third Annual Conference on Editorial Problems, University of Toronto, 6–7 November 1987*, ed. John N. Grant, 121–162. New York.

1989b. "Silver Threads Among the Gold: A Problem in the Text of Ovid's *Metamorphoses*." *ICS* 14 (1/2):103–117.

1991. Review of *L'étude des auteurs classiques latins au xie et xiie siècle*, by Birger Munk Olsen. *Speculum* 66 (4):930–936.

1992. "Nights at the *Copa*: Observations on Language and Date." *HSCP* 94:331–347.

1995a. "Greek and Roman in the Tragedies of Seneca." *HSCP* 97:215–230.

1995b. "The Editing of Classical Latin Literature." In *Scholarly Editing: A Guide to Research*, ed. D. C. Greetham, 94–148. New York. (Also published in a French version: 1993. "L'edition de la littérature latine classique." In *Les problèmes posés par l'édition critique des textes anciens et médiévaux*, ed. J. Hamesse, 1–56. Louvain.)

1995c. "*Da Capo* Structure in Some Odes of Horace." In *Homage to Horace: A Bimillenary Celebration*, ed. S. J. Harrison, 32–49. Oxford.

1995d. "Ovid and the Failure of Rhetoric." In *Ethics and Rhetoric*, ed. Doreen Innes, Harry Hine, and Christopher Pelling, 63–74. Oxford.

1995e. "The *Narrationes* of 'Lactantius' and the Transmission of Ovid's *Metamorphoses*." In *Formative Stages of Classical Traditions: Latin Texts from Antiquity to the Renaissance*, ed. Oronzo Pecere and Michael D. Reeve, 83–115. Spoleto.

1995f. "The Silence of Cephalus: Text and Narrative Technique in Ovid, *Metamorphoses* 7.685ff." *TAPA* 125:99–111.

1996. Review of *Horace: Behind the Public Poetry*, by R. O. A. M. Lyne. *BMCR*, August 15, 1996.

1997a. "Aspects of Virgil's Reception in Antiquity." In *The Cambridge Companion to Virgil*, ed. Charles Martindale, 56–72. Cambridge.

1997b. "Poetry and Power: Virgil's Poetry in Contemporary Context." In *The Cambridge Companion to Virgil*, ed. Charles Martindale, 169–187. Cambridge.

1998. "Parenthetically Speaking (in Virgil and Other Poets)." In *Style and Tradition: Studies in Honor of Wendell Clausen*, ed. Peter Knox and Clive Foss, 141–157. Beiträge zur Altertumskunde 92. Stuttgart.

1999. "Nicolaas Heinsius and the Rhetoric of Textual Criticism." In *Ovidian Transformations: Essays on Ovid's Metamorphoses and its Reception*, ed. Philip Hardie, Alessandro Barchiesi, and Stephen Hinds, 288–300. Cambridge.

2000. "The Soldier in the Garden and Other Intruders in Ovid's *Metamorphoses*." *HSCP* 100:425–438.

2001. Review of *Analisi e interpretazione dell'Hercules Oetaeus*, by Silvia Marcucci. *CW* 94 (4):417–418.

2002a. "Charles Segal in Memoriam." *MD* 48:5–8.

2002b. "Ovid and Ancient Literary History." In *The Cambridge Companion to Ovid*, ed. Philip R. Hardie, 13–33. Cambridge.

2002c. "Chaos in Ovid's *Metamorphoses* and its Neronian Influence." *Arethusa* 35:349–360.

2004a. *P. Ouidi Nasonis. Metamorphoses*. Oxford Classical Texts. Oxford.

2004b. "The Last Book of the *Aeneid*." *Syllecta Classica* 15:103–129.

2005. "Roads Not Taken: Untold Stories in Ovid's *Metamorphoses*." *MD* 54:65–89.

2006a. "Propertian Textual Criticism and Editing." In *Brill's Companion to Propertius*, ed. Hans-Christian Günther, 45–65. Leiden.

2006b. "Seeing Seneca Whole?" In *Seeing Seneca Whole: Perspectives on Philosophy, Poetry and Politics*, ed. Katharina Volk and Gareth D. Williams, 1–17. Leiden.

2007a. "Horace and Roman Literary History." In *The Cambridge Companion to Horace*, ed. Stephen Harrison, 63–76. Cambridge.

2007b. "Ancient Receptions of Horace." In *The Cambridge Companion to Horace*, ed. Stephen Harrison, 277–290. Cambridge.

2007c. Review of P. *Ovidius Naso. Carmina amatoria*, ed. Antonio Ramírez de Verger. *CR* 57 (1):102–104.

2008. Review of *Marginal Scholarship and Textual Deviance: The "Commentum Cornuti" and the Early Scholia on Persius*, by J. E. G. Zetzel. *CR* 58:480–483.

2010. Entry in *The Classical Tradition*, ed. Anthony Grafton, Glenn W. Most, and Salvatore Settis: "Karl Lachmann." Cambridge, MA.

2012a. *Virgil. Aeneid Book XII*. Cambridge Greek and Latin Classics. Cambridge.

2012b. "*Lyricus vates*: Musical Settings of Horace's *Odes*." In *Reception and the Classics*, ed. William Brockliss, Pramit Chaudhuri, Ayelet Haimson Lushkov, Katherine Wasdin, 72–93. Yale Classical Studies 36. New Haven, CT.

2013. Entries in *The Virgil Encyclopedia*, ed. Richard F. Thomas and Jan M. Ziolkowski: "Codex," "Gates of Sleep," "Helen Episode," "Interpolation," "La Cerda," "Latinus," "Mozart," "Musical Reception, 16th Century Onward," "Parenthesis," "Propertius," "Punctuation," "Sacrilege," "Text and Transmission," "Tolumnius," and "Vida." Chichester, UK.

2014. Review of *Horace. Odes, Book I*, ed. Roland Mayer. *Mnemosyne* 67 (3):500–504.

2015a. "Virgil and Vergilius in Horace *Odes* 4.12." In *Virgilian Studies: A Miscellany Dedicated to the Memory of Mario Geymonat*, ed. H.-C. Günther, 429–452. Studia classica et mediaevalia 10. Nordhausen.

2015b. Review of *Properzio. Elegie*, ed. and trans. Giancarlo Giardina. *Gnomon* 87 (8):754–756.

2016a. *Texts, Editors, and Readers: Methods and Problems in Latin Textual Criticism*. Roman Literature and its Contexts. Cambridge.

2016b. "The Protohistory of the Text of Horace." In *From the Protohistory to the History of the Text*, ed. Javier Velaza, 223–244. Studien zur klassischen Philologie 173. Frankfurt.

2016c. "A New Critical Edition of Horace." In *Latin Literature and its Transmission: Papers in Honour of Michael Reeve*, ed. Richard Hunter and S. P. Oakley, 291–321. Cambridge.

2017. "*Custode rerum Caesare*: Horatian Civic Engagement and the Senecan Tragic Chorus." In *Horace and Seneca: Interactions, Intertexts, Interpretations*, ed. Martin Stöckinger, Kathrin Winter, and Andreas T. Zanker, 93–112. Berlin.

2018a. "Editing Ovid's *Metamorphoses*: Past, Present and Future." In *Vivam! Estudios sobre la obra di Ovidio / Studies on Ovid's Poetry*, ed. Luis Rivero García, María Consuelo Álvarez, and Rosa María Iglesias, 21–45. Exemplaria classica supplements 10. Huelva.

2018b. "Transmission of Greek and Latin Literature." In *Oxford Bibliographies Online*, https://doi.org/10.1093/obo/9780195389661-0302.

2018c. Review of *Horace. Odes*, trans. D. R. Slavitt. *Exemplaria Classica* 18:279–284.

2018d. Review of *Horace. Odes Book II*, ed. S. J. Harrison. *JRS* 108:275–276.

Forthcoming a. *Horace's Odes*. Oxford Approaches to Classical Literature. New York.

Forthcoming b. *Q. Horati Flacci. Carmina*. Oxford Classical Texts. Oxford.

Forthcoming c. Review of *Victorian Horace*, by S. J. Harrison. *CP*.

Forthcoming d. Review of *Horace. Odes*, trans. Stanley Lombardo. *BMCR*.

Forthcoming e. Review of *Virgil. Aeneid 8*, ed. Lee M. Fratantuono and R. Alden Smith. *Exemplaria Classica*.

PART ONE

EDITING

EDITING ANCIENT HANDWRITING

Rebecca R. Benefiel

WHEN I THINK BACK TO MY TIME AT HARVARD, I think of that first semester of my graduate studies and the Proseminar: sitting in Boylston on Monday afternoons and watching the sun set completely before our class finished, and we headed into the darkness of a Cambridge early winter evening. Shorter days were a very visible reminder that time was precious. There was a lot to learn and only so many hours in a day. The Proseminar was a fabulous grand tour—a rich, energizing experience of encountering one discipline after another within the field of Classics—a new adventure every week. Richard Tarrant taught our cohort textual criticism, and what an amazing opportunity it was. To learn textual criticism from Richard at the *moment* that he was working on the edition of Ovid's *Metamorphoses*! I remember wanting to ask some fairly basic questions. Of course Richard was patient, encouraging, and supportive in his answers. And thus began a wonderful education.

Where am I today? I am an epigrapher who blends topography, cultural history, Roman society, and text into an understanding of Latin and the ancient population that created it. One of my major projects involves editing the wall inscriptions of Pompeii and Herculaneum.[1] My

My thanks go to the organizers of the conference and the editors of this volume. The conference was a wonderful celebration of Richard Tarrant and the impact he has had on our lives, and I am very happy to have been part of it.

[1] Several years ago, I was invited by Silvia Orlandi to prepare the digital edition of the handwritten wall inscriptions of Pompeii and Herculaneum for the Epigraphic Database Roma (EDR), http://www.edr-edr.it/. As I began the undertaking, it became clear how fundamental archaeological context was for understanding these personalized writings. I therefore began the AGP to provide additional information specific to ancient graffiti and tools designed for research on these handwritten texts. My team and I continue to prepare the digital critical editions of these inscriptions for both projects.

work has earned two multiyear grants from the National Endowment for the Humanities, including a Scholarly Editions award. So I thought I would take this opportunity to discuss how I am editing these hand-written, 1st-century inscriptions, and what this project contributes to the field of Classics.

First, some background. As archaeological excavations expanded in Rome and in Pompeii during the late 18th and early 19th centuries, excavators began to notice tiny scratches of writing on the wall plaster. A term was coined to describe these small, scratched writings—"iscrizioni graffite" (from the Italian *graffiare*, "to scratch"), and this became a technical term for the handwritten inscriptions found in ancient Roman sites. During the mid-20th century, the term broadened to denote any writing on a wall. When I discuss graffiti, I will be talking about the original technical term of ancient, scratched, handwritten texts.

Even a quick glance reveals that ancient graffiti have little in common with their modern-day counterparts. Ancient examples contain overwhelmingly positive wishes (e.g., *feliciter!*), they are usually quite small and inconspicuous, and they are anything but anonymous. Personal names and greetings between friends were inscribed frequently among a wide variety of other content from quotations of literature to shopping lists, from personal prayers to word games. These messages were as personalized and unique as the people who wrote them.[2]

However, ancient graffiti are notoriously difficult to understand. Figure 1 presents some straightforward texts, examples of what ancient graffiti *can* be, while figure 2 offers other examples, which show how extraordinarily difficult texts can be to decipher.

There are a number of obstacles to understanding ancient graffiti. First, preservation. Although Pompeii and Herculaneum were preserved remarkably well by the eruption of Mt. Vesuvius, the destruction of these towns was still a cataclysmic event. Walls were

---

[2] For more on the variety of content among ancient graffiti, see Franklin 1991; Benefiel 2018.

knocked down, glass was shattered, items went flying.[3] Many walls that held inscriptions were already damaged when the graffiti were discovered.[4] Secondly, ancient graffiti are usually small and *very* lightly incised. They can be hard to find, letters can be difficult to make out, and they are nearly impossible to photograph. Thirdly, the texts are usually brief, and these messages are hand*written*. Just as reading modern handwriting can be a challenge, the same holds true for ancient texts. They can contain idiosyncratic abbreviations, flourishes, and other elements unique to the writer. It is not simple for anyone, even epigraphers, to immediately understand certain ancient graffiti.

And so, with the Ancient Graffiti Project (AGP), my team and I are reediting, studying, and analyzing material that holds great potential for illuminating Roman society but that has sometimes been set aside because its value was not recognized. We are creating critical editions of these texts. We are updating them with current epigraphic conventions and up-to-date bibliographies. And we are creating tools and aids that help students and scholars approach and understand these writings.

In this chapter, I present a few examples of texts that highlight our unique approach to editing ancient handwriting. The first example presented below, a prayer to Venus, illustrates the need to check and revise the texts for the inscriptions of Herculaneum. Beyond editing the text, when an inscription still survives, we create and curate a series of illustrations, including enhanced photographs and line drawings. These images allow readers to evaluate a potentially contested reading for themselves and offer the opportunity to study the appearance and paleography of the inscription. Readings can be improved even when the inscription itself has disappeared. With the second example below, a simple message presenting a personal name, we encounter challenges

---

[3] A large stone basin was launched across a room in the Suburban Baths in Herculaneum and illustrates the immense impact of the eruption felt in that town. See illustration in Wallace-Hadrill 2011:163.

[4] The editors of the *Corpus Inscriptionum Latinarum* noted, for example, that the exterior wall of the basilica in Pompeii held a large number of inscriptions, but since the plaster was damaged (*corroso tectorio*), many inscriptions were mutilated and illegible (*mutilatae et oblitteratae; CIL* IV, note at 1774–1777).

1893. 1894 ante 1891 sed paullo superius.

1893   SVRDA · SIT · ORANTI · TVA · IANVA · LAXA · FERENTI · AVDIAT · EXCLVSI · VERBA · RECEPTVS · aMANs

1894   IANITOR · AD · DANTIS · VIGILET · SI · PVLSAT · INANIS · SVRDVS · IN · OBDVCTAM · SOMNIET · VSQVe SERAM

1944 sub 1942c.

FYRRHICVS ALCIMO SAL

10558 In peristylii pila, quae est in angulo inter septentrionem et occidentem spectante, in tectorio albo

0,031	COSTIVS	0,004—0,022

10697 Ad d. 10693, superius

0,11	PORTVNNVS · AMAT · AMPLIANDA	0,003—0,013
0,115	IANVARIVS · AMAT · VIINIIRIA	0,003—0,007
0,095	ROGAMVS · DAMNA · VIINVS	0,003—0,009
0,095	VT · NOS · IN · MIINTII · HABIAS	0,003—0,01
0,115	QVOD TII · MODO · INTRORGAMVS	0,003—0,007

Della Corte p. 303 n. 811. Vidi.

V. 1 potius FORTVNATVS, v. 5 INTRORGAMVS legi potest vel INTIRORGAMVS.

4 Cf. 2013. 5 "pro *interrogamus*".

Figure 1. Examples of straightforward texts from ancient graffiti (*CIL* IV 1893 and 1894, 1944, 10697). Reproduced by kind permission of the *Corpus Inscriptionum Latinarum*, Berlin-Brandenburgische Akademie der Wissenschaften.

concomitant with a casual medium, where the way Latin is spoken or written in daily life might differ from a standard format. In such cases, our aim is not to replace what was written but instead to represent both standard and nonstandard forms. A third example demonstrates that even with partial, damaged, or incomprehensible text, all is not

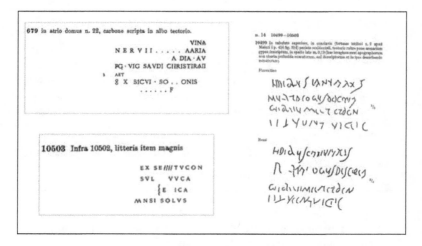

Figure 2. Examples of partial or only partially understood texts among ancient graffiti (*CIL* IV 679, 10499, 10503). Reproduced by kind permission of the *Corpus Inscriptionum Latinarum*, Berlin-Brandenburgische Akademie der Wissenschaften.

lost. The brevity of graffiti can deter a reader who encounters a difficult or uncertain reading. I designed AGP instead to encourage researchers. We provide a brief summary and a translation for each graffito, so that whatever information can be confirmed is available at a glance; we also make clear in all three instances—text, summary, and translation—what is known and what is uncertain. The text itself is always at the heart of the edition, while context and illustration will enhance understanding of these individualized writings.

I. A PRAYER TO VENUS

The first example presents a prayer to Venus. Here is the text as it is printed in the fourth volume of the *Corpus Inscriptionum Latinarum* (*CIL* IV) (fig. 3).

We can see that careful attention went into its inscription, as interpuncts are inserted between every word. The five lines of text are roughly equal in length, and we encounter the names of four individuals

Rebecca R. Benefiel

10697 Ad d. 10693, superius

0,11	PORTVNNVS·AMAT·AMPLIANDA	0,003—0,013
0,115	IANVARIVS·AMAT·VIINIIRIA	0,003—0,007
0,095	ROGAMVS·DAMNA·VIINVS	0,003—0,009
0,095	VT·NOS·IN·MIINTII·HABIAS	0,003—0,01
0,115	QVOD TII·MODO·INTRORGAMVS	0,003—0,007

Della Corte p. 303 n. 811. Vidi.
  V. 1 potius FORTVNATVS, v. 5 INTRORGAMVS legi potest vel
INTIRORGAMVS.
  4 Cf. 2013. 5 "pro *interrogamus*".

Figure 3. A prayer to Venus, as presented at *CIL* IV 10697. Reproduced by kind permission of the *Corpus Inscriptionum Latinarum*, Berlin-Brandenburgische Akademie der Wissenschaften.

before we arrive at the intention of the prayer. This text is of inherent interest as a rare example of a personal prayer. It can be translated thus: "Portunnus loves Amplianda. Ianuarius loves Veneria. We ask mistress Venus that you keep us in mind (and) what we now ask of you."

But the way the text has been edited has led to misinterpretations. Heikki Solin alerted scholars to problems with the publication of this inscription and others in his meticulous review of *CIL* IV, fascicles 3 and 4, which present the wall inscriptions of Herculaneum. There, he issued 20 pages of revisions, comments, and warnings as to the accuracy of the material and the way it was presented.[5]

First, the editorial comments in *CIL* do note that the final verb could be read as INTRORGAMUS or INTIRORGAMUS, and they explain that the form should be understood as the Latin *interrogamus*. There is no comment about the form *damna* in line 3, however. In other instances, an editor might alert a reader to a nonstandard spelling like this one, *damna* for *domina*, through use of the term *sic* or an exclamation point.

---

[5] Solin 1973. In addition to the numerous problems he flags and discusses in his review, he provides a long list of other inscriptions with problems. One of these will be discussed below.

CIL leaves this form without comment. There is also no explicit guidance on the decision to transcribe the text as it appears, with two vertical strokes to denote the letter *E*. This is one way to write the letter *E* in antiquity, but both this version and the version with three horizontal strokes were used equally, sometimes even within the same word.[6]

The most misleading decision, however, is the way the editor chose to comment on the first line of the inscription: *V. 1 potius FORTVNATVS. Potius* is not commonly used as an editorial term, and one might suppose that the editor meant *potius quam* (or "rather than"), i.e. *Portunnus* in line 1 should be read "rather than" *Fortunatus.* The less favorable form would be presented in the critical apparatus.

In fact, it seems that Pio Ciprotti, the editor of this section of *CIL*, has followed *the opposite* of standard practice and put his preferred reading in the apparatus while keeping a reading that should be discounted in the main text field. This practice can be confirmed by going back to Matteo Della Corte's original publication and seeing that he reads only Portunnus; there is no mention of Fortunatus.[7] By using *potius*, it seems, Ciprotti intended to communicate that the reading should, *rather*, be "Fortunatus." Yet the way he edits *CIL* here is confusing and even inscrutable for the reader.

In this case, we are extremely fortunate that the inscription itself still survives. That fact allows us to check the readings and determine that *Fortunatus* is the correct text, as is INTRORGAMUS. But given the tools and resources now at our disposal, we can correct the reading, update the critical apparatus, and do even more.

I have mentioned that it is difficult to photograph graffiti; however, it is not impossible. The prayer to Venus is not visible to someone standing a few feet away (fig. 4). Yet, with strong raking light and a digital camera with a macro lens, we can zoom way in and capture a much better image that allows us to see the actual ancient handwriting and letter forms (fig. 5). Including a scale allows viewers to understand

---

[6] A reader familiar with the conventions of ancient handwriting found on wax tablets will recognize *II* as the letter *E*; others tend to misunderstand the text as *ii*.

[7] Della Corte 1958:303n811.

Figure 4. The location of the inscribed prayer to Venus in Herculaneum, along the ramp leading up to the city from the terrace of Nonius Balbus. Photograph by The Ancient Graffiti Project, published by permission of the Ministero dei Beni e delle Attività Culturali per il Turismo – Parco Archeologico di Ercolano. Reproduction is expressly forbidden.

how small this inscription is. Each letter here is roughly half-a-centimeter high. (The ancient plaster is itself flaking off and impedes the legibility of the inscription. Nevertheless, it is remarkable that this inscription has survived as well as it has since it is exposed to the elements and in a highly trafficked area of the site.)

Even with this detailed level of photography, it can be challenging to identify and read the ancient writing. I therefore decided to create a series of illustrations to go along with the photograph and thereby enhance the visibility of the graffito and legibility of the text for the reader. I first created an enhanced photograph with an overlay articulating the ancient text (fig. 6). I then created line drawings and removed the background noise to allow a reader to focus on the paleography and appearance of the text (fig. 7). With my colleague in computer science,

Figure 5. Detailed photograph of the prayer to Venus, showing the minute size of the text (with 1cm scale). Photograph by The Ancient Graffiti Project (ancientgraffiti.org), published by permission of the Ministero dei Beni e delle Attività Culturali per il Turismo – Parco Archeologico di Ercolano. Reproduction is expressly forbidden.

we then designed a photo gallery in which to display these images at http://ancientgraffiti.org.[8] A viewer can click to move back and forth among the images. Toggling from the enhanced image with overlay to the unaltered photograph helps bring into greater focus the small scratched writing that is visible on the wall. The photo gallery thereby allows a viewer to be able to identify for him or herself the ancient letter strokes that may not be visible at first glance.

[8] The example of the prayer to Venus is found at: http://ancientgraffiti.org/Graffiti/ graffito/AGP-EDR140983. We submit our high-resolution photos to the Epigraphic Database Roma (http://www.edr-edr.it/), which has a memorandum of understanding with the Italian Ministero dei Beni Culturali to display images of this cultural heritage. The photos are stored on the EDR server; the AGP webpages then point to EDR. Cf. Benefiel et al. 2017.

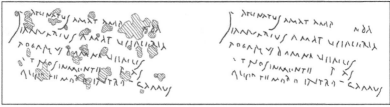

Figures 6 and 7. Enhanced photographs and line drawings of *CIL* IV 10697, created by and displayed at The Ancient Graffiti Project (ancientgraffiti.org). Permission granted from The Ancient Graffiti Project.

As can be seen in figure 8, when we present a graffito in AGP, we display additional material along with the text of the inscription. This decision is intended to help readers understand that ancient graffiti are in fact textual artifacts in the physical environment. So, we include a map to show where in the city of Herculaneum this graffito appears, and we have created hyperlinks so that one can explore what kind of graffiti appear nearby, or one can assemble all the graffiti in this one location to study them.

Graffiti are not just simple text. They are also cultural artifacts: material objects with a specific, fixed location and physical features

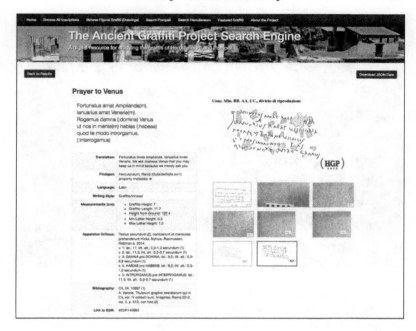

Figure 8. *CIL* IV 10697, a prayer to Venus, inscribed in Herculaneum, as presented by AGP (ancientgraffiti.org) with text, translation, apparatus, image gallery, and additional information. Permission granted from The Ancient Graffiti Project.

determined by handwriting and the writer's design. When a graffito is reduced to typescript and represented simply as text on a page, all of this essential physical information is lost—the very information that an ancient observer would have had available when he or she viewed the text in person.

II. IDENTIFYING *COSTIVS*

Since these handwritten wall inscriptions were inscribed on perishable material that has been exposed to the elements, many have now disappeared. Fortunately, it is still possible to improve readings even when the original is lost.

Figure 9. Photograph of the Casa dei Cervi at Herculaneum, looking through to the peristyle that once held *CIL* IV 10558. Published by permission of the Ministero dei Beni e delle Attività Culturali per il Turismo – Parco Archeologico di Ercolano. Reproduction is expressly forbidden.

Such is the case with *CIL* IV 10558, an inscription that was once visible in the peristyle of the House of the Stags (Casa dei Cervi) at Herculaneum. This house is one of the largest and most luxurious in the city, with an enviable position directly on the coastline overlooking the sea (fig. 9). In this peristyle were found the many sculptures of stags for which the house was named.[9] We searched for the inscription in 2016, but the remaining plaster is quite weathered and now reduced to its lower layers and consequently no text remains.

The text of *CIL* IV 10558 is deceptively simple: *COSTIVS*. *COSTIVS* ends in -*us* and looks like it could be a masculine Roman name. But is it? Well, no. It turns out that there *is* no Roman name, *Costius*. However,

---

[9] Reproductions of these sculptures are located on-site in the peristyle of the residence, visible in fig. 9.

praenomina were abbreviated to a single letter. Might this graffito present a combination of praenomen and nomen together? Could we have here the abbreviation *C.* for *Gaius* and then the gentilicium, *Ostius*? Della Corte suggested such identification in his initial publication of the graffito; Ciprotti printed the suggestion at *CIL* IV 10558 (*C. Ostius*).

However, it turns out there is no evidence for *Ostius* in use as a Roman name either. But there is the name *Hostius*. It is quite rare. This gentilicium, *Hostius*, is attested at Capua among the *magistri* inscriptions of the late 2nd and early 1st centuries BCE.[10] Beyond the Republic, it appears only a handful of times among a few cities in southern Italy.[11]

One of those cities is Puteoli, not far away, where a *Gaius Hostius Primogenes* is attested in roughly the same period as our graffito, the early to mid 1st century CE.[12] One other document, a wax tablet from the archive of the Sulpicii, was discovered at Moregine just outside Pompeii (*TPSulp.* 61) and lists a certain *Gaius Hostius Maro* as one of the witnesses for the transaction. That tablet dates to the same period as well; it can be precisely dated to the year 43 CE.[13] Outside of southern Italy, the name *Hostius* is virtually unknown.[14] There is, therefore,

---

[10] *CIL* I² 681 (2), cf. p. 932; 686, cf. p. 726, p. 933; 2947, cf. p. 930. Cf. also *CIL* X 4177 and 4295, and EDR105301 (also from Capua).

[11] Abellinum (*CIL* X 1172 = EDR102294: *C. Hostius Clemens*), Aricia (Nemi) (*CIL* XIV 4201 = EDR147352: *Q. Hostius Capito, rhetor*), Atella (*CIL* X 3748 = EDR161477: *Q. Hostius Eros*), and Puteoli (*CIL* X 1934, 2530, 2752; *Eph. Epigr.* VIII.405 and 406).

[12] EDR080834 (This inscription was not published in *CIL* vol. X (1883); it was first published in *AJA* 1898 [Dennison 1898, p. 396] and did not receive a *L'Annee Epigraphique* reference until *AE* 1988.299). *Gaius Hostius Primogenes* is named as one of the freedmen who benefits from the tomb that the freedwoman *Plotia Helena* built for herself, her friends and family.

Other inscriptions from Puteoli likewise include the praenomen Gaius with the gentilicium. *CIL* X 1934: *C. Hostius*; *Eph. Epigr.* VIII.405: *C. Hostius, mercator* and 406: *C. Hostius Protogenes* and *C. Hostius Helius.*

[13] EDR103845; Camodeca 1999, 154.

[14] These few and isolated instances underscore the regional presence of this otherwise incredibly rare name. The name *Hostius* is attested only once in Rome (*CIL* VI 37148) and once in Ostia (*CIL* XIV 46a). Search conducted via the Epigraphic Database Roma (www.edr-edr.it), July 27, 2019.

Except for one instance in Thessaloniki (*Inscriptiones Graecae* [*IG*] 10.2.1.386bis) and one in Pannonia (*CIL* III 3441), the name is not found outside the Italian peninsula. Search conducted via the Epigraphic Database Heidelberg (edh-www.adw.uni-heidelberg.de), July 26, 2019.

sufficient support to understand our inscription at Herculaneum as representing the name *Gaius Hostius* but inscribed as the name was being pronounced rather than how it was spelled.

My aim with the AGP is not to "correct" the text so that this graffito is in line with other attestations of the name; rather, I am editing these handwritten inscriptions in order to represent both *what is written* and *what is meant*. Many ancient graffiti contain nonstandard or nonliterary forms. Such words are frequently dismissed as misspellings or mistakes, but to do so misses the fact that these spontaneous writings illustrate a daily, living use of Latin and can reveal casual expressions or regional pronunciation. These texts are not formal monuments displayed in public or works of published literature. In an official inscription, this individual might be named *C. Hostius*, with an *H*, but in this informal medium, he or someone else can write his name as it was being pronounced, *Ostius*. Graffiti are a valuable source for studying language change, and we can see in these writings from the middle of the 1st century that Latin is already trending toward the Romance languages. The letter *H* is only sometimes pronounced, as is final -*m* for accusative forms. The letters *B* and *V* are sometimes interchanged, which tells us that *V* has switched from vocalic to consonantal.[15]

The standard epigraphic convention used to be to insert a correction into the transcription—to focus on and represent what a stonecutter likely meant. But to do that is to replace the ancient text and so to erase this valuable perspective onto ancient literacy and language variation.

With AGP, we present the text the way it has been written, *Ostius*, and we then include a note to show the normalized way that name would be understood: *Hostius*. This way, if someone wants to study all examples of the gentilicium *Hostius*, he or she would find this example. Moreover, if someone wants to find this particular *Ostius* or anyone else who writes his name this way, that is possible too.

Personal names are one area where we have been able to offer a number of explanations and corrections. For example, the comment at

---

[15] Some of these shifts are listed in the index to *CIL* IV, Supp. 2 (XIII. Grammatica), 777–780. Väänänen (1959) is the standard reference for language variation among the Pompeian graffiti.

CIL IV 10577 that ΠΡΟΚΛΑ, written in Greek, represents the Latin name *Proc(u)la* is misleading, since Πρόκλα itself is a perfectly fine Greek name that was flourishing at exactly this time: the early Empire.[16] Or we could consider *CIL* IV 10588b, which presents the word ΦΙΛΙΠΠΙ but supplies no editorial comment. The final letter of the word has been understood as an *iota*, but no form of the Greek second declension ends in an *iota*. If the graffito itself still survived (unfortunately, it does not), it would be worth looking to see if there were any curve, in which case, it could be the beginning of an *omicron*. If, furthermore, we consider the medium here and the way graffiti are inscribed, it is possible that the writer stopped writing before completing the entire word, as happens often among graffiti. The final stroke might be the vertical of an *epsilon*, for the vocative of the name *Philippos*: *Philippe*. There is a danger in treating a typescript transcription as straightforward and settled, which misunderstands the way these texts were created, and so we have tried to highlight what is known and what is less certain in our presentation of these inscriptions.

One last example in this category of personal names is a graffito that gives details about wool working, amounts of material, and finished products (*CIL* IV 10645, fig. 10). Limited damage to the wall was recorded before the five letters of the first word, *ANTHI*, and so the genitive form *[X]anthi* was proposed as a supplement. While *Xanthus* is a name known from literature, the moniker *Anthus* is, in fact, a much more popular name at this point in time—and particularly in this city. The Album of Herculaneum is the description given to a group of large marble tablets found near the forum of Herculaneum that feature the names of more than five hundred people. These lists offer us a uniquely detailed and personalized view onto the broad population of the town.[17]

[16] Cf. Benefiel and Sypniewski 2018, 222. The name Πρόκλα, virtually unknown during the classical period, became popular during the Roman Empire (especially the first and second centuries CE). The *Lexicon of Greek Personal Names* lists 80 attestations; the Epigraphic Database Roma lists another six examples of the name in Rome. Results retrieved from http://clas-lgpn2.classics.ox.ac.uk/name/Πρόκλα and www.edr-edr.it, July 27, 2019.

[17] For more about the Album of Herculaneum and the populations it features, see especially Camodeca 2008, as well as De Ligt and Garnsey 2012.

10645 In conclavi H apud Maiuri I p. 342 fig. 271 (cf. *ibid.* p. 344 sq.), in pariete septentrionali, in podii fascia flava

0,064	// A N T H I	0,004—0,008
0,054	T R A M A	0,005—0,01
0,026	P I X	0,009—0,01
0,042	S T A M E	0,005—0,012
0,028	P V I I	0,005—0,009
0,029	V I I I	0,011—0,014

Della Corte p. 277 sq. n. 472.

1 "[X]*anthi*". 2 Cf. 1507. 3 "*P(ondo) IX*". 4 "*Stame(n)*"; cf. 1507 et 9109. 5 "*P(ondo) VII*".

Figure 10. Graffito about wool working (*CIL* IV 10645). Reproduced by kind permission of the *Corpus Inscriptionum Latinarum*, Berlin-Brandenburgische Akademie der Wissenschaften.

No other attestations of the name *Xanthus* are known in Herculaneum, but the name *Anthus* appears on the lists of the Album as the cognomen of three different individuals.[18] Given the popularity of this name in Herculaneum, it is possible that the graffito about wool working named not *Xanthus* but an *Anthus*.

III. HANDWRITING AND ENDURING MYSTERIES

Other handwritten inscriptions work hard to retain their mystery. The handwriting itself can prove challenging and even inscrutable at times. The first issue of *CIL* IV (1871) included many line drawings that illustrated the appearance of wall inscriptions in tables at the end of the volume. Similar tables of illustrations were not printed in the later supplements to *CIL* IV and accordingly many fewer line drawings were printed. If a line drawing appears in *CIL* IV, Supp. 3, fasc. 4, where the wall inscriptions of Herculaneum are published, it is likely included

---

[18] EDR076983 (*CIL* X 1403b, i, k), col. III, line 16: [*A(ulus) A]ttius A. l. Anthus*; EDR135457 (*CIL* X 1403a), col. II, line 2: *M(arcus) Nonius M. l. Anthus*; EDR140728 (*CIL* X 1403d), col. II, line 4: *Sex(tus) Pompeius Anthus*.

because there is some uncertainty about how to read it, although unfortunately this is never made explicit.[19] Indeed, despite the fact that the graffiti published in the second half of the 20th century contain many difficult and uncertain readings, the way they were published often conceals doubts as to their readings. As mentioned previously, Solin highlighted numerous problems and proposed emendations for a number of texts in his magisterial review of *CIL* IV, Supp. 3, fasc. 3–4. Still other readings were so problematic that Solin included a list of inscriptions that were "wholly or partially uncertain" or that had "incorrect readings or interpretations."[20] Below, I present how we have decided to edit one of the inscriptions from this list.

CIL IV 10499 (fig. 11) was discovered early on in the large-scale excavations of Herculaneum, which began in the 1920s; Della Corte documented the wall inscriptions that were revealed as the excavations then progressed over several decades.[21] In 1929, as the upper story of the building that would come to be known as the Casa a Gratticio (III.14) was being excavated, a graffito was discovered that Della Corte could not access himself. He sent two staff members to record it separately and then created his own reading based on a combination of their drawings. In his original publication of the inscription, Della Corte mentioned this process but presented only his reading, acknowledging that he had read lines 1–2 "con sicurezza" but lines 3–4 "con approssimazione."[22] When Pio Ciprotti later edited Della Corte's work for publication in *CIL* IV, Supp. 3, fasc. 4, he decided to publish both line drawings on which Della Corte's reading was based, but he unhelpfully removed Della Corte's stated doubts from the transcription. *CIL* IV 10499 therefore reads: *Idibus Ianuaris / mystagogus docens / Gebeum et Etoen / lucian[ ] vici[ ]*.

---

[19] Cf. *CIL* IV 10554–10556, 10601–10602.

[20] Solin 1973, 276: "Hier noch eine Liste weiterer Inschriften, die ganz oder teilweise unsicher bleiben oder falsche Lesungen und Interpretationen aufweisen."

[21] His decades of work recording the wall-inscriptions of Herculaneum were eventually published in a summary article: Della Corte 1958.

[22] Della Corte recounts how the documentation took place by the "funzionari Sigg. Rossi e Fiorentino" on July 29, 1929 (Della Corte 1958, 242). The line drawings are attributed to each of the two men in *CIL* IV at 10499.

n. 14   10499—10503

10499 In tabulato superiore, in conclavis (fortasse biclinii n. 2 apud Maiuri I p. 416 fig. 354) pariete occidentali, tectorio rubro pone armarium gypso inscriptum, in spatio lato m. 0,19 (hae imagines sunt apographorum non charta perlucida exaratorum, sed descriptorum et in ipso describendo minutorum)

Fiorentino

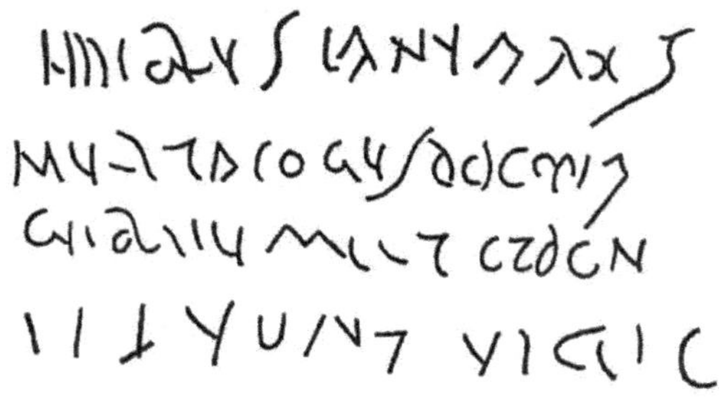

²/₃

Rossi

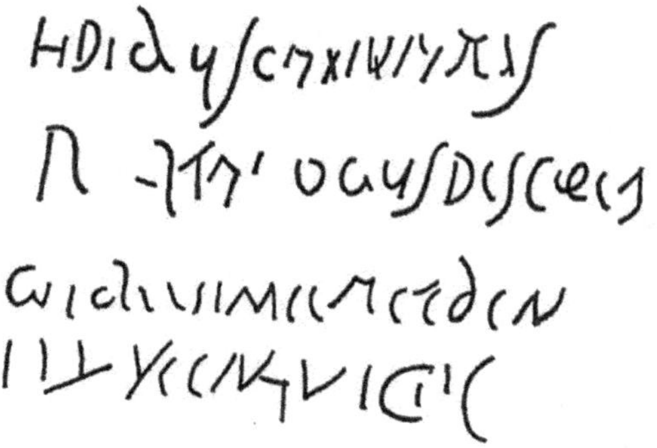

²/₃

Della Corte p. 242 n. 6 ex apographis a Fiorentino et a Rossi factis, v. 2 DOCENS Fiorentino, DISCENS Rossi.

Idibus Ianuaris / mystagogus docens / Gebeum et Etoen / lucian[   ] *vici*[   ].

Figure 11: Graffito from the Casa a Gratticio (*CIL* IV 10499). Reproduced by kind permission of the *Corpus Inscriptionum Latinarum*, Berlin-Brandenburgische Akademie der Wissenschaften.

The transcription of an inscribed text is a powerful tool. It represents the editor's best and final thoughts about the ancient text. The transcription will influence any scholar who seeks out the text of an inscription; it will likely be the first and it may be the only place a researcher will look. Since the transcription is typed on the page, it often belies the certainty of a reading, making it seem clear and decided when, in fact, it is not. This happens much more frequently for inscriptions written by hand on a wall surface than it does for inscriptions formally carved on stone.

In my work editing these inscriptions for the AGP, I wish to make clear how certain—or precarious—a reading actually is. At the same time, I do not want to scare people away from these complicated and intriguing texts. I therefore aim to communicate to the audiences who use AGP, from scholars to students, how much we can learn from graffiti even when the text may not be 100 percent clear.

First, why the difficulty in reading this graffito in the first place? The Casa a Gratticcio is one of only two buildings in Herculaneum that are in such a precarious state that they are off-limits to all. Our team was therefore unable to inspect the inscription itself during our campaigns; however, it is likely that this inscription no longer exists and probable that it disappeared soon after its discovery since it had been written in chalk.[23] Chalk was a far less precise material for writing than a stylus, and the medium almost certainly affected the legibility and appearance of the message. Certain wall inscriptions written in chalk or charcoal were discovered during excavations in Herculaneum and Pompeii, but these faded quickly when exposed to the elements. They therefore occur in much smaller numbers than handwritten inscriptions that were incised or scratched into wall plaster.

Another challenge with this graffito is its length. Longer handwritten inscriptions tend to become somewhat less legible in their final line(s). The further down one writes on the vertical surface of a wall, the more difficult the angle at which one is writing. The result is that lower lines can often be less legible than the first lines written. This inscription presents four lines of text, and the writing is more

---

[23] Della Corte 1958:242: *tracciate col gessetto.*

difficult to understand in the third and fourth lines. My colleague, Holly Sypniewski, and I analyzed this inscription for the AGP and carefully considered both line drawings; we made the following decisions about how best to present the uncertainty of the inscription.[24]

The line drawings made by the two staff members, Sig. Fiorentino and Sig. Rossi, agree on many points. Both drawings, for example, are in agreement that the first word of the inscription was written as *HDIBUS*. This is not a standard form, yet neither Della Corte nor Ciprotti offered any comment. Della Corte simply presented the initial word as *Idibus* ("on the Ides"). The word certainly contains a reference to the Ides of the month, although it is unclear why the first character was written as a form that resembles the letter *H*. The letter *E* was frequently inscribed as two vertical strokes: ||. Perhaps the writer was writing *Eidibus*, and the horizontal bar was an extraneous mark on the plaster.[25] This pronunciation was still current in the early 1st century as is attested among Pompeian graffiti. References to a day before the Ides of the month were written in many Pompeian graffiti as *Eidus* (instead of *Idus*), a characteristic signaling that the diphthong *ei* had not yet collapsed into -*ī*.[26] Or it might be that the writer was influenced by Greek and began pronouncing *Eidibus*, hearing the letter *eta*, and continued writing in Latin from there. Since the text no longer exists, we unfortunately cannot evaluate the writing itself to determine if the horizontal bar was extraneous, a later addition, or integral to the text. We therefore present the text both as it was written and then make explicit the standard form, *HDIBUS (:Idibus)*.

Along the same lines, we make clear that the ancient writer wrote *IANYARIS* for (:*Ianuarias*) and *MYSTACOGUS* for (:*mystagogus*). The entry in *CIL* had kept *Ianuaris* and presented it without explanation while at

---

[24] See the publication at: http://ancientgraffiti.org/Graffiti/graffito/AGP-EDR140254. Cf. also Benefiel and Sypniewski 2018:211, 242.

[25] *Eidibus* might have included three vertical strokes. The writer might have begun with an E and changed his mind. Another possibility is he began writing and crossed out the first letter(s).

[26] Cf. *CIL* IV 2437, 3882, 4276, 4428. *Idibus* is the ablative "on the day of the Ides"; the form *Idus* was used when references where given to so many days before the Ides of the month, e.g., *a(nte) d(iem) VII Idus*.

the same time replacing *mystacogus* with the "corrected" *mystagogus* in the transcription. Our decision to present not one or the other but both forms means that we avoid the risk of overwriting what the ancient writer actually wrote as well as leaving unexpected forms unexplained to potentially confuse the modern reader. The term *mystacogus* in fact requires a bit more explanation since it is a Greek word transliterated into Latin.[27] We therefore provide the additional explanation when explaining the text *mystacogus (:mystagogus, μυσταγωγός)* and then make explicit in our apparatus: *MYSTACOGUS pro MYSTAGOGUS* (i.e., *verbum Graecum μυσταγωγός Latine scriptum*).[28]

The names in line three are a trickier case since they are presented without any alert to the reader, yet neither name is unproblematic. In fact, neither name is otherwise attested anywhere else. More than that, neither word is close to sound or letter clusters that are found in Latin. Here we face two different issues. The first word is reasonably legible. The two versions illustrate that the third line began with the letters *GEB*. The *G* in line three is consistent with the *G* in *mystacogus*, the *B* is consistent with the *B* in *Hdibus*, and the *E* is the common alternate form where the letter is written with two vertical strokes. The two line drawings agree in this much. They are also mostly similar in the letters that follow: *EVM*. Ciprotti therefore prints *Gebeum*, presumably a name in the accusative singular. Yet, the name *Gebeus* is completely unknown. Indeed, the sound cluster *GEB* appears in Latin almost exclusively for verb forms. There is a single inscription from Rome that features the name *Gebonia*,[29] and a version of Mercury was honored in Germany with dedications: *deo Mercurio Gebrinio*.[30] Beyond these two attestations, however, the string *GEB* only occurs when a second or third conjugation

---

[27] Benefiel and Sypniewski 2018:211n13.

[28] Full entry and critical apparatus at: http://ancientgraffiti.org/Graffiti/graffito/AGP-EDR140254.

[29] EDR108893 = *CIL* VI 7952, cfr. p. 3439: *Gebonia P(ubli) l(iberta)/ Numphe / M(arcus) Perperna M(arci) l(ibertus) / Numphius.*

[30] At least eight of these dedications are known, dating to the later 2nd and first half of the 3rd century CE. Results from the Epigraphische Datenbank Heidelberg, July 30, 2019. These inscriptions have also been compiled by the project *Keltische Götternamen in den Inschriften der römischen Provinz Germania Inferior* (https://gams.uni-graz.at/context:fercan).

verb is used in the imperfect tense. Since the letter forms of *Gebeum* are legible but the word itself has no meaning, we use the epigraphic convention of rendering the text in all capital letters. That is the current convention to identify the sort of problematic text in a manuscript that might be obelized by a textual critic.

The second part of line three is problematic in its own way: even the letter forms here are incomprehensible. Della Corte identified an *et* from the line drawing of Rossi, although it is far less secure in Fiorentino's drawing. The characters that follow, however, are extremely difficult to identify. The only sure letter is the final one: *N*. Those that precede it could be *CTDC*; Della Corte reconstructed this series as *Etoen*. It should be pointed out that in his original publication Della Corte had included a "?" at the beginning of line 3. Ciprotti, without having seen the inscription himself, removed the question mark when he printed the transcription in *CIL* IV. Since the identities of the characters themselves are problematic, we have given Della Corte's proposal but with underdots below every letter except the final *N* to denote that the readings of these characters are ambiguous or uncertain.[31]

The fourth line is almost entirely incomprehensible, even though the two line drawings are in general agreement about the shape of the characters. It is difficult to look at the line drawings and see how Della Corte read *lucian*. The punctuation printed in *CIL* is also misleading. In Della Corte's original publication, he presented his reading as *LUCIAN*

---

[31] In her *Cambridge Manual of Latin Epigraphy*, Alison Cooley (2012:350–355) discusses the system of epigraphic conventions, which has varied but came closest to universal agreement with the publication of the Krummery-Panciera system (Krummery and Panciera 1980). The underdot remains a special case. In Greek epigraphy, it denotes a character that might be uncertain for a range of reasons: "characters ambiguous outside of context, damaged, illegible, or otherwise uncertain" (cf. http://Papyri.info/conventions.html). The EpiDoc conventions for text mark-up are similar: "character of which at least traces survive, but not adequately to identify the letter unambiguously outside of its context" (http://www.stoa.org/epidoc/gl/latest/trans-ambiguous.html). Latin epigraphy generally has no convention to denote an unintelligible letter or character; the underdot instead communicates a damaged character that could not be recognized on its own but can be inferred from context. With the AGP, we use the underdot for the former, broader range of circumstances. To make all punctuation clear to a reader, we provide a key to the epigraphic conventions used in each particular inscription (on the individual graffito page) as well as a link to the full list of epigraphic conventions.

- - *VICI* - - - and his transcription as *Lucian(...) vici(...)*. When Ciprotti then published the inscription in *CIL*, he used square brackets: *lucian[ ] vici[ ]*.[32] In current epigraphic conventions, square brackets denote damage to the support. Yet Della Corte and Ciprotti seem to intimate not that something has been lost but, rather, that additional markings existed after the two words (or strings of letters) they identified. At the end of line four, it seems clear that the final character was something akin to the letter *C* or a lunate *sigma*. Della Corte may have found a final *C* problematic since Latin words do not end in *C*.[33] The two line drawings also agree in the marking that would have followed Della Corte's *lucian*. Here, the issue is that the marking does not appear to be a standard alphabetic letter. The mark presents a form similar to a *7* but with a vertical, not diagonal, downstroke, or a capital *T* that is missing the right side of the horizontal bar, and in both drawings this character is lower than the rest of the characters of the line. In both cases, therefore, it seems the editors were unsure what to do about puzzling characters.

As this text demonstrates, then, handwriting poses significant challenges for an editor. An inscription on stone is usually planned in advance and is the product of someone hired to create it, and so it does not include the inscrutable writing or personal idiosyncrasies frequently found among ancient graffiti. We therefore do our best to apply epigraphic standards and conventions to this less formal, personalized text. For the final line of this inscription, our solution was to include a plus sign for the nonalphabetic character to denote "an illegible or unclear character," and to write out *VIÇIC* in all capital letters to denote "clear letters of incomprehensible meaning."[34]

We therefore make clear the uncertainty of readings in the Latin text by means of capitalization and punctuation. We also provide a translation that further underscores what is certain and what is tenuous by explaining as much as we can, with editorial comments in parentheses:

---

[32] Note that in Ciprotti's transcription at *CIL* IV 10499, *lucian* is no longer capitalized.

[33] Exceptions are the deictic pronouns *hic, haec,* and *hoc,* but it would be unusual for one of these to end a sentence.

[34] We did also include an underdot below the middle *C* of *VIÇIC* to denote that the reading of that character is not absolutely certain.

Hdibus (:Idibus) Ianyaris (:Ianuarias)
mystacogus (:mystagogus, μυσταγωγός) docens
GEBEUM et Ẹtọẹn
lụcịạn+ VIÇIC

On the Ides of January, the guide (religious guide?)
teaching Gebeus(?) and Etoe(?) (neither name is otherwise
known) (... other letters here ...).

In this way, the translation presents the first line with certainty,
reveals the two possible meanings for *mystagogus* (simply a guide or a
type of religious guide), points out the uncertainty regarding the otherwise unattested names in line three, and makes evident that the fourth
line is at present completely incomprehensible with the phrasing *(other
letters here ...)*.

Despite all these uncertainties, however, all is not lost. This is still a
four-line message that aimed to communicate something. Since those
who approach ancient graffiti for the first time can be overwhelmed
with nonstandard forms and how much this Latin departs from Latin
literary texts, we compose a short description for each graffito for AGP
so that students and scholars derive an immediate sense of the character of the message. This short description appears above the relevant
text on the results page immediately after any search. It also appears
as the heading for the webpage displaying the detailed information
for an individual graffito. For this inscription, we decided to focus on
the confirmed information and describe it thus: "Graffito mentioning a
date and someone teaching."

Sometimes it takes a while, but a mystery is eventually solved, as
occurred when Antonio Varone recently unraveled the meaning behind
one unusual graffito.[35] Here, the handwriting was key to detecting
a hidden meaning. Fortunately, the text had been published with a
line drawing at *CIL* IV 10580 since the presentation of the letters was
unusual (fig. 12). *CIL* presented Della Corte's best guess at understanding the text as: *ex sept(em?)* (from seven?). The first two letters

---

[35] Varone 2016.

10580 In latrinae pariete occidentali

$^1/_5$

Della Corte p. 272 n. 412. V. 3 litterae secunda E vel I, tertia P vel T vel I legi possunt.
"*Ex sept(em?)*".

Figure 12. Graffito whose initial reading has been revised (*CIL* IV 10580). Reproduced by kind permission of the *Corpus Inscriptionum Latinarum*, Berlin-Brandenburgische Akademie der Wissenschaften.

EX were written vertically on the wall, one below the other. The other letters were inscribed in somewhat of a jumble.

Varone solved the puzzle by recognizing that the graffito was written as an anagram.[36] Rather than *SEPT*, the letters below *EX* should be read as *SETRI* with letters in nexus. In this instance, the handwriting is key to understanding the message. The jumble of letters and ligatures hint at a scrambling of the text. The fact that the letters of that text had not been correctly recognized had further obfuscated the character of the message. Once the letters SETRI are recognized and then unjumbled, they could be read as *EXTERSI* (I wiped myself), a message that made sense taking into account where it was found (a latrine) and for which Varone found a parallel with a recently discovered graffito in Stabiae.[37] For both of the inscriptions just discussed, the

[36] For fuller discussion, including references to other anagrams among the graffiti, see Varone 2016. Matthew Panciera has discussed the act of writing names backwards on the walls of Pompeii (2011). For discussion of magic squares and other flexible ways of reading and writing among ancient graffiti, see Benefiel 2012.

[37] Varone 2016:115–119. Varone suggests that the anagram may have had an apotropaic significance.

critical apparatus explains the previous hypotheses put forth, allowing a reader to find the backstory.

The AGP is therefore one of the scholarly tools available to epigraphers, philologists, and ancient historians. *CIL* will always provide the main reference and identification number for the inscriptions that have been published therein.[38] *CIL* presents the text as it was determined at the time of its publication. Yet, certain inscriptions have been reinterpreted, as is the case with Varone's reevaluation of *CIL* IV 10580. The Clauss-Slaby online database presents the texts of ancient inscriptions in a simple format, and is efficient for a quick text search, but it does not make clear if a reading has been revised or explain what the source of a reading is.

With AGP, we present the text of *CIL* as well as any updates that have been made since its publication. We also offer further analysis along with possible explanations of forms or content for the handwritten inscriptions of Herculaneum and Pompeii. Context is an exceedingly important part of understanding these handwritten inscriptions but multiple revisions to the system of addresses in Pompeii over the past 150 years have made it very difficult to determine the location of a graffito and nearly impossible to ascertain and study the locations of groups of handwritten inscriptions. AGP, therefore, has performed the correlations from earlier location identifications and naming systems to the current system of addresses to provide an accurate location for each graffito. We also categorize graffiti by the type of building in which they are found (house, shop, workshop, bakery, etc.), so that scholars can research and compare inscriptions in different types of spaces.[39] Finally, our analysis of inscriptions is based on fieldwork and autopsy whenever possible. For those inscriptions that remain visible today, we provide photographs, enhanced line drawings, and a series of illustrations, which not only allow scholars to evaluate aesthetic presentation and visual impact but also provide the material for paleographic studies.

---

[38] Trismegistos is another reference identification system that is now expanding from papyri to provide identification numbers for inscriptions as well.

[39] For more about our methods and design decisions for building AGP as a scholarly resource, see Benefiel et al. 2017.

This, then, is how I am editing these precious examples of ancient handwriting. The texts are best understood with as much context as possible and some degree of explanation. There are pieces to put together and puzzles to solve—or not—but it is very exciting to be able to encounter the actual handwriting from these Roman towns. It always communicates something more than text on a printed page.

My ambitious goal is therefore to give these fascinating texts their due by creating an accurate, up-to-date critical edition and a platform to make them widely available so that this handwritten material might be more accessible, more instructive, and more comprehensible for scholars, students, and the general public. We have more than twelve hundred inscriptions edited and available online so far, and the work continues.

I have been very fortunate to have the opportunities that the study of Classics has provided me. I have had excellent role models. I have learned from talented, generous, inspiring teachers, and I try to emulate them in my own teaching and research. During my first semester teaching at Harvard as a Teaching Fellow, I had a student come up to me at the end of a recitation section and ask, "Do you know Professor Tarrant?" I said yes. He said to me, "You should try to lead a discussion like him." I thought to myself, "Well, of course!" Classics is my intellectual home. I might have made it to Pompeii, and I may have discovered these understudied and fertile inscriptions, but I do not think I would be editing ancient texts now if I had not had the chance to study with Richard and hold him as a model.

WASHINGTON AND LEE UNIVERSITY

WORKS CITED

Benefiel, R. R. 2012. "Magic Squares, Alphabet Jumbles, Riddles, and More: The Culture of Word-games among the Graffiti of Pompeii." In *The Muse at Play: Riddles and Wordplay in Greek and Latin Poetry*, edited by D. Petrain, J. Kwapisz, and M. Szymanski, 65–80. Munich.

———. 2018. "Gladiators, Greetings, and Poetry: Graffiti in First Century Pompeii." In *Scribbling through History: Graffiti, People, and Places from Antiquity to Modernity*, edited by E. F. C. Ragazzoli, Ö. Harmansah, and C. Salvador, 101–116. London.

Benefiel, R., S. Sprenkle, H. Sypniewski, and J. White. 2017. "The Ancient Graffiti Project: Geo-Spatial Visualization and Search Tools for Ancient Handwritten Inscriptions." In *DATeCH2017: Proceedings of the 2nd International Conference on Digital Access to Textual Cultural Heritage*, 163–168. Göttingen.

Benefiel, R. R., and H. M. Sypniewski. 2018. "Greek Graffiti in Herculaneum." *AJA* 122:209–244.

Camodeca, G. 2008. "La popolazione degli ultimi decenni di Ercolano." In *Ercolano: Tre Secoli di Scoperte*, ed. M. P. Guidobaldi, 86–103. Naples.

———. 1999. *Tabulae Pompeianae Sulpiciorum: Edizione critica dell'archivio puteolano dei Sulpicii*. 2 vols. Vetera 12. Rome.

Cooley, A. E. 2012. *The Cambridge Manual of Latin Epigraphy*. Cambridge.

De Ligt, L., and P. Garnsey. 2012. "The Album of Herculaneum and a Model of the Town's Demography." *Journal of Roman Archaeology* 25:69–94.

Della Corte, M. 1958. "Le iscrizioni di Ercolano." *Rendiconti della Accademia di Archeologia Lettere e Belle Arti (Napoli)* 33:239–308.

Della Corte, M. and P. Ciprotti, eds. 1952–1970. *CIL* IV, *Supplementi pars III: Inscriptiones Pompeianae Herculanenses parietariae et vasorum fictilium*, fasc. 1.–4. (Supp. 3). Berlin.

Dennison, W. 1898. "Some New Inscriptions from Puteoli, Baiae, Misenum, and Cumae." *AJA* 2:373–398.

Franklin, J. L., Jr. 1991. "Literacy and the Parietal Inscriptions of Pompeii." In *Literacy in the Roman World*, ed. J. H. Humphrey, 77–98. Ann Arbor, MI.

Krummery, H., and S. Panciera. 1980. "Criteri di edizione e segni diacritici." *Tituli* 2:205–215.

Mau, A, ed. 1898. *CIL* IV, *Supplementi pars II: Inscriptiones parietariae et vasorum fictilium* (Supp. 2). Repr. 1968. Berlin.

Mommsen, T., ed. 1883. *Corpus Inscriptionum Latinarum*. Vol. 10, *Inscriptiones Bruttiorum, Lucaniae, Campaniae, Siciliae, Sardiniae Latinae (CIL X)*. Berlin.

Panciera, M. 2011. "Hamillus/Sullimah: Sex, Fiction, and the Significance of Ananyms in Pompeii." *CP* 106:53–59.

Solin, H. 1973. "Review of CIL IV, supplementum III, 3., 4. Lieferung." *Gnomon* 45:258–277.

Väänänen, V. 1959. *Le Latin Vulgaire des inscriptions Pompéiennes*. Berlin.

Varone, A. 2016. "Newly Discovered and Corrected Readings of iscrizioni "privatissime" from the Vesuvian Region." In *Inscriptions in the Private Sphere in the Greco-Roman World*, ed. R. Benefiel and P. Keegan, 113–130. Leiden.

Wallace-Hadrill, A. 2011. *Herculaneum: Past and Future*. London.

Zangemeister, C., ed. 1871. *Corpus Inscriptionum Latinarum*. Vol. 4, *Inscriptiones parietariae Pompeianae Herculanenses Stabianae (CIL IV)*. Repr. 1957. Berlin.

———, ed. 1898. *CIL IV, Supplementi pars I: Tabulae ceratae Pompeiis repertae* (Supp. 1). Repr. 1968. Berlin.

CHRISTIAN GOTTLOB HEYNE AS A VIRGILIAN TEXTUAL CRITIC

Gian Biagio Conte

Translated by
Irene Peirano Garrison and Nebojša Todorović

THE YOUNG GOETHE was determined to attend Christian Gottlob Heyne's lectures in classical philology in Göttingen, a university which the British crown was held in high regard during the years of its personal union with the state of Hannover. Goethe's father, however, preferred to send his son to Leipzig to pursue more profitable studies in law. Goethe himself recounts these memories in his conversations with J. P. Eckermann as well as in his autobiographical work.[1] Between the last 30 years of the 18th century and the beginning of the 19th century, Heyne was a beacon for classical studies in Europe. Quite a few young members of the German bourgeoisie and aristocracy were drawn to his teaching. Heyne's *Altertumskunde*—such was the term before his pupil Friedrich August Wolf renamed it *Altertumswissenschaft* just a few decades later—had already blossomed into a full-fledged discipline with the capacity to embrace Western thinking on antiquity and particularly on the Mediterranean world. Thanks to Heyne, classical philology, understood as a discipline encompassing the entire history of the Greco-Roman literary tradition, emerges as a field fully emancipated from theological studies and could now assert itself as the formative ideal of the new secular knowledge.[2]

---

[1] See Riedel 1998.
[2] See the influential collected volume by Bäbler and Nesselrath 2014, as well as the outstanding essays by Fornaro: Fornaro 2011 and 2016a, with ample bibliography.

It would be incorrect to consider Heyne's work an unsophisticated prelude to what would soon become a transformative age of German classical studies. He is, rather, already part of this new era—he inaugurates it and nourishes it. He is not moved by romantic ideals; in him the spirit of the Enlightenment is fused with the liveliest sensitivity of neoclassical culture. Above all, he possesses a living sense of history and an assured taste for poetry.

After his death, it was easy for the subsequent generation of pupils (with all the arrogance typical of innovators) to move beyond the recent past altogether and deny Heyne his status as a true pioneer. Heyne was considered too backward and obsolete for the new era that his detractors aspired to inaugurate.[3] Wilhelm von Humboldt and Friedrich Schlegel chose to forget that Heyne was their teacher and did not hesitate to belittle his merits in order to promote the innovations of which they felt themselves to be harbingers.[4] Even Friedrich August Wolf—anxious to proclaim himself the father of a new, systematic *Altertumswissenschaft*—was reluctant to admit how much his own intervention in the "Homeric question" owed to the lessons of his teacher. Instead, Wolf claimed for himself the title of founding father of German classical philology and a role as its eponymous hero. In the meantime, the creation of the University of Berlin (where Wolf himself was invited to teach) enshrined the birth of a new center of studies that aimed to replace Göttingen, satisfying the dawning German nationalism.

It is undeniable that the program of studies drawn up by Wilhelm von Humboldt and Friedrich Schlegel was wide-ranging, insofar as they were both proponents of a comprehensive cultural reform; likewise undisputable is Wolf's influence over German romantic literature.[5] Although the specific intellectual projects of each thinker developed in different ways, the same "missionary" consciousness, typical of the greatest promoters of culture, animated them. Heyne's encyclopedism, on the contrary, embodied the everyday wisdom of the artisan, who increases his knowledge through a constant honing of his own work.

---

[3] See Fornaro 2016b.

[4] See the illuminating treatment in Fornaro 2013.

[5] See Maufroy 2011.

Thomas Carlyle, an iconic figure for many modern cultural heroes, puts it well: "... Heyne's best teacher was himself."[6] Two key achievements should suffice to assure him undying admiration: first, the sheer abundance of pioneering studies of different myths and their sources—for which he adopted a comparative methodology of investigation *avant la lettre*;[7] second, his monumental commentary on Virgil.[8] This titanic effort is the focus of this study.

Heyne's formidable abilities as an exegete of Virgil are well-known:[9] they are grounded not only in a great familiarity with Virgil's poetry but also in an innovative aesthetic vision. From Swiss critic Johann Jakob Breitinger (*Critische Dichtkunst*, 1740) and German philosopher Alexander Gottlieb Baumgarten (*Aesthetica*, 1750–58), he learned that the "concrete particular" is a key element of every artistic expression: Heyne is, therefore, invested in painstakingly explaining in his commentary the effects of the expressive defamiliarization that characterizes Virgilian poetic diction. In so doing, he leads his reader to appreciate the poet's extraordinary artistic achievements.

A clear principle inspires Heyne's work, which makes him a precursor of historicism on par with Lessing and Herder: for him, Virgil's originality lies in his expression of a mature and self-reflexive classicism. He is not imagined to be (like Homer) the champion of a primogenital and unconditional experience: his poetics must be judged as the product of *inuentio in delectu*. The commentator is aware that Virgil's first step toward the creation of great poetry lies in his emulation of Homer, but also that Virgil's *Kunstwollen* evolves beyond engagement with Homer and offers a new conception of the world. Nourished by the contrast with Homer, then, Virgil's poetry enables

---

[6] Carlyle 1870:119.

[7] See Fornaro 2017.

[8] The first edition, in four volumes, was published in Leipzig in 1767; the second edition, also in four volumes, was published in Leipzig in 1788; the first version of a third edition appeared in London in 1794 in four volumes; the second version of the third edition appeared in Leipzig between 1797 and 1800 in six volumes. The fourth edition (in five volumes) was published posthumously in Leipzig and London in 1830, edited by G. P. E. Wagner. I cite the text from the latter reproduced by Olms, Hildesheim, 1968, in 4 volumes (Heyne and Wagner 1968).

[9] See Döpp 2014.

the emergence of human and poetic values that are different from the Homeric ones. In simpler terms, a comparison between the two poems allows the reader to measure the differences between the two. At the same time, Heyne is nonetheless invested in the *synkrisis* with the Homeric model (a legacy of the critical tradition of 18th-century commentaries)[10] to such an extent that, despite his intellectual and emotional veneration of the *Aeneid*, which results at times even in an outpouring of admiration, he occasionally seems to undermine the strong creative originality of the poem.

The merits of Heyne's textual editing are less celebrated than his exegetic skills. As a critic, his main ambition was to craft a modern commentary that would prove informative in all literary and historical questions and explain difficulties of language and style while doing justice to Virgil's poetic virtuosity.[11] He did not consider it necessary to commit to preparing a new edition of Virgil. In effect, he accepted the text of the Heinsius-Burman edition, albeit with careful revisions, convinced that it was to some extent definitive insofar as it engaged with many contributions (general as well as particular) that Virgilian criticism had been distilling over time. This decision reflects the common prejudice that Virgil's text, transmitted by authoritative ancient and medieval manuscripts, was preserved almost without damage; another commonly held false belief at the time was that Virgil's text did not descend from ancient or late antique manuscripts but went back to Varius's edition *recta uia*. (Centuries later, Remigio Sabbadini would be a victim of the same fabrication.[12]) As a matter of fact, it is undeniable that the Virgilian text suffered inevitable damage during its transmission, albeit in smaller proportion compared to less fortunate authors: the presence of interpolations, corruptions, banalizations, and lacunae calls for the critical care of a meticulous *emendatio*.

After his death, Heyne's reputation, as well as that of his exegetical masterpiece, fell victim to the spitefulness of certain scholars who did not hesitate to pour scorn at his abilities as textual critic, even

[10] See Knauer 1964:84–93.
[11] See the excellent entry on Heyne in *Enciclopedia Virgiliana*: Chiarini 1985.
[12] See Conte 2017:67n2.

though his text was always judiciously and meticulously thought out. It is thanks to Sebastiano Timapanaro, independent scholar *sans pareil*, that the question was properly reformulated: he was the first to point out that, as a textual critic of Virgil, Heyne was far less naive than had been unfairly suggested by some after his death.[13] One must point out, however, that Heyne's work, while seemingly infused with a modern sensitivity and divorced from the tradition of editions *cum notis uariorum*, remains nevertheless a product of the 18th century.

Within a few years, German philology, determined to introduce new scientific rigor to philological methodology, perfected the rules of the stemmatic method. Named after Karl Lachmann, this approach was based (to speak in broad terms) on the reconstruction of a common archetype from which the manuscript tradition of a certain author descended. The rapid progress that this methodology brought about in textual criticism seemed destined to make Heyne's work on the Virgilian text obsolete simply because it preceded Lachmann's revolution.

But this assumption is only true to a point, for it is well-known that the Virgilian manuscript tradition is unique. Disregarding the large volume of medieval and humanistic witnesses, one is left with a group of authoritative, mutually independent manuscripts from late antiquity. These do not, therefore, allow the textual critic to reconstruct a common archetype, thus rendering the parameters of the stemmatic method unusable in the reconstruction of Virgil's text. There was, therefore, no good reason why Heyne's pre-Lachmannian philology should be delegitimated by the arrival of this new, more sophisticated critical methodology.

After all, Heyne's philology was based on exemplary "artisanal" methods of textual analysis that had transformed textual criticism into a real art. This type of textual criticism relied not only on a more rigorous logical-linguistic analysis but also on the commentator's

---

[13] See Timpanaro 1981:33n45: "Alla fama di Heyne come critico del testo, e come filologo in generale, nocque il tono sprezzante che verso di lui assunsero, in gran parte ingiustamente, i suoi scolari Wolf e Lachmann (e, in un ambito meno tecnico, Friedrich Schlegel); quanto al Lachmann in particolare vedi *Kl. Schr.*, II, p. 106."

extraordinary capacity to elucidate meanings implicit in the verbal texture of the poem and to pick between variants with acute stylistic sensibility. Heyne had evaluated with careful critical attention each proposal that his predecessors made before accepting any one of them: his philology was chiefly founded on a solid *iudicium*. In his commentary, he verified the letter of the text step-by-step. Always attentive to linguistic meanings, Heyne also tried to unveil the text's more expressive effects—one could say that he operated like a seismographer, capable of registering even the slightest vibrations in the author's poetic formulation.

Obviously, Heyne's textual choices are disputable and open to question. The introduction by Philip Wagner (a devoted student of Heyne) to the fourth edition of his teacher's commentary is a case in point. Wagner apologizes for having to deviate from Heyne's text, pointing out that he did not intend to accuse him of philological ineptitude. He writes: *Heynium satis constat interpretationis maxime rationem habuisse, rem criticam non aeque curasse.*[14]

Although this might sound like a harsh accusation, in the following sentence Wagner clarifies that Heyne's apparently scarce interest in textual criticism seemed only to be so because of his gentlemanly temperament: Heyne was not prone to the quarrels so dear to textual critics, and he feared that defending his own carefully thought-out choices would have devalued, by contrast, those of others.[15] He had the silent discretion of the critic who, convinced that his only duty is to the poet, does not indulge in the drama of polemics—he feared that such controversies would distract the reader from appreciating Virgil's poetry. He brought every single judgment of his to bear on the text itself. Satisfied with his thorough decision-making process, he preferred to avoid bitter scholarly quarrels. In the larger landscape of philological studies at the time, Heyne's rejection of polemics appears absolutely exceptional. Wagner picks up on this and gives him credit:

[14] Heyne and Wagner 1968: vol.1, VII.

[15] Heyne and Wagner 1968: vol.1, VII: "Erat nimirum id Heynii ingenium, ut in edendis a se scriptoribus antiquis eam potissimum rationem sequendam sibi putaret, quae ad ipsam lectionem intellectumque esset fructuosissima, ab omni contentione—rem criticam tractanti necessario subeunda—alienissimus."

> fuit ea istius aetatis, qua inclarescere ille coepit, labes,
> ut quidam acres inter se exercerent inimicitias critici
> rusticeque se invicem exagitarent. Quae res Heynium ...
> non potuit non vel invitum deterrere ab ea re, quam
> rixarum atrocitas invisam reddere deberet homini nec
> alienis meritis invidenti obtrectantique, nec suam famam
> in anceps certamen committere cupienti.[16]

After his death, despite this lack of interest in controversy,[17] Heyne was made the object of an ungenerous depreciation by some scholars. Inspired by the call to arms of the insurgent positivist revolution, this new school of philology showed increasing skepticism toward the authoritative texts of many a classical author and considered the ecdotic technique of the previous age disingenuous and inadequate.

If we grant that there exists a form of emotional intelligence in response to art (and Heyne's interpretative abilities in this respect are excellent), we should remember that emotions are also elicited from scientific intelligence, which derives the rules of its critical method from an empiric *obseruatio*. It is to this objective form of judgment that Lachmann and his comrades aspired. However, they assumed incorrectly that this demand for rigor was extraneous to Heyne's philological approach.

Between 1859 and 1868, Otto Ribbeck published his critical edition of Virgil for the *Bibliotheca Teubneriana*, arguably the first scientific edition of the modern age.[18] In the textual history of Virgil, this edition is undoubtedly a milestone; the *Prolegomena critica* is also an invaluable supplement with its inexhaustible collection of materials, data, observations, and reasoned arguments. His philological method is of a "Robespierrean" rigor. Student of both Lachmmann and Ritschl, Ribbeck shows great intellectual intransigence, even moral intransigence. The urge to purify Virgil's text emerges in his determination to unmask previously unnoticed corruptions, to repair dislocations of lines, and to denounce interpolations. His autonomy of judgment,

---

[16] Heyne and Wagner 1968: vol.1, VII.

[17] Cf. Chiarini 1985.

[18] See Conte 2017.

however, spills into a cerebralism that causes him to carry out arbitrary changes—Ribbeck transposed or suppressed lines just because they seem to go against the logical order he postulated.

The absolute rationalism that inspired the new methods of the post-Heyne generation of philologists could easily lapse into hyper-skeptic intellectualism. The most conspicuous damage of this critical behavior was suffered by the text of the *Georgics*, based on unsupported rumors of a second redaction at the hands of Virgil himself. This false premise contributed not only to Ribbeck's hunt for additional lines but also for presumed authorial revisions inserted in the previous text. Conington peremptorily labelled Ribbeck's conjectural inventiveness "a perverse application of cleverness."[19] Although it does not always marry prudence with subtlety of inquiry, Ribbeck's edition was founded on a collation of all ancient and medieval manuscripts, amply corroborated by a limpid critical apparatus and endowed with a rich inventory of *testimonia*. As such, it offers an incomparable comprehensiveness of supporting evidence and remains an imposing monument of learning.

I proceed by comparing specific choices made by Ribbeck with Heyne's edition. A comparison with the Heinsius-Burman edition would make little sense because its text, even after careful revision, undergoes few changes. Rather than comparing Heyne with his predecessors, I juxtapose his text to that of subsequent editors. The comparison with Ribbeck ought to show the degree to which the old-school philological approach of the Göttingen teacher endured the changing textual methodologies of 19th-century German philology and remains available to us, having withstood the test of time.

Heyne often provided satisfying solutions to problematic passages, but scholars of the following generations were not always capable of taking full advantage of them: they did not understand the merit of his decisions and ended up accepting a corrupt text. The following passage from *G.* 2.69–72 is a case in point: here, the poet addresses the topic of

---

[19] Conington's review first appeared in the *Cambridge Journal of Philology* in 1868. As a testament to the value he attached to polemics against those whom he viewed as extremists, he reprinted it as an appendix in his 1871 commentary to Virgil's works: Conington 1871:477. See further Conte 2017:63.

the grafts that transform the ability of trees to bear fruits. Ribbeck's edition reads:

> Inseritur uero et nucis arbutus horrida fetu,
> et steriles platani malos gessere ualentes,   70
> castaneae fagos; ornusque incanuit albo
> flore piri, glandemque sues fregere sub ulmis.

G. 2.69–72

This passage presents two difficulties, one at line 69 and one at line 71. Both are caused by metrical particularities. The main witness, the *codex Mediceus* (**M**), reads *inseritur uero et fetu nucis arbutus horrida* (the bristly arbutus is grafted with the fruit of the walnut). A late editor of **M**, the humanist Pomponius Laetus, who corrected the manuscript with red ink around the second half of the 15th century, thought that the text was corrupt and wanted to eliminate the anomaly of this hypermetric line. He did not realize, however, that the last syllable of the line *horrid(a)* undergoes synalepha with the *et* of the following line; he then recuperated the "normalizing" intervention of a second-hand Carolingian manuscript (γ) and edited the line as *nucis arbutus horrida fetu*. Heyne knew that Macrobius quotes the line as it appears in the Mediceus (*Sat.* 5, 14, 4) and that Servius too corroborates such a reading.[20] For this reason, he did not hesitate to disregard the metrical anomaly and printed the correct version, *fetu nucis arbutus horrida*. But Wagner, a zealous as well as a myopic student (the number of inferior readings he introduces in his revision of Heyne's edition is not small), changed the text and accepted the transposition. Ribbeck followed his mistake.

Another mistake that Ribbeck made is at line 71, where he reads *castaneae fagos*, a brief colon that allows him to create a syntactic parallel with the previous line *steriles platani malos gessere ualentes*: "[thanks to the drafting] sterile plane trees bore strong apple trees, the

---

[20] Servius *ad G.* 2.69: *FETU NUCIS ARBUTUS HORRIDA: uersus dactylicus: name male quidam 'horrens' legunt*; Macrobius, *Sat.* 5.14.4: Ὑπερκαταληκτικοὶ *syllaba longiores sunt ... 'arbutus horrida.'* Macrobius cites two other cases of hypermetric lines with synaphea: *G.* 1.295 *Vulcano decoquit umorem*; 3.449 *spumas miscent argenti uiuaque sulpura.*

chestnut trees bore the beech-trees." Two nominative plurals and two accusative plurals in apparent correspondence share the verb *gessere*. However, this reading implies that an infertile plant (the beech tree) is grafted onto a fruitful one (the chestnut tree), a practice that goes against common sense as well as against the examples of *insitio* that Virgil discusses in this very passage. To remedy this absurdity, Scaliger emended the text to *castaneas fagus*, taking *fagus* to be the fourth declension form of the nominative plural. [21] The accusative *fagos*, however, is a product of corruption. Priscian, as well as two Carolingian manuscripts, transmit the correct reading *fagus*, in which the final syllable is subject to a lengthening in arsi before a caesura (and resulting in a syntactical break).[22] To remedy this metrical anomaly, someone corrected to *fagos*, thus making the accusative dependent on the verb *gessere* and creating a syntactic parallel with the previous line. This innovation became authoritative and ended up influencing almost the entire manuscript tradition. To make sense of the lines, one must punctuate after *gessere ualentes* and let a new sentence begin; thus, *fagus* turns out to be, in coordination with *ornus*, the subject of *incanuit*, while *castaneae* is a genitive governed by *flore*, in parallel with *piri*.[23] Heyne's exegesis of this line is simple and precise: "*fagus flore castaneae et ornus albo piri flore incanuit:* h. e. castanea inseritur in fago (cf. Plin. *HN* 17.10.10) et pirus in orno."

Once again, Wagner's revision of Heyne's text is wrong,[24] and this mistake contributed to Ribbeck's disorientation, leading him away from the correct solution which had been proposed by Heyne:

> Inseritur uero et fetu nucis arbutus horrida,
> et steriles platani malos gessere ualentis;   70
> castaneae fagus ornusque incanuit albo
> flore piri, glandemque sues fregere sub ulmis.

---

[21] Scaliger 1600:9. This emendation is accepted in recent times by Thomas 1988.

[22] See discussion in Conte 2016:5.

[23] The first person to arrive at the correct reading (punctuating after *ualentis* and establishing the parallelism between *fagus* and *ornus*, both of which govern *incanuit ... flore*) seems to have been the Venetian humanist Naugerius (Andrea Navagero).

[24] See Wagner's discussion in his *Quaestiones Vergilianae* XII.14: Heyne and Wagner 1968: vol. 4, 428.

In their OCTs, Hirtzel and Mynors followed Ribbeck, neglecting Heyne.

To give one further example, equally unfavorable to Ribbeck, there is the case of *Aen.* 10. 303–305:

> namque inflicta uadi dorso dum pendet iniquo,
> anceps sustentata diu, fluctusque fatigat,
> soluitur atque uiros mediis exponit in undis.   305

Aen. 10.303–305

The poet is describing the docking of the Etrurian fleet, allied to Aeneas. In a rush to get to land, Tarcon's flagship hits shallow waters: the ship remains suspended on a shoal's protrusion (*dorso*) and wavers until dashing and throwing all the ship's occupants into the sea. Most manuscripts read *uadis*; only **P** reads *uadi* (corrected to *uadis* by a second hand). Servius Danielis argues that Probus too supported the reading *uadi dorso*—it is not clear whether this was an emendation or if he found this *lectio* somewhere.[25] For this reading to work, one must be convinced that *uadi dorso* is governed ἀπὸ κοινοῦ both by *inflicta* (understood as a dative) and by *pendet* (understood as an ablative), which would be a linguistic absurdity. One must also bear in mind the strong preference that Virgil shows for the plural *uada* when referring to shallow waters' shoals: the use of the singular *uadum* in this sense would be at the very least improbable.

Let us look closely at the passage. The *caesura semiquinaria* divides the lines in two halves: *namque inflicta uadis / dorso dum pendet iniquo*. For the second part of the line, the poet could have chosen the isometric variant *dum dorso pendet iniquo*, which would have underscored more clearly the syntactic articulation of the two hemistiches. For metrical reasons, however, he chose the sequence *dorso dum*, inverting the expected order as he has done in other similar circumstances: the very first line of the poem, where we have *Troiae qui* instead of *qui Troiae*, is a famous example. In this case, the verbal order is governed by "Marx's law," which notes that: "If after a *caesura semiquinaria* in a hexameter

---

[25] The best discussion of the problem is Delvigo 1987:55–62. See also Timpanaro (1986:89–90), who, however, leans towards *uadi dorso*. He seems to have later changed his mind, while still holding on to a measure of doubt: Timpanaro 2001:66–68.

a long monosyllable is associated with a spondaic word, the spondaic word precedes in the sequence."[26] The conjuction *dum* follows *dorso*, but logically it opens the subordinate clause which includes *dorso*.

Heyne understood the syntax of the line and did not hesitate to reject Probus's reading (noting: *Probus apud Seruium: male*). He correctly printed: *Namque, inflicta uadis, dorso dum pendet iniquo*. Ribbeck mistakenly followed Probus's version and thereby influenced many subsequent editors: Ladewig-Schaper-Deuticke, Hirtzel, Sabbadini, Geymonat, and Paratore; Conington and Mynors instead chose Heyne's text.

Respect for the indirect tradition and for Probus's readings in particular pushed Ribbeck to make this choice. It is this same awe for the indirect tradition which rightly determined his choice of *floros* over *flauos* at 12.605, [27] *umbrae* over *umbra* in 1.441, *arma relinquunt* over *arma reliquens* in 11.830, *uelati limo* over *uelati lino* in 12.120. [28] He did not make a similar choice in *G*. 3.230: here, the Virgilian manuscripts read almost unanimously *pernix*, whereas Servius Danielis registers also the variant *pernox* (*DS ad G*. 3.230 *et aliter: legunt et 'pernox', sed 'pernix' melius, id est pertinax*). Servius comments on *pernix*, without mentioning *pernox* (Servius *ad G*. 3.230 *pernix autem perseuerans a pernitendo tractum est*). A fanciful etymology for *pernix* is devised, assigning a meaning that this word does not and could not have: Servius (or perhaps someone before him) improvises a verb *pernitor*, which supposedly means "to insist in making an effort"; from this verb would come the meaning defined by the gloss *perseuerans*.

After all, the only meaning that the adjective *pernix* has in all its occurrences (since it derives from *perna* [leg or thigh]) implies speed: one must read "quick, speedy, agile," definitely not *pertinax* or *perseuerans*. Without giving it too much thought, Ribbeck welcomes

---

[26] Conte 2016:26, with further bibliography.

[27] See the magisterial treatment in Timpanaro 2001:77–93; see also Delvigo 1987:81–96; Reeve 1985:90.

[28] Heyne's preference for *limo* is noteworthy in that it entailed revising the text by Heinsius-Burman, which instead read *lino*. The note in which Heyne explains his choice is a masterful display of antiquarianism that demonstrates his deep knowledge of Roman religious ritual.

pernix into his text, even though he remembers in the critical apparatus that Scaliger had defended the reading *pernox*.[29] Heyne did not hesitate to reject *pernix*, finding that its assumed meaning was unacceptable in the context of the passage (he also notices that the verb *iacet* excluded an attribute that properly indicates quick movement): he understood that the pseudo-etymology proposed by the grammarians was nothing but an erudite mirage to be discredited.[30]

Still, in making this choice, Heyne relied on the indirect tradition. This decision was not accidental. There are at least three other cases in which he diverged from the manuscripts' readings, judging them to be the outcome of banalizations. According to him, the correct reading was preserved outside the direct tradition. For example, at *Aen.* 5.720, Ribbeck prints *tum uero in curas animo diducitur omnis*. Most codices (with the exception of a few Carolingian ones) read *animo*, whereas the indirect tradition (Servius and pseudo-Probus) prefers *animum*. The choice is not easy: generally speaking, Virgil loves the "middle passive" accusative, an elegant syntactic Graecism that replaces the ablative of respect especially when the verb refers to body parts: for example, in *Aen.* 1.579 *his animum arrecti dictis*; 1.658 *faciem mutatus et ora Cupido*; 1.561 *tum breuiter Dido uultum demissa profatur*; 6. 156 *Aeneas maesto defixus lumina uultu*; 12. 224 *[Iuturna]* ... *formam adsimulata Camerti*. It is also true that reasons of metrical convenience or syntactic convenience play an important role in most of these passages (e.g., *Aen.* 3.65 *Iliades crinem de more solutae*; 3.47 *ancipiti mentem formidine pressus*; 6.470 *nec magis incepto uultum sermone mouetur*; 1.713 *expleri mentem nequit [Phoenissa]*; 8.265 ... *nequeunt expleri corda tuendo*.) In any event, I endorse Heyne's choice, which in adopting the accusative *animum*, preserves a peculiarity of the high register that would have been exposed to easy banalization.[31] All other editors neglected Heyne's decision, wrongfully so.

[29] Scaliger 1600:9.

[30] See Conte 2016:61–68. It seems possible that the reading *pernox* was initially glossed as *perseuerans* or *pertinax* in order to explain how the defeated bull "lies awake all night long enclosed in his resentment" and that from this gloss some grammarian derived the idea of a verb **perniti* and a derivative *pernix* interpretable as *perseuerans*.

[31] On the middle-passive accusative, see Courtney 2004; Landgraf 1896–98; Löfstedt 1956: vol. 2, 421–422; see also Conte 2016:33–34.

Another case in which Heyne prefers a *lectio* from the indirect tradition is *Aen.* 7.109–110: *instituuntque dapes et adorea liba per herbam / subiciunt epulis* (*sic Iuppiter ipse monebat*). Ribbeck, Hirtzel, Sabbadini, Mynors, and Geymonat all accept this reading based on the manuscript tradition; *sic Iuppiter ille monebat* is supported by Priscian, Servius, Servius Danielis (*ad.* 1.617), and Tiberius Donatus,[32] as well as by the most authoritative editor of the codex Mediceus, the consul Asterius, who carefully emended it toward the end of the 5th century. The expression *Iuppiter ille*, as well as *Pater ille*, implies reverence and becomes a ritual formula of well-wishing: in ancient times, *Iuppiter* was "deictically" summoned ("Jupiter up there!"), pointing a finger to the sky or raising hands in an act of devotion.[33] The origins of this formula are archaic (see, for example, Plaut. *Mostell.* 398 *ita ille faxit Iuppiter*),[34] and it occurs only in passages of marked religious solemnity, such as the ending of the terrifying prophecy announced by the harpy Celaeno in Book 3. The *adorea liba* (wheat flatbread) of the subsequent line are also words with an archaic resonance (Plin. *HN* 18.81 *far quod adoreum ueteres appellauere*); the entire passage is thus infused with sacred language.[35] Emphasizing liturgical Latin's lively style, Heyne accepted *ille* and rejected the banalizing *ipse*. Only Conington followed his lead.

The risk of banalization is indeed quite frequent; in addition to the abovementioned example, the indirect tradition offered Heyne many other occasions to find a fitting remedy. I am now convinced that in *Aen.* 7.98 the reading *venient* (commonly proposed by editors) is a result of an easily made banalization, which was spread due to contamination in the collation of all late antique manuscripts. The correct reading is indicated by Servius, who has *uenient* in the lemma, as his exemplar read, but in his note writes: *melius "ueniunt," ut iam eos uenire significet* (Servius *ad Aen.* 7.98). The reading *ueniunt* appears also in pseudo-Probus (Keil, *Gramm. Lat.* IV 233.25), but a large number of the Carolingian

---

[32] It seems therefore clear that Donatus was already reading *ille*.

[33] See *TLL* 7.1.357.5ff.

[34] I give many examples including Plautus, Cicero, Ovid, and Virgil himself in Conte 2016: 34–35.

[35] The popular etymology associated *ador* with *adorare*, as if it were the same word belonging to religious ritual: see Ernout-Meillet 1967:9; Maltby 1991:9.

manuscripts also read *ueniunt*, probably under the influence of Servius's note. In this passage, King Latinus, worried that the inauspicious portents might signify an obstacle to an imminent wedding between Lavinia and Turnus (7.58 *sed uariis portenta deum terroribus obstant*; cf. verses 7.68–80), interrogates the oracle of his father, Faunus; the answer is quite explicit: *ne pete conubiis natam sociare Latinis / ... thalamis neu crede paratis; / externi ueniunt generi* ("Do not seek to join your daughter in a Latian marriage / ... do not entrust her to the marriage bed that has been prepared; / foreign sons in law are coming"). This interpretation is certainly the correct *lectio*; Servius is right: it could not be a conjectural reading (either by him or some predecessor) because evidently "mancava lo stimolo a congetturare."[36]

I must confess that I regret accepting the future *ueniet* in my first critical edition (in the second edition I read *ueniunt*). I had neglected to consider the limpid exactitude of Heyne, who notes: "sed bene iam Serv. vidit *veniunt* melius convenire vaticinio, quod, quae futura sunt, ut praesentia nuntiat." He also does not fail to notice how oracular style tends to link the "prophetic present" (*ueniunt*) with the "categorical plural" (*externi ... generi*): this is how oracles speak. The present *ueniunt* is at the same time more incisive and more irrevocable than the future *ueniet*, which is nothing more than a flat variant. The present contains the idea that the prophesized event is about to manifest, that it is already taking place. After all, few lines earlier another *uates*, questioned by King Latinus, had replied (7.68–69): *... externum cernimus ... / aduentare uirum* ("we see that a foreign man is coming")—a man whom the soothsayer's inspired eyes already see as if he were present in front of them. Many of us editors—all, in fact—did not reflect enough on Heyne's choice: once again, the Göttingen teacher showed not only independence of judgment but also an incisive ability to interpret the Virgilian text to its core.

The cases in which Ribbeck seems to lack Heyne's refined interpretative abilities are not small in number—a comparison between the two is often very unfavorable to the former. One further example will illustrate how the correct textual choice seems to be traceable back to

---

[36] Timpanaro 2001:124.

Heyne's uncommon linguistic sensibility. In the scene of the final duel
between Aeneas and Turnus, Ribbeck reads lines 12.788–790 (in agreement with the great majority of editors) as follows:[37]

> Olli sublimes, armis animisque refecti,
> hic gladio fidens, hic acer et arduus hasta,
> adsistunt contra certamina Martis anheli.

> *Aen.* 12.788–790

Nothing strange, considering that this is the text transmitted unanimously by the direct tradition. Servius, however, notes: *alii "certamine"*
legunt, ut sit sensus: adsistunt contra se in Martis anheli certamine (Servius
ad Aen. 12.790). The defenders of the reading *certamina* are compelled to
interpret: "They face the panting combat of Mars."[38] However, this idea
of "rising up before Mars's combat" does not seem to make much sense,
and even the poetic plural *certamina* is not convincing. It is probable
that the reading *certamina* stems from the error of someone who was
misled by the usual construction of *contra* + accusative, thus making
contra a preposition rather than an adverb to be joined with *adsistunt*
(see, for example, *constiterant contra* at line 12.271). The expression
certamine Martis forms a lexical unity insofar as it corresponds to an
Homeric formula that Virgil here reproduces (ἔριδα ... Ἄρηος at *Il.*
5.861 e 14.149 or ἔργον Ἄρηος at *Il.* 11.734)—these are formulae that
indicate a heroic duel. Therefore, the attribute *anheli* does not belong
to the "closed" structure of the formula, but it is a nominative plural
governing *certamine Martis* ("they are standing against one other,
panting because of Mars' combat.") Servius preserves this reading but
does not accept that *certamine* is governed by *anheli*; in fact, he translates *in Martis anheli certamine* (*ad Aen.* 12.790), inventing a figurative
locative construction (*in certamine*). It is interesting to observe that
even in this case Heyne found his path independently from Heinsius
because he diverged from his text, a text which he tends to follow in
many other instances: Heinsius accepts the reading *certamina*.

---

[37] With the important exception of Conington.
[38] Traina 1997:171.

This example is not the only occasion when Heyne diverges from his edition of choice: his departures always entailed careful and responsible revisions. The case of *G.* 1.383–387 is, in this respect, emblematic. Heinsius-Burman reads:

> Iam uarias pelagi uolucres et quae Asia circum
> dulcibus in stagnis rimantur prata Caystri
> certatim largos umeris infundere rores;   385
> nunc caput obiectare fretis, nunc currere in undas
> et studio incassum uideas gestire lauandi.

> *G.* 1.383–387

Late antique manuscripts (one must, however, keep in mind that a long part of the text is missing in the Palatinus manuscript) read *uariae ... uolucres*. In his lemma, Servius gives *uarias*, which he defends by saying: *haec est uera lectio ... nam si 'iam uariae' legeris, sensus nulla ratione procedit* (Servius *ad G.* 383). In other words, he takes *uarias ... uolucres* to be governed by *uideas*. But the *lectio* attested in Servius has all the appearance of a normalizing conjecture, while the nominative *uariae ... uolucres* has the merit of being a *lectio difficilior*; as a matter of fact, many editors had chosen it, justifying it in different ways. Among the most recent editors, Mynors believes that the passage contains an anacoluthon: the period would begin with a nominative destined to remain pending, followed by a series of infinitives (*infundere ... obiectare ... currere ... gestire*), all governed by *uideas*. In fact, after *Caystri* at the end of line 384, he inserts a long dash, signaling a pause and change of construction. This solution does not seem particularly viable: I do not believe that such an anacoluthon is attested outside popular and colloquial language. Sabbadini, followed faithfully by Geymonat, proposes a convenient, yet quite bizarre, compromise: "structura haec est: quae uariae pelagi sunt uolucres et quae in stagnis rimantur, eas infundere uideas." For this odd reading to work, one would have to imply *sunt* and to retrospectively extract from the coordinate copulative clause *et quae ... in stagnis rimantur* a relative circumlocution: (*quae*) *uariae pelagi uolucres* (*sunt*). All this is quite unlikely.

In both cases, the mistake consists in assuming that the four infinitives constitute a homogeneous syntactic series. This interpreation is not the correct reading. The first part of the image—lines 383–385, *iam uariae ... uolucres ... infundere rores*—is governed by the descriptive infinitive *infundere* and aims at providing the bigger picture of the scene: "then the multicolored birds pour upon the sea." The second part—the three infinitives *nunc obiectare ... nunc currere ... et gestire*—is governed by the verb *uideas* and focalizes ("you could see") the single details of the merry spectacle offered by the birds flying in and out of the waves. The proper function of the descriptive infinitive is to represent a scene vividly.[39] Heyne points out this fact with effective brevity: "*infundere* pro *infundunt* dictum ... Ita nova sententia facienda: *nunc caput obiectare ... uideas*."[40] This time, Ribbeck understood that Heyne, distancing himself from the Heinsius-Burman edition, had found the correct solution and rightly followed his reading. He should have done this more often.

I have provided some examples attesting to Heyne's autonomy of judgment and to his exceptional critical sensibility, but I could give more without difficulty. I have presented some that best bear witness to his attentive and acute intelligence that did not settle for an acceptable text but always worked in the service of interpreting Virgil's expressive art, which is always so limpid and unexpected. As Heyne writes at the beginning of his work:

> Difficile est Virgilium et sine interprete recte legere, et cum interprete. Sunt enim multa in doctissimo poeta, quae ... viros satis acutos exercitatosque, etiam in repetita lectione, tenere, aut quae, cum non sine multarum rerum

---

[39] Cf. e. g. *Aen.* 2.97–99: *... hinc sempre Ulixes / criminibus terrere nouis, hinc spargere uoces / in uulgum ambiguas et quaerere conscius arma*; 132–133 *Iamque dies infanda aderat; mihi sacra parari / et salsae fruges et circum tempora uittae*; cf. also *G.* 1.200. For more on the descriptive infinitive, see Leumann-Hofmann-Szantyr 1972:367: "Dieser absolute Inf. ist in seinem Wesen schildernd und malend."

[40] In the *apparatus criticus* of my edition, I tried to offer a syntactical interperation of the Virgilian image: "si post *rores* (385) satis fortiter distinguitur, haec sententia pro uerbo habet infinitum descriptiuum *infundere* et pro subiecto *uariae uolucres*. Postquam cupidas lauandi aues poeta indistincte descripsit, eas per aquam uarie lusitantes oculis subicit (*nunc ... nunc ... uideas*)."

scientia nec sine subtiliore et subacto iudicio cognosci possint, legentis oculum fugere soleant, quamvis sint summa cum arte posita, pulcerrime a poeta dicta et ad sensum iucundissima.[41]

A simplistic reading, one that lacks a fine and exercised *iudicium* (*sine subtiliore et subacto iudicio*), might not appreciate the minutiae of an extremely elaborate style.

When faced with this confrontational use of language, which is such a defining characteristic of Virgil's style, Ribbeck (as well as some subsequent editors) did not usually show a perceptiveness comparable to Heyne's. Through this style, the poet manages to create and recreate, over and over, an artistically defamiliarizing and dramatically original poetic diction. It is almost a paradox that, in virtue of their painstaking textual exegesis, commentators often appear better equipped to think through the different readings of a text than the editors who are supposed to construe it. Ribbeck's edition certainly attests to the progress of critical knowledge about Virgil's text. But Heyne can claim to have built a monument of undying philological science—a science fortified by a subtle acumen and nourished by an intense devotion to Virgilian poetry.

Scuola Normale Superiore, Pisa

WORKS CITED

Bäbler, B., and H. G. Nesselrath, eds. 2014. *Christian Gottlob Heyne: Werk und Leistung nach zweihundert Jahren*. Abhandlungen der Akademie der Wissenschaften zu Göttingen, Neue Folge 32. Berlin.

Carlyle, T. 1870. "The Life of Heyne." In *Critical and Miscellaneous Essays by Thomas Carlyle*, 115–127. New York.

Chiarini, G. 1985. "Heyne, Christian Gottlob." In *Enciclopedia Virgiliana*, vol. 2, 846–849. Rome.

Conington, J. 1871. *P. Vergili Maronis. Opera.* Vol. 3. 2nd ed. London.

---

[41] Heyne and Wagner 1968: vol.1, 14.

Conte, G. B. 2016. *Critical Notes on Virgil: Editing the Teubner Text of the Georgics and the Aeneid*. Berlin.

———. 2017. "Ribbeck e Sabbadini editori di Virgilio." *Materiali e Discussioni per l'Analisi dei Testi Classici* 78:51–68.

Courtney, E. 2004. "The 'Greek' Accusative." *CJ* 99:425–431.

Delvigo, M. L. 1987. *Testo virgiliano e tradizione indiretta: Le varianti probiane*. Pisa.

Doepp, S. 2014. "Es lohnt sich, bei Heyne 'anzufragen': Zu Heynes monumentalem Vergilkommentar." In Bäbler and Nesselrath 2014, 43–61.

Ernout, A., and A. Meillet. 1967. *Dictionnaire étimologique de la langue latine*. 4th ed. Paris.

Fornaro, S. 2011. "Christian Gottlob Heyne dans l'histoire des études classiques." In *La Philologie allemande, figures de pensée*, ed. M. Espagne and S. Maufroy, 15–26. Revue Germanique Internationale 14. Paris.

———. 2013 "Christian Gottlob Heyne und Friedrich Schlegel." In *Friedrich Schlegel und die Philologie*, ed. U. Breuer, R. Bunia, and A. Erlinghagen, 45–57. Schlegel Studien 7. Padeborn.

———. 2016a. "Christian Gottlob Heyne e le nuove vie dello 'studio degli antichi.'" In *Storia della Filologia Classica*, ed. D. Lanza and G. Ugolino, 49–70. Rome.

———. 2016b. "Christian Gottlob Heyne et Wilhelm von Humboldt." In *L'hellénisme de Wilhelm von Humboldt et ses prolongements européens*, ed. M. Espagne and S. Maufroy, 15–29. Paris.

———. 2017. "The Apollodorus of Christian Gottlob Heyne." In *Apollodoriana: Ancient Myths, New Crossroads; Studies in Honour of Francisco J. Cuartero*, ed. J. Pàmias, 219–226. Berlin.

Heyne, C. G., and G. P. E. Wagner. 1968. *P. Vergili Maronis. Opera*. 4th ed. 4 vols. Hildesheim.

Knauer, G. N. 1964. *Die Aeneis und Homer: Studien zur poetischen Technik Vergils mit Listen der Homerzitate in der Aeneis*. Göttingen.

Landgraf, G. 1896–98. "Der Accusativ der Beziehung nach passiven Verbis." *Archiv für lateinische Lexicographie und Grammatik mit Einschluss des älteren Mittellateins* 10:215–24.

Leumann, M., J. B. Hofmann, and A. Szantyr. 1972. *Lateinische Syntax und Stilistik*. Vol. 2. Munich.

Löfstedt, E. 1956. *Syntactica: Studien und Beiträge zur historischen Syntax des Lateins*. 2 vols. Lund.

Maltby, R. 1991. *A Lexicon of Ancient Latin Etymologies*. ARCA. Leeds.

Maufroy, S. 2011. "Friedrich August Wolf, un modèle philologique et ses incidences européennes." In *La philologie allemande, figures de pensée*, ed. M. Espagne and S. Maufroy, 27–39. Revue Germanique Internationale 14. Paris.

Reeve, M. 1985. Review of *Latin Textual Criticism in Antiquity*, by J. Zetzel. *CP* 80:85–92.

Ribbeck, O., ed. 1894–1895. *P. Vergili Maronis. Opera*. 4 vols. Leipzig.

Riedel, V. 1998. "Antike." In *Goethe Handbuch*, vol. 4, pt. 1, 56. Stuttgart.

Sabbadini, R., ed. 1930. *P. Vergili Maronis. Opera*. 2 vols. Rome.

Scaliger, J., ed. 1600. *M. Manilii. Astronomicon libri quinque*. Leiden.

Thomas, R. 1988. *Virgil. Georgics*. Cambridge.

Timpanaro, S. 1981. *La genesi del metodo del Lachmann*. 2nd ed. Padua.

———. 1986. *Per la storia della filologia virgiliana antica*. Rome.

———. 2001. *Virgilianisti antichi e tradizione indiretta*. Florence.

Traina, A. 1997. *Virgilio: L'utopia e la storia; Il libro XII dell'Eneide e antologia delle opere*. Turin.

ON (AUTHORIAL AND OTHER) PARENTHESES IN CAESAR'S *COMMENTARII*

Cynthia Damon

I TOOK MY CUE for this paper from our honorand's marvelous and wittily titled essay "Parenthetically Speaking (in Virgil and Other Poets)," in which he builds an impressive case for "the expressive potential of parenthesis" in Hellenistic and Roman poetry, discussing the figure's role in communicating both empathetic involvement and ironic detachment.[1] With a wonderful selection of examples, he shows that these verbal gestures, generally associated with conversation and informal discourse, also have their place, indeed a prominent place, in high poetic art. His colleague Kathleen Coleman, in her illuminating paper on "Parenthetical Remarks in the *Siluae*," brings out the utility of parentheses for *sententiae* and "learned footnotes."[2] And Wendell Clausen, the dedicatee of Richard's paper, notes their aura of spontaneity in his commentary on the *Eclogues*.[3] Of the characteristics mentioned so far—empathy, irony, conversation, informality, poetic art, sententiousness, learned footnotes, spontaneity—not one is readily associated with Caesar's *Commentaries*, so my readers may be prepared to go along with a generalization in a standard Latin grammar asserting

I am grateful to the organizers for the invitation to participate in the conference and contribute to the present volume; questions and comments from the audience in 2018, especially from our honorand himself, materially improved my argument. I am likewise grateful to Harm Pinkster for giving me access and permission to quote from his helpful discussion of parentheses in advance of the eagerly awaited publication of the second volume of the *Oxford Latin Syntax*.

[1]   Tarrant 1998:144.

[2]   Coleman 2010:307–314.

[3]   Clausen 1994 (ad Virgil *Ecl*. 1.31). In an age hostile to parentheses, the figure was even associated with disorganized thought (Lennard 1991:84–90).

that parentheses are "extremely infrequent" in Caesar.[4] But that would be a mistake. The implication of that (unsupported) generalization is that Caesar's parentheses are uninteresting as well as infrequent, and yet they are neither.

Consider the following sentence:

> Conclamant legionis tertiae decimae, quae aderat, milites—hanc enim initio tumultus euocauerat, reliquae nondum conuenerant—sese paratos esse imperatoris sui tribunorumque plebis iniurias defendere.[5]
>
>   *BCiv.* 1.7.8
>
> A shout went up from the soldiers of the thirteenth legion, which was at hand—for he had summoned this legion at the start of the emergency; the rest had not yet arrived—that they were ready to protect their commander and the tribunes from injury.

The soldiers' shout demands attention. Caesar, known for his regular verb-final clauses, starts *this* sentence with the main verb. So Caesar sets his men shouting, but he is in no hurry to deliver the content of their shout. And yet the reader will be waiting for content, since Caesar usually supplies it when he uses *conclamare* elsewhere.[6] In our passage, however, a six-word subject intervenes (*legionis tertiae decimae, quae aderat, milites*), and that subject initiates an eight-word parenthesis (*hanc enim initio tumultus euocauerat, reliquae nondum conuenerant*),

---

[4] "In der klass. Zeit sind sie (*sc.* Parenthesen) äußerst selten bei Caes. und Sall" (Leumann, Hofmann, and Szantyr 1972–1979: vol. 2, 472), echoed (from an earlier edition) by Schwyzer 1939:96.

[5] Passages from the *BGall.* and *BCiv.* are punctuated according to Hering 1987, and Damon 2015b, respectively, unless another source is indicated.

[6] Caesar uses the verb in 16 other passages. In seven the content is a military order such as *ad arma!* (*BGall.* 7.70.6; *BCiv.* 1.69.4) or *uasa!* (*BCiv.* 1.66.2, 3.37.4, 3.38.3; this formula is reduced to *conclamari* at *BCiv.* 1.67.2, 3.75.2). Once he supplies a direct object (*BGall.* 5.37.2 *uictoriam conclamant*), and twice he pairs *conclamare* with a second verb that governs the content of both (*BGall.* 7.26.4 *conclamare et significare de fuga Romanis coeperunt*; 7.38.6 *conclamant Haedui et Litauiccum obsecrant ut sibi consulat*). In the remaining six passages *conclamare* introduces *oratio obliqua* (*BGall.* 1.47.6, 3.18.5, 5.26.4, 7.21.1, 7.66.7; *BCiv.* 3.6.1).

where the demonstrative *hanc* and the postpositive *enim* make it clear that Caesar restarted the syntax after *milites*. With the asyndetic *reliquae*, he restarts it again, carrying us on to *conuenerant*. Only then do we hear what the soldiers shouted. And it was worth waiting for, given its importance to Caesar's implicit argument about the legitimacy of the war he has just begun: they shouted "that they were ready to protect their commander and the people's tribunes from injury."[7] In effect, Caesar interrupts his soldiers in mid-shout, and the interruption is arguably more important than the just-in-time delivery of background information about the timing of his summons to the legions; the resulting hyperbaton increases the impact of the declaration of loyalty to Caesar's cause. Of course the existence of one effective parenthesis does not constitute a rebuttal of "extremely infrequent," but the appendix in which I have collected more than one hundred Caesarian parentheses can perhaps do that. My aim here is to persuade you that Caesar uses parentheses for a variety of expressive effects, and more importantly, that their collective impact makes a significant contribution to his rhetoric.

I. *CONTINVATIONI SERMONIS MEDIVS ALIQVI SENSVS INTERVENIT*

The parentheses listed in the appendix are those found in Wolfgang Hering's 1987 Teubner of the *Bellum Gallicum* and my 2015 OCT of the *Bellum ciuile*. If I had used other editions the list would have been slightly different,[8] but parenthesis is not an artifact of punctuation. It was a figure of speech as familiar to ancient grammarians as it was popular among Greek and Roman writers. Quintilian, for example, defines "parenthesis" as a figure of speech in which "some intervening

---

[7] He uses a similar structure at a similar juncture in the *BGall.*, when the Gauls reaffirm their confidence in Vercingetorix's leadership after a defeat (the parenthesis is underlined): 7.21.1 *conclamat omnis multitudo et suo more armis concrepat, quod facere in eo consuerunt, cuius orationem approbant, summum esse Vercingetorigem ducem nec de eius fide dubitandum nec maiore ratione bellum administrari posse.*

[8] Punctuation for parentheses is not standardized, and even within editions, punctuation "rules" sometimes yield precedence to other editorial priorities. For similar cautions about their poetic material, see Albrecht 1964:23–25, and Tarrant 1998:142–143.

idea interrupts the continuity of an utterance" (9.3.23 *quod interposi-tionem uel interclusionem*[9] *dicimus, Graeci* παρένθεσιν *<siue>* παρέμπτωσιν *uocant, cum continuationi sermonis medius aliqui sensus interuenit).*[10] Both the adjective *medius* and the threefold prefix *inter-* signal the key feature of a parenthesis, the fact that it interrupts an ongoing utterance.[11]

It is helpful to consider this ancient definition of parenthesis in light of the description in a modern functional grammar:

> A parenthetical constituent (or: parenthesis) is a linguistic unit that is inserted inside another linguistic unit (its "host"), but which does not belong to and has no influence on the internal syntactic structure of its host, nor is its own internal structure determined by the host.[12]

In this description, taken from the forthcoming second volume of Harm Pinkster's monumental *Oxford Latin Syntax*, the interrupting quality of a parenthesis is again primary: it is "a linguistic unit that is inserted inside another linguistic unit."[13] (I should perhaps say, parenthetically, that I use Pinkster's analysis of the parenthesis in preference to that in

---

[9] *Interclusio*, the second of Quintilian's Latin equivalents for *parenthesis*, occurs nowhere else in this sense (see *TLL* 7.1.2170.50–54) but seems to stress the shutting off of the initial utterance (cf. Cic. *De orat.* 3.181 *clausulas ... et interpuncta uerborum animae inter-clusio atque angustiae spiritus attulerunt*). Schwyzer's (1939:591) proposed emendation to an equivalent for παρέμπτωσιν, the otherwise unattested *intercasionem*, has not found favor.

[10] Albrecht (1964:13–25) provides a useful overview of parenthesis as a feature of literary texts.

[11] For other ancient definitions of *parenthesis*, see *TLL* 10.1.368.42–61, with Roschatt 1884:190–195, Kitzmann 1907:3–13, Schwyzer 1939:4–7, Albrecht 1964:13–17, and Panico 2001.

[12] Pinkster, forthcoming: §22.44. Earlier discussions of the syntax and rhetorical figure include Kühner-Stegmann 1962, vol. 2, 248–249 (on *Satzapposition*); Leumann, Hofmann, and Szantyr 1972–1979: vol. 2, 472–473, 634–635, 728–729; and Lausberg 1998:§860.

[13] Pinkster (forthcoming) discusses various categories of parenthetical constituent: verbs and expressions of perception, cognition, and communication (§22.46); curses and swear words (§22.47); interjections (§22.48–52); forms of address (§22.53) Cf. Bolkestein 1998:1: "There are very few restrictions on the type of linguistic expression which can be parenthetically inserted into some host clause."

other grammars because in the past the construction has tended to get what Michael von Albrecht has called a "step-motherly treatment.")[14]

Both the ancient and the modern grammarian are interested in the function of this intrusive constituent. According to Quintilian, it is one of the figures of speech that "attract attention to themselves and keep the listener from being bored" (9.3.27 *Haec schemata ... conuertunt in se auditorem nec languere patiuntur*); he likens them to seasoning in food, agreeable to the consumer if not used in excess.[15] Pinkster's account is less metaphorical and more detailed:

> Parentheses often contain information that supports, qualifies, rectifies, justifies, or constitutes an authorial comment on the content (or part of it) of the host clause or sentence, or, more generally, situates that content in a wider context. ... They may also appeal to the knowledge of the addressee, invoke the sympathy of the addressee, or have a text structuring function.[16]

These and other functions of parenthesis will become clearer when we look at representative parentheses from Caesar's *commentarii*.[17]

II. PARENTHESIS EST QVOTIENS REMOTA DE MEDIO SENTENTIA INTEGER SERMO PERDVRAT?

In adapting the parenthesis for the historiographical genre, Caesar's predecessors prepared the ground for his use of its content delivery

---

[14] See Albrecht 1964:21: "Die stiefmütterliche Behandlung der P[arenthese] durch die Grammatiker."

[15] Quint. 9.3.4: *uelut asperso quodam condimento iucundior* [sc. *sermo*]; cf. 9.3.27 *habent* (sc. *schemata*) *quandam ex illa uitii similitudine gratiam, ut in cibis interim acor ipse iucundus est. Quod continget si neque supra modum multae fuerint nec eiusdem generis aut iunctae aut frequentes, quia satietatem ut uarietas earum, ita raritas effugit.*

[16] Pinkster, forthcoming: §22.45. Albrecht (1964:196) disputes the utility of dividing informational and interactional functions: "Weiterhin zeigt sich hier auch die Fragwürdigkeit der herkömmlichen Zweiteilung der P[arenthese]n in 'logische' und 'psychologisch-rhetorische' ... : gerade diesen 'logischen' P[arenthese]n dienen Ovid mit Vorliebe dazu, den Hörer anzusprechen und sein Denken zu beleben."

[17] Henceforth I use the term "brackets" for the punctuation mark, reserving the term "parenthesis" for the figure of speech.

and interactional functions, for example, by increasing the proportion of authorial parentheses beyond that in narrative poetry, where a robust proportion of the total occur in character speech.[18] Some rough numbers will suggest the scale of this change. According to Stephen Harrison, about two-thirds of the parentheses in the first six books of the *Aeneid* (46 of 65) occur in character speech.[19] In the first six books of Livy's *Ab urbe condita*, by contrast, 11 of 108 parentheses occur in character speech,[20] while in what survives of the first six books of Tacitus's *Annals* there are 6 character-speech parentheses from a total of 52.[21] For the ten Caesarian commentaries, which contain roughly 75 percent as many words as Livy's first six books, the statistics are complicated by the fact that one of the characters is "Caesar" himself, but even so the basic character/narrator breakdown is seven character-speech parentheses from a total of roughly a hundred parentheses.[22] In other words, Caesar uses more parentheses per page than Livy and gives a greater percentage of his parentheses to the narrator than any of the other authors mentioned.[23] In the remainder of this paper, we will be

[18] For surveys of the use of parenthesis by Herodotus, Thucydides, and Xenophon, see Schmitt 1913.

[19] Harrison 2010:269n4: "Of the sixty-five parentheses usually marked in modern editions of *Aeneid* 1–6, forty-six occur in direct discourse"; also Tarrant 1998:151: "There [*sc.* in the *Aeneid*] ... more than half of the parentheses appear in speeches ... and are thus a means of rendering, in however stylized a way, the rhythms of direct speech." On Ovid's use of parenthesis in the service of characterization, see also Albrecht 1964:143–156; on Statius's selective use of parentheses in character speech in the *Siluae*, see Coleman 2010:302–305.

[20] The total represents the parentheses set off by paired dashes in the Ogilvie and Walters/Conway OCTs of Livy 1–6. Eckert (1911:66) finds 170 parentheses in the first decade, rarely in speeches: "Adnotandum videtur parentheses a Livio in orationibus satis raro esse adhibitas."

[21] I hope to publish a discussion of Tacitus's parentheses elsewhere. The total (52) is my count of intraclausal parentheses in *Annals* 1–6. Schmitt (1913:62) notes that Thucydides uses no parentheses in speeches.

[22] Character-speech parentheses are marked with quotation marks (";") in the appendix.

[23] And yet parenthesis is cited by Oakley as a regular feature of Livy's style (1997–2005: vol. 1, 132–133): "A further device which adds to the complexity of L.'s sentence structure (both in periodic sentences and elsewhere) is his fondness for parenthesis; in his hands this becomes another method of subordination, to be used alongside ablative absolutes, participles, and adverbial and relative clauses." On Livy's "characteristic boldness

trying to listen in on the conversation that occurs between brackets in Caesar's *commentarii*. I begin with a parenthesis that communicates Caesar's grasp of reality, however unpalatable.

Late in the summer of 55 BCE, Caesar's bold and underprepared expedition to Britain reached a crisis after a violent storm: his fleet lay shattered on the beach, and his army had no way to return to Gaul and no supplies for a winter in Britain:

> Compluribus nauibus fractis, reliquae cum essent funibus, ancoris reliquisque armamentis amissis ad nauigandum inutiles, magna, id quod necesse erat accidere, totius exercitus perturbatio facta est.

> *BGall.* 4.29.4

> Many boats had broken up, and since the remainder, having lost stays, anchors, and the rest of the tackle, were unfit for sailing, there developed significant—the thing that was bound to happen—dismay in the entire army.

The parenthesis *id quod necesse erat accidere*, like many a subordinate clause in periodic sentences, appears after the opening word of the main clause, delaying the arrival of its subject and verb. But *id quod necesse erat accidere* is not a subordinate clause. It is an independent sentence, unconnected to the context except by sense: the referent of *id* is the main clause of the host sentence, *magna ... perturbatio facta est.* In other words, this is an instance of the construction called *Satzapposition*, *apposition de phrase*, or now, clausal apposition:[24] the parenthesis stands in apposition to its host sentence.[25] It is, in Pinkster's terms, an extra-clausal constituent, its alien status signaled by the demonstrative *id*,

---

in the use of parenthesis," see Oakley 1997–2005, vol. 3, 465. In his commentary on Book 6, Oakley "hazard[s] the guess that no previous Latin writer used parentheses so extensively as L." (vol. 1, 133n119).

[24] Pinkster, forthcoming.

[25] See Kühner and Stegmann 1962: vol 2, 248–249; Longrée 2007; and Pinkster, forthcoming: §18.27. These extraclausal constituents need not be parenthetical, indeed they gravitate to the end of sentences: e.g., *BGall.* 2.35.4: *quod ante id tempus accidit nulli*, 5.33.1 *quod plerumque eis accidere consueuit, qui in ipso negotio consilium capere coguntur*; *BCiv.* 3.32.5 *quod in bello plerumque accidere consueuit uniuersis imperatis pecuniis*, etc.

which restarts the syntax before the main clause initiated by *magna* reaches its conclusion. Like most appositional expressions, this one is punctuated with commas.[26] The statement "was bound to happen" is of course part of Caesar's apologia for his army's panic: it was inevitable. But he is not really on the defensive here; indeed the hyperbaton forces us to dwell on *magna*. This maneuver is the opposite of sweeping a problem under the rug. However, the bigger the problem, the greater the credit for solving it, as Caesar eventually does: repairs were initiated (4.31.2–3) and the ships reached the mainland safely (4.36.3: *quae [sc. naues] omnes incolumes ad continentem peruenerunt*).[27] With this bland-looking parenthesis, Caesar simultaneously demonstrates his imperturbability in a crisis and magnifies the predicament in which he found himself.

Two further examples of clausal apposition will show that Caesar's legates, too, are credited with or claim insight into the ways of the world and demonstrate the author's expertise with parenthetical rhetoric.

The first example shares many features with the previous one. Early on in the civil war, before Caesar has even reached Spain, a sudden storm and the bridge washout that ensued stranded a large foraging party on the wrong side of a river, vulnerable to a Pompeian attack. The Pompeians do attack, but disaster is prevented by the foresight of Caesar's legate, C. Fabius, who had sent two legions across the river by a different bridge. He did so, says Caesar,

> ... suspicatus fore—id quod accidit—ut duces aduersariorum occasione et beneficio Fortunae ad nostros opprimendos uterentur.[28]

> *BCiv.* 1.40.7

> ... suspecting that it would be the case—the thing that happened—that the enemy leaders would use the occasion and Fortune's gift to crush our men.

---

[26] Examples of parenthetical clausal apposition are marked with an asterisk (*) in the appendix.

[27] On Caesar's preemptive explanations, see Rambaud 1966:151–173.

[28] Klotz (1926) punctuates with commas instead of dashes.

The parenthesis *id quod accidit*, which stands in apposition to the *fore ut* clause, i.e., to the object of *suspicatus*, assures us that Caesar's men were in good hands. It is an implicit comment on Fabius's foresight offered from the perspective of a narrator who, in hindsight, sees that Fabius got it right.[29] And the sequel validates the narrator's approval: when the legions arrive, the battle breaks up, and everyone returns to camp (*BCiv.* 1.40.8).

Admittedly, the syntax could be construed differently here: one could take *id* as the subject of *fore* and the *ut* clause as standing in apposition to the demonstrative. This is how the sentence is construed and translated by Fabre, the editor of the Budé edition:

> ... suspicatus fore id quod accidit, ut duces aduersariorum occasione et beneficio Fortunae ad nostros opprimendos uterentur.

> ... il avait pressenti qu'il se produirait ce qui avait eu lieu en effet, que les généraux ennemis mettraient à profit l'occasion et l'avantage que leur offrait la Fortune pour surprendre les nôtres.

However, Fabre has included an indicative verb within *oratio obliqua* and rendered that verb, *accidit*, rather loosely.[30] So I think that Klotz and I are justified in construing *id quod accidit* as a parenthesis.

If we test *id quod accidit* against Servius's definition of the parenthesis, it passes muster:

> Parenthesis est quotiens remota de medio sententia integer sermo perdurat.

Servius ad Aen. 1.65

> A parenthesis occurs when the sense persists unchanged after a sentence has been removed from the middle.

---

[29] On this episode, see Rambaud 1976. He considers it to have been "avec toutes les ressources de l'apologétique césarienne" (34) but does not discuss the parenthesis.

[30] Longrée (2007:13–14) agrees with Fabre, citing *BGall.* 5.33.6 as a parallel. A better parallel is on offer at *BGall.* 4.31.1. On retained indicatives, see Leumann, Hofmann, and Szantyr 1972–1979: vol. 2, 547–548, Pinkster 2015:669–671.

Without *id quod accidit*, the syntax of the host clause is indeed intact:

> * ... suspicatus fore ut duces aduersariorum occasione et beneficio Fortunae ad nostros opprimendos uterentur.

> * ... suspecting that it would be the case that the enemy leaders would use the occasion and Fortune's gift to crush our men.

However, the overall sense is not, for *id quod accidit* is one of a series of comments about the predictability of events, the cumulative effect of which is to reassure the reader that humans, though subject to the unexpected, are not helpless, at least not if they have the right leaders.[31]

Later on in the *Civil War* a similar parenthesis helps Caesar show that Labienus is *not* one of the right leaders:

> "Noli" inquit "existimare, Pompei, hunc esse exercitum qui Galliam Germaniamque deuicerit. Omnibus interfui proeliis neque temere incognitam rem pronuntio. Perexigua pars illius exercitus superest. Magna pars deperiit, quod accidere tot proeliis fuit necesse, multos autumni pestilentia in Italia consumpsit, multi domum discesserunt, multi sunt relicti in continenti."

> *BCiv.* 3.87.1–2

> "Do not suppose, Pompey, that this is the army that conquered Gaul and Germany," says Labienus. "I took part in all of the battles; I am not speaking at random about something unfamiliar to me. The surviving portion of that army is exceedingly small. Most of it has perished, as was bound to happen in so many battles. Disease took many in the fall in Italy, many went home, many were left behind on the mainland."

---

[31] In addition to the passages cited in the text and in notes 25 and 30: *BGall.* 5.39.2: *quod fuit necesse*; *BCiv.* 1.85.4: *Accidisse igitur his quod plerumque ... accidere soleat*; 3.41.4 *ut accidit*; 3.44.3 *idque accidit*.

Labienus's *quod accidere tot proeliis fuit necesse* is one of the relatively rare parentheses in character speech in the *commentarii*. It looks and sounds similar to what the narrator said about Caesar in Britain and Fabius in Spain.[32] But its effect is quite different since the preceding narrative shows that Labienus's assertion about the character of Caesar's troops is false, at least insofar as pertains to the experience gained in Gaul and Germany. For as Caesar tells it, the troops considered themselves to be the very men who fought at Alesia and Avaricum (*BCiv.* 3.47.5). So it is irrelevant whether many had perished, as Labienus says was "bound to happen." Labienus knows that leaders are supposed to express reassuring inferences in parentheses, and his bid to sound like Caesar succeeds in the moment: Pompey and his council of war "felt that victory was theirs since on so important a matter, it seemed impossible that the assurances given by so experienced a commander were empty" (*BCiv.* 3.87.7). But empty they were, and the parenthesis backfires badly with Caesar's readers, who know that Labienus is wrong as he speaks.[33]

These three examples indicate something of Caesar's skill with parentheses and give a glimpse of the editor's role in ensuring that the reader is alert to the presence of an additional layer of communication from the author. The editorial parenthesis (alluded to by "other" in my titular parenthesis) will be the subject of Part III of this paper, but first I review some other categories of authorial parenthesis in the *commentarii*.

Parentheses commencing with the particle *nam*, common everywhere in Latin, ostensibly supply explanatory material.[34] But they also help establish a connection with the reader, as is particularly clear in a siege scene near the end of *BGall.* 2, where Caesar provides a paraphrase of the words of the besieged Aduatuci, who are bemused by the sight of Romans building a siege tower too far from their wall to threaten it:

---

[32] The demonstrative pronoun in such appositional expressions is optional (see notes 25 and 30–31 above), so its absence here is not a significant difference.

[33] At Pharsalus the reader discovers the cost of Pompeian overconfidence (*BCiv.* 3.96.1: *nihil eos de euentu eius diei timuisse*).

[34] Parentheses signaled by *nam* and post-positive *enim*: (*nam*) *BGall.* 1.18.10, 2.14.1, 2.16.3, 2.23.1, 2.30.4, 4.14.5; *BCiv.* 3.95.2; (*enim*) *BGall.* 2.17.4, 5.52.1 (as emended), 6.34.3; *BCiv.* 1.7.8, 2.22.1.

> Quibusnam manibus aut quibus uiribus praesertim
> homines tantulae staturae—nam plerumque omnibus
> Gallis prae magnitudine corporum suorum breuitas
> nostra contemptui est—tanti oneris turrim in muro sese
> posse conlocare confiderent?

BGall. 2.30.4

> For what exertions or strength make them confident,
> especially men of such puny stature—for by comparison
> with the size of their own bodies our short stature gener-
> ally arouses contempt in all Gauls—that they can position
> so heavy a tower against the wall?

In the parenthesis opened by *nam* the narrator interrupts the mockery and addresses the Roman reader, speaking in the present tense about "us." So when Caesar's men roll the tower up to the wall, as they do in short order, his readers can take vicarious pleasure in the comeuppance of the Aduatuci (*BGall.* 2.31–33).

Caesar also introduces parentheses with connecting relatives.[35] In these interruptions the author often speaks sotto voce,[36] as in a report from another scene of military panic, this one in North Africa:

> Sed tantus fuit omnium terror ut alii adesse copias Iubae
> dicerent alii cum legionibus instare Varum iamque se
> puluerem uenientium cernere—quarum rerum nihil
> omnino acciderat—alii classem hostium celeriter aduola-
> turam suspicarentur.

BCiv. 2.43.2

> But so great was the universal terror that some were
> saying that Juba's forces were at hand, others that Varus

---

[35] Parentheses signaled by connecting relatives: *BGall.* 3.13.6, 3.20.2, 3.21.3, 3.26.4, 5.12.2, 5.20.1, 5.33.6, 5.39.2, 5.54.4, 5.58.4, 6.15.1, 7.44.3, 7.55.4; *BCiv.* 1.5.3, 1.6.6, 1.6.7, 1.7.6, 1.18.1 1.56.2, 1.58.3, 2.5.2, 2.6.1, 2.22.1, 2.25.6, 2.43.2, 3.1.4, 3.4.5, 3.23.1, 3.26.4, 3.51.5, 3.64.3, 3.87.2, 3.111.3.

[36] Cf. John Ash, in his *Grammatical Institutes*, from 1761 (quoted by Lennard 1991:89): "A Parenthesis ... denotes a Suppression of the Voice, and a hasty Pronunciation."

and his legions were imminent and that the dust cloud of their approach was already visible to them—and of these things not one had happened—and others suspected that the enemy fleet was going to sail against them soon.

Caesar, who was not present at this debacle, interrupts the flying rumors with a reality check, communicating both the soldiers' panic and the narrator's almost clinical detachment from it.[37]

Sometimes a parenthesis is used to inject emotion into a scene, for example, when characters' words break through the narrative surface.[38] From Herodotus onwards, historians have used free-floating snippets of indirect statement for this purpose.[39] A Caesarian example is found at a moment of high drama in Spain, where Caesar's army has a chance to crush their Pompeian enemy:

> Totis uero castris milites circulari et dolere—hostem ex manibus dimitti, bellum necessario longius duci—centurionesque tribunosque militum adire atque obsecrare ut per eos Caesar certior fieret: ne labori suo neu periculo parceret.
>
> *BCiv.* 1.64.2

> Throughout the camp soldiers clustered and lamented—the enemy was slipping away, they said, the war was necessarily going to be further prolonged—and approached the centurions and staff officers and pleaded that they inform Caesar that he should not spare them effort or danger.

The soldiers' asyndetic protests interrupt the sequence of well-connected historical infinitives. The protests could be removed without harm to the syntax here but not without harm to the scene.

---

[37] There is a similar parenthesis at *BCiv.* 1.7.6.

[38] Parentheses containing *oratio obliqua*: *BGall.* 1.39.1, 3.9.3, 5.34.4, 6.8.1, 6.42.1, 7.20.2; *BCiv.* 1.64.2, 2.4.3, 2.5.2, 3.28.4, 3.31.4, 3.82.4, 3.102.7.

[39] For parenthetical "snippets of *oratio obliqua*" in the Greek historians, see Schmitt 1913:40 (Herodotus), 42 (Thucydides), 44 (Xenophon).

The parentheses considered so far range in length from three to twelve words, and their average is close to the average length—roughly eight words—for the parentheses listed in the appendix.[40] Brevity is necessary in this figure, says Quintilian, in order to prevent obscurity.[41] However, in the same breath Quintilian also says that orators and historians use long parentheses, and Caesar is no exception.[42] Some of his parentheses run on for more than 20 words,[43] and some also differ from those discussed so far in falling not within a clause but between sentences.[44] But according to Quintilian, at least, they are still parentheses. Indeed his example of an objectionably long parenthesis of the sort used by orators and historians is a four-line, two-sentence Vergilian parenthesis that stands between two independent sentences (8.2.15, quoting *G.* 3.79–83). Caesar's description of the port of Nymphaeum is an example of the type:

> Nacti portum qui appellatur Nymphaeum, ultra Lissum milia passuum tria, eo naues introduxerunt. (Qui portus ab africo tegebatur, ab austro non erat tutus, leuiusque tempestatis quam classis periculum aestimauerunt.) Quo simul atque intro est itum ... auster ... in africum se uertit.

> *BCiv.* 3.26.4–5

> Coming to a harbor called Nymphaeum, three miles beyond Lissus, they put in there. (This harbor was protected from a southwest wind but not safe from a south wind, and in their reckoning there was less danger

---

[40] Caesar's intraclausal parentheses tend to be longer than those of Tacitus, which average about five words in length; Tacitus's shortest is one word (*H.* 2.76.3 *fateor*), his longest runs for sixteen (*Ann.* 1.10.2) or possibly seventeen words (*Ann.* 4.16.2, a difficult passage).

[41] Quint. 8.2.15: *Etiam interiectione, qua et oratores et historici frequenter utuntur ut medio sermone aliquem inserant sensum, impediri solet intellectus, nisi quod interponitur breue est.*

[42] Schmitt (1913:19–20 and 40–44) lists instances of such parentheses in Herodotus, Thucydides, and Xenophon.

[43] Long intraclausal parentheses: *BGall.* 3.9.3 (17 words), 5.20.1 (27 words), 5.54.4 (21 words), 6.8.1 (24 words).

[44] Parentheses falling between sentences: *BCiv.* 1.7.6 (20 words), 1.44.2 (15 words), 1.61.3 (41 words), 3.26.4 (16 words), 3.79.4 (6 words), 3.111.3 (35 words).

from the storm than from the enemy fleet.) The moment
they entered, ... the south wind ... turned into a south-
west wind.

The sentence about the orientation of the port and the strategy of the
ships' commanders intervenes between a connecting relative (*quo*) and
its antecedent (*eo*) and is thereby relegated to the status of background
information, comparable to that of many of the intraclausal parentheses discussed earlier.

In the examples we have considered so far and in the majority
of those listed in the appendix, Caesar's parentheses are well sign-
posted: by demonstratives such as *id*, by particles such as *nam* or *enim*,
by connecting relatives or other subordinating conjunctions, or by
a connective that signals the postponement of expected syntax. Even
when they arrive unannounced, however, as nearly 40 of them do,[45]
their interrupting effect is generally secured by the structure that they
force open, as for example *eo* ... *quo* in the passage just discussed, or
alii ... *alii* at *BGall.* 6.40.2:

> Alii cuneo facto ut celeriter perrumpant censent—
> quoniam tam propinqua sint castra, et si pars aliqua
> circumuenta ceciderit, at reliquos seruari posse
> confidunt—alii, ut in iugo consistant atque eundem
> omnes ferant casum.
>
> *BGall.* 6.40.2

> Some proposed forming a wedge, then breaking through—
> since the camp was so close at hand and they were confi-
> dent that, even if some portion fell, the rest could be
> saved—, others that they make a stand on the ridge and all
> endure the same fate.

---

[45] The proportion of unannounced parentheses in Tacitus is lower: 53 out of about 200.

Equally clear are interruptions sandwiched between a verb and the subject it requires (*BCiv.* 1.32.2) and those that follow a quantity or category that calls for glossing.[46]

That suffices to suggest the range of Caesar's parentheses. It may be surprising to find so many in the works of a well-organized writer who values clarity, and perhaps this is why they have been all but invisible. Be that as it may, I now turn to some Caesarian parentheses that were quite invisible until editors helped them emerge from the manuscript tradition.

III. "A PARENTHESIS (TO BE AVOIDED AS MUCH AS POSSIBLE)"?[47]

The following statement about some rather alarming German opportunists provides an example:

> Non hos palus—in bello latrociniisque natos—, non siluae morantur.[48]
>
> *BGall.* 6.35.7

> The swamps did not hold them up—men born amidst war and banditry—, nor did the woods.

These Germans had heard that everyone was welcome to plunder the hated Eburones, the tribe that annihilated 15 Roman cohorts in 54 BCE. So they crossed the Rhine and hastened toward the tribe's territory, despite the obstacles of the terrain. The strange initial negative

---

[46] E.g., *BCiv.* 1.18.2 *uniuersi*; 1.80.5 *complures milites*; 2.34.3 *qui una procurrerant*; 3.4.4 *D ex Gabinianis*; 3.44.1 *omnem apparatum belli*; 3.53.1 *VI proeliis factis*; 3.78.3 *iis copiis*; 3.101.1 *duas partes*; 3.102.2 *omnes ... iuniores*; 3.103.1 *duobus ... milibus*; and perhaps also the rather abrupt parenthesis glossing *quae inanes remitterentur* at *BGall.* 5.23.4. Even the longest of Caesar's parentheses, a 41-word sentence at *BCiv.* 1.61.3, is bounded by two references to Celtiberia (1.61.2 *in Celtiberiam*; 1.61.4 *Hic*). Abrupt parentheses: *BGall.* 1.7.2; *BCiv.* 1.4.4, 1.48.5, 3.30.1, 3.44.4, 3.65.2, 3.70.1; the most abrupt is an editorial aside at *BCiv.* 3.71.4.

[47] This line is the witty opening to a section on parenthesis in the *Grammatical Institutes* of John Ash (1761), quoted by Lennard 1991:89. The italics are original.

[48] Neither of the emendations recorded in Meusel (1893)—*paludes* in place of *palus*, excision of *in*—affects the point at issue here.

suggests that the German advance was uncanny but leaves the reader uncertain as to what is being negated (*hos? palus?* something else?). The following words, *in belli latrociniisque natos*, delay the clarification that arrives with the second *non*, which shows that the construction is an emphatic anaphora.[49] In effect, while insisting that the Germans are not delayed, Caesar delays his reader; he is not just explaining here. Most editors, unlike Hering, use a comma, the non-committal comma, as I call it,[50] to punctuate this clause. Granted, *in bello latrociniisque natos* does not fit Pinkster's requirements for the independence of the parenthesis (see above) since *natos* needs *hos*.[51] But the phrase does satisfy Quintilian's definition with its "intervening idea" (9.3.23 *continuationi sermonis medius aliqui sensus interuenit*) and also that of Servius (see above) since it could be removed from its host sentence. Furthermore, if *in bello latrociniisque natos* were simply a description of the object of *morantur*, the demonstrative *hos* would be superfluous. But in my view, Hering's brash dashes make it easier for the modern reader to see what Caesar is doing here: opening up a window in the text through which one can hear his ominous aside on the Germans, who are about to change course and threaten a Roman camp instead of the Eburones (*BGall.* 6.35.8–41).

I now turn to two passages where Caesar's editors mark a parenthesis instead of emending the text, one from the *BGall.* and one from the *BCiv.*

The first passage comes at a turning point in Caesar's dash to rescue Quintus Cicero from a Gallic attack in *BGall.* 5. Caesar, who managed to draw the attack onto himself and drive the Gauls off, refrained from

---

[49] For the emphatic *non ... non* structure, cf. *BGall.* 5.40.5, 6.34.1; *BCiv.* 2.37.6, 3.47.6, 3.72.2–4.

[50] Cf. George Campbell, *The Philosophy of Rhetoric*, 1776, quoted by Lennard 1991:93: "Others ... have carried their dislike to the parenthesis only so far as to lay aside the hooks by which it is commonly distinguished, and to use commas in their place. But this is not avoiding the fault, if it be a fault, it is only endeavouring to commit it so as to escape discovery, and may more justly be denominated a corruption in writing than an improvement."

[51] At the conference in 2018 where this paper was first presented, Richard Thomas suggested to me that one might have expected a parenthesis comparable to *BCiv.* 3.95.2, e.g., *nam erant ... nati*.

pursuit. Here is the passage as it appears in Meusel's 1893 edition, with the information from his critical apparatus:

> Longius prosequi ueritus, quod siluae paludesque inter-cedebant [neque etiam paruulo detrimento illorum locum relinqui uidebat] omnibus suis incolumibus copiis eodem die ad Ciceronem peruenit.

BGall. 5.52.1

> Afraid to pursue too far, since woods and swamps inter-vened, he reached Cicero that same day with all of his own troops safe.

> prosequi noluit, ueritus β / illum *SM²* : ullum *Lambin.* : suorum *Jurin.* / locum eos β / uidebat ω : uolebat *Lamb., Jur.* / neque etiam ... relinqui uidebat *del. Bentl.*

You can see that Bentley—this is the Thomas Bentley who published an edition of the *commentarii* in 1742, not the Bentley of critical fame—excised a sizeable chunk of the Latin. The text he excised, *neque etiam paruulo detrimento illorum locum relinqui uidebat,* is unlikely to have originated as a gloss,[52] but in excising it, Bentley cut a Gordian knot of complications visible in the apparatus.[53] Oudendorp dubs this a

---

[52] Klotz (1921 [but not 1952], ad loc.) comments *del. Bent. nulla probabilitate.*

[53] The complications are also manifest in the widely divergent translations or para-phrases of the transmitted text. Oudendorp (1737, ad loc.) paraphrases the *mens Caesaris* thus: *se reuertisse, quia uerebatur insidias in siluis; quia eum siluestrem locum ab iis non relinqui uidebat, paruo accepto detrimento.* That is, Oudendorp supplies a reference to Caesar's turning around. Like Oudendorp and many others, Schönberger (1990) takes *locum* liter-ally, but he associates it with Caesar, not the enemy: "und er den Feinden voraussicht-lich nicht einmal geringe Verluste zufügen konnte, wenn er den Platz verließ." Raaflaub (2017) continues the association with Caesar but takes *locum* metaphorically: "and he realized that there was little opportunity left (*sc.* for him) to inflict further harm upon them." Constans (1926, "et voyant d'ailleurs qu'il n'était plus possible de leur faire le moindre mal") and Ciaffi and Griffa (2008, "e d'altra parte vedeva che i nemici non gli lasciavano possibilità d'infliggere loro neppure un piccolo danno") envisage the scenario similarly but add adverbs to dissociate the two imperfects. Nipperdey, who like many other editors places no punctuation before *neque,* deems Caesar's language careless here (1847:145, "neglegentia"). Seel (1961, ad loc.) has a helpful note about its ambiguity: "*totam parenthesin* neque ... videbat *secl. (solito more) Meu. et Fu.: verba* parvulo detr. *ancipitia sunt: subaudiri enim potest aut:* sed nullo, *aut:* sed magno detr.; *illud editoribus omnibus,*

"locus ... intricatissimus" in 1737.[54] The main issue is the apparently parallel status of *intercedebant* and *uidebat* in the *quod* clause: the former explains Caesar's fear, but the latter explains his (unstated) decision to march in the other direction.[55] If this were Tacitus, we might assign significance to the deceptive parallelism, but for Caesar we are more likely to echo an 18th-century editor in saying that the passage lacks Caesar's elegance and clarity.[56]

But here is the passage with a parenthesis, as presented by Klotz (4th ed., 1952; followed by Hering) and Seel (1961):

> Longius prosequi ueritus, quod siluae paludesque inter-cedebant—neque enim paruulo detrimento illorum locum relinqui uidebat—, omnibus suis incolumibus copiis eodem die ad Ciceronem peruenit.[57]

> Fearing to pursue (*sc.* the enemy) too far, since woods and swamps intervened—<u>for he saw that no opportunity remained for doing them slight damage</u>—he reached Cicero that same day with all of his own troops safe.

---

ambiguitatem omnino neglegentibus, hoc mihi patere videtur; intell.: 'Caes. videbat locum illum, quo nunc erat, a Romanis non nisi magno (Romanorum) detrimento hostes persequendi causa relinqui posse.' quae sequuntur (... pervenit) minime obstant. (He prints *illum*, not *illorum*.)

[54] Echoed by Bentley 1742, ad loc.: *Est in istis aliquid intricati, quod exsolvere non possum. Nihil sane extricant Interpretes, qui tamen immane quantum scripserunt.*

[55] Other issues are the negation *neque* (what does it negate?), the usage of *etiam* (why *neque etiam paruulo* instead of *et ne paruulo quidem*?), the syntax of *detrimento* and *illorum*, and whether to take *locum* as "place" or "opportunity." As a parallel for the latter meaning Stock (1898, ad loc.) cites *BGall.* 6.42.1 (—*ne minimum quidem casu locum relinqui debuisse*—), itself a parenthesis containing a snippet of *oratio obliqua*.

[56] Clark, 1712, quoted by Oudendorp 1737, ad loc.: *neque haec neque illa lectio, utrouis modo explicata, Caesaris elegantiam et perspicuitatem sapit.*

[57] In his first edition, Klotz (1921) already had dashes, but he also replaced *illorum* with *suorum*. Hering (1987) prints the same text as Klotz (1952), but as is his wont, he minimizes the history of textual scholarship, noting only this: "enim] etiam ω *corr.* *Ciacc.*" Yet Ciacconius's actual suggestion (at least as reported in Meusel 1893) was to read *neque enim uel paruulo detrimento*, etc.; it was Klotz who proposed *enim* alone (he claimed it as his own emendation in 1921 but credited it, rather misleadingly, to Ciacconius in 1952). In my view "*corr.*" is a rather high-handed dismissal of previous scholars' work on this passage, especially since without *uel* the emendation is imperfect (see n. 59 below).

Longius prosequi ueritus, quod siluae paludesque intercedebant—neque etiam paruulo detrimento illum locum
relinqui uidebat—, omnibus suis incolumibus copiis
eodem die ad Ciceronem peruenit.

Fearing to pursue (*sc.* the enemy) too far, since woods
and swamps intervened—<u>and he saw that leaving that
location was going to come at no small cost</u>—he reached
Cicero that same day with all of his own troops safe.

With two small dashes these editors remove *uidebat* from the *quod*
clause and create the main clause that Bentley made by excision. As you
can see, their repairs to other problems in the passage have a significant effect on the meaning: Klotz makes the parenthesis less abrupt by
emending *etiam* to *enim*,[58] Seel follows Lambinus in emending *illorum*
to *illum*, and as a result the content of their respective parentheses
is strikingly different.[59] But for the main issue, their solution is the
same: they create an apologetic subtext. Caesar's readers expect that
Caesar will pursue a routed enemy, but he does not because he fears
the terrain ... and because he saw either that there was nothing to be
gained or that there was much to be lost in pursuit. With the introductory negative *neque*, Caesar validates the reader's expectation before
presenting the logic of his decision, saying, in effect, "and it's not what
you thought, but rather this, that I didn't see, etc." I am inclined to view
this parenthesis as a particularly subtle manifestation of what Hirtius
called Caesar's "veritable science of explaining his plans" (*BGall.* 8 pr.,
uerissima scientia suorum consiliorum explicandorum), not as something
that merits the knife.

My last example also concerns a passage that has attracted much
critical attention.[60] Here I will focus on the punctuation, which declares

---

[58] *Neque enim* occurs parenthetically only once elsewhere in the *commentarii* (*BGall.*
2.17.4), but it is more common in this position in Livy (around nineteen times) and
Tacitus (around eight times).

[59] The passage is arguably better off without either emendation. If one reads *enim*
instead of *etiam*, it is harder to understand *paruulo* (unless *uel* is also added), and with
illum in place of *illorum*, it is much harder to explain the present passive infinitive.

[60] For discussion, see Damon 2015a:291–292.

a problematic stretch of text a parenthesis. The passage in question comes from the description of Caesar's preliminary battle line at Pharsalus:

> Superius tamen institutum in equitibus quod demonstrauimus seruabat, ut quoniam numero multis partibus esset inferior adulescentes atque expeditos ex antesignanis—electos milites ad pernicitatem—armis inter equites proeliari iuberet.

> *BCiv.* 3.84.3

> He maintained the previous arrangement among the cavalry that I mentioned: since he was numerically inferior by a wide margin, he ordered young and unencumbered men from the front-line fighters—soldiers chosen for speed—to do battle in the midst of the cavalry.

> electos milites ad pernicitatem armis *ed. pr., quod dubitanter accepi (u. 3.75.5, Fron. Str. 2.3.22 et cf. 3.91.4, BAlex 16.5)* : electis m- ad p- a- ω : electos m- ad p- [a-] *Oudendorp* : electis [m-] ad p- a- *Nipperdey* : m- electis ad p- a- *Menge, alii alia* / iuberet μ : iubet ν

In addition to creating a parenthesis by adding dashes here, I accepted the emendation of *electis* to *electos*, as you can see from the apparatus. You can also see that I do not have a lot of confidence in this repair. But it seemed to me worth trying something new since none of the repairs on offer is problem-free. In defense of this parenthesis, an admittedly abrupt one, I will say that with *quod demonstrauimus* the author has already signaled his presence in the passage and that the aside has something in common with Caesar's comment about those uncanny Germans, *in bello latrociniisque natos.*[61] Both comments simultaneously explain what precedes and prepare the ground for what comes next. In the *BGall.* passage the aside on "men born amidst war and banditry" sets up the sudden German threat; in the *BCiv.* passage the inserted characterization sets up the unexpected success Caesar had with this

---

[61] There is more parenthetic language at the end of the paragraph (*BCiv.* 3.84.5 *Namque ... interfecit.*). On parentheses of this extent, see section II above.

unusual fighting formation, which allowed his 1000-strong cavalry to withstand some attacks by Pompey's 7000 horsemen (*BCiv.* 3.85.4). It also provides an implicit defense for the general when these troops fail to withstand an attack in the final battle (*BCiv.* 3.93.4): he had used the best men available, "soldiers chosen for speed." I could have placed *electos milites ad pernicitatem* between commas, in apposition to *adulescentes atque expeditos.* But in my view these commas would have made it harder for the reader to see how awkward the expression is—*milites* is particularly otiose—and how it benefits from being treated as an aside.[62]

According to Quintilian, the appeal of the parenthesis lies—paradoxically—in its proximity to faults of style: figures such as parenthesis, he says, "have a certain charm precisely because they look like mistakes" (9.3.27 *habent quandam ex illa uitii similitudine gratiam*). In part the *gratia* must be a consequence of the apparent artlessness of the awkward or abrupt parentheses that, as we have seen, cause problems for Caesar's readers and editors. The artlessness of parentheses is an illusion, of course; in Caesar's hands it is one of his many devices for cultivating the reader's attention and trust. Our honorand compliments the "unobtrusive skill with which the device is normally handled" by Ovid, and perhaps you may now feel that something similar could be said about Caesar.[63]

UNIVERSITY OF PENNSYLVANIA

APPENDIX

This appendix includes all parentheses placed between brackets or dashes in Hering 1987 and Damon 2015b, plus comma-punctuated parentheses of the clausal apposition type (indicated by *). Character-speech parentheses are indicated by quotation marks. Some possible parentheses not punctuated as such by Hering or Damon are included between double brackets, [[]]. At the recommendation of our honorand

---

[62] On asides and afterthoughts in Caesar, see Damon 2015a:107. For some particularly abrupt examples, see n. 46 above.

[63] Tarrant 1998:157.

I have included in a separate section the parentheses from *BGall.* 8 (by Aulus Hirtius) and the *Bellum Alexandrinum* (of unknown authorship) to facilitate future comparison with Caesarian usage; the former are from Hering 1987, the latter from the text that I am preparing for the Library of Digital Latin Texts (https://digitallatin.org/library-digital-latin-texts). The relative frequency (35 in 78 chapters) and length (ten words on average) of the parentheses in the *Bellum Alexandrinum* is immediately obvious.

TABLE 1: PARENTHESES IN CAESAR, *BELLUM GALLICUM*

LOCATION	PARENTHESIS	# OF WORDS
1.7.2	—erat omnino in Gallia ulteriore legio una—	7
1.16.2	—quod Gallia sub septentrionibus, ut ante dictum est, posita est—	10
1.18.10	—nam equitatui, quem auxilio Caesari Haedui miserant, Dumnorix praeerat—:	9
1.39.1	—saepenumero sese ... dicebant ferre potuisse—,	14
""1.44.12	—id se ab ipsis per eorum nuntios compertum habere—,	9
2.14.1	—nam post discessum Belgarum dimissis Haeduorum copiis ad eum reuerterat—	10
2.16.3	—nam his utrisque persuaserant uti eandem belli fortunam experirentur—	9
2.17.4	—neque enim ad hoc tempus ei rei student, sed quicquid possunt, pedestribus ualent copiis—,	14
2.23.1	—nam his ea pars obuenerat—	5
2.30.4	—nam plerumque omnibus Gallis ... nostra contemptui est—	12
3.9.3	—legatos, quod nomen ... fuisset, retentos ab se et in uincula coniectos—,	17
3.13.6	—quod est magis ueri simile—	5

LOCATION	PARENTHESIS	# OF WORDS
3.13.8	—tanta in iis erat firmitudo—,	5
3.20.2	—quae sunt ciuitates Galliae prouinciae finitimae, ex his regionibus—	9
3.21.3	—cuius rei sunt longe peritissimi Aquitani, propterea quod ... aerariae secturaeque sunt—,	15
*3.26.4	, quod plerumque in spe uictoriae accidere consueuit,	7
4.14.5	—nam cum omnibus suis domo excesserant Rhenum transierant—	8
*4.29.4	, id quod necesse erat accidere,	5
5.12.2	—qui omnes fere eis nominibus ciuitatum appellantur, quibus orti ex ciuitatibus eo peruenerunt—	13
5.20.1	—ex qua Mandubracius ... uenerat, ... ipse fuga mortem uitauerat—	27
5.23.4	—[et] prioris commeatus ... et quas postea Labienus faciendas curauerat numero LX—	12
*5.33.6	—quod fieri necesse erat—	4
[[5.34.4	; leuitate armorum et cotidiana exercitatione nihil eis noceri posse;]]	
*5.39.2	—quod fuit necesse—	3
5.52.1	—neque enim paruulo detrimento illorum locum relinqui uidebat—,	8
5.54.4	—quos praecipuo semper honore Caesar habuit, alteros pro ... fide, alteros pro ... officiis—	21
*5.58.4	—quod fore, sicut accidit, uidebat—	5
6.8.1	—longum esse ... exspectare, neque suam pati dignitatem ut ... adoriri non audeant—	24
[[6.12.6	, quod ii, qui se ad eorum amicitiam adgregauerant, ... aequiore imperio se uti uidebant,]]	

LOCATION	PARENTHESIS	# OF WORDS
*6.15.1	—quod fere ante Caesaris aduentum quotannis accidere solebat, uti ... illatas propulsarent—,	16
6.30.3	—ut sunt fere domicilia Gallorum, qui uitandi aestus causa ... fluminum petunt propinquitates—	15
6.34.3	—nullum enim poterat uniuersis <a> perterritis ac dispersis periculum accidere—,	10
6.35.7	—in bello latrociniisque natos—,	4
6.40.2	—quoniam tam propinqua sint castra, et ... reliquos seruari posse confidunt—	16
""6.42.1	—ne minimum quidem casu locum relinqui debuisse—	7
[[7.20.2	; non haec omnia ... accidere potuisse; regnum illum Galliae malle ... ipsorum habere beneficio—]]	
*7.44.3	—quod iam ipse Caesar per exploratores cognouerat—	7
7.55.4	—quod est oppidum apud eos maximae auctoritatis—,	7
""*7.66.5	—id, quod magis futurum confidat—	5
7.75.1	—ut censuit Vercingetorix—	3
""7.77.6	—tantum apud me dignitas potest—,	5

TABLE 2: PARENTHESES IN CAESAR, *BELLUM CIVILE*

LOCATION	PARENTHESIS	# OF WORDS
1.4.4	—et quod neminem dignitate secum exaequari uolebat—	7
1.5.3	—quique <pro> consulibus sunt ad urbem—	6
*1.6.6	—quod superioribus annis acciderat—	4
*1.6.7	—quod ante id tempus accidit numquam—	6

LOCATION	PARENTHESIS	# OF WORDS
1.7.6	(Quarum rerum illo tempore nihil factum, ne cogitatum quidem: nulla ... secessio facta.)	20
1.7.8	—hanc enim initio tumultus euocauerat, reliquae nondum conuenerant—	8
1.18.1	(quod oppidum a Corfinio VII milium interuallo abest)	8
1.18.2	—et oppidani et milites—	4
1.32.3	—contradicentibus inimicis, Catone[m] uero ... dies extrahente[m]—	13
*1.40.7	—id quod accidit—	3
1.44.2	(Quod fere fit, quibus quisque in locis miles inueterauerit, ut ... consuetudine moueatur.)	15
1.48.5	—neque multum a maturitate aberant—	5
1.56.2	—de quibus supra demonstratum est—	5
1.58.3	—qui repente ex onerariis nauibus erant producti—	7
1.61.3	(Huic consilio suffragabatur etiam illa res. ... Caesaris autem erat in barbaris nomen obscurius.)	41
1.64.2	—hostem ex manibus dimitti, bellum necessario longius duci—	8
1.80.5	—etiam nonnulli centuriones—	3
1.86.1	—ut ex ipsa significatione cognosci potuit—	5
2.4.3	—extremo tempore ciuitati subuenirent—	4
2.5.2	—quos integros superauissent ut uictos contemnerent—	6

LOCATION	PARENTHESIS	# OF WORDS
2.6.1	—quibus in pugna uitae periculum acciderat—	6
2.17.1	—cognitis iis rebus quae sunt in Italia gestae—	7
2.22.1	—panico enim ... omnes alebantur quod ... antiquitus paratum in publicum contulerant—	18
2.22.1	—quos in Caesaris potestatem uenisse cognouerant—	6
2.25.6	—quae stabant ad Vticam numero circiter CC—	7
""2.32.13	—en Africi belli praeiudicia!—	4
2.34.3	—leuis armatura—	2
2.34.5	—ut memoria tenerent milites ea quae pridie sibi confirmassent—	9
2.43.2	—quarum rerum nihil omnino acciderat—	5
3.1.4	—quae iudicia aliis audientibus iudicibus aliis sententiam ferentibus ... erant perfecta—	12
3.4.4	—Gallos Germanosque quos ibi A. Gabinius ... reliquerat—	11
3.4.5	—cui magna Pompeius praemia tribuit—	5
3.13.2	—quod properans noctem diei coniunxerat neque iter intermiserat—	8
3.14.1	—ut erat praeceptum a Caesare—	5
3.20.1	—ut Caesar praesens constituerat—	4
3.22.1	—ea quae faceret iussu atque imperio facere Pompei, quae mandata ... delata essent—	16
3.23.1	—qua necessarius nostris erat egressus—	5

LOCATION	PARENTHESIS	# OF WORDS
3.26.4	(Qui portus ab africo tegebatur, ab austro non erat tutus, leuiusque ... periculum aestimauerunt.)	16
3.28.4	—nihil his nocituros hostes—	4
3.30.1	—iter secundum eas terras derexerant—	5
3.31.4	—sese contra hostem si ducerentur ituros, contra ciuem et consulem arma non laturos—	13
3.32.6	—sed in singulos conuentus singulasque ciuitates—	6
3.43.3	—quod angusta re frumentaria utebatur quodque Pompeius multitudine equitum ualebat—	10
3.44.1	—tela arma tormenta—	3
3.44.4	—ne quo loco erumperent Pompeiani ac nostros post tergum adorirentur timebant—	11
*3.51.5	—quae res tamen fortasse aliquem reciperet casum—	7
3.53.1	—tribus ad Dyrrachium, tribus ad munitiones—	6
3.60.3	—et fortasse non se liberari sed in aliud tempus reseruari arbitrati—	11
*3.61.1	—quodque nouum et praeter consuetudinem acciderat—	6
""*3.64.3	—quod ante in exercitu Caesaris non accidit—	7
3.65.2	—significatione per castella fumo facta, ut erat superioris temporis consuetudo—	10
3.70.1	—quod haec praeter spem acciderant eius qui paulo ante ex castris fugientes suos conspexerat—	14

LOCATION	PARENTHESIS	# OF WORDS
3.70.1	—atque his a Caesaris militibus occupatis—	6
3.71.4	—ostentationis, ut uidebatur, causa quo maior perfugae fides haberetur—	9
3.78.3	—frumento ac commeatu—	3
3.79.4	(Haec ad id tempus Caesar ignorabat.)	6
3.82.4	—praestaret quod proficiscenti recepisset ne per eius auctoritatem deceptus uideretur—	10
3.84.3	—electos milites ad pernicitatem—	4
""*3.87.2	, quod accidere tot proeliis fuit necesse,	6
3.95.2	—nam ad meridiem res erat perducta—	6
3.101.1	—dimidiae parti praeesset P. Sulpicius ... dimidiae M. Pomponius ad Messanam—	13
3.102.2	—Graeci ciuesque Romani—	3
3.102.7	—ex his locis discederent—	4
3.103.1	—partim quos ... delegerat, partim a negotiatoribus coegerat, quosque ... idoneos existimabat—	19
3.105.3	—repetitis atque enumeratis diebus—	4
3.111.3	(Quarum erant L auxilio missae ad Pompeium,. ... Praeter has, XXII ... constratae omnes.)	35

TABLE 3: PARENTHESES IN HIRTIUS,
BELLUM GALLICUM 8

LOCATION	PARENTHESIS	# OF WORDS
*8.3.1	, quod imparatis disiectisque accidere fuit necesse,	6
8.5.1	—nuper enim deuicti complura oppida dimiserant—,	6
8.7.2	—namque esse undique diligenter demigratum—,	5
*8.10.3	—id quod accidere erat necesse—,	5
*8.12.1	—quod plerumque accidit diuturnitate—,	4
8.14.2	—magna enim multitudo carrorum etiam expeditos sequi Gallos consueuit—	9
8.15.5	—namque in acie sedere Gallos consuesse superioribus commentariis Caesaris declaratum est—	10
8.36.3	—ut barbarorum fere consuetudo est—	5
*8.41.5	—id enim nullis operibus effici poterat—,	6
8.44.3	—crebro enim ... se committebat, quod ... uidebatur, cum ... esset, quam ... deberet ... habere—,	24
8.46.6	—cognoscendi enim ... facultatem habebat, quali quisque fuisset animo ... , quam sustinuerat ... —,	19

TABLE 4: PARENTHESES IN [INCERTUS],
BELLUM ALEXANDRINUM

LOCATION	PARENTHESIS	# OF WORDS
1.5	(Quarum alterius rei copiam exiguam, alterius nullam omnino facultatem habebat.)	10
2.4	—erat autem quadrato extructus saxo neque minus XL pedes altitudinis habebat—	11
5.3	—specibus ac puteis extracta—	4
7.2	—neque fallaces esse neque temerarii—	5
13.5	—nam decem missis una in cursu litore Aegyptio defecerat—	9
14.5	(Sic enim praedicant, partem esse Alexandriae dimidiam Africae.)	8
""15.4	—neque tuum iudicium fallemus—	4
19.3	(Non enim plures consistere angustiae loci patiebantur. Reliquae copiae ... stationem obtinebant.)	13
*25.1	—quod nondum auditum Caesari erat—	5
25.3	—nulla etiam parum feliciter—	4
26.2	—namque tota Aegyptus maritimo accessu Pharo, pedestri Pelusio ... existimatur—,	12
34.3	(Quarum altera in bello Alexandrino non occurrit quod itinere terrestri per Syriam erat missa.)	14
36.3	—quod oppidum positum in Armenia minore est plano ipsum loco, montibus tamen ... remotis—	23
39.2	—quibus tamen angustissimum interuallum frontis reliquit—	6

LOCATION	PARENTHESIS	# OF WORDS
42.2	—quod magnam curam suscipiebat ne quo temere progrederetur—	8
42.3	—quae etsi erat tenuis tamen in tanta prouinciae desperatione erat grata, praesertim uirtute parta—	14
43.2	—in oppidum maritimum, quod ciues Romani fortissimi fidelissimique incolebant—	9
44.3	—quarum numerus erat satis magnus, magnitudo nequaquam satis iusta ad proeliandum—	11
44.4	—quorum magnam copiam habebat ... , qui ... relicti erant ... cum exercitus ... transportaretur—	18
47.5	—prouincia recepta et Cornificio reddita, classe aduersariorum ex illo toto sinu expulsa—	12
49.3	—qui modo aliquam iacturam facere posset—	6
52.2	—nam is latus Cassi tegebat—	5
57.5	—namque id uarie nuntiabatur—	4
57.5	—quae fuerant Cordubae—	3
58.1	—qui Caesaris nomine maioribus uiribus uti uidebatur—	7
61.3	—namque Vlia in edito monte posita est—	7
61.4	—cuius si rei facultas esset resistere incitatis militibus non poterat—	10
63.5	—si tamen in omnibus fuit Cassius: nam de huius conscientia dubitabatur—	11
64.3	—nihilo periculosius se nauigaturum credens—	5
65.4	—qui omnes ad eum concurrerant—	5

LOCATION	PARENTHESIS	# OF WORDS
67.1	—quod ei ... concessum esse ceteri tetrarchae contendebant, sine dubio ... appellatus—	20
69.1	—excepta enim legione ... , quam secum abduxerat ... deminutam ut minus mille ... in ea esset—	32
71.1	—nemini enim erat ignotum plurimis de causis ad urbem Caesarem reuocari—	11
73.1	—quae multo erant propiora regis castris—	6
78.2	—nam eum Mithridates, rex Asiae ... secum asportauerat in castra multosque retinuerat annos—	17

WORKS CITED

Albrecht, M. v. 1964. *Die Parenthese in Ovids Metamorphosen und ihre dichterische Funktion*. Hildesheim.

Bentley, T. 1742. *Caii Julii Caesaris de bello gallico et ciuili nec non A. Hirtii aliorumque de bellis Alexandrino, Africano, et Hispaniensi commentarii: Notas et animaduersiones addidit Tho. Bentleius; Accessere conjecturae et emendationes Jacobi Jurini*. London.

Boldt, H. 1884. *De liberiore linguae graecae et latinae collocatione verborum capita selecta*. PhD diss., University of Göttingen.

Bolkestein, A. M. 1998. "Between Brackets: Some Properties of Parenthetical Clauses in Latin; An Investigation of the Language of Cicero's *Letters*." In *Latin in Use: Amsterdam Studies in the Pragmatics of Latin*, ed. R. Risselada, 1–17. Amsterdam.

Ciaffi, R., and L. Griffa. 2008. *Gaio Giulio Cesare. Opere*. Turin. (orig. pub. 1952 and 1973).

Clausen, W. V. 1994. *A Commentary on Virgil, Eclogues*. Oxford.

Coleman, K. 2010. "Parenthetical Remarks in the *Silvae*." In Dickey and Chahoud 2010, 292–317.

Constans, L.-A. 1926. *César. Guerre des Gaules*. 2 vols. Paris.

Damon, C. 2015a. *Studies on the Text of Caesar's Bellum Ciuile*. Oxford.

———. 2015b. *C. Iuli Caesaris commentariorum libri III de bello ciuili*. Oxford.

———. 2016. *Caesar. Civil War*. Loeb Classical Library 39. Cambridge, MA.

Dickey, E., and A. Chahoud, eds. *Colloquial and Literary Latin*. Cambridge.

Eckert, W. 1911. *De figurarum in Titi Livi ab urbe condita libris usu*. PhD diss. University of Breslau.

Fabre, P. 1936. *César. Guerre civile*. 2 vols. Paris. (rev., ed. A. Balland, 2006.)

Harrison, S. J. 2010. "*Sermones Deorum*: Divine Discourse in Virgil's *Aeneid*." In Dickey and Chahoud 2010, 266–278.

Hering, W. 1987. *C. Iulii Caesaris commentarii rerum gestarum*. Vol. 1, *Bellum Gallicum*. Leipzig.

Kitzmann, H. 1907. *Über parenthetische Sätze und Satzverbindungen in den Reden des Demosthenes*. Regensburg.

Klotz, A. 1921. *C. Iuli Caesaris commentarii*. Vol. 1, *Commentarii belli gallici*. 1st ed. Leipzig. (4th ed., 1952.)

———. 1926. *C. Iuli Caesaris commentarii*. Vol. 2, *Commentarii belli civilis*. 1st ed. Leipzig. (2nd ed., 1950.)

Kraner, F., W. Dittenberger, and H. Meusel. 1960. *C. Iulii Caesaris commentarii de bello gallico*. 2 vols. Dublin.

Kühner, R., and C. Stegmann. 1962. *Ausführliche Grammatik der lateinischen Sprache*. 4th ed. revised by A. Thierfelder. Munich.

Lausberg, H. 1998. *Handbook of Literary Rhetoric: A Foundation for Literary Study*. Trans. M. T. Bliss. Leiden.

Lennard, J. 1991. *But I Digress: The Exploitation of Parentheses in English Printed Verse*. Oxford.

Leumann, M., J. B. Hofmann, and A. Szantyr. 1972–1979. *Lateinische Grammatik*. 3 vols. Munich.

Longrée, D. 2007. "*Mirum dictu*: Les appositions de phrase chez les historiens latins." In *Éléments "asyntaxiques" ou hors structure dans l'énoncé latin*, ed. C. Bodelot, 1–19. Clermont-Ferrand.

Meusel, H. 1893. *Coniecturae caesarianae*. Berlin.

Nipperdey, K. 1847. *C. Iulii Caesaris commentarii*. Leipzig.

Oakley, S. P. 1997–2005. *A Commentary on Livy, Books VI–X*. 4 vols. Oxford.

Oudendorp, F. 1737. *C. Julii Caesaris. De bellis gallico et civili pompejano: Nec non A. Hirtii aliorumque De bellis alexandrino, africano et hispaniensi commentarii ad MSStorum fidem expressi, cum integris notis Dionysii Vossii, Joannis Davisii et Samuelis Clarkii cura et studio Francisci*

Oudendorpii qui suas animadversiones ac varias lectiones adjecit. Leiden.

Panico, M. 2001. "La 'digressio' nella tradizione retorico-grammaticale." *BSL* 31:478–496.

Pinkster, H. 2015. *Oxford Latin Syntax*. Volume 1, *The Simple Clause*. Oxford.

———. Forthcoming. *Oxford Latin Syntax*. Volume 2. Oxford.

Raaflaub, K. A. 2017. *The Landmark Julius Caesar: The Complete Works*. New York.

Rambaud, M. 1966. *L'art de la déformation historique dans les commentaires de César*. Paris.

———. 1976. "Le camp de Fabius près d'Ilerda: Un problème césarien (*Bellum ciuile* I, 40)." *Les études classiques* 44:25–34.

Roschatt, A. 1884. "Über den Gebrauch der Parenthesen in Ciceros Reden und rhetorischen Schriften." *Acta seminarii philologici erlangensis* 3:189–244.

Schmitt, J. 1913. *De parenthesis usu Hippocratico, Herodoteo, Thucydideo, Xenophonteo*. Greifswald.

Schönberger, O. 1984. *C. Iulius Caesar. Der Bürgerkrieg*. Munich.

Schwyzer, E. 1939. *Die Parenthese im engern und im weitern Sinne*. Abhandlungen der Preussischen Akademie der Wissenschaften, Philosophisch-historische Klasse, nr. 6. Berlin.

Seel, O. 1961. *C. Iulii Caesaris commentarii rerum gestarum*. Vol. 1, *Bellum gallicum*. Leipzig.

Stock, St. G. 1898. *Caesar. De bello gallico: Books I-VII*. Oxford.

Tarrant, R. J. 1998. "Parenthetically Speaking (in Virgil and Other Poets)." In *Style and Tradition: Studies in Honor of Wendell Clausen*, ed. Peter Knox and Clive Foss, 141–157. Beiträge zur Altertumskunde 92. Stuttgart.

INTERPOLATION HUNTING IN SENECAN TRAGEDY, OVID, AND HORACE

S. J. HEYWORTH

AMONG THE MANY DISTINGUISHED CONTRIBUTIONS that Richard Tarrant has made to the study of Latin poetry—the insightful commentaries, the informed and cautious textual criticism—his work on interpolation stands out. In the 20th century, there had been a deep divide between those critics (e.g., Jachmann, Knoche) for whom this had been the essential approach, the way to solve most textual problems, and those equally radical critics for whom deletion was an insult to their conjectural prowess.[1] Other scholars, such as Zwierlein in his work on Senecan tragedy and Nisbet on Juvenal, had combined both techniques, but what Richard did in two papers in the 1980s[2] and again in his elegant little volume *Texts, Editors, and Readers* (2016) was to provide a theoretical underpinning based on a good sense of how transmission works. Central to this is the move away from loaded language of forgery and fraudulence:[3] interpolators are readers interacting with the text and trying to improve the experience of reading by correcting, annotating, or collaborating with the perceived aims of the author— in short they behave like philologists. But because their work has had effects on the manuscript tradition, it can seem pernicious: such

I am grateful to Irene Peirano and Lauren Curtis for the invitation to participate in the book, even though I was unable to attend the conference; and to Tristan Franklinos and Tobias Reinhardt, who read the whole piece and suggested a number of improvements. Tobias and I have together conducted classes on the textual criticism of Seneca tragedy since 2005, and I owe much to our discussions in those.

[1] Cf. Tarrant 2016a:86 on Shackleton Bailey.

[2] Zwierlein 1986a and b; Nisbet 1995, items 2, 15, 17. And see Tarrant 1987, 1989a. Tarrant 1989b concentrates on verbal substitutions.

[3] Tarrant 1987:283–284; revisited at Tarrant 2016a:87.

adjectives should be reserved for the results, however, not the motivation. The sublime climax of this approach came in the observation that "the first reader of the *Metamorphoses* to introduce a 'collaborative' interpolation in it may have been Ovid himself."[4]

How better to pay honor than to use the skills I have learned from reading and applying these lessons? What follows are notes on poetic texts on which Richard has worked and is working: the tragedies of Seneca, Ovid's *Metamorphoses*, and Horace. All the notes discuss interpolation, though in one or two there are other focal points. As we shall see, the *Agamemnon*, the subject of Richard's first commentary, still seems a rich hunting ground: though the edition puts 545–546 and 548 in square brackets[5] (the latter deleted by Leo, the former by Richard himself), full boldness in following the quarry's tracks seems to have developed later, mainly through work on the *Metamorphoses*, where the presence of alternative and additional lines in a number of passages forces the editor to confront what readers and scribes have been doing to the text.

I. SENECA *AGAMEMNON* 92–101

Nubibus ipsis inserta caput
turris pluuio uapulat Austro,
densasque nemus spargens umbras
annosa uidet robora frangi;   95
feriunt celsos fulmina colles,
corpora morbis maiora patent,
et cum in pastus armenta uagos

---

[4] Tarrant 1987:297.

[5] Also the unmetrical 934, an obvious sententious intrusion (see Fitch 2004b). In 545–546 *superasse nunc pelagus atque ignes iuuat, / uicisse caelum Palladem fulmen mare*, we have a metrically defective line, an obvious doublet, and in *Palladem*, an unparalleled form and a name that distracts from the direction of Ajax's speech before he addresses the goddess in 550. An alternative to deleting both lines would be to suppose that the doublet has resulted from embellishment of Senecan material: perhaps the speech opened with *uicisse* (or *superasse*) *caelum pelagus atque ignes iuuat*.

> uilia currant[6],
> placet in uulnus maxima ceruix: 100
> quidquid in altum Fortuna tulit,
>   ruitura leuat.[7]

The chorus reflects on how taller structures and larger creatures are more vulnerable to storms, lightning, selection for sacrifice, and, in short, the whims of fortune. Within this verse, line 97 stands out as unconventional and inaccurate: larger bodies are more open to storms and thunderbolts but not obviously to disease, to which "all bodies are vulnerable"[8]: compare the passage of Arellius Fuscus pater, quoted by the Elder Seneca at *Suasoriae* 6.6, arguing for Cicero to accept death: *nihil aliud intercidet quam corpus fragilitatis caducae, morbis obnoxium, casibus expositum, proscriptionibus obiectum.* Richard's commentary cites *Florus* 1.45 *corpora quo maiora erant, eo magis gladiis ferroque patuerunt* and the vaguer περισσὰ … σώματα | πίπτειν βαρείαις … δυσπραξίαις from Sophocles *Ajax* 758–759: no parallels for *morbis* here. According to Richard's apparatus, Stuart[9] conjectured *maius*, but (besides the lack of complement for *patet*) this is not normal Latin—*magis* is the adverbial form, and there is no adequate parallel in Seneca. This looks like an interpolation, a reader's expansion of a sententious sequence; but it is also possible that it began from something like *corpora maiora patent*, a gloss summing up the sequence, with *morbis* added to turn the words into an anapaestic dimeter.

---

[6] The *currunt* of some later manuscripts is appealing here: the *cum* clause is not causal, and the opposition between this and *placet in uulnus maxima ceruix* seems stronger if the sense is temporal ("when the common herd is running into the open pasture, the highest neck is the one that pleases for sacrifice") rather than concessive. Tarrant (1976a:191) and Fitch (2004a:133) both use "while" for *cum*, which nicely fudges the distinction.

[7] "The tower that sets its head amidst the very clouds is beaten by the rainy South Wind, and the wood that spreads dense shade sees its aged timber broken; thunderbolts strike high hills, bigger bodies are exposed to diseases, and though the common herd runs into the grazing pastures, the loftiest neck pleases for sacrifice: whatever Fortune has raised up high, she lifts to dash down again."

[8] Tarrant 1976a:191.

[9] It does not appear in Stuart's publications of either 1911 or 1912, so I assume it comes from his unpublished dissertation.

II. SENECA *AGAMEMNON* 610

Another gnomic intrusion in a choral passage of the Agamemnon comes in one of the polymetric odes (604–610, with Zwierlein's text and numeration):

> Solus seruitium perrumpet omne
> contemptor leuium deorum,   605
> qui uultus Acherontis atri,
> qui Styga tristem non tristis[10] uidet
> audetque uitae ponere finem:
> par ille regi, par superis erit.
> O quam miserum est nescire mori![11]   610

> 604 solus seruitium perrumpet omne *Zwierlein*:
> p- o- seruitium *E*: p- o- solus *A*

So ends the first, generalizing section of the ode, before the chorus of Trojan women begin to describe their experiences in enduring the city's fall. Truly heroic is the individual who dares to seek death, in the manner of Hercules, Socrates, or Cato, and indeed of Astyanax and Polyxena, as readers of Seneca may observe (cf. *Tro.* 1102 *sponte desiluit sua*; 1151–1159). The sequence comes to an effective climax with line 609. And then line 610 gives a surprising twist: how miserable by contrast is the one who does not know how to die. As the chorus are alive and miserable, this may seem relevant; but the diction, which reprises *miseros libera mors uocet* (591), gives less point to *miser*, which now reflects on the ignorance of others and not the misery of the chorus.[12] The words are to be condemned, not only for their

---

[10] *trepidus* Giardina, perhaps rightly: the assimilation would be easy. Wills (1996:229–230) has nothing especially similar to the phrasing here (but note Ovid *Pont.* 3.9.35 *cano tristia tristis*).

[11] "Only the man who scorns the unreliable gods shall break out of all servitude, he who sees the face of dark Acheron and without sadness the sad Styx and dares to put an end to life: he is equal to a king and to the gods. Oh, how unhappy it is not to know how to die."

[12] I owe this point to Tristan Franklinos.

isolation from the run of thought but also for their meter: this is the only anapaestic verse in the two polymetric odes in the play.

III. SENECA *OEDIPVS* 709–712

Amid the polymetric sections of the *Oedipus* too, there is just one anapaestic line (709):

> Non tu tantis causa periclis,
> non haec Labdacidas petunt   709
> fata, sed ueteres deum
> irae secuntur.[13]

This is the very start of the song, and the second half of the ode reverts to anapaests (738–763), so the inconcinnity is less marked, and the parallelism of phrasing does more to integrate the line within the context. Boyle 2011:278 comments on the absence of the copula; he compares *Herc.* 1122, but in any case *tu es* is easily conjectured here. And yet something seems to be wrong: on the one hand, *non tu* and *non haec* are in parallel; on the other, *non haec … fata* has its sense determined by the contrasting *sed ueteres deum / irae*. What follows in the ode will illustrate the divine-sent monstrosities that have dominated Theban history; *haec fata* are today's ill-omened pronouncements reported by Creon from the mouth of Laius's ghost (626–658; n.b. *non ira deum*, 630). Leo conjectured *hinc* for *haec*, which Zwierlein rejects as un-Senecan in a causal sense.[14] *Nunc* might be a better alternative, to contrast with *ueteres*.[15] But deletion of 709 would simply remove the initial confusion—and also the conversational *tu* as Oedipus departs (708), unorthodox at the start of a choral ode, and the very vague use of *periclis*. The line is a reader's attempt to make the chorus engage with Oedipus, summarizing, if imprecisely, the substance of the ode.

---

[13] "It is not you that are the cause of such perils, these fates are not aimed at the descendants of Labdacus, but ancient manifestations of divine anger are in pursuit."

[14] Zwierlein 1986b:248.

[15] Tristan Franklinos suggests *nec nunc*.

IV. SENECA *AGAMEMNON* 159

Mythology is another area that incites embellishment. Let us examine the debate between the nurse and Clytemestra at *Agamemnon* 155–163:

Nut.	At te reflectat coniugi nomen sacrum.	155
Clyt.	Decem per annos uidua respiciam uirum?	
Nut.	Meminisse debes sobolis ex illo tuae.	
Clyt.	Equidem et iugales filiae memini faces	
	et generum Achillem: praestitit matri fidem.	
Nut.	Redemit illa classis immotae moras	160
	et maria pigro fixa languore impulit.	
Clyt.	Pudet doletque: Tyndaris, caeli genus,	
	lustrale classi Doricae peperi caput![16]	

Clytemestra is committed to capping her adultery with a greater crime, and (as happens typically in the second episode of the tragedies[17]) the subordinate figure, here the nurse, tries to restrain her. In this passage she reminds her to respect the institution of marriage and then to remember who the father of her children is. Clytemestra responds that her husband has been away for ten years and left her a widow, and to the second point, she says that what she remembers is Iphigenia's wedding ceremony. The nurse argues that she brought an end to the calm and the fleet's inactivity, and Clytemestra in turn regrets that she has reduced her glorious line to being a source of sacrificial victims. This text all flows with rhetorical aptness—as long as we omit 159. That

---

[16] "'Let the sacred name of marriage turn you back.'—'After ten years of being a widow am I to think of my husband once more?'—'You ought to remember your children by him.' 'For my part I remember the wedding torches of my daughter, and my son-in-law Achilles: she (*or* he) showed loyalty to a mother.'—'She bought an end to the delaying of the stationary fleet and set in motion seas frozen by sluggish inactivity.'— 'It shames and grieves me: daughter of Tyndareus, offspring of heaven, yet I have given birth to a sacrificial victim to purify the Greek fleet.'"

[17] So Medea and her nurse in the *Medea*; Phaedra and her nurse in the *Phaedra*, Atreus and his "satellite" (*satelles* E; *seruus* A) in *Thyestes*; Deianira and her nurse in *Herc. Oet.*; Octavia and her nurse in the *Octavia*. Tarrant (1976a:192) sees the origin of such figures in the nurse of the Euripidean *Medea*; but there is presumably a rich history (Euripides's *Phaedra* also has a nurse as confidante, and family slaves regularly play important supporting roles in comedy).

Achilles was the intended bridegroom is not relevant for Clytemestra's argument, but the real problems come in the second half of the line. Fitch translates "he kept true faith with the mother" and helpfully explains that "he" is Agamemnon (so too Tarrant).[18] This cannot be right: normally in such a sentence *matri* would refer to the mother of the subject; more fundamentally two individuals have been mentioned since Agamemnon, and one of them is Clytemestra's daughter. Before lighting on Agamemnon, the reader or audience has to reject Achilles and Iphigenia as subjects, having determined that neither, in any relevant way, kept faith with their mother. There is also a grammatical point: after *memini* Seneca follows the norm that puts human beings in the genitive (e.g., 157, *Phaedra* 242). Richard's commentary sees that the shift of subject is very abrupt, considers emendation and positing a lacuna, but ends up retaining the transmitted text: "Here Seneca achieves compression at the expense of point." No, this is the embroidery of another, weakening the rhetorical concision with a display of mythological information.

V. SENECA *AGAMEMNON* 120

Deleting verse 159 deals with an acknowledged problem. It will be more controversial to find an interpolation in this passage from the soliloquy[19] with which Clytemestra opens the scene (*Agamemnon* 116–124):

> Tecum ipsa nunc euolue femineos dolos,
> quod ulla[20] coniunx perfida atque impos sui
> amore caeco, quod nouercales manus

---

[18] Fitch 2004a.

[19] The audience is told that the speech is to be understood as an internal monologue, partly by *tecum* (in your own mind) in 116 and then explicitly by the Nurse in 126–128 *quid tacita uersas ... ? licet ipsa sileas, ...*

[20] Tarrant (1976a:196–197) notes how unorthodox this usage is: "S. otherwise restricts *ullus* to negative, interrogative, and conditional utterances; here, if sound, it would probably be emphatic ('what *any* unfaithful wife has ever dared')." In the parallels he cites from Lucan, *ullus* is pronominal, and *lex ulla* at Juvenal 10.315 comes in a comparative sentence. We should look for a conjecture: *ausa* perhaps, parallel to *ausae* in 119?

ausae, quod ardens impia uirgo face
Phasiaca fugiens regna Thessalica trabe: 120
ferrum, uenena—uel Mycenaeas domos
coniuncta socio profuge furtiua rate.
Quid timida loqueris furta et exilium et fugas?
soror ista fecit: te decet maius nefas.[21]

118 caeca *Bentley*[22]   120 trabe *A*: graue *E*: rate *recc.*

Clytemestra urges herself to produce a dastardly plan, running through
the crimes women have committed, the wife uncontrollably blinded
by love, the stepmother, the maiden burning with desire that leads her
to act against her family's or her country's interest, deeds produced
by the sword or poison—or she might just choose to sail away from
Mycenae with her lover. But stealing away into exile is a timid act, the
kind of thing her sister Helen did. A greater crime suits Clytemestra.
Part of the pleasure of such evocative generalizations is that they
encourage the audience to find particular examples to match the
type figures. Clytemestra illustrates the technique when she rejects
adulterous flight because Helen has already done it. To my mind, it
detracts from the climactic effect of that if the *ardens uirgo* has already
been specified as Medea. Richard suggests Stheneboea and Phaedra as
possible identities for the *coniunx* and the *nouerca*; Medea too exhibits
love for her husband when she gets Pelias killed by his daughters; and
later she is a wife whom love drives to commit infanticide as revenge
on her husband; Procne's love of her sister Philomela will cause her
to commit a similar crime. Medea (again) attempts to get her stepson
Theseus killed by his father. As for the *uirgo*, the fratricidal Ariadne fits
the description given in 119. Verse 120 then rules that out and distracts
us from seeing Medea as the answer also to the earlier puzzles. It is a

[21] "Now in your mind scroll through the tricks of women, what has been dared by any
wife who was treacherous and out of self-control though blinding love, what the hands
of a stepmother, what the maiden burning with disloyal passion as she fled the kingdom
of Phasis in a Thessalian boat: blade, poison—or steal away on a boat from your home in
Mycenae accompanying your partner. Why do you timidly talk of stealing, and exile, and
flight? Your sister did such things: a greater crime suits you."

[22] For the source of this and other conjectures, see Billerbeck and Somazzi 2009.

verse written by a reader playing the collaborative game, but included in the text, it spoils that game.

VI. SENECA *AGAMEMNON* 267–277

(Clyt.)	Det ille ueniam facile cui uenia est opus.	
Aeg.	Ita est? Pacisci mutuam ueniam licet?	
	ignota tibi sunt iura regnorum aut noua?	
	Nobis maligni iudices, aequi sibi,	270
	id esse regni maximum pignus putant	
	si quidquid aliis non licet solis licet.	
Clyt.	Ignouit Helenae: iuncta Menelao redit	
	quae Europam et Asiam paribus afflixit malis.	
Aeg.	Sed nulla Atriden uenere furtiua abstulit	275
	nec cepit animum coniugi obstrictum suae.	
	iam crimen ille quaerit et causas parat.[23]	

267 dat *Bentley*　　　　　　lacunam ante 273 *Tarrant, Axelson*
273 sed] hunc *Damsté*: tunc *Tarrant*

The speech of Clytemestra that ends with line 267 has excused Agamemnon's exploiting his rights as victor and pointed out that she can scarcely take a hard line on adultery when she is aware of her own culpability. My inclination is then to print Bentley's *dat* in 267: the indicative makes for a more positive *sententia* and fits better with the adverbial *facile* ("he easily offers forgiveness who needs forgiveness"). If we read *det*, Agamemnon is denoted by *ille*: "he, who needs forgiveness, would easily grant forgiveness"; yet Aegisthus seems to take the *sententia* as applying to Clytemestra as well as Agamemnon when he responds with skepticism about "mutual indulgence" (268).

---

[23] "'Let him easily give forgiveness who has need of forgiveness.' — 'Is that it? Can one arrange mutual forgiveness? Are the rules of kingship unknown or alien to you? As judges they are grudging towards us, generous to themselves, and they think this the greatest benefit of kingship, if something not allowed to others is allowed to them.' — 'He pardoned Helen: beside Menelaus she returns, who ruined Europe and Asia with equal disaster.' — 'But no woman stole the son of Atreus away in a secret affair nor captured his heart, which was bound to his wife. He is already seeking an accusation and preparing a case.'"

As he points out, Agamemnon is a king, and kings do not expect to be held to the same standards of behavior as their subjects. Yet, the word *reges* never appears, even though kings are thought of as human actors, judging others and biased towards themselves (270); the subject for *putant* has to be extracted from *regnorum* in 269, a noun that is then repeated in 271 (*regni*). The combination of a superfluity and a lack points to corruption, and I suggest that Seneca wrote *ignota tibi sunt iura regum uel noua* in 269.[24] He writes *uel* for metrical convenience where simple alternatives are presented and *aut* could otherwise have been used (*Oed.* 928, *Tro.* 363, 1085). With *regni* below and *noua* later in the line, I suspect that a scribe wrote *regnorum* for *regum*, and then *uel* was changed to *aut* to mend the meter. Or the synonym *aut* was written instead of *uel*, and the noun then adjusted.[25] Here therefore I postulate a metrical interpolation.

In the OCT Zwierlein adopted Richard's suggestion of a lacuna before 273, in which Menelaus was introduced as the focus, thus allowing *Atriden* in 275 to refer to him. However, this leaves *ille* obscure in 277, and the reference to Menelaus by name in 273 is awkward if he has already been introduced as the subject. Fitch thus prints Damsté's *hunc* in 275,[26] which at a single stroke removes the essential problems, pointing to the more recently named son of Atreus and setting up the contrast with *ille*.[27] The picking up of *Menelao* by *hunc ... Atriden* would be even clearer if 274 were omitted.[28] Moreover, the verse is irrelevant for Clytemestra's argument and Aegisthus's response: Helen's adultery has been pardoned—why not hers? And though Helen's guilt is compounded by the effects it has had, in this rhetorical context the notion that she has brought equal pain to Asia conflicts with the point. Richard cites a similar passage of Dracontius, *Orestes* 200–202, where

[24] Giardina (2009) prints his own conjecture *Atridarum*, but the lines are surely generic.

[25] As monosyllabic synonyms, the conjunctions easily interchange (*Georgics* 1.288 *aut*] *uel* R; *Georgics* 4.313 *aut*] *uel* bc).

[26] Fitch 2004a.

[27] Fitch 2004b:159.

[28] The line has one unusual feature: the elision of *quae*, not otherwise elided by Seneca when it stands "first in both the verse and its clause"; so Tarrant 1976a:224 (nor is *hae* elided). But as he goes on to note, *qui* (*Herc.* 593, 604) is elided in this position; and *quae* itself is elided at *Herc.* 674, *Thy.* 978.

Clytemestra uses as evidence that she and Aegisthus may thrive after the assassination *Lacaenam / interfectricem tot regum, tot populorum, / uiuere felicem post funera tanta quiete.* This phrase may imply that 274 was in the text of the *Agamemnon* by the 5th century; it does not prove that Seneca wrote it.[29] If 274 is interpolated, it too may be classed as a mythological embellishment.

VII. SENECA *AGAMEMNON* 456–484

The expansion of conventional scenes is a frequent source of intrusive lines,[30] as one can see in the storm described by Eurybates later in the *Agamemnon*. Richter deleted 481; Zwierlein and Fitch concur;[31] discussion in our classes on the play led Tobias Reinhardt and me to doubt all of 479–484, an attempt to list the winds with their various weapons (cf. 477 *sua quisque mittunt tela*). Another tricky sequence in the messenger speech is 456–464, which uses anaphora of *iam* to describe the increasing effects of distance and the westering sun, an effect spoiled to my mind by the overemphatic and incoherent 461 *in astra iam lux prona, iam praeceps dies*, a doublet of 460 *iam lassa Titan colla releuabat iugo*.

VIII. OVID *METAMORPHOSES* 1.299–308

Similar phenomena can be found in the text of Ovid:

> Et, modo qua graciles gramen carpsere capellae,
> nunc ibi deformes ponunt sua[32] corpora phocae.   300
> Mirantur sub aqua lucos urbesque domosque
> Nereides, siluasque tenent delphines et altis
> incursant ramis agitataque robora pulsant.

[29] Cf. Tarrant 1989a:139 (on the presence of Ovid *Met.* 8.87 in Priscian 5.16) and 143n45.

[30] See e.g. Tarrant 1989a:140–150.

[31] Zwierlein 1986b:272; Fitch 2004b:166.

[32] *sua* ought to be emphatic; if so, its force is apparently to apply *deformes* to *corpora* too: "now shapeless seals place the bodies characteristic of them (i.e. shapeless)." For such uses of *suus*, see *Fasti* 3.80 (*suis* = *bellicis*), Heyworth 2007:192, Heyworth and Morwood 2011 (on Propertius 3.13.16, 3.19.8).

Nat lupus inter oues, fuluos uehit unda leones,
unda uehit tigres; nec uires fulminis apro,   305
crura nec ablato prosunt uelocia ceruo;
quaesitisque diu terris ubi sistere possit,
in mare lassatis uolucris uaga decidit alis.[33]

At *N.Q.* 3.27.14 Seneca praises Ovid's vision of the universal flood,
quoting 292 *omnia pontus erat, deerant quoque litora ponto* (everything was
sea, even shores were lacking to the sea), before complaining about his
failure to maintain such grandeur:

Ni tantum impetum ingenii et materiae ad pueriles
ineptias reduxisset:

Nat lupus inter oues, fuluos uehit unda leones.   [304]

Non est res satis sobria lasciuire deuorato orbe
terrarum. Dixit ingentia et tantae confusionis imaginem
cepit, cum dixit:

Exspatiata ruunt per apertos flumina campos,   [285]
cumque satis arbusta simul pecudesque virosque
tectaque cumque suis rapiunt penetralia templis.[34]
Si qua domus mansit,[35] culmen tamen altior huius
unda tegit, pressaeque labant[36] sub gurgite turres.   [290]

Magnifice haec, si non curauerit quid oues et lupi faciant.[37]

---

[33] "And where slender goats recently plucked the grass, there now shapeless seals
place their bodies. The Nereids wonder at groves beneath the water, and cities and
houses, and dolphins occupy woods and run up against high branches and move the oak-
trees that they strike. A wolf swims amid sheep, the waves carry tawny lions, the waves
carry tigers; nor is the power of the thunderbolt of use to the boar nor swift legs to the
stag when they have been swept away; and, having sought long for the lands on which it
might settle, the wandering bird falls into the sea, its wings exhausted."

[34] *templis* Z (Genève BPU Lat. 77): *sacris* codd. Ouidiani.

[35] Here Z omits the words *potuitque resistere tanto / indeiecta malo*, and it is not unthink-
able that they were not in the text of the *Met.* known to Seneca or written by Ovid.

[36] *labant* ZHPRW: *latent* F (presumably a sign of contamination), codd. Ouidiani.

[37] "If he [Ovid] had not reduced such force of inspiration and content to childish
follies: 'a wolf swims amid sheep, the waves carry tawny lions.' It is not entirely reasonable to be playful when the whole earth has been engulfed. He spoke impressively and
conceived an image of enormous confusion when he said: 'Rivers spread out and flood

Verses 286–289 and the first two words of 290 are absent from all the manuscripts save **Z**, a mid-12th century copy now in Geneva and the sole source for one half of the tradition at this point (see Hine's stemma[38]). Given that the omitted material is no less sublime (especially 286–287), it seems more likely that the lack is due to a medieval scribe than to Seneca.[39] The presence of 304 in the Senecan text is evidence to support its authenticity. However, the discussion refers only to the first half of the line and not the lions of the second half; and the words *fuluos uehit unda leones* are in fact absent from **Z**, the source that has been judged more reliable in its handling of 285–290. In the direct tradition of the *Met.*, the two half-lines *fuluos uehit unda leones* and *unda uehit tigres* were omitted in **HMN**; and in the Berne anthology, the oldest source at this point, these clauses are reordered into a separate line and placed before 306, thus:

Nat lupus inter oues; nec uires fulminis apro,
unda uehit tigres, fuluos uehit unda leones,
crura nec ablato prosunt uelocia ceruo.

The similarity of the ending of *tigres* to that of *oues* could explain an initial omission, ineptly corrected in Berne 363. But these two half-lines are pointlessly repetitive and have none of the engaging paradox present in *nat lupus inter oues* or the observation that neither power nor speed are of advantage in the Flood; in this context the epithet *fuluos*, conventional for lions, is especially inert.[40] It is therefore tempting to think that in the omission and reordering the Ovidian

---

over the open plains, and snatch up trees along with crops, herds, men, buildings, and sanctuaries with their temples. If any house remained, higher than its roof the wave still covers it, and under the pressure towers slip beneath the water.' This is sublimely said, if he had not bothered with what the sheep and wolves are doing."

[38] Hine 1996:XIII.

[39] There are a number of similar cases in the text of Macrobius: for example the omission of (probably) two and a half lines from Euripides *Troades* 25–27 at *Sat.* 5.22.7, where the ensuing *qui uersus docent* shows that more than three words must have been cited initially, and *discessisse deos a ciuitate iam capta* picks up phrasing from 26 and 27.

[40] Contrast the instances where sight matters, such as Verg. *Aen.* 4.159 (Ascanius hopes to spot one), or the image of Hercules is in question (*Fasti* 2.339; Verg. *Aen.* 2.722, 8.552). Even at *Met.* 10.551 *impetus est fuluis et uasta leonibus ira* the combination of bright color and anger suggests the fieriness of lions, as touched on by Lucretius at *D.R.N.* 5.901.

tradition reflects the addition of these clauses to the original text; and the presence of *fuluos uehit unda leones* in some of the manuscripts of *Naturales Quaestiones* is due to contamination from interpolated copies of Ovid; none of the Senecan manuscripts date from before the 12th century,[41] by which time the tradition of the *Metamorphoses* was widely established.

IX. OVID *METAMORPHOSES* 2.531–541

Di maris adnuerant: habili Saturnia curru
ingreditur liquidum pauonibus aethera pictis,
tam nuper pictis caeso pauonibus Argo,
quam tu nuper eras, cum candidus ante fuisses,
corue loquax, subito nigrantes uersus in alas.   535
Nam fuit haec quondam niueis argentea pennis
ales, ut aequaret totas sine labe columbas,
nec seruaturis uigili Capitolia uoce
cederet anseribus nec amanti flumina cycno.
Lingua fuit damno: lingua faciente loquaci   540
qui color albus erat nunc est contrarius albo.[42]

532 aethera *HMNUG*: aera *MᵛBFLPᶜ*   541 qui] cui *NᵃᶜUB*

Juno has received the assent of the gods of the sea: they will not allow the *paelex* Callisto to pollute the sea as well as the sky (ironically, she thus of course becomes one of the most familiar constellations, the Great Bear, always circling round the pole). Her approach to them has begun in the *aether* (512–513 *quaeritis aetheriis quare regina deorum /*

The phrase *fuluos ... leones* is part of an obviously interpolated passage at *Heroides* 10.85 (Sedlmayer deleted 83–88, rightly, I believe).

[41] Hine (1996:VI) dates the rediscovery to this period.

[42] "The gods of the sea had nodded in agreement: Juno in her nimble chariot advances into the clear sky on painted peacocks, peacocks as recently painted after the slaughter of Argus, as you had recently been transformed into black wings, talkative raven, though you had been previously white. This bird was once silvery with snow-white feathers, so as to equal entirely spotless doves, and not to yield to the geese that would protect the Capitol with their vigilant cry nor the river-loving swan. The tongue did the damage: the talkative tongue bringing it about, the color that was white is now the opposite of white."

sedibus hic adsim?), and it may well be the *aether* to which she returns in
532; but Juno in the *Aeneid* is associated with the *aër*, recalling the allegorical anagram of Hera, and it would be effective to have her returning
to mid-air, where the narrative will leave her until, half a book later, she
rises from her throne, covers herself in cloud, and appears on Semele's
doorstep (3.256–274).[43] Despite the contrast drawn at 1.23 *liquidum
spisso secreuit ab aëre caelum*, we may compare 4.667, 11.194, *Am.* 2.6.11
for *liquidum ... aër.*[44]

More troubling is the presence of two parallel ablatives with
ingreditur: though *ingredi* normally refers to walking (or at least self-
propelled movement), there is a parallel for *curru* at 13.251–252 *atque ita
captiuo, uictor uotisque potitus, / ingredior curru laetos imitante triumphos*,[45]
but it is surprising to have the additional *pauonibus*. Perhaps Ovid wrote
inuehitur: then *habili curru* could be taken as a locative or associative
ablative with Saturnia, and *pauonibus pictis* will be the instrumental
with the verb: cf. 14.538 *perque leues domitis inuecta leonibus auras*; 14.597
perque leues auras iunctis inuecta columbis.

Mention of the peacocks takes the narrative in an extraordinary
direction, back not to the transformation of their tails with the addition of Argus's eyes (1.722–723) but to something that happened "as
recently" (*tam nuper ... / quam ... nuper*, 533–534). The changing of the
raven from white to black is the start of a completely new narrative
sequence, and the dislocation of time (which will continue as we head
back into the past in 551–595) is introduced by comparisons evoking
the distant future (geese protecting the Capitol, 538–539)[46] and then
the recent past, the swan, created from Cycnus, friend of Phaëthon,
who becomes a river-loving bird out of hatred for fire (2.373–380). The
presence of an anachronistic simile here recalls the exemplum drawn

---

[43] Cloud = ἀήρ/*aër* = Hera [by anagram] = Juno; see, e.g., Feeney 1991:132.

[44] *liquidum aether* is transmitted, and surely correct, at 1.67 and *Rem.* 6.

[45] Even here the ending of *imitante* might imply that it forms an ablative absolute
with *curru* (as with *ingreditur iactatis aethera pennis* in 2.835), though the word order, with
captiuo ... curru embracing *ingredior*, stands against that.

[46] These lines are the last reference to Rome until Book 14. For good discussions of
the narrative complexities of the wider sequence, see Keith 1992:39–52, 137–46; Tissol
1997:157–162; Wheeler 1999:130–132; Feeney 1999:27; Zissos and Gildenhard 1999;
Barchiesi 2005:279–282 (the last four focusing particularly on the play with time).

from the future in Ovid's model, Callimachus *Hecale*, fr. 74.10–20 Hollis: the day will come "when the raven, which now would compete even with swans and milk in color and the pure crest of a wave, will have a gloomy wing on him as dark as pitch, as the reward Phoebus shall grant one day for his news" about Coronis.

The last two lines are, however, the reason for including this discussion here. "The tongue caused the damage; the talkative tongue bringing it about, the color which was white is now the opposite of white." Verse 541 is obvious nonsense: it is not the color white that has become the opposite of white, but the bird that was white. Grammatically that puzzle can be solved by reading *cui*, but the lack of antecedent is a little awkward, especially when the sentence has begun with a repetitive ablative absolute, and the gender of the bird, feminine in 536, returns to the masculine of the *coruus* (535). The change of gender would be eased if we read *hic* not *haec* in 536 ("He was once a silvery bird"): assimilation of the pronoun to the complement is common, but not universal,[47] and here it may be a change made in transmission.[48] The apparent problem of construing *contrarius* may also explain the intrusion of the unnecessary half line *qui color albus erat*: to readers thinking of the bird as a feminine *ales* or *auis*, the masculine *contrarius* needed a noun, and *color*, in its clause, provided that noun. Once we comprehend that *coruus* is the relevant noun, *qui color albus erat* can be omitted as an interpolation, and along with it will go the line-filling doublet *lingua faciente loquaci*.[49] Bömer points out that the employment of *faciente* to expand an ablative of cause is otherwise not recorded till rather later,[50] in grammatical and patristic texts.[51] For the brief resumptive sentence, returning to the dominant subject

---

[47] Roby (1889:28) cites Livy 2.38.5 and 3.38.3 as counterexamples; cf. also Vergil, *Aen.* 3.173 *nec sopor illud erat.*

[48] Anderson (1997) notes that *ales* takes the alternative, masculine gender in 544–545 *ales ... Phoebeius.*

[49] Cf. 8.190 *a minima coeptas, longam breviore sequente*, rightly deleted by Merkel and omitted by Hollis 1970, and Tarrant 2004.

[50] Bömer 1969:372.

[51] See Hofmann and Szantyr 1965:133–134.

(534–535), one could compare *Fasti* 6.362 *spes erat in cursu: nunc lare pulsa suo est*, where *nunc* introduces a reprise of *Alpino Roma sub hoste iacet* in 358.

X. HORACE *ARS POETICA* 374–378

Another place where I suspect that grammatical supplementation[52] has led to an interpolated verse is *Ars Poetica* 376:

> Ut gratas inter mensas symphonia discors
> et crassum unguentum et Sardo cum melle papauer   375
> [offendunt, poterat duci[53] quia cena sine istis:]
> sic animis natum inuentumque poema iuuandis,
> si paulum summo decessit, uergit ad imum.[54]

A reader has supplied *offendunt* as a verb to be read within the *ut* portion of the sentence, and the causal clause was subsequently added to complete the verse and provide what was seen as offensive in *symphonia discors*, etc. Wrongly: if you are enjoying a pleasant dinner, the last thing you want is a band playing out of tune. You would not be able to enjoy the company or the music, and the party would quickly turn to disaster (*uergit ad imum*): just so with poetry—it only works when the reader is confident that it is excellent and gives pleasure. Trickier within this run of thought are the perfume too thick to pour and the roasted poppy seeds coated with unpleasant flavored honey— judgment here is less absolute and, unlike the cacophonous music, the guest could simply avoid them, as verse 376 says. Perhaps Horace, the *bon viveur*, has added two pet hates to his list of things to avoid when giving a party, or perhaps this is a prior interpolation, due not to the poet but to a later reader. Without 375 (as well as 376), the sequence is

---

[52] On perceived syntactical incompleteness as a motive for interpolation, see Tarrant 1987:288–289.

[53] Brink (1971) questions the soundness of the verb.

[54] "Like discordant music at a pleasant dinner party, and a thick perfume and poppy-seeds with Sardinian honey [offend, because the meal could continue without them], so poetry, born and created to delight the mind, heads to the depths once it has fallen a little from the heights."

easy to read, and it may be that here, as elsewhere,[55] one interpolation has provoked another.

XI. HORACE *SERMONES* 1.4.2

Richard rightly stresses as a feature of interpolation "the use of language found elsewhere in the same author, often in the same work."[56] An apparently unidentified instance comes in Horace *Sermones* 1.4.1–5:

> Eupolis atque Cratinus Aristophanesque poetae
> atque alii, quorum comoedia prisca virorum est,
> siquis erat dignus describi, quod malus ac fur,
> quod moechus foret aut sicarius aut alioqui
> famosus, multa cum libertate notabant.[57]   5

The poets of Old Comedy freely named those who deserved to be described as criminals or bad characters. Though Eupolis, Cratinus, and Aristophanes were not the only writers of Old Comedy, it is hard to see why Horace has amplified these exemplary names[58] with the "vague etcetera" of verse 2.[59] The ungainly phrasing is an obvious reworking of *Serm.* 1.10.16:

> Ridiculum acri
> fortius et melius magnas plerumque secat res.   15
> Illi scripta quibus comoedia prisca viris est
> hoc stabant, hoc sunt imitandi.[60]

---

[55] See Tarrant 2016a:98. Of course, the theory, though valid in itself, opens the way to an infinity of editorial pruning.

[56] Tarrant 2016a:100.

[57] "The poets Eupolis, Cratinus and Aristophanes, and the other men to whom Old Comedy belongs, if anyone deserved to be depicted, on the basis that he was a rogue or thief, an adulterer or murderer or in some other way a figure of ill-repute, they used to point him out with considerable freedom."

[58] The three poets appear together as the canonical figures (equivalent to Aeschylus, Sophocles, and Euripides) also at Velleius Paterculus 1.16.3 *una* [scil. *aetas illustrauit*] *priscam illam et ueterem sub Cratino Aristophaneque et Eupolide comoediam.*

[59] Gowers 2012:153.

[60] "Ridicule generally cuts through important topics better and more firmly than severity. Those by whom Old Comedy was written based themselves on this, in this they are to be imitated."

This line is clearly the original of the two: it has a function—providing the subject for *stabant* and *sunt*—and it carries the meaning "the writers of Old Comedy" just as the sequence of names does in 1.4.1. Once again we see interpolation arising from a habit of commentary, in this case the cross-reference.

XII. HORACE *EPODES* 5.29–40

Abacta nulla Veia conscientia
    ligonibus duris humum   30
exhauriebat, ingemens laboribus,
    quo posset infossus puer
longo die bis terque mutatae dapis
    inemori spectaculo,
cum promineret ore, quantum exstant aqua   35
    suspensa mento corpora;
exsuca[61] uti medulla et aridum iecur
    amoris esset poculum,
interminato cum semel fixae cibo
    intabuissent pupulae.   40

Rudd's translation in the Loeb runs as follows:

> Veia, inhibited by no sense of guilt, dug a hole in the ground with an iron mattock, grunting with exertion, so that the boy might be buried up to his face (as a swimmer's body floats with its chin just clear of the water), and suffer a slow death gazing at food that was changed two or three times in the course of the long day. Their intention was that, when his eyeballs had finally rotted away from staring at the forbidden food, his dried-up marrow and liver should be cut out and used as a love charm.

---

[61] So Cunningham 1721, and some later editors: see Brink 1982:37–38. Despite the translation "dried-up," Rudd prints *exsecta*, "cut out" (2004:282).

Watson notes that *quo* to introduce a purpose clause is archaic and cites no parallel;[62] it seems worth wondering whether it has replaced *cui* (perhaps written *quoi*), which would give the dative found elsewhere of burial in the earth, e.g., Vergil, *Aen.* 11.204–205 *corpora* ... / *multa uirum terrae infodiunt*.[63] In either case the text presents one final clause (*exsuca uti medulla* etc., 37–40) as dependent on another (32–36); this might explain why Horace chose to use *quo* for *ut*, but the inelegance would be lessened if the first clause was introduced with a relative. Rudd's sense of elegance has separated the long sentence into two, and brought forward the implications (but hardly the phrasing) of 35–36. With *cui* 32–36 would mean "in which the boy might be buried and die amid the sight of food changed two or three times in the course of the long day when he was sticking out by the length of his face as much as bodies suspended by the chin stand above water." Within this the couplet 35–36 is redundant, tautological, and awkward. In the first place, what is the force of *cum*? Surely "while"; and we could print *dum* (the subjunctive being attributable to the purpose clause). But more serious problems rather commend deletion: the *quantum* clause simply duplicates *promineret ore*; and what are these bodies "hung by the chin"? Mankin thinks there is an evocation of Tantalus here, and the water washing against his chin at *Odyssey* 11.583;[64] but *suspensa* indicates a comparison to bodies floating in water, which rules out Tantalus, who is standing (ἑσταότα, 583). On the other hand, bodies do not float with heads sticking above the water, and yet *suspensa mento corpora* is hardly a natural way to evoke swimmers. Without the couplet, the text tells us all that we need to know: the boy is to be buried alive but with his face uncovered so that he can see (34, 39–40). A reader's attempt to draw out the implication precisely has been turned into the ugly tautology transmitted.

WADHAM COLLEGE, OXFORD

---

[62] Watson 2003:211.
[63] *OLD* s.v. *infodio* 1 adds later examples.
[64] Mankin 1995:120.

WORKS CITED

Anderson, W. S. 1997. *Ovid. Metamorphoses Books 1-5.* Norman, OK.

Barchiesi, A. 2005. *Ovidio. Metamorfosi.* Vol. 1. Rome.

Billerbeck, M., and M. Somazzi. 2009. *Repertorium der Konjekturen in den Seneca-Tragödien.* Mnemosyne suppl. 316. Leiden.

Bömer, F. 1969. *P. Ovidius Naso. Metamorphosen: Kommentar, Buch I-III.* Heidelberg.

Boyle, A. J. 2011. *Seneca. Oedipus.* Oxford.

Brink, C. O. 1971. *Horace on Poetry: The Ars Poetica.* Cambridge.

———. 1982. "Horatian Notes III." *PCPS* 28:30–56.

Cunningham, A. 1721. *Q. Horatii Flacci Poemata.* The Hague.

Feeney, D. C. 1991. *The Gods in Epic.* Oxford.

———. 1999. "*Mea tempora*: Patterning of Time in the *Metamorphoses*." In Hardie, Barchiesi, and Hinds 1999, 13–30.

Fitch, J. G. 2004a. *Seneca. Tragedies.* 2 vols. Cambridge, MA.

———. 2004b. *Annaeana Tragica: Notes on the Text of Seneca's Tragedies.* Leiden.

Giardina, G. 2007–2009. *Seneca. Tragedie.* 2 vols. Pisa.

Gowers, E. 2012. *Horace. Satires Book I.* Cambridge.

Hardie, P., A. Barchiesi, and S. Hinds, eds. 1999. *Ovidian Transformations: Essays on Ovid's Metamorphoses and its Reception.* Cambridge.

Heyworth, S. J. 2007. *Cynthia: A Companion to the Text of Propertius.* Oxford.

Heyworth, S. J., and J. H. W. Morwood. 2011. *A Commentary on Propertius Book 3.* Oxford.

Hine, H. M. 1996. *L. Annaei Senecae Naturalium quaestionum libros.* Stuttgart.

Hofmann, J. B., and A. Szantyr. 1965. *Lateinische Syntax und Stilistik.* Munich.

Hollis, A. S. 1970. *Ovid. Metamorphoses Book VIII.* Oxford.

Keith, A. M. 1992. *The Play of Fictions: Studies in Ovid's Metamorphoses, Book 2.* Ann Arbor, MI.

Mankin, D. 1995. *Horace. Epodes.* Cambridge.

Nisbet, R. G. M. 1995. *Collected Papers on Latin Literature.* Oxford.

Roby, H. J. 1889. *A Grammar of the Latin Language from Plautus to Suetonius.* Part 2. London.

Rudd, N. 2004. *Horace. Odes and Epodes.* Cambridge, MA.

Shackleton Bailey, D. R. 1953. "Some Recent Experiments in Propertian Criticism." *PCPS* 2:9–20.

Stuart, C. E. 1911. "Notes and Emendations on the Tragedies of Seneca." *CQ* 5:32–41.

———.1912. "The MSS. of the Interpolated (A) Tradition of the Tragedies of Seneca." *CQ* 6:1–20.

Tarrant, R. J. 1976a. *Seneca. Agamemnon.* Edited with a commentary. Cambridge Classical Texts and Commentaries 18. Cambridge.

———. 1987. "Toward a Typology of Interpolation in Latin Poetry." *TAPA* 117:281–298.

———. 1989a. "The Reader as Author: Collaborative Interpolation in Latin Poetry." In *Editing Greek and Latin Texts: Papers Given at the Twenty-Third Annual Conference on Editorial Problems, University of Toronto, 6-7 November 1987,* ed. John N. Grant, 121–162. New York.

———. 1989b. "Silver Threads Among the Gold: A Problem in the Text of Ovid's *Metamorphoses.*" *ICS* 14 (1/2):103–117.

——— .2004. *P. Ouidi Nasonis Metamorphoses.* Oxford.

———. 2016a. *Texts, Editors, and Readers: Methods and Problems in Latin Textual Criticism.* Roman Literature and its Contexts. Cambridge.

Tissol, G. 1997. *The Face of Nature: Wit, Narrative, and Cosmic Origins in Ovid's Metamorphoses.* Princeton.

Watson, L. C. 2003. *A Commentary on Horace's Epodes.* Oxford.

Wheeler, S. M. 1999. *A Discourse of Wonders: Audience and Performance in Ovid's Metamorphoses.* Philadelphia.

Wills, J. 1996. *Repetition in Latin Poetry: Figures of Allusion.* Oxford.

Zissos, A., and I. Gildenhard. 1999. "Problems of Time in *Metamorphoses* 2." In Hardie, Barchiesi, and Hinds 1999, 31–47.

Zwierlein, O. 1986a. *L. Annaei Senecae Tragoediae.* Oxford.

———. 1986b. *Kritischer Kommentar zu den Tragödien Senecas.* Stuttgart.

IVPPITER IMPERATOR?

MICHAEL D. REEVE

CICERO'S "FOURTH VERRINE," the fourth speech, that is, in his *actio secunda* against Verres, fascinates archaeologists and art historians because it describes many statues and other artifacts that Cicero accuses Verres of misappropriating. I read it in my teens but not again until a few years ago, when I had Gianluigi Baldo's commentary to review.[1] Among the statues that Verres allegedly looted from temples in Syracuse was one of *Iuppiter Imperator*, a designation that appears twice more in the passage (2.4.128–130)[2]:

> Quid? ex aede Iovis religiosissimum simulacrum <u>Iovis Imperatoris, quem Graeci Urion nominant</u>, pulcherrime factum nonne abstulisti? ... <u>Iovem</u> autem <u>Imperatorem</u> quanto honore in suo templo fuisse arbitramini? Conicere potestis si recordari volueritis quanta religione fuerit eadem specie ac forma signum illud quod ex Macedonia captum in Capitolio posuerat <T.> Flamini<n>us. Etenim tria ferebantur in orbe terrarum signa <u>Iovis</u> <u>Imperatoris</u> uno in genere pulcherrime facta, unum illud Macedonicum quod in Capitolio vidimus, alterum in Ponti ore et angustiis, tertium quod Syracusis

After checking with Mary Beard that my argument was not unduly eccentric, I gave an earlier version of this paper in May 2017, at a seminar in Naples organized by Mariachiara Scappaticcio and chaired by Arturo De Vivo, and I owe helpful comments to the participants, especially Giancarlo Abbamonte. It was a privilege to have the opportunity of giving the present version at an event in honour of a long-standing and deeply respected friend who in two of his finest works, an edition of Ovid's *Metamorphoses* and a commentary on the last book of the *Aeneid*, came to know Jupiter quite well.

[1] Baldo 2004; Reeve 2013.

[2] My text differs from Baldo's only in punctuation.

ante Verrem praetorem fuit. Illud Flamininus ita ex aede
sua sustulit ut in Capitolio, hoc est in terrestri domicilio
Iovis poneret. Quod autem est ad introitum Ponti, id, cum
tam multa ex illo mari bella emerserint, tam multa porro
in Pontum invecta sint, usque ad hanc diem integrum
inviolatumque servatum est. Hoc tertium quod erat
Syracusis, quod M. Marcellus armatus et victor viderat,
quod religioni concesserat, quod cives atque incolae
colere, advenae non solum visere verum etiam venerari
solebant, id C. Verres ex templo Iovis sustulit.

Did you not carry off from the shrine of Jupiter a deeply
venerated image of Jupiter the Ruler, or 'the Favourable' as
the Greeks call him, a work of supreme craftsmanship? ...
As for Jupiter the Ruler, what esteem do you think he
enjoyed in his very own temple? You can imagine if you
care to recall the veneration once accorded to that statue
of the same form and appearance that Titus Flamininus
took from Macedonia and placed on the Capitol. There
were reported, I should explain, to be three statues of
Jupiter the Ruler in the world, all alike and of supreme
craftsmanship: the one from Macedonia that we saw on
the Capitol, another where the Black Sea narrows to a
strait, and a third at Syracuse before the governorship of
Verres. Flamininus removed the first from its shrine only
to place it on the Capitol, the earthly residence of Jupiter.
The one at the entrance to the Black Sea, despite all the
wars issuing from there and exported there, has remained
intact and unmolested to this day. The third, the one at
Syracuse that I am talking about, seen by Marcus Marcellus
under arms and in victory, spared by him for its holiness,
habitually worshipped by citizens and residents and not
just viewed but venerated by visitors—well, Caius Verres
removed it from the temple of Jupiter.

Cicero says that the statue was one of only three in the world that
represented Jupiter in the same way. One of the other two was the

Capitoline statue brought to Rome from Macedonia in 197 BCE by T. Quinctius Flamininus.

In his commentary Baldo cites Livy 6.29.8–9:[3]

> T. Quinctius, semel acie victor, binis castris hostium, novem oppidis vi captis, Praeneste in deditionem accepto Romam revertit triumphansque signum Praeneste devectum <u>Iovis Imperatoris</u> in Capitolium tulit. Dedicatum est inter cellam Iovis ac Minervae, tabulaque sub eo fixa, monumentum rerum gestarum, his ferme incisa litteris fuit: "Iuppiter atque divi omnes hoc dederunt ut T. Quinctius dictator oppida novem caperet."

The passage concerns the Capitoline statue of Jupiter brought to Rome by another T. Quinctius in 380 BCE from Praeneste. As it seems unlikely, despite the propensity of families to create or maintain traditions, that two statues of *Iuppiter Imperator* were brought to the Capitol on occasions nearly two centuries apart, each by a T. Quinctius, scholars have debated frequently and sometimes at great length which account, if either, was right.[4] Justus Lipsius, who initiated the debate four hundred years ago in his commentary on Pliny's *Panegyricus*,[5] suggested that Cicero and Livy interpreted a plain *T. Quinctius* in different ways, but most contributors to the debate have agreed on two other things. One is that less trust should be placed in Livy than in his likely source, the antiquarian Cincius,[6] who according to Festus reported that the dictator T. Quinctius, the earlier bearer of the name, dedicated a crown:

> *Trientem tertium* pondo coronam auream dedisse se Iovi donum scripsit T. Quintius dictator cum per novem dies totidem urbes et decimam Praeneste cepisset. Id

---

[3] Text from Walters 1919.

[4] Among recent works, see especially Champeaux 1982:83–91, Riemann 1983:233–255, Oakley 1997:607–609.

[5] Lipsius 1613: vol. 2, 252n42. His preface is dated 1600, and he died in 1606.

[6] On this writer, first distinguished by Martin Hertz in 1842 from the historian Cincius Alimentus and usually thought to have worked no earlier than the 1st century BCE, see Cornell 2013: vol. 1, 181.

significare ait Cincius in Mystagogicon lib. II duas libras
pondo et trientem.

Festus p. 498.4–9 Lindsay

The other thing that contributors to the debate have agreed on is that,
as Stephen Oakley puts it, "We would not expect such a fine piece of
hellenized sculpture [as Cicero describes] to be found even at Praeneste
in the early 4th century."[7]

Surely the most puzzling feature of Cicero's account, though,
comes right at the beginning: *Iovis imperatoris, quem Graeci Urion nomi-
nant*. The Greek epithet means "giving fair wind," "favourable." Why
should its Latin equivalent be *imperator*? By 1831, when C. T. Zumpt in
his edition of the *Verrines* devoted a long note to *Imperator*, as many as
four conjectures had been proposed, none even remotely plausible:
Imbricitor, "rain-bringer," an epithet of Jupiter known from Apuleius
De mundo 37; *Temperator*, "controller"; *Impuber*, "not yet adult," on the
comical assumption that this was abbreviated as *imp.* and then wrongly
expanded; and *Imberbis*, "beardless," for reasons that escape me. It
had also been suggested that *imperator* was an understandable equivalent of οὔριος because Jupiter *imperium habuerit in ventorum rabiem
et indomitas undas*, "had power over raging winds and ungovernable
waves."[8] Cicero's choice is the more surprising because an older bilin-
gual inscription from Delos acceptably renders οὔριος as *Secundanus*, an
epithet of Jupiter also known to Martianus Capella (1.47).[9] Did the three
statues that Cicero mentions resemble each other so closely (129 *eadem
specie ac forma … uno in genere*) that he had no alternative in spite of the
semantic difference? Whatever gave him the idea that in the known
world there were just three statues of the same kind, he may well have
seen those at Rome and Syracuse.[10] He was 23 when the temple on the
Capitol went up in flames, and in 75 BCE, when he served as quaestor
in western Sicily, he paid a visit to Syracuse, where he famously uncovered the tomb of Archimedes (*Tusc.* 5.64).

---

[7] Oakley 1997:608.
[8] Zumpt 1831:786–788. See also Drakenborch 1738:390–392.
[9] Dessau, *ILS* 9237, *CIL* I2 2236, *IDélos* 1754, *ILLRP* 760.
[10] Riemann 1983:235n10, 236.

Though Baldo's commentary is thorough and useful and he set up his own text, he did no serious work on the manuscripts, even though none had been done for a century. Not for the sake of this passage, I decided it was time to do it.

J. N. Madvig showed in 1828 that the medieval tradition of the *Verrines* splits into a French family, no member of which is complete, and an Italian family, most of whose members are complete, among them the one that has since turned out to be the oldest.[11] Study of the medieval witnesses leads me to believe that at this point in the seven speeches, where 82 survive, only three have authority: the oldest member of the French family present, **R** of the 9th century, and two members of the Italian family, **P** of the eleventh and a manuscript that I will call **M**, written round about 1400.[12] This is my stemma:

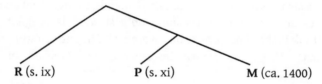

R (s. ix)   **P** (s. xi)   **M** (ca. 1400)

It has been on record since Jordan's edition of 1854 that on the first occurrence of *Iuppiter imp-* **R** has *impetratoris*.[13] That on the first and third occurrence **P** also has *impetr-* was first reported by Bardon in 1964,[14] and in fact it has *impetr-* all three times.[15] So has **M**.[16] Even though **R** has *imper-* on the second and third occurrence as editors imply,[17] the evidence of the three witnesses speaks louder for *impetr-* than for

---

[11] Madvig 1828:7–10.

[12] Reeve 2016. **R** is Paris BN Lat. 7774A, **P** is Paris BN Lat. 7776, **M** is Modena Est. Lat. 328 (α F 8 6).

[13] Orelli, Baiter, and Halm 1854:371. Bursian provided Halm with a further collation of **R**; see p. 323.

[14] Bardon 1964:78. Like Klotz (1923), he calls the manuscript **P**, and it does not deserve the humiliation of the lower-case *p* bestowed on it by the first editor to recognize its importance, Émile Thomas; see Thomas 1885:1–2, 25.

[15] **P** is available at www.gallica.bnf.fr.

[16] I am much obliged to the Biblioteca Estense for quickly supplying me with a digital reproduction. **M** is absent from the list of manuscripts drawn up in Lopez (1973:83–95).

[17] I thank Giliola Barbero for checking.

imper-. Zumpt was therefore quite mistaken when he said of *imperator* that "one should be wary of correcting it because the name is there three times with no variant," *a corrigendo deterret nomen ter sine ulla varietate scripturae positum.*[18]

Naturally I checked modern editions of Livy, but they print *imperator* and say nothing in the apparatus. I therefore went to the *Oxford Latin Dictionary* and looked up *impetrator*: nothing. The *Thesaurus*, however, has an entry for the word and gives five citations, four of them from late antiquity.[19] A legal measure of 349 in the *codex Theodosianus* and two passages of Augustine concern obtaining *beneficia*. A passage of a writer on types of stone has a message for those of us who are authors or prospective authors: *lapis galactites* (milkstone, I suppose) *auctorem gratiosum facit semper et peritum et facundum et efficacem et impetratorem et persuadentem omnibus hominibus.*[20] Honesty demands, though, that I pass on to you a warning from the *Thesaurus* on *galactites*: "lapis ignotus" (though I think Richard must have discovered it). The fifth citation for *impetrator* in the *Thesaurus* is from an inscription, which I looked up:

IOVI

IMPETRATORI

A · L · C

It appears on both sides of a marble *cippus* found in September 1889 among rubble cleared from the bed of the Tiber. Though reported to be "in good lettering," it is undated and so cannot safely be assigned to the period that the *OLD* covers. Publishing it a few years later, Vaglieri added these comments[21]: "Unparalleled is the title *impetrator* given to Jupiter, an epithet that must be taken in the sense not of requesting or obtaining the god's favour but of being the god who granted it. Perhaps the same epithet should be recognized in an inscription from Milan." He quotes one that begins *Herculi inpetra. sacr.*, where *inpetra.* is usually expanded, he says, to "the commoner and more natural *impetrabilis.*"

---

[18] Zumpt 1831:787.
[19] *TLL* 7.1.598.50–56 (J. B. Hofmann).
[20] Abel 1881:190 (Damigeron 34).
[21] Vaglieri 1896:44.

This expansion is attested, I add, by the next inscription in *CIL* (V 5769), another dedication to Hercules found at Milan. "Indeed," says Vaglieri, "one might wonder if in our inscription too, carefully written though it is, *impetratori* should be put down to an error." Vaglieri would therefore have made a good speaker for a conference held on September 20–21, 2018, at the Ambrosiana in Milan, *L'errore in epigrafia*. Incidentally, no one to my knowledge has offered any other explanation of *A · L · C* than Vaglieri's suggestion that these are the initials of the dedicant.[22] Back, though, to *impetratori*. Reporting Vaglieri's publication of the inscription, Cagnat tacitly replaced it with *IMPERATORI* and drew attention to the epithet, "qui est nouvelle,"[23] but Vaglieri's transcription was soon confirmed from autopsy by Huelsen.[24] I imagine Cagnat's *IMPERATORI* was an oversight and the supposed novelty really *IMPETRATORI*. Certainly in the 1890s the epithet *Imperator* was anything but new: editors of Cicero and Livy had been printing it for centuries.

At this point it seemed advisable to take a closer look at the text of Livy. The medieval stemma of Books 1–10 remains controversial, but I believe it to be this[25]:

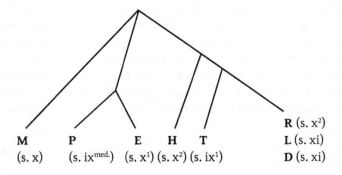

$$
\begin{array}{ccccccc}
\mathbf{M} & \mathbf{P} & & \mathbf{E} & \mathbf{H} & \mathbf{T} & \mathbf{R}\ (\text{s. x}^2) \\
& & & & & & \mathbf{L}\ (\text{s. xi}) \\
(\text{s. x}) & (\text{s. ix}^{\text{med.}}) & & (\text{s. x}^1) & (\text{s. x}^2) & (\text{s. ix}^1) & \mathbf{D}\ (\text{s. xi})
\end{array}
$$

[22] Vaglieri 1896:44 ("Nomi de' dedicanti, scritti con sole iniziali, come qui nel terzo verso, ricorrono in altri monumenti").

[23] Cagnat 1896:18 no. 75.

[24] *CIL* 6.4.30935.

[25] Reeve 1996; see also Reeve 1995:499–505 = Reeve 2011:287–291 (in the latter, correct the stemma on p. 289 by removing **M** and putting λ where the lines from **H** and **RLD** meet).

Oakley inclines to agree.[26] Most of these manuscripts are now available online,[27] and Oakley kindly lent me films of others.[28] It turned out that **P, E, H**, and **T**, all have *impetr-*. If you do the stemmatic arithmetic, **HT** outweigh **RLD**, and **PEHT** then outweigh **M**; and even if, as some editors hold, the stemma is bipartite, with **M** on one branch and the rest on the other, the evidence is no stronger for *imper-* than for *impetr-*.

Throw in the question *utrum in alterum abiturum erat?* (which was going to turn into the other?), and it becomes plainer still that both Cicero and Livy, no less than the engraver of the inscription, twice, wrote *Impetr-*. For corruption of *impetr-* to *imper-*, one need look no further than a 12th-century manuscript of the *Verrines*, **S**, which descends from **R** but has *imper-* all three times.[29] True, *impetrare* is a common enough verb, even if less common than *imperare*, and the *Thesaurus* illustrates corruption in both directions.[30]

Goodbye, then, to any Republican *Iuppiter Imperator*. What should be made, however, of *Iuppiter Impetrator*? The epithet is a closer match for οὔριος but still by no means an exact one, even if taken, as Vaglieri wanted, in the sense of granting rather than winning favours. That sense, however, is not only unattested but hardly compatible with the formation. The passages of Livy and Festus concern a place that readily allows the usual sense: Praeneste. The best-known cult there was that of Fortuna, treated in local inscriptions as Jupiter's daughter.[31] How better to procure her favour than by asking him to intercede?

Perhaps, though, in waving goodbye to any Republican *Iuppiter Imperator*, I have offended an imperial one. When Lipsius initiated the debate on the passages of Cicero and Livy, he did not cite Festus, but

[26] Oakley 1997:152–327; see esp. pp. 321–324 and his stemma on p. 325, fuller than the one that I sketch here.

[27] **P** (Paris BN Lat. 5725) and **T** (Paris BN Lat. 5726) at www.gallica.bnf.fr; **M** (Laur. 63.19) and **D** (Laur. S. Marco 326) at www.teca.bmlonline.it; **R** (Vat. Lat. 3329) at www.digivatlib.

[28] **E** (Einsiedeln 348) and **L** (Leiden B.P.L. 6A), and **T** and **R** before they came online. I have checked **H** (B.L. Harl. 2672) on the spot.

[29] **S** (Paris BN Lat. 7775) is available online at gallica.bnf.fr.

[30] *TLL* 7.1 582.83–84 (O. Prinz), 599.11–12 (J. B. Hofmann).

[31] *CIL* I2 60, XIV 2862–2863, 2868. At *Div.* 2.85 Cicero describes an image at Praeneste of Fortuna suckling two babies, and Champeaux (1982:72–73, 82–83) accepts his identification of them as Jupiter and Juno, but Riemann (1983:240) dismisses it as arbitrary.

he was commenting on a passage ignored by recent contributors to the debate. In his *Panegyricus* 5.1–5, the Younger Pliny regales Trajan with this story about his departure for Germany in 96 CE:[32]

> An fas erat nihil differre inter <u>imperatorem</u> quem homines et quem di fecissent? quorum quidem in te, Caesar Auguste, iudicium et favor tunc statim cum ad exercitum proficis-cereris et quidem inusitato \<omine\> enotuit. Nam ceteros principes aut largus cruor hostiarum aut sinister volatus avium consulentibus nuntiavit; tibi ascendenti de more <u>Capitolium</u> quamquam non id agentium civium clamor ut iam principi occurrit, siquidem omnis turba quae limen insederat, ad ingressum tuum foribus reclusis, <u>illa quidem, ut tunc arbitrabatur, deum, ceterum, ut docuit eventus, te consalutavit imperatorem</u>, nec aliter a cunctis omen acceptum est. Nam ipse intellegere nolebas; recusabas enim <u>imperare</u>, recusabas, quod erat bene imperaturi.

> Would it have been right and proper for there to be no difference between an *imperator* created by men and one created by the gods? Their judgement in your favour, Caesar Augustus, was revealed not a moment later than your departure for active service, and revealed by a novel omen. Other *principes* have been announced in rites of inquiry by a gush of blood from sacrificial victims or by birds flying on the left, but you, as you went up in the traditional way to the Capitol, were greeted by cheering citizens, who were just going about their business, as if you were already *princeps*. When the doors were thrown open for your entry, the whole crowd occupying the threshold hailed the god, or so they thought at the time, but actually, as the sequel showed, it was you that they were hailing as *imperator*, and that is how everyone took the omen. As for you yourself, you declined the interpretation, refusing to command, a refusal that befitted a good *imperator*-to-be.

[32] Text from Mynors 1964.

Zumpt even suggested in his commentary on the *Verrines* that the passage was a way of bridging the gap between οὔριος and *Imperator*: Trajan was embarking on a journey, and so too perhaps were the people waiting at the doors. Even more ingeniously, he ventured an etymological link: did the *pera* of *imperator* perhaps come from the Greek verb περᾶν (cross)?[33] I hope to have shown, though, that οὔριος needed linking not with *imperator* but with *impetrator*; so let us forget Zumpt and come back to Lipsius. Already in play when Lipsius wrote his commentary was this notion, propounded by Catanaeus:[34]

> Traianum ... Capitolinum templum ingredientem Romanorum turba consalutavit, quamquam tunc non id intenderet; putabat enim consalutasse Iovem optimum max., sed eventus docuit consalutasse Traianum, cui deinde cognomen optimi est inditum et maximus omnium factus.

> The Roman crowd hailed Trajan as he entered the Capitoline temple, though that was not their intention at the time; they thought they were hailing Jupiter Optimus Maximus, but the sequel showed that they had hailed Trajan, who was later given the designation *optimus* and became the greatest of all.

Pliny has already mentioned at 2.7 that the senate conferred on Trajan the designation *Optimus*, and he will elaborate at 88.4-10; *Maximus* never formed part of his titulature, but *optimus maximusque* does appear in some honorific citations.[35] Adducing the passages of Cicero and Livy, however, Lipsius gave a new explanation:[36]

---

[33] Zumpt 1831:787.

[34] Catanaeus 1506:clxxviii verso.

[35] Eck 2015:454, 457. Fell (1992:52–75) discusses both the formal and the informal applications of *optimus* to Trajan and observes that *optimus maximusque* puts him on a level with Jupiter.

[36] The other passage that he adduces, from *Regio* VIII in "P. Victor, De regionibus urbis," must have been a medieval or humanistic interpolation from Livy, because nothing of the kind appears in Nordh (1949:84–86).

Ingressa turba "salve imperator" clamavit, sed ad Iovem. Quia tamen ipso puncto ingressus Traianus, omen ad illum haud vane tractum.

The crowd entered and called out *salve imperator*, but to Jupiter. At that very moment, though, Trajan entered, and so the omen was applied not unsuitably to him.

Doubtless that is what Pliny intended when he wrote *te consalutavit imperatorem*, but does it even prove that there was a cult of *Iuppiter Imperator* at the time, let alone before any of the three fires that had ravaged the temple on the Capitol, in 83 BCE (Cic. *Catil.* 3.9, Tac. *Hist.* 3.72), 69 CE (Tac. *Hist.* 3.71), and 80 CE (Suet. *Dom.* 5)? That the statue of *Iuppiter Impetrator* succumbed to the first of these fires is suggested by the *vidimus* that editors rightly print in the *Verrine* (129: *unum illud Macedonicum quod in Capitolio vidimus*). The manuscripts have *videmus*, which in the present discussion it would be circular to reject on historical grounds; but the tense in the phrase *quanta religione fuerit* just above (129: ... *si recordari volueritis quanta religione fuerit ... signum illud quod ex Macedonia captum in Capitolio posuerat <T.> Flamini<n>us*) does require *vidimus*, which in addition not only creates a better clausula (a double cretic rather than a ditrochee preceded by another trochee) but also gives a sharper point to Cicero's remark that the Pontic statue "has been preserved intact and unmolested to this day," *usque ad hanc diem integrum inviolatumque servatum est* (130), even if that is sufficiently explained by the contrast both with frequent upheaval in the region and with Verres's appropriation of the Syracusan statue. Over a century and a half after the statue of *Iuppiter Impetrator* went up in flames, and when two more fires had occurred in the recent past, how faithful is any restoration of the temple on the Capitol likely to have been, and how much continuity is likely to have been maintained in observances there? I must leave the answer to archeologists and historians of religion, and specifically perhaps, had he not died in 1992, to Hans Riemann, who 35 years ago, in the Roman section of the *Mitteilungen* *des deutschen archäologischen Instituts*, published an article of 106 pages entitled—what? Yes, you've guessed: *"Iupiter imperator."*[37]

PEMBROKE COLLEGE, CAMBRIDGE UNIVERSITY

WORKS CITED

Abel, E. 1881. *Orphei Lithica: Accedit Damigeron de lapidibus.* Berlin.

Baldo, G. 2004. *M. Tulli Ciceronis in C. Verrem actionis secundae liber quartus (de signis).* Florence.

Bardon, H. 1964. *M. Tulli Ciceronis actionis secundae in Verrem liber IV.* Milan.

Cagnat, R. 1896. *L'année épigraphique* (orig. pub. 1895). Paris.

Catanaeus, I. M. 1506. *Caii Plinii Caecilii Secundi epistolarum libri novem ... eiusdem Panagyricus Traiano Caesari dictus.* Milan.

Champeaux, J. 1982. "Religion romaine et religion latine: Les cultes de Jupiter et Junon à Préneste." *REL* 60:71–104.

Cornell, T. J. 2013. *The Fragments of the Roman Historians.* Oxford.

Corpus Inscriptionum Latinarum (CIL). 1863–. Berlin.

Degrassi, A. 1965. *Inscriptiones latinae liberae rei publicae (ILLRP).* Berlin.

Dessau, H. 1892–1916. *Inscriptiones latinae selectae (ILS).* Berlin.

Drakenborch, A. 1738. *T. Livii Patavini historiarum ab urbe condita libri qui supersunt omnes.* Vol. 2. Leiden.

Dürrbach, F. 1923–37. *Inscriptions de Délos (IDél).* Paris.

Eck, W., M. Heil, J. Heinrichs, and K. Wachtel. 2015. *Prosopographia imperii Romani saeculi I, II, III (PIR)* 8.2. Berlin.

Fell, M. 1992. *Optimus princeps? Anspruch und Wirklichkeit der imperialen Programmatik Kaiser Traians.* Munich.

Klotz, A. 1923. *M. Tulli Ciceronis scripta quae manserunt omnia.* Vol. 5. Leipzig.

Lindsay, W. M. 1913. *Sexti Pompei Festi de verborum significatu quae supersunt cum Pauli epitome.* Leipzig.

Lipsius, J. 1613. *Iusti Lipsii opera.* Lyon.

---

[37] Riemann 1983.

Lopez, G., and L. Piacente. 1973. "Inventario dei mss. delle orazioni ciceroniane contro Verre." *Arcadia: Accademia Letteraria Italiana, Atti e memorie*, ser. 3, 6(2):83–95.

Madvig, J. N. 1828. *Ad virum celeberrimum Io. Casp. Orellium epistola critica.* Copenhagen.

Mynors, R. A. B. 1964. *XII Panegyrici Latini.* Oxford.

Nordh, A. 1949. *Libellus de regionibus urbis Romae.* Lund.

Oakley, S. P. 1997. *A Commentary on Livy Books VI–X.* Vol. 1, *Introduction and Book VI.* Oxford.

Orelli, J. C., J. G. Baiter, K. Halm. 1854. *Marci Tullii Ciceronis opera quae supersunt omnia.* Zürich.

Reeve, M. D. 1995. Conclusion to O. Pecere and M. D. Reeve, eds., *Formative Stages of Classical Traditions: Latin Texts from Antiquity to the Renaissance*, 497–511. Spoleto.

———. 1996. "The Place of P in the Stemma of Livy 1–10," *Medieval Manuscripts of the Latin Classics: Production and Use*, ed. C. A. Chavannes-Mazel and M. M. Smith, 74–90. Los Altos Hills.

———. 2011. "Inspecting the Foundations: Reflections on Lupus's Edition of Livy I–X." In *Manuscripts and Methods*, 285–295. Rome.

———. 2013. Review of Baldo 2004. *Gnomon* 85: 25–30.

———. 2016. "The Medieval Tradition of Cicero's *Verrines.*" *Exemplaria Classica* 20:19–90.

Riemann, H. 1983. (I cite the title of the article elsewhere and withhold it here).

Thomas, É. 1885. *Discours de Cicéron contre Verrès: Seconde action—livre 5, De suppliciis.* Paris.

Vaglieri, D. 1896. *Atti della R. Accademia dei Lincei, Classe di scienze morali, storiche e filologiche: Notizie degli scavi*, ser. 5, 3(2):44.

Walters, C. F., and R. S. Conway. 1919. *Titi Livii ab urbe condita.* Vol. 2. Oxford.

Zumpt, C. T. (= K. G.) 1831. *M. Tullii Ciceronis Verrinarum libri septem.* Vol. 2. Berlin.

PART TWO

SENECA, OVID, AND OTHER INCURSIONS IN LATIN LITERATURE

READING CEYX AND ALCYONE IN THE MEDIEVAL SCHOOL TRADITION ON OVID

FRANK T. COULSON

THE STORY OF CEYX AND ALCYONE (Ovid *Met.* 11.410–748) represents one of the most important episodes in the *Metamorphoses*. Among the longest, at some five hundred lines, it has always been appreciated by scholars for its literary qualities. Comprising the vivid storm scene and the description of the cave of Morpheus, it develops many of the themes important to Books 1 through 10, namely conjugal love, loss, separation, and unity in death. Further, it forms an important structural bridge in the epic between the stories concerned with Athens in Books 8 and 9, and those dealing with the Trojan War in Books 12 and 13. In the present article, I trace how this fable was explicated in the medieval schoolroom by focusing, in particular, on the Vulgate Commentary, composed in the Orléanais ca. 1260, and the allegorical treatment of Pierre Bersuire, entitled the *Ovidius moralizatus*, written a century later (ca. 1348) at Avignon. In my discussion of the story in the Vulgate Commentary, I shall emphasize three specific categories: first, what I call "the teacher in the medieval classroom," that is to say, how the medieval master clarified points of grammar and reading for his student so as to facilitate his understanding of the text; second, I shall detail some of the commentator's interests in matters of more literary import and look particularly at Ovid's perceived influence on late antique and medieval writers; and third, I shall conclude the section on the Vulgate Commentary by touching more briefly on the allegorical interpretation of the myth advanced by the Vulgate commentator. This third topic serves as an apt segue to the second section of the article which treats the *Ovidius moralizatus* of Pierre Bersuire, who in the mid-14th century developed multiple allegories to explain the hidden meanings of the pagan fables for the medieval reader.[1]

From 1200 to 1500, the *Metamorphoses* served as one of the significant school texts in the medieval classroom. It was read at multiple levels, from the most elementary (the prose paraphrase), through the most utilitarian (the grammatical commentary) and most encompassing (the Vulgate Commentary), to the most spiritually allegorical (the *Ovidius moralizatus*). The Vulgate Commentary was arguably the most widely circulated and sophisticated post-classical interpretation of Ovid's epic. Not only did it give the schoolboy access to the text at all levels (combining the prose paraphrase and the grammatical, literary, and allegorical exposition), it has also been credited with being the Latin commentary through which Dante read his Ovid.[2] The commentary was widely read and disseminated in France and Italy. Spanning the late 13th to the 15th century, twenty-two copies of the text have now been identified.[3] As no critical text of the Vulgate Commentary for the Ceyx and Alcyone episode has yet been published, I transcribe excerpts from manuscript Vat. lat. 1598, a late 13th-century manuscript that transmits the best text of the commentary. The *Ovidius moralizatus* of Pierre Bersuire, on the other hand, assumed a much narrower focus, enveloping Ovid's sophisticated literary text in a veil of Christian truth revealed through spiritual allegory. The episode of Ceyx and Alcyone, with its expansive narrative, complex structure, rhetorical embellishment (particularly in the storm scene), and potential for allegorization (due to the virtues of Ceyx and Alcyone) seemed a particularly apposite choice for our investigations.

---

[1]   The Vulgate Commentary remains unedited. Sections of Book 1 (the Creation Myth) and Book 10 (Orpheus and Eurydice) have been edited in Coulson 1991. An edition (based on Engels 1962) and translation of Pierre Bersuire's *Ovidius moralizatus* by Coulson and Justin Haynes is forthcoming from Harvard University Press. All citations and translations of the Latin text of the *Ovidius moralizatus* have been taken from that forthcoming work.

[2]   See, particularly, Ghisalberti 1966.

[3]   See Coulson 1985; Coulson and Roy 2000:123–125.

I. THE VULGATE COMMENTARY

I.A. The Teacher in the Medieval Classroom

Like any good commentator, the Vulgate commentator was interested in elucidating the structure of the narrative, detailing how the story fits into the larger patterns of Book 11 and how Ovid chooses to develop his narration within the story. This emphasis on the structure of the *Metamorphoses* is particularly dear to the Vulgate commentator and is much in evidence throughout the text. For example, he notes the use of the overlapping narrative between Books 1 and 2, where the story of Phaethon bridges the two books, as well as the narrative overlap of the story of the river god Achelous between books 8 and 9:

> Prelibacio est prime mutacionis sequentis libri, sicut ante nonum[4] librum de Acheloo dicit: *Quid moror externis?* [*Met.* 8.879]

> *Ad Met.* 1.750; Vat. lat. 1598, fol. 11r

Here we have a foretaste of the first transformation of the following book, just as before Book 9 he says about Achelous: *Why do I linger over tales of others?*

In the tale of Ceyx and Alcyone, Ovid frequently switches narrative focus between the two characters. At 11.474, he moves from a vivid description of Alcyone's foreboding upon her husband's departure to the scene detailing the storm that shipwrecks Ceyx. In the text of the *Metamorphoses*, the section dealing with Ceyx's return begins with the keyword *portibus* (at verse 474), and the Vulgate commentator introduces this section with the following comment:

> Alterutro calle procedit actor. Postquam enim locutus est de Alcione, loquitur de Ceice, ostendens quomodo periclitata est nauis Ceicis, et est intelligendum quod hoc fuit

---

[4] Vat. lat. 1598 mistakenly writes *octauum.* I have corrected the text.

in reditu illorum a Claro insula. Dicit ergo *portubus* [Met.
11.474].

Ad Met. 11.474; Vat. lat. 1598, fol. 117r

The author proceeds on first one and then the other
path. For after he spoke about Alcyone, he speaks of Ceyx,
showing how his boat was threatened. We must understand that this took place during their return from the
island of Claros. And so he says: "*They had just left harbor.*"

Similarly, at the end of the Ceyx and Alcyone tale, the Vulgate
commentator carefully maps the transition to the fable of Aesacus, the
son of Priam, who is transformed into a diving sea bird, the *mergus*:

Sequitur mutatio de Esaco in mergum mutato, et con-
tinuat se per precedentia dicens: *proximus* post illum qui
primo uiderat illos, *aut idem* senior, id est ille ipse qui
laudabat amores Ceicis et Alciones, *dixit* [Met. 11.749].

Ad Met. 11.749; Vat. lat. 1598, fol. 121r

The transformation of Aesacus into the diver follows, and
Ovid links this to the preceding section saying *the next*,
after him who had first seen them, or *the same*, old man,
that is the man who praised the love of Ceyx and Alcyone,
said.

The commentator is also quite conscientious in pointing out small
points of Latinity that might trip up the more elementary student. At
verses 11.661 to 662, for example, the ghost of Ceyx says to his wife:

Nil, opis, Alcyone, nobis tua uota tulerunt,
Occidimus.

Ovid *Met.* 11.661–662

Alcyone, your prayers availed us nothing, I am dead.

And the Vulgate dutifully comments:

Occido, dis, media correpta, idem est quod cado, dis.
Occido, dis, media producta, idem est quod interficio, cis,
et sunt ambo tercie coniugationis.

Ad Met. 11.662; Vat. lat. 1598, fol. 119v

Occido when the middle syllable is short means to die. But
when it is long, it means to kill, and both are of the third
conjugation.

In other sections of the myth, the medieval student was confronted
with multiple possibilities for translating and interpreting a verse,
and the Vulgate commentator expends quite a lot of ink going over
the various possibilities, usually introducing the passage with words
like *multipliciter potest legi* (the passage can be read in multiple ways).
Let us look briefly at two such examples, though I stress that there are
numerous places in the Ceyx and Alcyone story where the Vulgate
commentator provides multiple interpretations. In verses 11.510–513,
the waves that attack the ship are compared to lions as they rage
against the weapons of hunters:

utque solent sumptis incursu uiribus ire
pectore in arma feri protentaque tela leones,
sic, ubi se uentis commiserat unda coortis,
ibat in arma[5] ratis multoque erat altior illis.

Ovid *Met.* 11.510–513

Like ferocious lions, with gathered strength, charging the
hunters' blades and levelled spears, so when the wave
engaged with the raging winds, it charged against the
armor of the ship and rose high above it.

The Vulgate commentator serves up several possible readings:

Sic ubi: uersus ille multipliciter potest legi. Primo ergo sic:
sic, id est tali modo sicut est de leone, *ratis in arma,* id est
in pericula, *ubi* postquam, *unda commiserat se uentis coortis,*

---

[5] Tarrant's OCT edition (2004a) prints *in alta,* but the medieval tradition gives *in arma.*

id est peruenerat ad impetum uentorum, *multoque erat*, unda scilicet, *altior illis*, id est per illos uentos. Vel aliter: *sic*, id est tali modo, *ratis in arma*, id est in scopulos et in lapides quibus allidebatur, *ubi se* etc., et *erat multo altior*, nauis scilicet, *illis*, scilicet scopulis, quia eam eleuabant fluctus. Vel aliter et melius: *sic*, id est tali modo sicut est de leone, *ubi*, postquam, *unda commiserat se uentis coortis*, id est fauerat impetui uentorum, *ibat*, scilicet unda illa, *in arma*, id est armamenta *ratis*, id est nauis, et *erat*, unda scilicet, *altior illis*, id est quam essent illa armamenta nauis, et tunc erit *ratis* genitiui casus.

Ad Met. 11.512; Vat. lat. 1598, fol. 117v

Just as when: this verse can be read in various ways. First thus: *so*, that is to say, in such a way as the lion, *the ship unto arms*, that is into danger, *when*, after, *the wave engaged with the raging winds*, that is came to the force of the winds, and *it was*, namely the wave, *much higher by them*, that is through the waves. Or read otherwise, *thus*, that is in such a way, *the ship onto arms*, that is boulders and rocks by which it was dashed, *when the wave* and so on, and *it was*, namely the ship, *higher than them*, namely the rocks since the waves held it up. Or read otherwise and this is the better way to take these lines: *thus*, that is in such a way as with the lion, *when*, after, *the wave entrusted itself to the raging winds*, that is favored the onslaught of the winds, *it went*, that is that wave, *onto the arms*, that is the *rigging of the boat*, that is ship, and *it was*, namely the wave, *higher than them*, that is the tackle of the ship, and in this case the noun *ship* is in the genitive case.

At the conclusion of the tale, at verses 742 to 743, Ovid emphasizes the bond of conjugal love that unites Ceyx and Alcyone even after transformation: *fatis obnoxius isdem, / tunc quoque mansit amor* (though they suffered the same fate still even then their love remained). The Vulgate commentator offers multiple interpretations of the phrase, based in part on the two possible readings transmitted by the manuscripts, *isdem* and *idem*:

> *fatis obnoxius isdem tunc quoque mansit amor*: multipliciter potest legi. Primo sic: *amor* illorum *mansit tunc quoque*, scilicet post tempestatem, *obnoxius isdem fatis*, id est isdem tempestatibus, quia tempestas erat quasi principalis causa amoris illorum quia tempestas Ceicem submerserat. Illa uero pre dolore mortis illius se precipitauerat et ideo miseratione deorum in auem mutata, ille uero prius, et ita tempestas erat causa sue mersionis et ideo amoris. Vnde bene amor obnoxius erat tempestati. Vel aliter: *amor* illorum, *tunc quoque*, etiam scilicet cum mutati essent, *mansit idem*, id est talis qualis fuerat prius, scilicet antequam mutati essent, *amor*, dico, obnoxius *fatis*. Multum enim debebat illorum amor fatis quia illos insimul mutauerant. Vel aliter: *amor* illorum *tunc quoque* post mutacionem scilicet, *mansit obnoxius*, id est iunctus unicus sibi inuicem, *isdem fatis*, id est in eadem mutatione. Amor enim unius obnoxius est amori alterius cum se inuicem diligunt, quia amor alterius est causa quare amatur et ita amor unius est obnoxius amori alterius.

> Ad *Met.* 11.743–744; Vat. lat. 1598, fol. 121r

Though they suffered the same fate, still even thus their love remained, this verse can be read in several ways. First thus: *love* of them *remained then also*, namely after the storm, *subject to the same fate*, that is storm, since the storm was, as it were, the main cause of their love since the storm drowned Ceyx. She, out of grief for his death, threw herself off and thus by the pity of the gods was changed into a bird, though he was changed beforehand, and thus the storm was the cause of their drowning and their love. Thus love was linked to the storm. Or read differently: *love* of those two, *then also*, namely after their transformation, *remained the same*, that is such as it had been before, namely before their transformation. *Love*, I say, subject to *fate*. For their love owed much to fate since it had changed them at the same time. Or read differently: *love* of both, *then also*, namely after the transformation, *remained bound*, that is joined one to another, *by the same fate*, that is the same transformation. For love of one was bound to love of the other since they loved each other because love for another inspires love and thus love of one person is bound to the love of another.

As any younger student of Ovid knows, there are passages in his poetry that are chock-full of unusual vocabulary. The Vulgate master, like any good teacher, explicates the specific meaning of those words that must have caused the medieval student some real difficulty. For example, at *Met.* 11.474–483, as the storm begins, Ovid regales the reader with his knowledge of the ship's riggings, citing in the space of five lines *rudentes* (ropes for raising a sail), *cornua* (yardarm), *malus* (the mast of a ship), *carbasa* (canvas), and *antemnae* (sail yard). All of these terms are relatively skillfully outlined by the Vulgate commentator, either in the interlinear gloss or in the marginal gloss surrounding the poem (fol. 117r of Vat. lat. 1598).

Further, the commentator carefully explains unusual words or allusions for the medieval reader. Allow me to reproduce two such examples selected at random. At *Met.* 11.584, where Juno invokes Iris to proceed to the cave of sleep, the Vulgate commentator defines a rainbow:

> Yris est rota solis que rotunda est et in nube impressa rotundum facit arcum. Vnde Lucanus: *Hinc imperfecto complectitur aera giro arcus* [*Bellum civile*, 4.78–80].
>
> *Ad Met.* 11.585; Vat. lat. 1598, fol. 118v

> Iris is the wheel of the sun which is round and when impressed in a cloud makes a rounded arch. Whence Lucan: *Next the rainbow spanned the air with its broken arch.*

At 11.610, Ovid introduces the abode of sleep with reference to the bed of ebony that lies in the central span of the cavern. The Vulgate commentator defines ebony so:

> Ebenus enim arbor est nigri coloris et nascitur in India et Ethiopia, que cesa durescit in lapidem, cuius cortex leuis est ut lauri. Hoc dicit Ysidorus [*Etym.* 17.7.36].

> *Ad Met.* 11.610; Vat. lat. 1598, fol. 119r

> Ebony is a black wood that grows in India and Ethiopia. When cut it hardens into stone and its bark is smooth like a laurel's. Isidore refers to this.

Lastly, the Vulgate commentator is aware of the way in which Ovid uses rhetoric for persuasion, as for example at verse 11.623 where Iris addresses Sleep:

> In hac oratione intendit Yris Sompni beniuolentiam acquirere ut ipsius precibus citius adquiescat dicens *Sompne.*

> *Ad Met.* 11.623; Vat. lat. 1598, fol. 119r

> In this speech, Iris plans to capture the goodwill of Sleep so as to fulfill her prayers, and she says *Sleep.*

I.B. Literary Qualities of the Episode

In many respects, the Vulgate Commentary reflects the scholarly preoccupations of the High Middle Ages.[6] As we have shown above, the text is often interested in explicating the poem at its most basic level: explaining grammar, providing synonyms for difficult vocabulary, or illuminating the background to the myth developed in a particular story. In one respect, however, the Vulgate Commentary is quite unique within the medieval commentary tradition, namely in its preoccupation with what might be termed literary aspects of the *Metamorphoses*. The commentator draws upon a long list of classical, late antique, and

---

6   See also Coulson 2016b.

medieval authors to illustrate points of comparison. Among classical and later antique authors, one may note Virgil, Statius, Horace, Juvenal, Valerius Flaccus, and Claudian. Among medieval authors, Bernard Silvester, Alan of Lille, and Walter of Châtillon are frequently cited.

In the Ceyx and Alcyone story, the commentator makes relatively judicious comments about Ovid's use of language or the way in which a particular scene evokes or recalls others in the poem. Near the end of the story of Ceyx and Alcyone, for example, Morpheus, in the guise of Ceyx, appears before Alcyone to announce Ceyx's death. As the ghost of Ceyx withdraws, Ovid writes at verses 11.686–87:

> Manusque
> ad discedentem cupiens retinere tetendi.
>
> Ovid *Met.* 11.686–687

> I stretched out my hands to him as he vanished, wanting to hold him back.

The Vulgate connects the scene with the shade of Eurydice that withdraws from the embrace of Orpheus in the beginning of Book 10:

> *manus ad discedentem cupiens retinere tetendi,* sicut Orpheo umbra uxoris sue. Vnde supra: *Brachiaque intendens prendique et prendere captans / nil nisi cedentes infelix attigit auras* [*Met.* 10.58–59].
>
> Ad *Met.* 11.686–687; Vat. lat. 1598, fol. 120r

> *I stretched out my hands to him as he vanished, wanting to hold him back,* just like the shade of his wife for Orpheus, hence above. *He stretched out his arms, eager to clasp her or feel her clasp. But the wretch touched nothing but the yielding air—.*[7]

---

[7]   The reader should note that the medieval tradition at *Met.* 10.58–59 presents a text different from Anderson's Teubner or Tarrant's OCT. The Vulgate Commentary transmits *captans*, against Anderson's and Tarrant's *certans* (adopted from manuscripts **M B**), while the Vulgate Commentary has *attigit* for Anderson's and Tarrant's *adripit*.

The Vulgate commentator also demonstrates an acute awareness of how medieval poets, particularly Walter of Châtillon, appropriated scenes and vocabulary from the *Metamorphoses*. Walter wrote his epic on Alexander the Great, the *Alexandreis*, around 1175 in imitation of Virgil, Lucan, and particularly Ovid. The Vulgate commentator has a relatively deep appreciation for the debt Walter owes to his predecessor in the *Alexandreis*. A particularly apt illustration may be found in the Vulgate commentator's note to *Met.* 9.76 where Ovid uses the adjective *precaria* in an unusual sense: *arma aliena moues, quem forma precaria celat* (a borrowed form conceals you, who fights with arms not your own). The *Oxford Latin Dictionary*'s entry to *precarius, a, um* 1,b notes this unusual usage ("not properly one's own, borrowed") and cites two later attestations of its use in Seneca and one in Apuleius. The Vulgate commentator is so astute as to link this unusual meaning with its use by Walter of Châtillon at *Alex.* 5.469:

> *precaria*: Simile in *Alexandreide*: *inter honoratos fulgere precaria uestis* [*Alex.* 5.469].

Ad Met. 9.76; Vat. lat. 1598, fol. 90r

> *borrowed* as we have in the *Alexandreis*: *among the honored they shone in their borrowed clothes.*

Similarly, in the tale of Ceyx and Alcyone, the commentator alludes to several places where Walter appears to have Ovid as a model, perhaps most notably at *Alex.* 4.438, where Walter models his cave of Sleep after the passage in Book 11:

> *tecta sub nube latentia*: Simile dicit magister Galterus de domo sompni: *Emicat extimplo, uelataque nubis amictu antra quietis adit et desidis atria Sompni* [*Alex.* 4 437].

Ad Met. 11.591; Vat. lat. 1598, fol. 118v

> *Cloud-concealed palace*: Master Walter uses similar language about the house of Sleep: *At once she sprang up and approached the caves veiled in cloud where all lay quiet and inactive Sleep held his court.*

I.C. ALLEGORY IN THE VULGATE COMMENTARY[8]

From 1100 to 1600, one of the most widespread ways of interpreting the *Metamorphoses* was to produce allegories on each story so that the reader might grasp the essential moral or spiritual truth veiled behind the pagan myth. More than 20 different allegorical treatments of the poem are extant,[9] ranging from Arnulf of Orléans's *Allegoriae*, written at Orléans about 1180,[10] through Giovanni del Virgilio's prosimetric version composed at Bologna about 1320,[11] to perhaps the most notorious example, the Latin *Ovidius moralizatus* of Pierre Bersuire, composed at Avignon and Paris between 1342 and 1360.

The allegories found in the Vulgate Commentary follow in the earlier tradition of Arnulf of Orléans. Arnulf was an important schoolmaster at Orléans around 1180 who wrote a grammatical commentary on the *Metamorphoses* as well as a series of what he calls "Allegories" (*Allegoriae*).[12] The latter text rarely conforms to the modern notion of allegory, but rather interprets each story in a historical (euhemeristic) or naturalistic or moral sense. Thus the story of Jupiter and Europa reveals that a king of Crete abducted a young maiden in his ship which had an image of a bull on its bow (*Allegoriae* 2.13). The Vulgate Commentary produces a naturalistic interpretation for the story of Ceyx and Alcyone, drawing on the earlier allegory of Arnulf of Orléans (*Allegoriae* 11.9). Ceyx and Alcyone drowned in the ocean and are said to be transformed into halcyons since the bird bears the same name as Alcyone:

> Rei ueritas est quod Ceix et Alcione submersi sunt in mare. Quod autem dicitur illos mutatos esse in aues, nichil aliud est quam quod Alcione uocata est quo nomine uocata est auis que frequentat occeanum, et est talis nature quod semel in anno, scilicet in hieme, per

---

[8] See further Coulson 2016a.
[9] These allegories are discussed in my forthcoming fascicle on Ovid's *Metamorphoses* for the *Catalogus translationum et commentariorum*.
[10] Edited in Ghisalberti 1932.
[11] Edited in Ghisalberti 1931.
[12] For Arnulf, see, in particular, Coulson 2011, and Gura 2015.

septem dies incubat super oua sua, et per illud tempus fit
mare tranquillum, et sic ad naturam spectat ista mutatio.

Ad Met. 11.746, Vat. lat. 1598, fol. 121r

In truth, Ceyx and Alcyone drowned at sea. They are said
to be transformed into birds because Alcyone has the same
name as the bird that journeys on the ocean, and the bird's
nature is to each year in winter nest its eggs for seven
days; the sea is tranquil during this time, and so this transformation looks to nature.

II. PIERRE BERSUIRE, *OVIDIVS MORALIZATVS*

A century after the Vulgate Commentary, Pierre Bersuire, a Benedictine
preacher at Avignon and Paris from 1342 to 1362, in his treatise *Ovidius
moralizatus* (The Moralized Ovid), developed an even fuller allegorical
treatment of the *Metamorphoses*.[13] The *Ovidius moralizatus* was arguably
one of the most important interpretations of Ovid in the High Middle
Ages. The text exists in about one hundred manuscript copies,[14] and
it was printed numerous times in the 16th century. The history of the
text's transmission is further complicated by the fact that Bersuire
produced three distinct versions of the *Ovidius moralizatus*: a primi-
tive version (labeled A_1 in the scholarly literature) written at Avignon;
a revised version of A_1 (labeled A_2) completed at Avignon; and a third
version (labeled **P**) composed after Bersuire's move to Paris after 1348,
wherein he incorporated many of the allegories found in the vernacular *Ovide moralisé*. In certain instances, Bersuire furnished a brief
euhemeristic account of the myth, but more often he concentrates on
the moral and spiritual significance of the story. The *Ovidius moralizatus*

---

[13] In spite of its relative importance, the *Ovidius moralizatus* remains unedited and
underexamined. Coulson and Haynes (forthcoming) have a projected edition and translation in the Dumbarton Oaks Medieval Library of Texts, from which the text and translation used here are drawn. The most important and interesting work on the *Ovidius
moralizatus* is currently being done by Marek Thue Kretschmer (2016) and Pablo Piqueras
Yagüe (forthcoming). See also Ghisalberti 1933, Hexter 1989, and Fumo 2014.

[14] Coulson and Roy 2000:24–27.

was a highly influential text, serving as a source for many later Latin and vernacular mythographic treatises, for example the *Arcana deorum* of the English cleric Thomas of Walsingham[15] and the anonymous French vernacular *la Bible des poètes*, composed in the 16th century.

One aspect of the *Ovidius moralizatus* that must have made it very attractive to medieval students is the fact that a succinct prose summary precedes each allegory. James Clark has noted that the *Ovidius moralizatus* was imported to England within a decade of its production and was intensely studied by English clerics.[16] Through the *Ovidius moralizatus*, then, the student was able to enter the world of the *Metamorphoses* both literally and allegorically.

The interpretation of the Ceyx and Alcyone tale begins with a relatively straightforward prose paraphrase:

> Cum Ceyx rex Thraciae fratrem suum Daedalionem mutatum in accipitrem videns, quam plurimum terreretur, volens placare numina contra voluntatem uxoris suae Alcyones mare navigaturus intravit, qui una cum navibus et comitiva interiit ita quod nullus ex eis remansit. Cum igitur Alcyone uxor eius pro eo sacrificaret dis omnibus et praecipue Iunoni, Iuno mandavit per Iridem nuntiam suam Somno deo dormientium, cuius domus erat in quodam antro secreto ab omni tumultu tecto, quod ipse unum de somniis suis ad Alcyonen mitteret et quod se in speciem Ceycis periclitantis transformaret, et sic uxorem de viri obitu et naufragio informaret. Quod et factum est. Propter quod Alcyone mane ad litus veniens corpus viri submersi ad litus fluctuando propinquare vidit. Quae dolore tacta super ipsum in mare se proiecit. Di autem utriusque miserti ipsos in aves quae *alcyones* vocantur mutaverunt quae adhuc mare frequentant et in mari super harenam nidum faciunt et ibidem pullificant. Unde Ovidius:

15 The text is edited in Van Kluyve 1968.
16 Clark 2011:177–196, esp. 187–188.

> *Superis miserantibus, ambo*
> *alite mutantur; fatisque obnoxius isdem*
> *tunc quoque mansit amor, nec coniugiale solutum*
> *foedus in alitibus. Coeunt fiuntque parentes,*
> *perque dies placidos hiberno tempore septem*
> *incubat Alcyone pendentibus aequore nidis.*
> *Tunc via tuta maris, ventos custodit et arcet*
> *Aeolus egressu praestatque nepotibus aequor* [Met. 11.741–748].
> Alcyone enim fuit filia Aeoli.

Pierre Bersuire, *Ovidius Moralizatus* 11.9

When Ceyx, the king of Thrace, saw his brother Daedalion turned into a hawk, he was greatly terrified and wanted to placate the divinities, though his wife Alcyone was opposed to it. So he set sail and, entering the sea, perished along with his ships and crew so that nothing remained of them. His wife Alcyone was offering sacrifices for him to all the gods and especially to Juno. Juno, therefore, through her messenger Iris, ordered Sleep, the god of sleeping people, whose house was in a secret cave hidden from all disturbance, to send Alcyone one of his dreams and to make himself look like Ceyx being shipwrecked. In this manner he was to inform Ceyx's wife of her husband's death by shipwreck. He did this, and as a result Alcyone went in the morning to the seashore where she saw the corpse of her drowned husband floating to shore. Overwhelmed by grief, she threw herself into the sea on top of him. The gods, however, took pity on both and changed them into birds called halcyons which still are found around the sea and make their nest on sand in the sea and there hatch their young. Hence Ovid:

The gods took pity and changed them both to birds. Though they suffered the same fate, their love still remained and their marriage bond was unbroken as birds. They still mate and become parents, and for seven peaceful days in winter Alcyone sits on her nest floating on the water. Then the sea is safe to travel, for Aeolus guards his winds and forbids them to escape and keeps the sea peaceful for his grandsons. For Alcyone was the daughter of Aeolus.

Bersuire then develops a spiritual allegory in which the soul, contemplating the death of Christ, is commanded through devotion to lie with Christ and be renewed through the Resurrection:

> Sic anima, Christi uxor, quando videt quod vir suus, Dei filius, navem crucis ascendit ubi periclitatus et mortuus fuit, cum videt et considerat ipsum mortuum, debet se super eum in mari, id est in amaritudine poenitentiae et confessionis, per devotionem ponere, et cum eo facto ave in resurrectione et ascensione simul renovari, et sic avis similitudinem induere, et per contemplationem ascendere et volare, ut sic sibi dicatur illud Psalmistae: *In mari via tua et semitae tuae in aquis multis* [Psalm 77:19].

Pierre Bersuire, Ovidius Moralizatus 11.20

> Thus when the soul, the wife of Christ, sees that its husband, the son of God, ascended the ship of the cross where he was shipwrecked and died, and when it contemplates his death, out of devotion it should place itself on top of him in the sea, that is in the bitterness of penitence and confession, and it should be renewed in the resurrection and the ascension together with her husband who had been made a bird, and thus it should adopt the appearance of a bird and should ascend and fly through contemplation. Just so may be spoken to her: *In the sea is your way and your paths in many waters.*

Bersuire, then, draws out the important themes of this episode, namely marital fidelity, the devotion of the spouses, and unity in death, but he develops them in an allegorical interpretation that goes much deeper than his predecessor, the Vulgate commentator, along the path of anagogical or spiritual allegory, in which characters and myths in the *Metamorphoses* may be viewed as illustrations of events in the life of

Christ and of the struggle of the Christian soul.[17] The spiritual interpretation is further strengthened by reference to an outside text, in this case the Psalms.

In 1979, when I was first introduced to the Vulgate Commentary by Richard Tarrant, little was known of the "medieval Ovid." Richard's work on the manuscripts of the *Metamorphoses*, undertaken in preparation for his magisterial Oxford Classical Text, has uncovered a rich store of untapped and unedited material now being investigated by a younger generation. All scholars who work on the *Nachleben* of Ovid are greatly in Richard's debt. We wish him a long and fruitful retirement.

THE OHIO STATE UNIVERSITY

WORKS CITED

Anderson, W. S. 1977. *P. Ovidii Nasonis Metamorphoses*. Leipzig.

Clark, J. G. 2011. "Ovid in the Monasteries." In *Ovid in the Middle Ages*, ed. James G. Clark, Frank T. Coulson, and Kathryn L. McKinley, 177–196. Cambridge.

Coulson, F. T. 1985. "MSS. of the *Vulgate* Commentary on Ovid's *Metamorphoses*." *Scriptorium* 39:118–129.

———. 1991. *The 'Vulgate' Commentary on Ovid's "Metamorphoses": The Creation Myth and the Story of Orpheus*. Toronto.

———. 2011. "Ovid's *Metamorphoses* in the School Tradition of France, 1180–1400: Texts, Manuscript Traditions, Manuscript Settings." In *Ovid in the Middle Ages*, ed. James G. Clark, Frank T. Coulson, and Kathryn L. McKinley. Cambridge.

———. 2015. *The Vulgate Commentary on Ovid's "Metamorphoses" Book 1*. Kalamazoo, MI.

———. 2016a. "Myth and Allegory in the Vulgate Commentary on Ovid." In *Lire les mythes: Formes, usages et visées des pratiques mythographiques de l'Antiquité à la Renaissance*, ed. Arnaud Zucker, Jacqueline Fabre-Serris, Jean-Yves Tilliette, and Gisèle Besson, 199–224. Villeneuve d'Ascq.

---

[17] See Moss 1982:24

———. 2016b. "Literary Criticism in the Vulgate Commentary on Ovid's *Metamorphoses*." In *Medieval Textual Cultures: Agents of Transmission, Translation, and Transformation*, ed. Faith Wallis and Robert Wisnovsky, 121–132. Berlin.

———. 2018. "The Allegories in the Vulgate Commentary." In *Ovidius explanatus: Traduire et commenter les Métamorphoses au Moyen Âge*, ed. S. Biancardi, P. Deleville, F. Montorsi, and M. Possamaï-Pérez, 23–38. Paris.

———. Forthcoming. "Ovid, *Metamorphoses*." In *Catalogus translationum et commentariorum*, ed. Greti Dinkova-Bruun. Toronto.

Coulson, F. T., and J. Haynes. Forthcoming. *The "Ovidius moralizatus" of Pierre Bersuire*. Cambridge, MA.

Coulson, F. T., and B. Roy. 2000. *Incipitarium Ovidianum: A Finding Guide for Texts Related to the Study of Ovid in the Middle Ages and Renaissance*. Turnhout.

Engels, J. 1962. *Reductorium morale Liber XV, cap. ii–xv: Ovidius moralizatus*. Utrecht.

Fumo, J. 2014. "Commentary and Collaboration in the Medieval Allegorical Tradition." In *A Handbook to the Reception of Ovid*, ed. John F. Miller and Carole E. Newlands, 114–128. Chichester.

Ghisalberti, F. 1931. "Giovanni del Virgilio espositore delle *Metamorfosi*." *Il giornale Dantesco* 34:1–110.

———. 1932. "Arnolfo d'Orléans, un cultore di Ovidio nel secolo XII." *Memorie del Reale Istituto Lombardo di Scienze e Lettere* 24:157–234.

———. 1933. "L' *Ovidius moralizatus* di Pierre Bersuire." *Studi romanzi* 23:5–136.

———. 1966. "Il commentario medioevale all'*Ovidius maior* consultato da Dante." *Rendiconti dell'Istituto Lombardo, Classe di Lettere e Scienze morali e storiche* 100:267–275.

Gura, D. T. 2015. "Living with Ovid: The Founding of Arnulf of Orléans' Thebes." In *Manuscripts of the Latin Classics, 800–1200*, ed. Erik Kwakkel, 131–168. Leiden.

Hexter, R. J. 1989. "The Allegari of Pierre Bersuire: Interpretation and the *Reductorium morale*." *Allegorica* 10:49–82.

Kretschmer, M. T. 2016. "L'*Ovidius moralizatus* de Pierre Bersuire: Essai de mise au point." *Interfaces: A Journal of Medieval European Literatures* 3:221–244.

Moss, A. 1982. *Ovid in Renaissance France: A Survey of the Latin Editions of Ovid and Commentaries Printed in France Before 1600.* London.

Piqueras Yagüe, P. Forthcoming. "Preliminary Comparison of the Use of the Sources in the *Ovide moralisé* and in Bersuire's *Ovidius moralizatus*." In *Ovid in the Vernacular: Translations of the Metamorphoses in the Middle Ages and Renaissance,* ed. G. Pelissa Prades and M. Balzi.

Tarrant, R. J. 2004a. *P. Ovidi Nasonis. Metamorphoses.* Oxford Classical Texts. Oxford.

Van Kluyve, R. A., ed. 1968. *Thomae Walsingham. De Archana deorum.* Durham.

Zeeman, N. 2009. "In the Schoolroom with the '*Vulgate*' *Commentary* on *Metamorphoses* I." *New Medieval Literatures* 11:1–18.

IT'S THE *ANIMAE*, STUPID

SENECA'S OVIDIAN AFTERLIVES

JAMES KER

IN THE FINAL CHAPTERS of his *Consolatio ad Marciam* (ca. 37 CE), Seneca impersonates the grieving mother's long-dead father, Cremutius Cordus, speaking down to her from the heavens. Cremutius reassures Marcia that the deceased, her adult son Metilius, has now joined him up above, in a *coetus sacer* (sacred company) that includes the disembodied souls of the Scipios, the Catos, and his own ancestors (*Marc.* 25.2–7).[1] As Williams observes of Seneca's dramatic ending, "The problem of doctrinal inconsistency ... succumbs to the larger rhetorical and therapeutic momentum of the exercise."[2] For within the space of a few chapters, Seneca has gone from presenting an Epicurean symmetry argument ("Death ... restores us [*reponit*] to the tranquility in which we lay before we were born," 19.5) to an image of the "souls/minds" (*animis*) of the deceased, "looking down upon human affairs, elevated and from on high" (*sublimes et ex alto*, 23.2).[3] Cremutius, speaking no longer in his role as a historian but now "in an elevated style matching his newly sublime position" (*ingenio ... tanto elatiore quanto est ipse sublimior*), calls upon Marcia to realize that even dying kings are "supremely happy" (*felicissimos*) if death rescues them from life's uncertainties (26.1–3). The father's final solace for his daughter is to describe the

I thank the organizers and participants in the conference where this paper was first presented, especially Richard Tarrant for his generosity on that occasion—as also during the time when we were colleagues (2002–4). The paper received helpful contributions from audiences at NYU and Penn and from the editors of this volume.

[1] On *Marc.* (= *Dial. 6*), see esp. Sauer 2014, Manning 1981, Favez 1928, and refs. below.

[2] Williams (forthcoming).

[3] My translations throughout. Note that *animis* is here masculine (cf. 23.2 *liberati*, etc.); the later use of *animas* (25.1) and *animae* (26.7) is thus quite marked.

commune fatum (shared destiny/destruction) that awaits: a climactic world-conflagration in which "we too, happy souls" (*nos quoque felices animae*) will have an end (26.6–7).

Scholars have debated Cremutius's doctrine(s),[4] but all are agreed in detecting here the literary model of Cicero's *Somnium Scipionis*,[5] where the living Scipio receives cosmological instruction from his adoptive grandfather and his father, who explains that virtuous living leads to the Milky Way, a celestial "company (*coetum*) of those who have already lived their lives and [are] now released from the body" (*Somn.* 16). Seneca creatively moves one step beyond Cicero's ending: he retains the encounter between deceased father (Cremutius) and child (Marcia), but the young man (Metilius) has *already* been beamed up.

Not all Seneca's models have yet been identified. *Animae*, whether as "souls," a semitechnical term in philosophy, or "spirits" of the dead in "a largely poetic sense,"[6] is a term absent from the *Somnium*. I will argue that beyond the *Somnium* and beyond other acknowledged models in Virgil and Ovid, another passage, Ovid's *Fasti* 1.295–310, is indispensable for our understanding of Cremutius's *animae*.[7] This passage equipped Seneca with a more explicitly "sublime" aesthetic for his consolatory repertoire. Furthermore, Seneca's allusive adaptation of Augustan poetic models in this early prose work resembles the method that would later be typical in his tragedies.

This essay touches upon topics that others have addressed more extensively, such as Seneca's eschatologies;[8] his Augustan intertexts;[9] and his personalized therapies.[10] Its inspiration is Richard Tarrant's essay "Seeing Seneca Whole?" (2006), which includes a section entitled "It's the *Animus*, Stupid," a concise yet wide-ranging sketch of Seneca's

---

[4] For Posidonian influence, see Abel 1964 (critique: Manning 1981:133–137), also Hoven 1971:93–102; on Platonic dimensions, Hoven 1971:118–123, Setaioli 1997:338–339.

[5] See esp. Armisen-Marchetti 2007, Setaioli 1997:340–347; Manning 1981:133–135.

[6] Mayer 2012 (on Hor. *Carm.* 1.10.17).

[7] Expanding upon Ker 2015:115–116.

[8] E.g., Williams (forthcoming); Smith 2014, esp. 357–360; Setaioli 1997; Hoven 1971:109–126.

[9] E.g., Trinacty 2014, Littlewood 2004, Schiesaro 2003, Tarrant 1978a; cf. Ker 2015.

[10] E.g., Gloyn 2017, Wilson 2013, Wilcox 2006, Langlands 2004, Shelton 1995; cf. Ker 2009:87–112.

inventive deployment of the *animus* in multiple dramatic configurations across his oeuvre. My point is more limited: I focus upon Seneca's mention of *animae*, referring to the souls of the dead, in passages from two texts—the *Consolatio ad Marciam* and the *Troades*—as a further opportunity for seeing Seneca whole.

I. CREMUTIUS CONSOLES FROM ABOVE
(SENECA *AD MARCIAM* 26.2–7)

In his account of the *commune fatum* that he hopes may offer further comfort for Marcia, Cremutius details how Time (*vetustas*) will disrupt and break down the world's physical fabric as well as the "company" (*coetum*) of the human race (*Marc.* 26.6). "And when," he says, "the time has arrived when the world, preparing to renew itself, will extinguish itself (*se mundus renovaturus extinguat*), ... whatever light shines in ordered array will burn up in one fire as all matter goes up in flames" (26.6). And all *means* all:

> Nos quoque felices animae et aeterna sortitae, cum deo visum erit iterum ista moliri, labentibus cunctis et ipsae parva ruinae ingentis accessio in antiqua elementa vertemur.
>
> Seneca Marc. 26.7

> We too, happy souls and destined to endure, when the god decides to construct these things over again—ourselves also, a small participant in the massive ruin as everything collapses, will be turned into the ancient elements.

Seneca caps Cremutius's speech with a closing exclamation, evidently in his own voice: "Happy is your son, Marcia, who now knows these things!" (*felicem filium tuum, Marcia, qui ista iam novit!*, 26.7).

Cremutius's words are in some ways an expansion upon the standard consolatory argument that "everything is mortal" (cf. *Marc.* 11). But who are the *felices animae*? What exactly happens to the world, and to them?[11]

---

[11] In this context it is important to acknowledge a later variant in Seneca's letters: "It is contrary to belief that souls enclosed and embodied should be happier (*feliciores*) than

The Stoics regarded the soul as corporeal and so ultimately subject to destruction; the soul, Zeno said, "is consumed by much time, to the point of vanishing."[12] But Chrysippus argued that "the souls of the wise" persist until the conflagration, while Cleanthes had allowed this for all souls.[13] The conflagration itself, when "the whole world is dissolved into fire," is "destruction" only in the sense of "natural change."[14] The commanding faculty of god persists in bodily form as the fire itself; Seneca himself would famously invoke the image of "Jupiter," after the dissolution of the world, "given over to his thoughts."[15] The conflagration is not just an ending but also the beginning of a new cosmic cycle, identical to the previous one.[16] Fire "transforms all things into itself" (*in se cuncta convertat*), Seneca reports in *QNat.* 3.13.1, "and when the fire goes out nothing is left in the universe except moisture (*umorem*); and in this lies the hope of the world to come (*in hoc futuri mundi spem latere*)." In a summary by Diogenes Laertius, the moisture envelops the spermatic ordering principle that is divine *logos*, which begins working upon matter and then "creates first of all the four elements, fire, water, air, earth."[17]

Cremutius refers to the conflagration as the world's self-destruction to be followed by self-renewal (cf. *se mundus renovaturus extinguat, Marc.* 26.6), and he alludes to the role of divine reason in the rebuilding (cf. *cum deo visum erit iterum ista moliri,* 26.7)—where *iterum* (over again) suggests cosmic recurrence. The same thing is to happen to "us," *even* us, the happy souls, despite our being "destined to endure" (*aeterna sortitae*)—where *aeternus* could mean not "everlasting" but simply "long-lasting."[18]

---

souls free and given over to the universe" (*Ep.* 76.25; cited by *TLL* 6.1.443.40 [Ammann]). But the discussion there is entirely hypothetical, being preceded by the qualifier "*if* souls released from bodies do actually persist" (*si modo solutae corporibus animae manent*).

[12] *SVF* 1.146.

[13] *SVF* 1.522 = D.L. 7.157. Doxography reviewed in detail by Williams (forthcoming); Smith 2014:358–359.

[14] Long and Sedley (henceforth L&S) 46K. On Senecan conflagration, Gauly 2014:370–378.

[15] Sen. *Ep.* 9.16 = L&S 46O; cf. L&S 46H.

[16] L&S 46F, 46G.

[17] Diog. Laert. 7.135–136 = L&S 46B.

[18] Cf. *OLD* s.v. *aeternus* 4: "in a weaker sense"; see esp. Hoven 1971:45n5, 110.

Cremutius's final words, *in antiqua elementa vertemur* (we will be turned into the ancient elements), primarily describe the souls' dissolution but may also point ahead to the regeneration that begins with the four elements.[19] If so, *aeterna* may, after all, gesture toward persistence. Cremutius's *commune fatum* includes the comforting thought that everything will return.

Cremutius's *felices animae* are "a select group"[20] referred to by Seneca already when he reassured Marcia that Metilius "runs amid the happy souls" (*inter felices currit animas*, 25.1). They are neither the souls of *all* the dead nor the souls of *only* the wise but "that sacred company (*coetus sacer*), the Scipios and the Catos and—among those who look down upon life and are free thanks to death—your own parent, Marcia" (25.2). In the *Somnium*, a path to the heavens is earned by exercising "justice" and "dutifulness" toward one's "fatherland" (Cic. *Somn.* 16). We may also think of a Roman funeral procession—Cremutius tells Marcia he has been reunited with "his own ancestors" (*maiores ... suos*, *Marc.* 26.2)—or of exemplary heroes such as are presented on Roman monuments or in *Aeneid* 6. And these *animae* are something different than "the lesser substance of the soul"[21] that persists of the wise in Stoic eschatology: the conceit of prosopopoeia seen in both the *Somnium* and Cremutius's speech draws on the literary and mythical tradition of the spirits of the dead, or shades (*umbrae*), speaking from the underworld, as well as the orator's trick of bringing back a dead person to address the living.[22] Seneca also indicates that the members of the *coetus sacer* mostly died resolute deaths, whether by suicide (e.g., Cremutius) or at an enemy's hand (Cremutius's father, 26.2–3). Metilius himself was heroic only in civic life (cf. 23.3–24.2), but he died "most fortunately" (*felicissime*, 26.3), in a *mors opportuna* (20.4).

More needs asking about the souls' *felicitas*. First, what is the implication of the *makarismos* ("Happy the man who ...") uttered by Seneca in the exclamation following Cremutius's speech, *felicem filium tuum,*

---

[19] Cf. Gauly 2014:371n31; Hoven 1971:83–84n6. *Contra* Smith 2014:360: "Seneca's purgation is preparation for an extended afterlife and not for rebirth."

[20] Manning 1981:152.

[21] Euseb. *Praep. evang.* 15.20.6 = L&S 53W2.

[22] On the rhetorical technique, see Manning 1981:148.

Marcia, qui ista iam novit! (Happy is your son, Marcia, who now knows these things!) (26.7)? The double-*makarismos* at the end of Virgil's *Georgics* 2 celebrated knowledge of natural philosophy before going on to idealize knowledge of agriculture as an escape from urban strife (*G.* 2.475–540). The first *makarismos* especially, *felix qui potuit rerum cognoscere causas* (Happy [is] he who has been able to learn the causes of things, *G.* 2.490), does a lot of what we see in Seneca: we see the emphasis on knowledge, and Virgil says this knowledge will free a person from fear of "death that cannot be deflected" (*inexorabile fatum*) and "the clamor of a greedy underworld" (*strepitum ... Acherontis avari*, *G.* 2.491–492).[23] In Virgil, of course, the knowledge is possessed by the philosopher-poet during life, whereas Seneca's Metilius "now (*iam*) knows these things" after dying and being instructed by Cremutius on the workings of the universe. Closer parallels are available in *makarismoi* celebrating safe arrival in the underworld after a trouble-free life (e.g., Thgn. 1012–1013) and initiation into the Eleusinian mysteries (Hom. *Hymn Dem.* 480), and more broadly in the common Greek use of *makares* to refer to the "blessed" dead.[24] One further comparison can be made from Hesiod's *Works and Days*: "Blessed and fortunate he, who knowing all these things (τάδε πάντα / εἰδώς) does his work without blame by the immortals" (*Op.* 826–827), an instance relevant both for its use of the deictic τάδε and for its function in closing Hesiod's poem as a whole—a function likely operative in *Georgics* 2 and certainly in Seneca's consolation, where *felicem filium tuum ... !* is the final line.[25]

Felix has implications within the rhetorical economy of Seneca's consolation. The uses of *felix* clustering at the end of the consolation (*Marc.* 25.1; 26.2, 3, 6) are the culmination of his long-gestated attempt to reverse Marcia's perceptions—a classic Senecan exercise in redefining evaluative terms. Earlier in the consolation, he had referred to the imperial mother Octavia as feeling that Marcellus's death (23

---

[23] On the reference of *G.* 2.490, not limited to Lucretius, see Thomas 1988:253. Seneca may also echo *G.* 2.493 *qui novit* (*Marc.* 26.7 *qui iam novit*) and *G.* 2.498 *perituraque regna* (*Marc.* 26.6 *licet surrectura, licet ruitura regna prospicere*).

[24] LSJ s.v. μάκαρ III.

[25] In Hesiod, "these things" likely refers back to the last part of the poem concerning days and to knowledge about bird signs; see West 1978:364.

BCE) deprived her of "the happiness (*felicitas*) promised her" (2.5), but he had also touted the positive example of Cornelia, who despite the *death* of her sons, maintained: "I will never cease to call myself happy (*felicem*): I gave *birth* to the Gracchi (*quae Gracchos peperi*)" (16.3). Marcia is being asked to understand *felicitas* in yet more selfless terms. As Gunderson observes on the consolation's end, "The translation between worldly and sublime also entails a translation between the *felicitas* of female fertility and the more abstract 'happiness' of unified masculine presence."[26] Seneca pivots from a focus on the *felicitas* of the grieving parent (cf. 12.6, 14.3) to the *felicitas* of the deceased, a *felicitas* that does not require a long life but can be "ringfenced" by death (cf. 20.1: *felicitatem includit*; 20.5, 22.1). He ties *felicitas* to non-existence in general: "If the happiest thing of all is not to be born (*felicissimum est non nasci*), the next happiest, I think, is for us to live out a brief life and be swiftly restored to a state of wholeness (*cito in integrum restitui*)" (22.3)—an idea that builds upon the symmetry argument (i.e., that death returns us to our pre-birth state). This assertion is immediately followed by Seneca's account of Cremutius's suicide (22.4–8). Cremutius's own speech, however, goes far beyond the symmetry argument, correlating *felicitas* not with the tranquility of freedom from pain but with an afterlife in the *coetus sacer*.

Within a broader, intertextual economy, *felices animae* activates memories from Augustan poetry. In an *AJP* note entitled "A Prose Hexameter in Seneca? (*Consolatio ad Marciam* 26.7)," Francis Dunn analyses the beginning of Cremutius's final sentence as "a hexameter altered to end with a prose rhythm":[27]

$$- \quad \cup \cup \; - - - \cup \cup \; - \quad - \; - \; \cup \; - \; - -$$

nos quoque felices animae et aeterna sortitae.

Dunn is reluctant to compare this Senecan sequence directly to prose hexameters in Roman historiographers and instead draws attention to two Augustan poetic passages. He compares the words of the Sibyl in

---

[26] Gunderson 2015:80; for the full argument, see pp. 79–87.

[27] Dunn 1989:489. The scansion shown here is Dunn's. Although his overall point is well taken, *(-ae) et* would ordinarily scan short.

Aeneid 6, as she asks the dead heroes and benefactors who now inhabit the Elysian fields: "Tell, happy souls (*felices animae*), and you most excellent seer [Musaeus], what region, what place, holds Anchises? For his sake have we come ..." (*Aen.* 6.669–670).[28] Dunn's other comparison is from Ovid's *Metamorphoses* 15, where Pythagoras concludes to Numa: "We too, a part of the world (*nos quoque, pars mundi*)—since we are not bodies alone, but also airborne souls (*volucres animae*)—can pass into bestial abodes and be buried in the bodies of cattle" (*Met.* 15.456–458). Dunn makes a compelling case for the relevance of both texts: while the dead Anchises's lessons for Aeneas offer a parallel to Cremutius-Marcia that even alludes to the doctrine of conflagration (*Aen.* 6.745–747), in Ovid Dunn sees a close grammatical parallel where "the emphatic *nos quoque* introduces the personal testimony of the father who has joined the blessed (*felices animae*), and of the philosopher who has changed bodies (*volucres animae*)"—though Pythagoras's speech "lacks the emotional directness of the speeches by Anchises and Cremutius to their children."[29]

In the 30 years since Dunn's brief note, we have learned more about Senecan intertextuality. Richard Tarrant has attuned us to how Seneca engages with Augustan poetic texts, in his "Senecan Drama and its Antecedents" (1978) and in the commentaries on *Agamemnon* (1976) and *Thyestes* (1985) and the essay "Chaos in Ovid's *Metamorphoses* and its Neronian Influence" (2002).[30] By the time of "Seeing Seneca Whole?" (2006), Richard was able to summarize Seneca's practice as follows: "In the tragedies, Seneca's allusions to Augustan poetry are far from inert echoes; in many cases they constitute radical reinterpretations of the original. In the prose works, correspondingly strong readings of Virgil and Ovid often take the form of imposing a sense quite foreign to that of the original."[31] He also notes, strikingly, "the presence of explicit citation of Augustan poets in close proximity to

---

[28] On *Aen.* 6 ~ *Marc.* 26, see also Setaioli 1997:esp. 342–343; also Horsfall 2013:459, glossing *felices* with "blessed because free of the bonds of mortality and settled in Elysium."

[29] Dunn 1989:489–490.

[30] Tarrant 1978a; 1976a; 1985a; 2002c.

[31] Tarrant 2006b:2–3.

allusive reference to the same texts."[32] Such observations have been confirmed and extended in subsequent case studies too numerous to mention here.

Dunn's inquiry, too, can be extended. For example, let us consider the final words of Cremutius's speech: that after the conflagration "we will be turned into the ancient elements (*in antiqua elementa vertemur*)" (*Marc.* 27.7). The form of that phrase, as it happens, is closely paralleled in words uttered by Tellus in the Phaethon episode of *Metamorphoses* 2: "If the seas perish, and the lands, and the skies' kingdom, then we are mixed up into the ancient chaos (*in chaos antiquum confundimur*)" (*Met.* 2.298–299). While Seneca was to repurpose this Ovidian description, as Richard showed, to evoke moral (not just material) chaos in an ode in *Thyestes* (*Thy.* 828–835),[33] Cremutius directs it in an entirely different direction, pointing ultimately toward the renewal of the cosmos in which "we" will participate again. The echoes noted by Dunn also offer further specific associations for this renewal. Dunn's comparison with *Metamorphoses* 15 ushers in the transmigration of souls and unceasing metamorphosis, and the key terms of Cremutius's *in antiqua elementa vertemur* (*Marc.* 26.7) may evoke technical terms from Pythagoras's speech—that "our very own bodies are being changed (*vertuntur*) always, without rest, and what we were before or what we are now we will not be tomorrow" (*Met.* 15.214–216); that with regard to the four elements (*elementa*), "all things come about from them and fall back into them" (15.244–245) and out of them "the same order is re-woven" (*idem ... retexitur ordo*, 15.249).[34] In *Aeneid* 6, in turn, Anchises's account of the conflagration (*Aen.* 6.745–751) belongs to his response to Aeneas's question, "O father, should we think that some souls (*aliquas ... animas*), being elevated (*sublimis*), go from here toward the sky (*ad caelum hinc*), and again return to sluggish bodies (*iterumque ad tarda reverti corpora*)?" (6.719–720)—where "toward the sky" takes them to a life on earth. Anchises concludes by describing how "we few"—that is, some blameless souls—"occupy the happy [i.e., Elysian] fields" (*pauci laeta arva*

---

[32] Tarrant 2006b:3.

[33] Tarrant 2002c:356.

[34] Likely echoed in Sen. *QNat.* 3.30.7: after the flood, *antiquus ordo revocabitur.*

tenemus, 6.744) and in the statement that they are recalled to the river Lethe "so they will begin to be willing to be returned into bodies (*in corpora ... reverti*)" (6.749–751).[35] This line is immediately followed by the pageant of future Roman heroes up to the time of Augustus (6.756–892). For the reader of Seneca's consolation, the Virgilian intertext may serve not just as a model for the *coetus sacer* to which Cremutius belongs but as the most optimistic possible comparand for the future that will follow cyclically *after* the conflagration.[36]

One limitation of Dunn's comparisons, however, is made evident in the closing words of his note. For he adds, without explanation, that "this is a striking example of the elevated or 'sublime' style in Seneca."[37] Certainly, Seneca's incorporation of the poetic imagery, sounds, and cosmological content from his intertexts in *Aeneid* and *Metamorphoses* raises the register of Cremutius's peroration. But the sublime elevation of Cremutius and the other souls in the *coetus sacer*, evidently inspired by the *Somnium Scipionis*, does not find any satisfying comparands in either *Aeneid* 6 or *Metamorphoses* 15. For Cremutius's sublime soul *and* celestial viewpoint, a more specific poetic reference point is available in Ovid's *Fasti* 1.

II. PRIAM'S HAPPY AFTERLIFE BELOW
(SENECA *TROADES* 142–163)

Before we turn to Ovid's sublime, however, let us consider an under-worldly parallel for *felices animae* that arises later in Seneca's own writings, during the initial ode of the *Troades* (*Tro.* 67–163).[38] As the responsional lament of Hecuba and the Chorus over a fallen Troy seems

[35] *Reverti* echoes a term referring to souls' cyclic movement in Cic. *Somn.* 13, 29.

[36] Cf. Ker 2009:95 on how *Marc.* figures Marcia's grief therapy through the teleological plot of the *Aeneid*.

[37] Dunn 1989:491. He cites, e.g., Currie (1966:84), who sees *Marc.* 26 reflecting the critical discourse on the sublime.

[38] Similarity between the *Consolatio ad Marciam* and the *Troades*, as both presenting multiple perspectives on death, has been noted by Williams (forthcoming) and Smith (2014:359n56) but without specific focus on *felices animae*. For commentary on the ode, see esp. Keulen 2001:157–164; Boyle 1994:144–145, 150–152; Fantham 1982:220–231. Line numbers are inevitably imprecise, given debated line breaks; I follow Fitch 2002–2004.

ready to culminate in sorrow for Priam, they instead express envy for him (142–163). Such an emphasis is absent, as Fantham notes, in the *Trojan Women* and *Hecuba* of Euripides; rather, as we will see, it is found in Seneca's Augustan antecedents.

"My Priam's death," Hecuba instructs the Trojan women, "is not to be lamented" (142–144): "Say 'Happy Priam,' all of you!" (*"felix Priamus" dicite cunctae*, 145). Her husband's death is a liberation: "He marches, free, to the spirits below, and will never bear the Greek yoke upon his conquered neck" (146–147). She details the indignities, culminating in an imagined triumphal procession in Mycenae, that Priam has eluded by his death (148–155). Whereupon the Chorus not only complies with Hecuba's instructions but turns her *felix Priamus* into a triple-*makarismos* that also makes mention of the *animae* whom Priam will join in death:

> "Felix Priamus" dicimus omnes:
> secum excedens sua regna tulit.
> Nunc Elysii nemoris tutis
> errat in umbris, interque pias
> felix animas Hectora quaerit.
> Felix Priamus;
> felix quisquis bello moriens
> omnia secum consumpta tulit.
>
> Seneca *Tro.* 156–163

> "Happy Priam!" all of us say:
> passing away he took his own kingdom with him.
> Now he wanders
> among the safe shadows of the Elysian grove,
> and happy among the dutiful souls
> searches out Hector.
> Happy Priam:
> happy anyone who, dying in war,
> has taken with him everything used up.

This logic of *felix Priamus* involves several fuzzy but discernible and characteristically Senecan notions: that Priam somehow kept his

kingdom intact and took it with him when he died; that in the underworld, among *pias ... animas* (dutiful souls), he may be reunited with
Hector; and that his heroic death in war coincided with the end of
"everything" (*omnia*) and so he is not missing out on anything.[39]

When I say that this passage offers a parallel for the Cremutius
speech in the *Consolatio ad Marciam*, I have in mind not simply the use
of *felix* to refer to the dead, and as part of a *makarismos*, but also its use
in close conjunction with mention of *animas* (*Tro.* 159). Taken together,
these points of similarity provide for revealing comparisons with
Cremutius's consolatory speech directed at Marcia.

The strident assertion of Priam's happiness, in stark opposition
to Priam's well-established role as a case study of happy lives gone
bad (cf. Arist. *Eth. Nic.* 1100a) has seeds in Virgil (*Aen.* 3.321–323 *felix
... Priameia virgo*) and more specifically in Ovid's *Metamorphoses* 13.[40]
There, Hecuba, addressing the dead Polyxena, asks: "Who could have
thought Priam could be said [to be] happy after the destruction of
Troy (*quis posse putaret / felicem Priamum post diruta Pergama dici*)? He
is happy, by his death (*felix morte sua est*)! He does not see you, my
daughter, destroyed, and he has left his life and his kingdom equally"
(*Met.* 13.519–521). Seneca's Hecuba and Chorus conspicuously utter
the exact words that the Ovidian Hecuba portrays as improbable: *felix
Priamus*. The logic of the Senecan ode picks up on the idea that it is
precisely Priam's death that makes him happy, even if Ovid's Hecuba
sees Priam as having left behind (*reliquit*) his (ruined) kingdom,
whereas Seneca's Chorus sees him as having taken with him (*secum ...
tulit*) his (real) kingdom.[41]

Scholars have pointed to another poetic model—Horace—for the
notion that happy Priam is among *pias ... animas* in the safety of the
Elysian grove. Horace mentions *pias ... animas* in the final stanza of his
hymn to Hermes/Mercury, which describes the god's role as a psycho-
pomp in Elysium: "You restore devoted souls to the blessed seat (*tu pias*

---

[39] For the third idea, compare *Thy.* 882–883 *vitae est avidus quisquis non vult / mundo secum pereunte mori*, cited ad loc. by Boyle 1994:151; the topos of the satiated guest is suggested by Keulen 2001:164.

[40] Noted by Jakobi 1988:21–22 and taken up by Boyle 1994; Keulen 2001.

[41] For the latter idea, see perhaps *Thy.* 390 *hoc regnum sibi quisque dat.*

laetis animas reponis / sedibus) and you herd the insubstantial crowd with your golden staff, pleasing to the gods above and the ones below" (*Carm.* 1.10.17–18).[42] The comforting image of the Horatian ode, including the idea that Hermes "restores" (*reponis*)[43] pious souls to their origin, helps Seneca to depict the blessed life that Priam is now enjoying. Scholars do not appear to have noted that the immediately preceding stanza in Horace's ode has described Hermes in another of his roles, not in the underworld (the topic of the final stanza) but during the Trojan War: "But even wealthy Priam leaving Troy (*Ilio dives Priamus relicto*) with you as guide (*duce te*) eluded ... the camp hostile to Troy" (*Carm.* 1.10.13–16). At Zeus's request, Hermes had helped Priam to arrive safely at the tent of Achilles without being noticed by the other Greeks and to retrieve the body of Hector (Hom. *Il.* 24.334–467). So the Senecan ode contaminates the two Horatian stanzas in a way that enhances the Chorus's consolation, as they apply the familiar image of Priam conducted safely through the camp by Hermes (a quasi-katabatic episode already in Homer) to the image of Priam in the underworld. When the Senecan Chorus describes how Priam in the underworld "searches out Hector" (*Hectora quaerit, Tro.* 160), we already have a mental image for Priam searching: his search for Hector's body outside the walls of Troy. Now he searches in a happier location.

Let us take stock of *felix Priamus* in the *Troades* and *felices animae* in Cremutius's speech. In both cases the reader or audience observes a woman (Marcia, Hecuba) grieving for a deceased family member (Metilius, Priam) and being reassured by a consolatory voice (Seneca/Cremutius, Hecuba/Chorus) with the thought that the deceased is *felix* in an afterlife among other happy *animae*, where he will in fact live a better life than the one here. In both cases the consoler seamlessly appropriates the language of two or more Augustan poetic models that

[42] The intertext is noted by Keulen 2001:163 and Jakobi 1988:22–23 but only with attention to the final stanza. Note that the Horatian text may help us in assessing (if not reconciling) the manuscript discrepancy *tutus* (A) vs. *tutis* (ε) at *Tro.* 158, where *tutis ... umbris* would exactly match Horace's *laetis ... sedibus*.

[43] Mayer (2012:116) follows Rudd in understanding *reponis* in an intensive sense ("duly installs"), but the idea of repetition/restoration is at least latent (Shorey and Laing 1919:176).

have their own optimistic viewpoints on death and the hereafter. Here we have several opportunities to "see Seneca whole." First, the fact that in Cremutius's speech we see allusion, rather than explicit citation, requires us to recognize that allusion is not at all exclusive to the tragedies but may permeate the prose works far more than has been realized even yet. Second, to say "It's the *animae*, stupid" is to note that both passages articulate a positive view of the afterlife drawing upon broadly the same mythic/cultural repertoire of people living on somewhere after death. Third, these scenarios both belong under larger umbrella categories of all Seneca's writings, such as the consolatory mode and "Come, Sweet Death."[44]

The two passages also emblematize broad differences between Seneca's philosophical prose and tragic poetry. For Hecuba and the Trojan women, the image of *animae* enjoying an afterlife is situated in the underworld, the conventional locus of the dead in mythic poetry. In the *Consolatio ad Marciam*, the underworld is no longer available as a haven since just a few chapters prior Seneca has deflated as "fiction" (*fabulas*) the very idea of the underworld (*Marc.* 19.4–5). When he presents Marcia with the most optimistic possibility of an afterlife and the image of her father's soul, the scene is not infernal but supernal. These infernal and supernal orientations are reflective of the two women's literary scenarios. Hecuba, on the one hand, is consoled by the idea of Priam happy in the underworld, but that particular conception of death has pernicious consequences in the play, which Hecuba herself lives on to witness, intensifying her grief still further.[45] Marcia, on the other hand, is offered a solace that may be exaggerated but is not ultimately contradicted in Seneca's philosophy; at worst, it must sit alongside agnostic eschatologies—as in Seneca's "Socratic alternative" that death is "either an end or a transition" (*aut finis aut transitus, Ep.* 65.24).[46] The image brought before Marcia is also in keeping with Seneca's recurring rhetoricized perspective, the "view from above,"

---

[44] Tarrant 2006b:16–17.

[45] These conflicting views of death in *Tro.* are set out by Williams (forthcoming); also Trinacty 2014:151–154; Stroh 2014.

[46] On the "Socratic alternative," see Smith 2014:360.

often associated with a sublime aesthetic.[47] Seneca, then, can be seen whole, but he is at the same time a "man of many genres":[48] he nimbly moves back and forth between tragic delusion and philosophical solace, showing what is similar about them—indeed how close they can come to resembling one another—but at the same time mapping each of them onto two broadly contrasting spheres of reference, the supernal and the infernal.

III. FROM ASTRONOMY TO ESCHATOLOGY (OVID *FASTI* 1.295–310)

For projecting the afterlife of Cremutius and other souls, Seneca found inspiration in another poetic locus distant from the Virgilian under-world. This is the sequence in Ovid's *Fasti* 1 that scholars have dubbed the "second proem" or "eulogy to astronomers" (*Fast.* 1.295–310), in which Ovid elaborates on the secondary topic of his poem—not the "times arranged through the Roman calendar together with their origins" of the first line, but the "constellations sinking below the earth and rising" (*lapsaque sub terras ortaque signa*) of the second line (*Fast.* 1.1–2).[49] Seneca did not need to populate Ovid's locus with *felices animae*. They are already there, in the eulogy's opening couplets:[50]

> Quid vetat et stellas, ut quaeque oriturque caditque,
>   dicere? Promissi pars sit et ista mei.
> Felices animae, quibus haec cognoscere primis

---

[47] See esp. Williams 2012:223. On Seneca and the sublime, see also Mazzoli 2016:15–25; Gunderson 2015, esp. 85–87 on *Marc.* On the sublime in general, Porter 2016 (with pp. 53–54 on a Senecan example).

[48] Ker 2006.

[49] Commentary in Green 2004:135–148; on the relevance of *Fast.* 1.2, see Ham 2013:245–246.

[50] See Ham 2013:236–251, esp. 248n607. I first learned of Ovid's mention of *felices animae* from Charles Ham in the spring of 2013, as he was completing his doctoral disser-tation on Empedocles and Ovidian elegiac poetry (Ham 2013). I am profoundly grateful to Charles for his sharing of citations and insights. As Irene Peirano Garrison points out to me, Horsfall's note on Verg. *Aen.* 6.669 (2013:459) refers to Ammann's *TLL* entry on *felix* (6.1.443.37–41), which already cites in support of the Virgil passage the following loci: Ov. *Fast.* 1.297; Sen. *Marc.* 25.1, 6.26; Sen. *Ep.* 76.25.

inque domos superas scandere cura fuit!

Ovid, *Fast.* 1.295–298

What forbids me also to tell of the constellations, as each rises
and sets? Let that also be part of my promise.
Happy souls, who took pains to be the first to learn these things
and to climb to the homes above!

If Seneca's consolation alludes to this passage, as I will argue, it is
important first to recognize a great difference. For while Seneca has
Cremutius apply *felices animae* directly to the disembodied souls of the
dead in a celestial afterlife, Ovid uses the same phrase to refer synec-
dochally to the astronomers who first discovered the risings and
settings of the constellations and whose scaling of the sky is simply a
metaphor for their intellectual feat. There has been extensive debate
about the identity of the *felices animae* to whom Ovid refers—"writers of
astronomical poetry," "astrologers," etc.[51]—and equally concerning how
the eulogy relates to Ovid's calendrical poem as a whole.[52] Regardless
of how these questions are answered, Seneca makes a significant adaptation. Ovid's metaphor referring to an epistemological feat is made
literal by Seneca, since he uses it to visualize the eschatological sublimation of the disembodied soul.

Seneca adapts much more than the one phrase, however: he draws
upon Ovid's entire eulogy, including its sublime aesthetics and its
sense of wonder, to enhance his portrait of the celestial *coetus sacer* to
which Cremutius and Metilius now belong. Most obviously, he retains
the *makarismos* formula which Ovid uses to justify the "happy" epithet,
felices animae, quibus haec cognoscere primis ... cura fuit (*Fast.* 1.297–298),
though it is the voice of Seneca himself that caps Cremutius's speech
with the exclamation, *felicem filium tuum, Marcia, qui ista iam novit!* (*Marc.*
26.7). Seneca's text thus retains the emphasis on an epistemological
gain even as he repurposes Ovid's language to describe eschatology.
Seneca's posthumous souls do not simply ascend and survive: in the

---

[51] Green 2004:135–136.
[52] Quotations from Green 2004:135–137. On these questions, see esp. Newlands
1995:32–43; Barchiesi 1997:178–180; Gee 2000:47–65; Herbert-Brown 2002:101–128.

process they gain philosophical knowledge about the nature of the world, not unlike Ovid's astronomers.

One of the more provocative features of Ovid's eulogy is that in the course of celebrating the astronomers, it verges on criticizing the human social sphere they have transcended—a touchy subject for an Augustan poet. Relatively uncontroversial is that they have left behind human weaknesses, pleasures, and enticements (*Fast.* 1.299–301, 303–304). Provocatively, however, their minds also went unbroken by "the duties of the forum or the work of soldiering" (*officiumque fori militiaeve labor*, 1.302). If Germanicus is a likely referent in Ovid's eulogy, then however much the *recusatio* may serve to characterize laudable values (intellectual focus, godlike accomplishments, and moral restraint), an abandonment of public life would be scandalous. It is no exaggeration to say, with Barchiesi, that "momentarily at least, Germanicus is forced to divide himself into two."[53] Seneca, however, is able to reuse several of the same terms in his consolatory portrait of Metilius without the same risk, since Metilius is split only between service *in life* and philosophy *after death*. Cremutius, whose transcendence of history is licensed by death, can scorn both the *arma* and the *forum* that he and Metilius have left behind them (*Marc.* 26.4).

Even before Cremutius's speech, in fact, Ovid's characterization of the astronomers as *felices animae* who have "raised their heads high above human weaknesses just as much as above human locations" (*pariter vitiisque locisque altius humanis exseruisse caput*, *Fast.* 1.299–300) and whose "sublime minds" (*sublimia pectora*) are "unbroken" (*non ... fregit*) by sex or wine (1.301), is reshaped by Seneca to characterize Metilius's eschatological condition:

> [Metilius] has fled intact (*integer*) and leaving behind no part of himself on earth (*nihilque in terris relinquens*); he has departed entirely (*totus*). And after lingering for a short while above us, while he was being purified and was shaking off the impurities that clung to him and all the stagnation of mortal life (*inhaerentia vitia situmque omnem*

---

[53] Barchiesi 1997:178.

mortalis aevi), he was then elevated to great heights (*ad excelsa sublatus*) and he runs among the happy souls (*inter felices currit animas*).

Seneca *Marc.* 25.1

This description, preceding Cremutius's speech, appears to be the first moment in the consolation at which Seneca alludes to Ovid's passage, and the resemblances are hard to miss, right down to the syllepsis *vitiis locisque* (Ovid) ~ *vitia situmque* (Seneca)—though Seneca's shift from the neutral term *locus* to the pejorative *situs* is characteristic of his moralizing turn.

One other major feature of Ovid's eulogy is redeployed by Seneca. After describing the astronomers' accomplishment ("They brought distant stars before the eyes of the mind and subjected to their intellect the upper sky") and preferring it over gigantomachic mountain-stacking ("*This* is the way to reach the heavens," *Fast.* 1.305–308), Ovid concludes by vowing to follow in their path:

Nos quoque sub ducibus caelum metabimur illis,
  ponemusque suos ad vaga signa dies.

Ovid *Fast.* 1.309–310

We too, under these tutors, will measure out the heavens
  and will give for the wandering signs their own days.

The line-initial phrase *nos quoque*, coming just a few lines after Ovid's *felices animae*, would seem to be the inspiration for the hexametric utterance that Seneca puts in Cremutius's mouth as he finishes consoling his daughter: *nos quoque felices animae* ... ("We too, happy souls," *Marc.* 26.7). Yet the resemblance is more one of form and sound than of substance. Ovid uses *nos quoque* here (*Fast.* 1.309) to link himself to the astronomers, while for Cremutius *nos* already refers to the group of *felices animae* to which he himself belongs, and his *quoque* links these souls to the rest of the physical world, emphasizing that *even we*, given the soul's corporeality, will be subject to the conflagration and renewal: "We too (*nos quoque*), happy souls and destined to endure, when the god decides to construct these things over again—ourselves also (*et ipsae*), a small participant in the massive ruin (*parva ruinae ingentis accessio*) as everything collapses, will be turned into the ancient elements" (*Marc.* 26.7). As it happens, *nos quoque* is a fairly common line-initial phrase in Ovid (25 times, cf. once in Virgil), and we might choose to understand it as a convenient marker and building block for the poetical language Seneca places in Cremutius's mouth. But a second look at the *Metamorphoses* 15 passage noted by Dunn offers a more substantial parallel: Pythagoras uses *nos quoque* to emphasize that "we too," that is human beings, are *pars mundi* (a part of the world) and *volucres animae* (airborne souls) and therefore can inhabit animals—a strong reason to avoid the killing and eating of animal flesh (*Met.* 15.453–478). The emphasis on human beings as *pars mundi* offers a close parallel for Cremutius's point, enhancing the connections to Pythagoras's speech.

Seneca's engagement with two Ovidian texts along with *Aeneid* 6 and the *Somnium Scipionis* should come as no surprise. More surprising, however, and certainly more interesting is Seneca's engagement with these two *specific* passages in Ovid: the eulogy to the astronomers (*Fast.* 1.295–310) and the speech of Pythagoras (*Met.* 15.75–78). At least one Ovidian scholar has noted the similar profile of these two passages: each is "at odds with" the rest of the content of the poem it bookends.[54] This factor surely attests to Seneca's sophisticated reading of Ovid's oeuvre.[55] Yet perhaps the greatest surprise is that Seneca should be found alluding to the *Fasti* at all. For in works on the tragedies, such as Jakobi's *Der Einfluss Ovids auf den Tragiker Seneca* (1988), there is scant reference to the poem; as for the prose, Mazzoli argues, in *Seneca e la poesia*, that "Ovid is for Seneca almost exclusively the poet of the *Metamorphoses*"[56] and even the rare traces of other Ovidian works traced by Mazzoli do not involve the *Fasti*.[57] Now that we have noted such a clear instance of Seneca engaging with the *Fasti*, it is plausible that further significant intertexts will be discovered. For now, however, let us recognize how Cremutius's speech, which has often been singled out

---

[54] Green 2004:136–137; Newlands 1995:33.
[55] A significant theme of Hinds 2011.
[56] Mazzoli 1970:239–240.
[57] Mazzoli 1970:238–247; quotation from 239.

as distinctive among all Seneca's writings for its detailed and positive vision of the afterlife, is distinctive also in that Seneca elaborates that vision by engaging with the sublime aesthetics of the *Fasti*'s programmatic eulogy.

IV. CONCLUSION

There is more to learn, surely, about the role of *Fasti* as a model for the *Consolatio ad Marciam*—works of almost the same era. I will conclude, however, by observing how Ovid's eulogy and Cremutius's speech together throw light on a much-discussed passage from late in Seneca's career, in the *Epistulae Morales* 21[58]—where Seneca also takes the ideas in a new direction. Seneca promises that if Lucilius persists in his Stoic studies, he will make him famous just as Cicero made Atticus famous, Epicurus gave fame to Idomeneus, and Virgil immortalized Nisus and Euryalus (*Ep.* 21.4–5). The alternative is to be forgotten:

> Profunda super nos altitudo temporis veniet, pauca ingenia caput exerent et in idem quandoque silentium abitura oblivioni resistent ac se diu vindicabunt.
>
> Seneca *Ep.* 21.5

> A profound depth of time will come over us. Only a few intellects will raise their head and—despite being destined to fade away into the same silence—will resist oblivion and for a long time will stake their claim.

Seneca's imagery is more suggestive of a flood than of sublimation or conflagration, but his portrayal of literary immortality shares several key features with Cremutius's speech and also with Ovid's eulogy. The "profound depth of time" is much like the *vetustas* mentioned by Cremutius, and it will ultimately overwhelm us and silence us *all*, much as Cremutius had indicated with "we too …, a small participant in the massive ruin" (*Marc.* 26.6–7). The gesture of self-preservation in which

---

[58] Expanding here on Ker 2015:119. Echoes of Ovid's phrasing at *Fast.* 1.300 in imperial literature, including Sen. *Ep.* 21.5, are briefly noted by Green (2004:138–139).

"only a few intellects" (*pauca ingenia*) will "raise their head" (*caput exerent, Ep.* 21.5) specifically recalls Ovid's eulogy with its reference to the astronomers who "raised their heads (*exseruisse caput*) high above ... human locations" and who "subjected to their intellect (*ingenio*) the upper sky" (*Fast.* 1.299–300, 306).[59]

Once again, then, Seneca repurposes Ovid's metaphorical, epistemological elevation to refer to an eschatological reality, but he also explicitly elaborates the *authorial* aspirations that were already present in Ovid's eulogy. The few *ingenia* that will survive are not simply intellects but authors who will live on, Seneca predicts, through their popularity with readers "in posterity" (*apud posteros, Ep.* 21.5). Where Ovid had used *felices animae* to celebrate the accomplishments of astronomer-poets without any explicit reference to their literary immortality, Seneca develops the image of an authorial afterlife by enlisting himself (in his own *nos quoque* moment) among the exclusive group of *pauca ingenia* whose afterlife in readership—albeit ultimately time-limited (since they will persist "for a long time" [*diu*], not always)—is bolstered by the best eschatology that Stoicism can provide.

UNIVERSITY OF PENNSYLVANIA

WORKS CITED

Abel, K. 1964. "Poseidonios und Senecas Trostschrift an Marcia (*dial.* 6, 24, 5 ff.)." *Rheinisches Museum für Philolgie* 107:221–260.

Armisen-Marchetti, M. 2007. "Echos du Songe de Scipion chez Sénèque." In *Munus quaesitum meritis: Homenaje a Carmen Codoñer*, ed. Gregorio Hinojo Andrés and José Carlos Fernández Corte, 71–79. Salamanca.

Barchiesi, A. 1997. *The Poet and the Prince: Ovid and Augustan Discourse.* Berkeley, CA.

Boyle, A. 1994. *Seneca's Troades.* Leeds.

---

[59] For *ingenio* at *Fast.* 1.306 plausibly meaning "poetic genius" rather than just "intellect," see Green 2004:142. For discussion of Sen. *Ep.* 21, I thank audiences at Wake Forest University, Oberlin College, and Indiana University.

Currie, H. M. 1966. "The Younger Seneca's Style: Some Observations." *Bulletin of the Institute of Classical Studies* 13:76–87.

Damschen, G., and A. Heil, eds. 2014. *Brill's Companion to Seneca, Philosopher and Dramatist*. Leiden.

Dunn, F. 1989. "A Prose Hexameter in Seneca? (*Consolatio ad Marciam* 26.7)." *AJP* 110:488–491.

Fantham, E. 1982. *Seneca's Troades*. Princeton.

Favez, C. 1928. *L. Annaei Senecae Dialogorum liber VI, Ad Marciam de consolatione*. Paris.

Fitch, J. G. 2002–2004. *Seneca. Tragedies*. 2 vols. Cambridge, MA.

Gauly, B. 2014. "Physics II: Cosmology and Natural Philosophy." In Damschen and Heil 2014, 363–378.

Gee, E. 2000. *Ovid, Aratus, and Augustus: Astronomy in Ovid's Fasti*. Cambridge.

Gloyn, L. 2017. *The Ethics of the Family in Seneca*. Cambridge.

Green, S. 2004. *Ovid. Fasti 1: A Commentary*. Leiden.

Gunderson, E. 2015. *The Sublime Seneca: Ethics, Literature, Metaphysics*. Cambridge.

Ham, C. 2013. *Empedoclean Elegy: Love, Strife, and the Four Elements in Ovid's Amores, Ars Amatoria and Fasti*. PhD diss., University of Pennsylvania.

Herbert-Brown, G. 2002. "Ovid and the Stellar Calendar." In *Ovid's Fasti: Historical Readings at its Bimillenium*, ed. G. Herbert-Brown, 101–128. Oxford.

Hinds, S. 2011. "Seneca's Ovidian Loci." *Studi italiani di filologia classica* 9:5–63.

Horsfall, N. 2013. *Virgil. Aeneid 6: A Commentary*. Vol. 2. Berlin.

Hoven, R. 1971. *Stoïcisme et stoïciens face au problème de l'au-delà*. Paris.

Jakobi, R. 1988. *Der Einfluss Ovids auf den Tragiker Seneca*. Berlin.

Ker, J. 2006. "Seneca, Man of Many Genres." In Volk and Williams 2006, 19–42.

------. 2009. *The Deaths of Seneca*. Oxford.

———. 2015. "Seneca and Augustan Culture." In *The Cambridge Companion to Seneca*, ed. S. Bartsch and A. Schiesaro, 109–121. Cambridge.

Keulen, A. J. 2001. *L. Annaeus Seneca. Troades: Introduction, Text, and Commentary*. Mnemosyne Supplement 212. Leiden.

Langlands, R. 2004. "A Woman's Influence on a Roman Text: Marcia and Seneca." In *Women's Influence on Classical Civilization*, ed. F. McHardy and E. Marshall, 115–126. New York.

Littlewood, C. 2004. *Self-Representation and Illusion in Senecan Tragedy*. Oxford.

Long, A. A., and D. N. Sedley. 1987. *The Hellenistic Philosophers*. 2 vols. Cambridge.

Manning, C. 1981. *On Seneca's Ad Marciam*. Mnemosyne Supplement 69. Leiden.

Mayer, R. 2012. *Horace. Odes Book 1*. Cambridge.

Mazzoli, G. 1970. *Seneca e la poesia*. Milan.

———. 2016. *Il chaos et le sue architetture: Trenta studi su Seneca tragico*. Palermo.

Newlands, C. 1995. *Playing with Time: Ovid and the Fasti*. Ithaca, NY.

Porter, J. I. 2016. *The Sublime in Antiquity*. Cambridge.

Sauer, J. 2014. "*Consolatio ad Marciam*." In Damschen and Heil 2014, 135–140.

Schiesaro, A. 2003. *The Passions in Play: Thyestes and the Dynamics of Senecan Drama*. Cambridge.

Setaioli, A. 1997. "Seneca e l'oltretomba." *Paideia* 52:321–367.

Shelton, J. 1995. "Persuasion and Paradigm in Seneca's *Consolatio ad Marciam* 1–6." *Classica et Mediaevalia* 46:157–188.

Shorey, P., and G. J. Laing. 1919. *Horace. Odes and Epodes*. Chicago.

Smith, S. 2014. "Physics I: Body and Soul." In Damschen Heil, 343–362.

Stroh, W. 2014. "Troas." In Damschen and Heil, 435–447.

Tarrant, R. J. 1976a. *Seneca. Agamemnon*. Edited with a commentary. Cambridge Classical Texts and Commentaries 18. Cambridge.

———. 1978a. "Senecan Drama and its Antecedents." *HSCP* 82:213–263.

———. 1985a. *Seneca's Thyestes*. Edited with introduction and commentary. American Philological Association Textbook Series 11. Atlanta, GA.

———. 2002c. "Chaos in Ovid's *Metamorphoses* and its Neronian Influence." *Arethusa* 35:349–360.

———. 2006b. "Seeing Seneca Whole?" In *Seeing Seneca Whole: Perspectives on Philosophy, Poetry, and Politics*, ed. Katharina Volk and Gareth D. Williams, 1–17. Leiden.

Thomas, R. F. 1988. *Virgil. Georgics I-II*. Cambridge.

Trinacty, C. 2014. *Senecan Tragedy and the Reception of Augustan Poetry*. Oxford.

Volk, K., and G. D. Williams, eds. 2006. *Seeing Seneca Whole: Perspectives on Philosophy, Poetry, and Politics*. Leiden.

West, M. L. 1978. *Hesiod: Works and Days*. Oxford.

Wilcox, A. 2006. "Exemplary Grief: Gender and Virtue in Seneca's Consolations to Women." *Helios* 33:73–100.

Williams, G. D. Forthcoming. "Eschatology in Seneca: The Senses of an Ending." In *Eschatology in Antiquity*, ed. H. Van Noorden, H. Marlow, and K. Pullman. London.

———. 2012. *The Cosmic Viewpoint: A Study of Seneca's Natural Questions*. Oxford.

Wilson, M. 2013. "Seneca the Consoler? A New Reading of his Consolatory Writings." In *Greek and Roman Consolations: Eight Studies of a Tradition and its Afterlife*, ed. H. Baltussen, 93–122. Swansea.

MARTIAL'S RETIREMENT AND OTHER EPICUREAN POSTURES IN BOOK 10

Alison Keith

I. *PROLEGOMENA*

Martial's tenth book of *Epigrams* is prefaced by a poem explaining the collection as a second edition, containing a few previously published epigrams newly "polished with a recent file" (*nota leges quaedam sed lima rasa recenti*, 10.2.3), but a greater number still of entirely fresh poems (*pars noua maior erit*, 10.2.4).[1] In his description of the original collection as "too hurried earlier," the poet implicitly justifies the reissued volume as a work of greater literary care (10.2.1–2): *festinata prius, decimi mihi cura libelli / elapsum manibus nunc reuocauit opus* (too hurried earlier, the care of my tenth little book has now recalled a work that slipped from my hands). Martial here draws on the familiar lexicon of Latin Callimacheanism (*cura libelli, opus, lima rasa*) to present his revised tenth collection as a work of literary craftsmanship in the tradition of Catullus (e.g., *libellus, c.* 1.1), Horace (e.g., *limae labor, Ars P.* 291), and Ovid (e.g., *opus, Am.* 1.1.14, 24).[2] The irony with which

---

I offer this paper to Richard Tarrant on the occasion of his retirement in gratitude for his wide-ranging learning in both Latin literature and Epicurean philosophy. Our conversations about the impact of the latter on the former have meant more to me than he perhaps realizes.

[1] I cite Martial's *Epigrams* from the OCT edition of Lindsay 1929; translations follow or adapt Shackleton Bailey 1993.

[2] Martial frequently cites Catullus as his model in the genre of epigram: 1. *Epist.*, 7, 61, 109; 2.71; 4.41; 5.5; 6.34; 7.14, 99; 8.73; 10.78, 103; 11.6; 12.44, 59. On the relationship between Martial and Catullus, see Barwick 1958; Ferguson 1963; Offermann 1980; Swann 1994, and 1998; Grewing 1998; Roman 2001; Fedeli 2004; Fitzgerald 2007:18–19, 78–79, 167–186. Although Martial cites Horace much less frequently by name (1.107, 8.18, 12.3), his debt to Horatian satire also has long been recognized: see Mendell 1922; Szelest 1963;

Martial customarily deploys the vocabulary of Callimachean aesthetics may be thought to be (at least momentarily) in abeyance in a work that advertises itself as the product of revision.[3]

The literary plot thickens in the following epigram, which disavows the work of "a certain anonymous poet" (*poeta quidam clancularius*, 10.3.5) who "spreads" (*spargit*, 10.3.5) "buffoons' quips, vulgar ill-will, and the foul abuse of a mountebank's tongue" (*uernaculorum dicta, sordidum dentem, / et foeda linguae probra circulatricis*, 10.3.1–2), and palms them off as the work of our epigrammatist (*et uolt uideri nostra*, 10.3.6). In introducing his revised collection in 10.2, Martial denies that "thefts harm his books" (10.2.11), but elsewhere he complains about the theft of his works and, conversely, the circulation of epigrams falsely imputed to him, with the concomitant threat to his reputation.[4] In the fifth epigram in the opening series, Martial curses "whoever he is" (*quisquis*, 10.5.1) who "has attacked his betters in impious verse" (*quos colere debet laesit impio uersu*, 10.5.2) and thereby traduced our famous epigrammatist, "known the whole world over" (*toto notus in orbe*, 1.1.2).[5] Taken in sequence, the opening series constructs a literary argument that repudiates invective as an appropriate subject for Martial's verses and announces an innovative program of poetic revision.[6]

Yet, a political motive for the reissue in 98 CE, under Trajan, of a collection originally put into circulation in 95 CE, under Domitian, is not far to seek.[7] For the last Flavian emperor was assassinated by his guard in a palace coup in September 96 CE, and the Senate elevated

---

Merli 2006; Pentzer 2019. Martial names Ovid in 1.61, 3.38, 5.10, 12.44, 14.192; on Martial's debt to Ovid, see Szelest 1999; Williams 2002; Fitzgerald 2007:186–190; Hinds 2007.

[3] Roman 2001; Rimell 2008:230, Index of subjects s.v. "Callimachean aesthetics." On Book 10, see Spisak 2002; Merli 2006; Rimell 2008:65–82.

[4] On plagiarism, see 1.29, 38, 52–53, 63, 66 and 72, with Rimell 2008:40–50; 2.20, with Williams 2004:91–93, ad loc.; cf. 7.77; 10.100, 102; 11.94; 12.63.

[5] On Martial's fame as an epigrammatist, see Citroni 1975 (on *Epigram* 1.1); and the essays collected in Grewing 1998.

[6] Spisak notes the literary program enunciated in the opening epigrams of the tenth book, though not the Callimachean posture (2002:132). On the thematic coherence of *Epigrams* 10, see also Sullivan 1991:44–52; Fearnley 2003. On Martial's literary self-consciousness, see Hinds 2007; Neger 2012.

[7] On the politics of Martial's tenth book, see Fearnley 2003.

one of their number, Nerva, to the imperial purple. The following year, under increasing pressure from the military, the new emperor adopted the Spanish general Trajan, and he in turn succeeded to power on the death of his "father" in January 98 CE. Martial hints at the recent regime change at the end of the second epigram, where a personified Rome reflects on the immortality of her poet's epigrams, by contrast with the monuments of statesmen:

> marmora Messallae findit caprificus et audax
>   dimidios Crispi mulio ridet equos:
> at chartis nec furta nocent et saecula prosunt,
>   solaque non norunt haec monumenta mori.

Mart. *Epigr.* 10.2.9–12

The fig tree splits Messalla's marble tombstone and the bold muleteer laughs at Crispus' halved horses: but thefts don't harm your pages and the centuries do them good. These are the only memorials that cannot die.

It is tempting to connect Martial's reflection on the destruction of partisan memorials over the passage of time not only to the important literary model of Horace's famous *envoi* to his three-book collection of *Odes* (3.30), but also to the contemporary political erasure of Domitian's name from his monuments as a result of the senatorial vote of *damnatio memoriae*.[8]

Martial broaches the subject of regime change directly in 10.6, where the introduction of the new prince to his imperial capital and to Martial's *Epigrams* is handled with unusual circumspection. Trajan, expected back in Rome from warfare on the Rhine, goes unnamed as Martial evokes the pageantry of the emperor's anticipated triumph in an epigram congratulating the senators selected to participate in an embassy to the new prince. The next poem offers a more effusive statement of imperial panegyric:

> Nympharum pater amniumque, Rhene,
>   quicumque Odrysias bibunt pruinas,

---

8   Rimell 2008:66.

sic semper liquidis fruaris undis
nec te barbara contumeliosi
calcatum rota conterat bubulci;   5
sic et cornibus aureis receptis
et Romanus eas utraque ripa:
Traianum populis suis et urbi,
Thybris te dominus rogat, remittas.

Mart. *Epigr.* 10.7

Rhine, father of nymphs and streams, and whoever drinks
Odrysian frosts, so may you ever enjoy flowing waves and
may the barbarian wheel of an abusive cattle-driver not
trample and destroy you; so may you go, with your golden
horns restored, Roman on either bank; and may you send
back Trajan to his peoples and the city—Tiber, your master,
asks you.

Invoking the river Rhine in the highest register of hymnic style,
Martial invites the conquered German watercourse to acknowledge the
Roman Tiber's dominion by returning Trajan to the imperial capital.
The *du-Stil* in which Martial hymns the Rhine is a carefully calibrated
displacement of the emperor-panegyric for which his epigrams to the
assassinated Domitian were known.[9]

Only much later in the book does Martial explicitly confront regime
change in his panegyric program, with the disavowal of flattery in his
verse:

Frustra, Blanditiae, uenitis ad me
adtritis miserabiles labellis:
dicturus dominum deumque non sum.
iam non est locus hac in urbe uobis;
ad Parthos procul ite pilleatos   5
et turpes humilesque supplicesque

---

[9] Coleman (1990[2000]:39) notes that "the atmosphere of sycophantic adulation
of the emperor is, if anything, intensified" under Trajan. On panegyric in Martial's
epigrams, see Lorenz 2002; Watson and Watson 2015:32–36.

pictorum sola basiate regum.
Non est hic dominus sed imperator,
sed iustissimus omnium senator,
per quem de Stygia domo reducta est   10
siccis rustica Veritas capillis.
Hoc sub principe, si sapis, caueto
uerbis, Roma prioribus loquaris.

Mart. Epigr. 10.72

In vain, Flatteries, do you come to me with complaints on
your shameless lips: I'm not going to celebrate the "Lord
and God." There's no place in this city for you; be off to the
turbaned Parthians, you base and abject suppliants, and
kiss the soles of painted kings. There is no "Lord" here, but
a general and the most just senator of all, through whom
rustic Truth, with her unpomaded locks, has been brought
back from the house of Styx. Under this prince, Rome, if
you're smart, beware of speaking in the language of earlier
days.

Domitian, the "Lord and God" of the earlier books of epigrams,[10] here
unnamed, has been condemned to *damnatio memoriae*, well and truly
displaced by the military commander-in-chief Trajan, whose respect
for the traditional Roman constitution Martial implies in the compli-
mentary turn of phrase, *iustissimus omnium senator* (9). Where Domitian
had styled himself *dominus et deus*, a title whose use Martial now
disavows as flattery, Trajan is a traditional Roman general and senator
(8–9), far removed from the hereditary monarchs of the autocratic
oriental east in Parthia (5–7).

Epigram 10.72 retrospectively lays bare the indirection with which
Martial approaches the political uncertainty of a period of regime
change at the outset of his reissued tenth book. The opening sequence
of epigrams is carefully ordered to emphasize in turn Martial's literary
artistry (10.2), the goodwill of his verse (10.3, 5), and the welcome owed

---

[10] See, e.g., 5.8.1, with Howell 1995:85; 7.34.8; and cf. Suet. *Dom.* 13.2, who preserves the
information that Domitian required this mode of address.

by a grateful populace to the guarantor of imperial stability, the new Caesar Trajan (10.6, 7). Many of the ensuing epigrams in the reedited collection rehearse themes that are familiar from the earlier books, even if Martial characterizes the majority as newly composed for the revised edition. In this way, the epigrammatist offers his public a reassuring picture of managed continuity in both imperial governance and authorial composition.

II. EPICUREAN THEMES IN THE "PROEMIO AL MEZZO" OF BOOK 10

Through his nuanced articulation of a program of literary revision in the opening sequence, Martial invites his readers to pay particular attention to his treatment of conventional themes in the reissued collection. At the centre of the revised book, moreover, he provides a "proem in the middle" that offers a key to the thematics of the collection in a statement of his philosophy of the happy life:[11]

> Vitam quae faciant beatiorem
> iucundissime Martialis, haec sunt:
> res non parta labore sed relicta;
> non ingratus ager, focus perennis;
> lis numquam, toga rara, mens quieta;   5
> uires ingenuae, salubre corpus;
> prudens simplicitas, pares amici;
> conuictus facilis, sine arte mensa;
> nox non ebria sed soluta curis;
> non tristis torus et tamen pudicus;   10
> somnus qui faciat breues tenebras:
> quod sis esse uelis nihilque malis;
> summum nec metuas diem nec optes.

Mart. *Epigr.* 10.47

---

[11] On the "proem in the middle," see Conte 1992. Spisak recognizes the programmatic importance of the location of 10.47 "midway in the book" (2002:134–137, esp. 134).

> Most delightful Martialis, these are the things that make a happier life: wealth not acquired from work but inherited; land not unproductive; a fire all year round; lawsuits never, infrequently wearing the toga, a mind at peace; gentleman's strength, a healthy body; thoughtful simplicity, friends of like station; easy company; a table without frills; a night not drunken but free of cares; a bed-mate not austere but nonetheless chaste; sleep that makes the shadows short; you should wish to be what you are and prefer nothing; don't fear your final day, nor desire it.

The epigram is among his most famous, and its Epicurean contours have long been recognized, though critics have rarely appreciated the depth and breadth of Martial's philosophical knowledge in the piece.[12] He draws throughout on statements of Epicurean doctrine, from his opening statement of what makes for the good life (*uita beatior*, 1), the goal of all ancient ethics;[13] through the renunciation of *negotium* (*toga rara*, 5) and embrace of tranquility (*mens quieta*, 5; *nox non ebria sed soluta curis*, 9; *somnus qui faciat breues tenebras*, 11)[14] in a country retreat (*non ingratus ager*, 4);[15] to the joys of friendship (*pares amici*, 7), congenial company (*conuictus facilis*, 8),[16] and plain fare at table (*sine arte mensa*, 8).

These principles are instantiated in the epigram that follows, a dinner invitation addressed to six of the poet's boon companions

---

[12] See Keith (2019) for detailed discussion of the Epicurean precepts on which Martial draws in 10.47, with full bibliography. Sullivan (1991) is typical in seeing here an intellectually debased Epicureanism in the epigram, which he calls "simply a manifesto of a cultivated Epicurean conformist" (216); cf. Holzberg 2002:81–85; Watson and Watson 2003:139–143; Damschen and Heil 2004:183–187; Spisak 2002:134–137, and 2007:81–90.

[13] Martial's phrasing takes up Hor. *Sat.* 2.4.95 (*uitae praecepta beatae*), discussed by Keith 2019:320–322. For the central problematic of the "good life" in classical philosophy, see Aristotle, *Eth. Nic.* 1.1, with Annas 1993:27–46. For pleasure as the highest good in Epicurean thought, see Woolf 2009; O'Keefe 2010:111–115. Cicero offers a concise statement of the Epicurean position at *De finibus* 1.29–42.

[14] Woolf 2009; O'Keefe 2010:117–127.

[15] Clay 2009.

[16] Glad 1996; Konstan 1997:108–113, 141–144; O'Keefe 2010:147–154; Armstrong 2011.

(10.48).[17] As a genre, the invitation poem has been identified as an Epicurean literary form and associated especially with Philodemus (*Epigr.* 27 Sider) and his young Roman literary friend Horace (cf., e.g., *Carm.* 1.20, 4.12; *Epist.* 1.5).[18] To his select company of friends, Martial proposes a simple repast of vegetarian appetizers (7–13), for the most part provender from his garden (... *mihi uilica maluas / adtulit et uarias quas habet hortus opes*, 7–8); a single main course (*una ponetur cenula mensa*, 13) consisting mostly of scraps (*offellae*, 15), more greens (*et faba fabrorum prototomique rudes*, 16), and leftovers (*cenisque tribus iam perna superstes / addetur*, 17–18); fruit for dessert (18); and a modest local vintage for the drinking party after dinner (19–20). The simplicity of Martial's menu aligns with his espousal of a plain table in the preceding epigram (10.47.8, quoted above), and the abundant vegetarian offerings are consistent with the evidence for Epicurean *conuiuia* in antiquity.[19] Over the wine, moreover, Martial promises the jokes and frank speech approved by the sect (21–24; cf. Phld. 27 Sider).[20] The two epigrams are among the most philosophically explicit in Martial's oeuvre and imply that an Epicurean ethical stance underwrites the tenth book.

Indeed, the programmatic salience of Epicurus's precepts to the book is hinted at already in 10.33, an elegant compliment to Munatius Gallus that reprises the literary agenda set out in the opening movement of the book.[21] Martial praises Gallus not only as "more guileless than the ancient Sabines," but also as one who "outdoes the

---

[17] Cf. Kropp *apud* Damschen and Heil 2004:190: "Das Epigramm [10.48] ... schließt sich an das wohl bekannteste Gedicht Martials (X 47) an und führt dessen Thema, die *vita beata* an einem konkreten Beispiel vor Augen." On cycles in Martial, all with further bibliography, see Barwick 1958; Sullivan 1991:218–219; Merli 1993, and 1998; Spisak 2002. On the Epicurean contours of 10.48, see Keith 2019; cf. Buongiovanni 2012:237. While I accept Vallat's estimation of 10.48 as promoting Martial's "quasi Epicurian" ideal (2008:65), he does not begin to do justice there to the epigrammatist's knowledge of Epicurean precepts and application of Epicurean principle in 10.47–48. On Epicurean themes in Martial, see Innocenti 1972; Adamik 1975; Heilmann 1984.

[18] See Tait 1941:68–70; Sider 1997:153; cf. Buongiovanni 2012:237–241.

[19] On Epicurus's vegetarianism, see Nisbet and Hubbard 1970:356, citing Cic. *Tusc.* 5.89: *ipse* [sc. Epicurus] *quam paruo est contentus! nemo de tenui uictu plura dixit* (with how little was he himself content! No one has spoken at more length about a restricted diet).

[20] See Phld. *On Frank Criticism*, in the edition of Konstan et al. 1998.

[21] On Munatius Gallus, see Vallat 2008:83.

old Cecropian in goodwill" (*Simplicior priscis, Munati Galle, Sabinis, / Cecropium superas qui bonitate senem,* 10.33.1–2). Shackleton Bailey has identified this Athenian ancient as Epicurus, rather than Socrates, on the basis of Diogenes Laertius's description of the former as exhibiting "unsurpassed good will to all men" and "unsurpassed qualities of goodness" (Diog. Laert. 10.9).[22] Martial strategically couples his addressee's good nature with the benign nature of his own verse:

> ut tu, si uiridi tinctos aerugine uersus   5
>   forte malus liuor dixerit esse meos,
> ut facis, a nobis abigas, nec scribere quemquam
>   talia contendas carmina qui legitur.
> Hunc seruare modum nostri nouere libelli,
>   parcere personis, dicere de uitiis.

Mart. Epigr. 10.33.5–10

If perchance evil envy has said that verses dipped in green verdigris are mine, please drive ill will away from me, as you do, and maintain that neither does anyone who is read write such poems. My little books know how to observe this limit: to spare persons, to tell of vices.

The epigram looks back to the programmatic opening sequence, especially 10.3, which disavows vituperative verse, and 10.4, which celebrates the practical human lessons on offer in the epigrams by contrast with the mythological *fabulae* on display in epic (10.4.9–10): *non hic Centauros, non Gorgonas Harpyiasque / inuenies: hominem pagina nostra sapit* (you won't find Centaurs, Gorgons, and Harpies here: my page smacks of humanity).[23] But in 10.33, Martial is unwontedly transparent about the Epicurean profile of his tenth epigram book—and not only in his coded

---

[22] Shackleton Bailey 1993: vol. 2, 347n58.

[23] Martial's mockery of the fantastical creatures of mythological epic in this couplet derives from the opening of Horace's *Ars poetica* (1–5), which derides such confusion of categories in markedly Epicurean terms (see Armstrong 1993). One of the editors reminds me that the verb *sapit* often has a philosophical valence, as a reference to *sapientia* (wisdom): see, e.g., Cic. *Leg.* 1.22.58: *ita fit, ut mater omnium bonarum rerum sit sapientia, a cuius amore Graeco uerbo philosophia nomen inuenit* (so it comes about that the mother of all good things is wisdom, from love of which philosophy takes her name in Greek).

allusion to Epicurus in the phrase "the Cecropian ancient" (10.33.2). For his reference to the limit (*hunc modum*, 10.33.9), which the literary program of his tenth book observes, recalls the fundamental principle of limit (Latin *finis*, *modus*) that underpins the systematization of both physics and ethics in Epicurus's thought. Lucretius's famous phrase "the deep-set boundary-stone" (*alte terminus haerens*, Lucr. 1.77) testifies to the limits of the physical universe and finds a parallel in the Epicurean ethical precept that empty (unnecessary and futile) desires are insatiable (i.e., fail to recognize the limits of true pleasure)[24] while natural desires are readily fulfilled (i.e., have a fixed term or limit; cf. Cic. *Fin.* 1.19 *finitas habet cupiditates*).

III. EPICUREAN THEMES IN BOOK 10

A recurrent opposition between city and country, the contrast familiar from *Epigrams* Book 3, has been identified as the overarching theme of the tenth book.[25] Epigrams on Trajan's military absence from the city (10.6) and the poet's request for the river Rhine to return him to the imperial metropole (10.7) align with this thematic, but Martial approaches it more fully in 10.12, a propempticon addressed to his friend Domitius on the occasion of his withdrawal from Rome to Vercellae, there to enjoy a summer's respite from the press of urban affairs:

> Aemiliae gentes et Apollineas Vercellas
>   et Phaethontei qui petis arua Padi,
> ne uiuam, nisi te, Domiti, dimitto libenter,
>   grata licet sine te sit mihi nulla dies:
> sed desiderium tanti est ut messe uel una   5
>   urbano releues colla perusta iugo.
>
> Mart. *Epigr.* 10.12.1–6

You who seek the people of the Aemilian Way, Apollo's Vercellae and the fields of Phaethon's river Po, Domitius, I

---

[24] Cf. Cic. *Fin.* 1.13 *inanium autem cupiditatum nec modus ullus nec finis inueniri potest* (but for empty desires neither is any limit nor end able to be discovered).

[25] Spisak 2002:132–140; Merli 2006; *contra* Rimell 2008:202–203.

wouldn't live happy unless I sent you off gladly, though no
day can please me without you: but missing you is worth it
so that for one summer you can relieve your neck, galled
by the urban yoke.

Martial sympathizes with his friend's desire to forego the oppres-
sive routine of *clientela* at Rome during the hot summer months and
memorably symbolizes his withdrawal from the imperial metropole to
the Po Valley as his release from the yoke of slavery. The poet figures
Domitius's rustic leisure in days of sunbathing and contrasts his
resulting tan with the pallor of Rome's urban denizens:

> i precor et totos auida cute conbibe soles—
>   o quam formonsus, dum peregrinus eris!
> et uenies albis non adgnoscendus amicis
>   liuebitque tuis pallida turba genis.   10
> sed uia quem dederit rapiet cito Roma colorem,
>   Niliaco redeas tu licet ore niger.

Mart. Epigr. 10.12.7–12

Go, I beg, and drink in whole days of sunshine with your
greedy skin—oh how handsome, while you're abroad!
You'll return unrecognizable to your pale friends, and the
pallid crowd will envy your cheeks. But Rome will quickly
snatch the colour which the road gave you, though you
return dark with the complexion of the Nile.

The strongly drawn contrast between Domitius's country leisure and
his friends' urban labour in 10.12 introduces the twin Epicurean themes
of living in undisturbed retirement in the countryside, apart from the
cares of public business in the imperial capital. Epicurus enjoined his
followers to "live unnoticed" (λάθε βιώσας),[26] explaining that "the
purest security is that which comes from a quiet life and withdrawal
from the many" (*RS* 14 *apud* Diog. Laert. 10.143 εἰλικρινεστάτη γίνεται

---

[26] Plut. *Mor.* 1128–9. On the doctrine Λάθε βιώσας (live unnoticed) and the misunder-
standings it has engendered, see Roskam 2007.

ἡ ἐκ τῆς ἡσυχίας καὶ ἐκχωρήσεως τῶν πολλῶν ἀσφάλεια).[27] As a site of rural *otium*, in explicit contrast with urban *negotium*, Domitius's country villa recalls the retirement recommended by Epicurus in his maxims (cf. Lucr. 2.20–36, 5.1366–1410) and instantiated in his garden outside Athens; we may compare Philodemus's presumed tenure at the Villa of the Papyri outside Herculaneum and Horace's enjoyment of his Sabine villa.[28]

The epigram includes other elements that look distinctively Epicurean. Martial's anticipation of Domitius's tan as a mark of his rural *otium* recalls the description of the complexion of a self-proclaimed Epicurean of an earlier generation (Hor. *Epist.* 1.4.15–16): *me pinguem et nitidum bene curata cute uises, / cum ridere uoles, Epicuri de grege porcum* (you will visit me, a porker from Epicurus's herd—fat and gleaming with well cared-for hide—when you want to laugh).[29] The *persona* of the author of *Epistles* 1 here embraces membership in the Epicurean sect and offers a self-characterization that bears out the introductory notice that "he lives retired in the countryside" (*latet abditus agro, Epist.* 1.1.5).[30] The Latin lexicon of Epicurean friendship also colors Martial's portrait of his relationship with Domitius, whose release from cares he does not begrudge despite his "longing" (*desiderium*, 10.12.5) for him.[31] The amatory undertones in Martial's description of their friendship bear all the hallmarks of his characteristically homosocial verse[32] and are especially reminiscent of Epicurean expressions of the close bond of

---

[27] I cite Diogenes Laertius from Dorandi 2013; translations follow or adapt Inwood and Gerson 1994.

[28] On Epicurean doctrine concerning the good life, drawing largely on Lucr., Cic. *Fin.* 1–2, and Diog. Laert. 10, see the contributions to Warren 2009; Fish and Sanders 2011.

[29] The explicitly Epicurean context of Horace's self-description here illuminates a similar reference to the Phaeacians' self-care earlier in the book (*Epist.* 1.29): *in cute curanda ... operata* (occupied with looking after their physical well-being; tr. Mayer 1994:116). On the Epicurean associations of the Phaeacians, see Gordon 2012:38–71.

[30] On the theme of the countryside in *Epistles* 1, see Mayer (1994:46–47), who notes its moral valence but not its specifically Epicurean import.

[31] On friendship in Martial, see Kleijwegt 1998; Spisak 1998; on Epicurean friendship, see the references collected in note 16 above.

[32] With the homosocial ambit of Martial's verse, we may compare Catullus (esp. *c.* 50) and the elegists (e.g., Prop. 1.5, 10, 13, 20): see Wray 2001:64–216; Keith 2008:115–138.

friendship. The sect espoused the value of friendship for the happy life, as Epicurus emphasizes in his maxims:

> 27. Ὧν ἡ σοφία παρασκευάζεται εἰς τὴν τοῦ ὅλου βίου μακαριότητα, πολὺ μέγιστόν ἐστιν ἡ τῆς φιλίας κτῆσις. 28. Ἡ αὐτὴ γνώμη θαρρεῖν τε ἐποίησεν ὑπὲρ τοῦ μηθὲν αἰώνιον εἶναι δεινὸν μηδὲ πολυχρόνιον, καὶ τὴν ἐν αὐτοῖς τοῖς ὡρισμένοις ἀσφάλειαν φιλίας μάλιστα κατεῖδε συντελουμένην.

Epicurus *RS* 27–28 *apud* Diog. Laert. 10.148

> 27. Of all the things which wisdom provides for the blessedness of one's whole life, by far the greatest is the possession of friendship. 28. The same understanding produces confidence about there being nothing terrible which is eternal or [even] long-lasting and has also realized that security amid even these limited [bad things] is most easily achieved through friendship.

The founder of the sect was himself celebrated by his followers for his exemplary friendship with a host of contemporaries (Diog. Laert. 10.10): οἳ [*sc.* φίλοι] καὶ πανταχόθεν πρὸς αὐτὸν ἀφικνοῦντο καὶ συνεβίουν αὐτῷ ἐν τῷ κήπῳ (Friends indeed came to him from all parts and lived with him in his garden).[33]

The contrast between city and country also animates the next epigram, which newly intimates the poet's own imminent withdrawal from Rome to Spain:

> Ducit ad auriferas quod me Salo Celtiber oras,
>   pendula quod patriae uisere tecta libet,
> tu mihi simplicibus, Mani, dilectus ab annis
>   et praetextata cultus amicitia,
> tu facis; in terris quo non est alter Hiberis   5
>   dulcior et uero dignus amore magis.

---

[33] The *Vatican Sayings* also bear witness to the importance of friendship in Epicurean philosophy (*Sent. Vat.* 23, 52, 78); cf. Phld. *Epigram* 27 Sider; and Hor. *Sat.* 1.5.39–44, with Armstrong 2014; Yona 2018.

tecum ego uel sicci Gaetula mapalia Poeni
  et poteram Scythicas hospes amare casas.
Si tibi mens eadem, si nostri mutua cura est,
  in quocumque loco Roma duobus erit.   10

Mart. *Epigr.* 10.13

The fact that Celtiberian Salonica draws me to its gold-
bearing shores, that it pleases me to visit the hanging
roofs of my fatherland, you Manius—beloved by me from
my youth and cultivated in a boyhood friendship—you're
the reason: there's none other sweeter than you in Iberian
lands or worthier of real love. With you I could love the
Gaetulian huts of the arid Carthaginian and Scythian
homes though a stranger. If you're of the same mind as me,
if you hold us in mutual affection, Rome will be in whatever place the two of us are.

Martial limns his return to Spain as the pleasing prospect (*libet*, 10.13.2)
of resuming his close friendship with Manius (*dilectus*, 3; *cultus amicitia*,
4; *dulcior et uero dignus amore magis*, 6; *amare*, 8; *nostri mutua cura*, 9).
The epigrammatist again recurs to the Latin lexicon of Epicurean
friendship, here to close the physical distance that has separated the
two friends; we may compare Horace's address to his great friend and
patron Maecenas in *Epistle* 1.7.12 (*dulcis amice*). In the light of Martial's
emphatic expressions of friendship for Domitius in 10.12 (*desiderium*,
5; *amicis*, 10) and Manius in 10.13 (3-4, 6, 9), and his repeated avowal
of pleasure at the prospect of withdrawal from the imperial capital,
whether Domitius's or his own (*libenter*, 10.12.3; *libet*, 10.13.2), it is
worth considering the possibility of a specifically Epicurean valence in
the urban/rural contrast not only in 10.12 and 10.13, but also in 10.30,
where Martial next broaches the theme.

The longest epigram in the book, 10.30 describes the delights of
a seaside villa belonging to Martial's friend Apollinaris (10.30.1-4): *O
temperatae dulce Formiae litus,* / *uos, cum seueri fugit oppidum Martis* / *et
inquietas fessus exuit curas,* / *Apollinaris omnibus locis praefert* (Temperate
Formiae, sweet shore—you, when he flees harsh Mars's town and,
tired out, discards unrestful cares, Apollinaris prefers to all places).

The opening lines contrast the harried life (*inquietas curas*, 3) of the inhabitants of the imperial metropole (*seueri oppidum Martis*, 2) with leisure on the sweet shore (*dulce litus*, 1) of Apollinaris's seaside villa outside Formiae. The Formian villa thus provides the pleasure and respite from cares that Lucretius characterizes as the goal of Epicurean philosophy:[34]

> nonne uidere
> nil aliud sibi naturam latrare, nisi utqui
> corpore seiunctus dolor absit, mensque fruatur
> iucundo sensu cura semota metuque?

> Lucr. 2.16–19

To think that you should fail to see that nature importunately demands only that the body may be rid of pain, and that the mind, divorced from anxiety and fear, may enjoy a feeling of contentment!

The younger Seneca confirms that the formulation was Epicurean in provenance (*Ep.* 66.45): *apud Epicurum duo bona sunt ex quibus summum illud beatumque componitur, ut corpus sine dolore sit, animus sine perturbatione* (In Epicurus there are two goods from which that highest blessing is achieved, namely that the body be without pain and the mind without disturbance).[35] The close correspondence in the description of Apollinaris's seaside villa with Epicurus's characterization of the tranquil life and Lucretius's description of the Epicurean philosophical project adumbrate the Epicurean character of Apollinaris's withdrawal to Formiae. The sweetness of the site of Apollinaris's villa (*dulce litus*, 1) also adds to the philosophical valence of the setting, for this quality often appears in Epicurean descriptions of the good life. In this regard, moreover, the villa at Formiae outstrips the famous retreats elsewhere on the Italian peninsula (10.30.5–7): *non ille sanctae dulce Tibur uxoris, /*

---

[34] I cite Lucretius from the OCT edition of Bailey, though I adopt the emendation *mensque* rather than *mente* printed by Bailey (1922): on the textual problem, see Fowler 2002:76. Translations are from Smith 2001.

[35] Cic. *Fin.* 1.49 similarly adapts Epicurean phrasing: *ista sequimur ut sine cura metuque uiuamus* (We follow these precepts of yours, in order to live without anxiety and fear).

nec Tusculanos Algidosue secessus, / *Praeneste nec sic Antiumque miratur* (he does not admire so much his chaste wife's sweet Tibur, nor the retreats of Tusculum or Algidum, nor Praeneste nor Antium).

Of particular interest in this context is Martial's characterization of rival Italian retreats as *secessus* (10.30.6), for this too was a technical term of Latin Epicureanism for the sect's preference for withdrawal from public life, famous from Epicurus's dictum to "live unknown." Indeed, Apollinaris's villa at Formiae furnishes the exemplary quietude characteristic of Epicurean retreat (10.30.11–15): *Hic summa leni stringitur Thetis uento;* / *nec languet aequor, uiua sed quies ponti* / *pictam phaselon*[36] *adiuuante fert aura,* / *sicut puellae non amantis aestatem* / *mota salubre purpura uenit frigus* (Here at Formiae, the surface of the sea is swept by a gentle wind; nor is the sea languid, but the living slumber of the deep bears a painted boat with the aid of a breeze, just as refreshing coolness comes when the purple fan of a girl who doesn't like the summer heat is moved). Martial evokes the goal of the Epicurean life in his description of the "quietude" (*quies*, 10.30.12) of the villa's seaside setting, like the safe havens (often, quite literally, ports)[37] of Epicurean community.

The concomitant pleasures of sex and the belly follow, the former hinted at in the reference to a girl who dislikes the heat (14–15), the latter elaborated in the catalogue of fish bred in the owner's own ponds for delivery to his table:

> ridet procellas tuta de suo mensa:
> piscina rhombum pascit et lupos uernas,
> natat ad magistrum delicata murena,
> nomenculator mugilem citat notum
> et adesse iussi prodeunt senes mulli.

Mart. Epigr. 10.30.20–24

---

[36] Martial's employment of the Greek word for a kidney bean–shaped watercraft, *phaselos* (10.30.13), in his limping iambics signals his debt to Catullus's *c.* 4, written in pure iambics, about the late republican poet's own return to his home from Bithynia, where he had served on the staff of the provincial governor L. Calpurnius Piso Caesoninus, in just such a watercraft. The term was current in Catullus's day (cf. Cic. *Att.* 1.13.1) but is sparingly deployed in Latin verse; in addition to Martial here, only Horace (*Carm.* 3.2.29) and Juvenal (15.127) use it.

[37] Cf., e.g., Diog. Laert. 10.6; *Sent. Vat.* 17; [Verg.] *Catal.* 5.8. On the trope, see Clay 2004.

The table, secure in its own stock, laughs at gales: the fish-pool pastures turbot and home-bred pike, the delicate sea-eel swims to its master, the slave in charge of names summons the well-known mullet, and old barbels come forth when bidden to appear.

Epicurus famously acknowledged "the pleasures of the belly,"[38] though he deprecated the carnal pleasures of sex and the table by comparison with the delights of mental tranquility and philosophical conversation.

> οὐ γὰρ πότοι καὶ κῶμοι συνείροντες οὐδ' ἀπολαύσεις
> παίδων καὶ γυναικῶν οὐδ' ἰχθύων καὶ τῶν ἄλλων,
> ὅσα φέρει πολυτελὴς τράπεζα, τὸν ἡδὺν γεννᾷ βίον,
> ἀλλὰ νήφων λογισμὸς καὶ τὰς αἰτίας ἐξερευνῶν πάσης
> αἱρέσεως καὶ φυγῆς καὶ τὰς δόξας ἐξελαύνων ἐξ ὧν
> πλεῖστος τὰς ψυχὰς καταλαμβάνει θόρυβος.

Epicurus *Ep. Men. apud* Diog. Laert. 10.132

For it is not drinking bouts and continuous partying and enjoying boys and women, or consuming fish and the other dainties of an extravagant table, which produce the pleasant life, but sober calculation, which searches out the reasons for every choice and avoidance and drives out the opinions that are the source of the greatest turmoil for men's souls.

In the context of this famous passage, it is perhaps no accident that Martial focuses particularly closely on fish in his enumeration of the delicacies to be enjoyed at Apollinaris's villa,[39] especially as the sting in

---

[38] Usener fr. 67: οὐ γὰρ ἔγωγε ἔχω τί νοήσω τἀγαθόν, ἀφαιρῶν μὲν τὰς διὰ χυλῶν ἡδονάς (For I cannot conceive of the Good if we are to eliminate the pleasures of the belly); cf. Diog. Laert. 10.6; *Sent. Vat.* 33: Σαρκὸς φωνή τὸ μὴ πεινῆν, τὸ μὴ διψῆν, τὸ μὴ ῥιγοῦν· ταῦτα γὰρ ἔχων τις καὶ ἐλπίζων ἕξειν κἂν <Διὶ> ὑπὲρ εὐδαιμονίας μαχέσαιτο (The cry of the flesh: not to be hungry, not to be thirsty, not to be cold. For if someone has these things and is confident of having them in the future, he might contend even with <Zeus> for happiness).

[39] Cf., e.g., Hor. *Sat.* 2.4, a discourse on the subject of good living, which consists of a recital of the pleasures of the table by Horace's fellow Epicurean Catius (identified by Porphyry as the author of *quattuor libros de rerum natura et de summo bono*; see Porph. *ad* Hor. *Sat.* 2.4) and is informed throughout by an ironic self-awareness of the dissolute

the epigram's tail implies that his friend all too rarely experiences the Epicurean felicity of withdrawal to his seaside villa and the pleasures of its well-stocked fish-ponds:

> Frui sed istis quando, Roma, permittis?   25
> quot Formianos inputat dies annus
> negotiosis rebus urbis haerenti?
> o ianitores uilicique felices!
> dominis parantur ista, seruiunt uobis.
>
> Mart. Epigr. 10.30.25–29

> But when, Rome do you allow him to enjoy these pleasures? How many days at Formiae does the year enter into the account of a man embroiled in the city's pressing affairs? O happy doormen and bailiffs! Though these pleasures are prepared for your masters, they serve you.

Martial frequently complains about the excessive demands of business at Rome (10.30.25–27), rehearsing the familiar Horatian contrast between the press of affairs at Rome and the tranquil pleasures of his Sabine villa. In Horace, the contrasts between city and country, *negotium* and *otium*, are freighted with Epicurean significance, and Martial's adoption of the satirist's characteristic tropes imparts a similarly Epicurean valence to his concluding lines. Apollinaris's villa provides all the appurtenances with which to support an Epicurean lifestyle, but it is his doormen and bailiffs (*ianitores uilicique*, 28) who actually enjoy the pleasures of their master's Epicurean villa. Martial's application of philosophical felicity to the master's slaves (*felices*, 28) is especially pointed as the final line ironically revisits Epicurus's paradox, quoted by Seneca (*Ep.* 8.7), that "to be truly free one must serve philosophy" (*philosophiae seruias oportet, ut tibi contingat uera libertas*).

---

reputation of the sect. For an Epicurean interpretation of Hor. *Sat.* 2.4, see Classen 1978; for Epicurean play on the sect's reputation for hedonism and dissolute living, see Gordon 2012, esp. 38–71; Yona 2018.

IV. EPICUREAN WITHDRAWAL

As we have seen, Martial sounds his impending departure from Rome to Spain as early as 10.13, and its motivation is implicit in the poems praising the villa retreats of his friends Domitius (10.12) and Apollinaris (10.30). Epigram 10.37 reprises the motif of the poet's retirement to Spain and combines it explicitly with the withdrawal of his friend Maternus to his country villa, in a newly emulative contrast between Italy and Spain:[40]

> iuris et aequarum cultor sanctissime legum,
>   ueridico Latium qui regis ore forum,
> municipi, Materne, tuo ueterique sodali
>   Callaïcum mandas si quid ad Oceanum—.

Mart. Epigr. 10.37.1–4

> Scrupulous devotee of law and just statutes, Maternus,
>   you who rule the Latin Forum with truth-telling mouth,
> if you entrust anything to your fellow townsman and old
>   companion for the Galician ocean—

The epigram's opening lines implicitly invite Maternus to inquire into the reason for his old friend's departure for Spain, but the epigrammatist goes on to supply the answer unprompted in the rest of the poem, which draws a detailed contrast between the idealized pleasures of his provincial retreat and the considerably less elegant offerings of his friend's Laurentine villa (10.37.5–19). Martial draws once again on an Epicurean frame of reference to articulate the contrast, both generally, in terms of the pleasures of the belly, and more particularly, in terms of a hierarchy of seafood delicacies:

> An Laurentino turpis in litore ranas   5
>   et satius tenues ducere credis acos
> ad sua captiuum quam saxa remittere mullum,
>   uisus erit libris qui minor esse tribus?

---

[40] On 10.37, see Kolosova 2000; Buongiovanni 2012:183–233. On the identification of Maternus, see Buongiovanni 2012:199–202, *contra* Kolosova 2000.

et fatuam summa cenare pelorida mensa
    quosque tegit leui cortice concha breuis   10
ostrea Baianis quam non liuentia testis,
    quae domino pueri non prohibente uorent?

Mart. Epigr. 10.37.5–12

Or do you think it better to pull out ugly frogs and slender needle fish on the shore of Laurentum than to throw back on its rocks a captured mullet that appears to be less than three pounds; and to dine on insipid peloris as *pièce de resistance* and the creatures that a small shell covers with a smooth coating rather than oysters that do not envy Baian jars, that the slaves devour unchecked by master?

The "ugly frogs" of Laurentum recuperate a Horatian expression (*Epod.* 5.19) from the enumeration of Canidia's catalogue of witchcraft supplies and imply not only Martial's aesthetic distaste for, but also his ethical renunciation of, Italy. The "ugly frogs and slender needle fish" of Maternus's Laurentine villa can in no way compare to Spanish mullets, deemed too small to harvest at a weight of three pounds (10.5–8).[41] The undistinguished shellfish (*fatuam peloridem,* 9) and mussels (10) of Laurentum likewise pale beside Spanish oysters of such size that Baiae envies them and of such abundance that slaves no less than their masters feast on them (10.37.11–12). Even Maternus's huntsman can provide only a smelly vixen for his table, readily outclassed by Martial's Spanish hares (10.37.13–16). The imagined context of the epigram is revealed in the final couplets:

Dum loquor ecce redit sporta piscator inani,
    uenator capta maele superbus adest:
omnis ab urbano uenit ad mare cena macello.
    Callaïcum mandas si quid ad Oceanum—   20

Mart. Epigr. 10.37.17–20

---

[41] The weight of three pounds is also chosen by reference to Horace, who praises as large a mullet of that weight at *Sat.* 2.2.33–34. On Martial's predilection for the fish and its frequent appearance in his epigrams, see Buongiovanni 2012:215–217.

> Even as I speak, here comes the fisherman back with an
> empty hamper, and here is the hunter, proud of having
> captured a badger. Every seaside dinner comes from the
> city market. If you have any message for the Galician
> ocean—

Martial sets the epigram at Maternus's villa, where he waxes eloquent
about the delights of his homeland even as his host's staff (in this case,
fisherman and huntsman) return, if not empty-handed, at least with
undistinguished fare for dinner. The sting in the tail of the epigram lies
in his friend's inability to provide even an unexceptional meal from his
Laurentine estate. Maternus must lay in provisions from the city, and
the fact that he does so inadvertently lends support to the epigrammatist's decision to return to Spain, as true withdrawal from the city
requires retirement from Italy altogether (10.37.20).[42]

Another epigram draws an implied contrast between the poet's
impending retirement and an old friend's departure from Rome:

> Quinte Caledonios Ovidi uisure Britannos
> et uiridem Tethyn Oceanumque patrem,
> ergo Numae colles et Nomentana relinquis
> otia nec retinet rusque focusque senem?

> Mart. Epigr. 10.44.1–4

> Quintus Ovidius, will you go to see the Caledonian Britons,
> green Tethys and father Ocean, and so you are leaving
> behind Numa's hills and Nomentan leisure, nor do country
> and hearth hold you in old age?

Ovid's departure to the ends of empire (cf. Catull. 11) mimics Martial's
proposed trip to Spain, but Ovid will have to forgo the Epicurean pleasures of home and hearth that Martial lauds in 10.47 (*non ingratus ager,
focus perennis*, 4) and anticipates in his retirement (10.96.7–8: *tepet igne
maligno / hic* [sc. *Latia in urbe*] *focus, ingenti lumine lucet ibi* [here (sc. in
Rome) the hearth warms with a grudging fire, there (sc. in Spain) it is

---

[42] The younger Pliny, by contrast, testifies to his enjoyment of *studiosum otium* at his
Laurentine villa in *Ep.* 2.17.

bright with a huge blaze], discussed below). For Martial's friend departs on business, deferring the pleasures of his Nomentan retirement out of friendship:

> gaudia tu differs, at non et stamina differt 5
>   Atropos atque omnis scribitur hora tibi.
> Praestiteris caro—quis non hoc laudet?—amico
>   ut potior uita sit tibi sancta fides.
>
> <div align="right">Mart. <i>Epigr.</i> 10.44.5–8</div>

> You postpone your joys, but Atropos does not put off her threads and every hour is written down to your account. You will have shown a dear friend—who wouldn't praise it?—that your sacred word is more important to you than life.

The couplets, with their contrast between personal pleasure (*gaudia tu differs*, 5) and its postponement in favor of honouring the call of a dear friend, recall the importance of friendship in Epicurean thought (Epicurus *RS* 27–28, *Sent. Vat.* 23, 52, 78) and Martial's own emphasis on this precept in 10.47.7–8 (*pares amici; / conuictus facilis*), even as the epigrammatist implies that Ovid's commitment to friendship may imperil his life (10.44.8). The tension between the principles of utility and pleasure in the definition of friendship was a frequent subject of discussion in Epicurean circles:

> 23. Πᾶσα φιλία δ' ἑαυτὴν αἱρετή· ἀρχὴν δὲ εἴληφεν ἀπὸ τῆς ὠφελείας.
>
> 28. Οὔτε τοὺς προχείρους εἰς φιλίαν οὔτε τοὺς ὀκνηροὺς δοκιμαστέον· δεῖ δὲ καὶ παρακινδυνεῦσαι χάριν φιλίας.
>
> <div align="right"><i>Sent. Vat.</i> 23, 28</div>

> 23. Every friendship is worth choosing for its own sake, though it takes its origin from the benefits [it confers on us].

28. One must not approve of those who are excessively eager for friendship, nor those who are reluctant. But one must be willing to run some risks for the sake of friendship.

Epicurus attempted to resolve the contradictions by underlining the advantages of friendship (*KD* 14; cf. Phld. *De oeconomia*, Coll. XIII.15–19, XV.3–6 [Tsouna 2012]), but the ambiguities were pressed by the sect's critics (e.g., Cic. *Fin.* 1.65–70).[43] Martial wittily enters the fray in the closing couplet, where he plays on the Epicurean advantage of friendship in his advice to Ovid that he include himself in the circle of his own friends (10.44.9–10): *sed reddare tuis tandem mansure Sabinis/ teque tuas numeres inter amicitias* (Do but return to your Sabine villa, to stay at last, and count yourself amongst your friendships).

More epigrams celebrating the prospect of withdrawal from Rome in Epicurean tones follow. In 10.51, Martial enumerates the delights on offer at Faustinus's country retreat. Winter has given way to spring (1–2; cf. Hor. *Carm.* 1.9.5–8), with its wealth of flora (3) and fauna (4) in full array, but Faustinus lingers in Rome, deprived of the Epicurean tranquility of his rural villa (5–6): *quos, Faustine, dies, quales tibi Roma †Ravennae†/ abstulit! o soles, o tunicata quies!* (What days, Faustinus, what [textual crux] has Rome taken from you! Ah suns, ah tunic-clad tranquility!). Tunic-wearing tranquility is precisely what Epicurean withdrawal to the countryside affords the Roman man of affairs—respite from wearing the *toga* on business (cf. 10.47.5, quoted above). Martial evokes the landscapes' beauties—glades and fountains (7), the shore and clear waters of Anxur (8), where the river flows gently into sea (9–10)—but Faustinus is detained in Rome on business in the city's theatres, baths, imperial fora, and temples (11–14). Martial imagines him demanding recompense from Quirinus, the patron divinity of the Roman citizen (15–16): *Dicere te lassum quotiens ego credo Quirino: / 'Quae tua sunt, tibi habe: quae mea, redde mihi'* (How often I believe you say, tired out, to Quirinus: "Keep what is yours; give me back what is mine").

---

[43] On the tensions, see Konstan 1997:109–112.

Epigram 10.58 similarly lauds the tranquility of the epigrammatist's stay at his friend Frontinus's seaside villa in Anxur, a "peaceful
retreat" (*placidos ... recessus*, 1) on the shore near Baiae, whose glades
and pools Martial enjoyed because there he could cultivate the Muses
(5–6). He contrasts the tranquil pleasures of withdrawal to Anxur with
the fervid cares of daily life in the imperial metropole, the urban grind
from which he is eager to escape:

> ... nunc nos maxima Roma terit.
> Hic mihi quando dies meus est? iactamur in alto
>   urbis, et in sterili uita labore perit.

Mart. *Epigr.* 10.58.6–8

> ... Now mightiest Rome wears me down. When is the day
> my own here? I'm buffeted in the city's ocean, and my life
> perishes in empty toil.

Martial's complaints here are closely aligned with the Epicurean goals
of pleasure and the avoidance of care (*cura*) and toil (*labor*),[44] and he
concludes with an epigrammatic restatement of the Epicurean moral
of *Vatican Saying* 14: Σὺ δὲ οὐκ ὢν τῆς αὔριον <κύριος ἀναβάλλῃ τὸν
καιρόν· ὁ δὲ βίος μελλησμῷ παραπόλλυται καὶ εἷς ἕκαστος ἡμῶν
ἀσχολούμενος ἀποθνήσκει. (You are not in control of tomorrow and yet
you delay your [opportunity to] rejoice. Life is ruined by delay and each
and every one of us dies without enjoying leisure).

The full roster of Epicurean pleasures is precisely what Martial
anticipates in his Spanish retirement:

> Saepe loquar nimium gentes quod, Auite, remotas
>   miraris, Latia factus in urbe senex,
> auriferumque Tagum sitiam patriumque Salonem
>   et repetam saturae sordida rura casae.
> Illa placet tellus in qua res parua beatum   5
>   me facit et tenues luxuriantur opes:
> pascitur hic, ibi pascit ager; tepet igne maligno

---

[44] Epicurus, *Ep. Men.* 128 (*apud* Diog. Laert. 10); Phld. *De oeconomia,* Col. 11 (Tsouna
2012); Lucr. 3.59–64, 5.1430–1433.

> hic focus, ingenti lumine lucet ibi;
> hic pretiosa fames conturbatorque macellus,
>   mensa ibi diuitiis ruris operta sui;   10
> quattuor hic aestate togae pluresue teruntur,
>   autumnis ibi me quattuor una tegit.
> I, cole nunc reges, quidquid non praestat amicus
>   cum praestare tibi possit, Auite, locus.

Mart. Epigr. 10.96

Does it surprise you, Avitus, that I, who have grown old in Latium's city, often speak of very far-off peoples, that I thirst for gold-bearing Tagus and my native Salo, that I am going back to the rough fields of a well-stocked cottage? Give me a land where a small competence makes me wealthy and narrow means are a luxury. Here the soil is supported, there it supports. Here the hearth warms with a grudging fire, there it is bright with a huge blaze. Here hunger is costly and the market makes men bankrupt, there the board is spread with the riches of its own countryside. Here four or more gowns wear out in a summer, there one covers me through four autumns. Go now, pay court to royal patrons, Avitus, when a place can provide you with all that a friend does not provide.

Martial elaborates a stark contrast between the life of Epicurean leisure he will enjoy upon his return to Spain and the careworn life antithetical to Epicurean precepts he leads in Rome, framing his desire to retire to Spain as a recovery of Epicurean principle in the absence of a truly Epicurean friend. The rough fields of his humble cottage (10.96.4) are sufficient for the Epicurean epigrammatist, who recognizes his wealth in a small holding (10.96.5–6) and sees his slender resources as a luxury (10.96.6). Martial's oxymoronic phrasing in these lines evokes Epicurean principles such as that expressed in *Vatican Saying* 25: Ἡ πενία μετρουμένη τῷ τῆς φύσεως τέλει μέγας ἐστὶ πλοῦτος· πλοῦτος δὲ μὴ ὁριζόμενος μεγάλη ἐστὶ πενία (Poverty, if measured by the goal of nature, is great wealth; and wealth, if limits are not set for it, is great poverty). The poet draws a contrast between the bright blaze of his Spanish hearth and the grudging Roman fireplace in language that seems indebted to Lucretius, both for the wordplay (*igne maligno*, 10.96.7; *lumine lucet*, 10.96.8) and for the imagery of illumination, while we have already seen the Epicurean provenance of the warm hearth (10.47.4, quoted above). Also familiar from Lucretius is the opposition in epigram 10.96 between costly urban banquets (10.96.9) and the true wealth of country fare (10.96.10). Even the skeptical note Martial sounds in the final couplet about friendship finds parallels in Epicurus's maxims, where the master tempers praise of friendship with practical concerns (*Sent. Vat.* 23, 28, quoted above), and in Diogenes Laertius's report of Epicurus's view that "without confidence there is no friendship" (Diog. Laert. 10.11: εἰ δ' ἀπίστων οὐδὲ φίλων).

V. *ENVOI*

The closing movement of the book returns to the literary concerns with which it opened. In 10.100, Martial asks why an author includes his stolen verses with his own (*quid, stulte, nostris uersibus tuos misces?*), in a reprise of the plagiarism motif of 10.3 and 10.5, while in 10.103, he invites the citizens of Bilbilis to glory in his fame just as Verona celebrates Catullus (10.103.5–6). The final epigram of the collection is addressed to his little book, urging it to take ship for Spain (10.104.1–7), there to seek out the poet's old friends in Bilbilis and Salo, especially Flavus (10.104.12–15): *et nostrum admoneas subinde Flauum / iucundos mihi nec laboriosos / secessus pretio paret salubri, / qui pigrum faciant tuum parentem* (and remind my good Flavus from time to time to find me a pleasant retreat not needing much work at a reasonable price, to make your father lazy). The poet instructs his little book to ask Flavus to secure for him an Epicurean retreat (*secessus*, 14), at once pleasant (*iucundos*, 13) and requiring no work (*nec laboriosos*, 13). The Epicurean themes of friendship, retirement, and the remission of care and toil thus merge in the poet's *envoi* to his book.

A year later, Martial writes to the satirist Juvenal from his retirement in Spain, where he claims to enjoy all that he had desired.

me multos repetita post Decembres
accepit mea rusticumque fecit
auro Bilbilis et superba ferro.
Hic pigri colimus labore dulci   10
Boterdum Plateamque—Celtiberis
haec sunt nomina crassiora terris—:
ingenti fruor improboque somno
quem nec tertia saepe rumpit hora,
et totum mihi nunc repono quidquid   15
ter denos uigilaueram per annos.
Ignota est toga, sed datur petenti
rupta proxima uestis a cathedra.
surgentem focus excipit superba
uicini strue cultus iliceti,   20
multa uilica quem coronat olla.
uenator sequitur, sed ille quem tu
secreta cupias habere silua;
dispensat pueris rogatque longos
leuis ponere uilicus capillos.   25
Sic me uiuere, sic iuuat perire.

Mart. *Epigr.* 12.18.7–26

Me my Bilbilis, proud of her gold and iron, revisited after
many Decembers, has received and made a rustic. Here
in idleness I exert myself pleasantly to visit Boterdus and
Platea (such are the uncouth names in Celtiberian lands).
I enjoy an enormous, indecent amount of sleep, often
unbroken till past the third hour, and pay myself back in
full now for my vigils of thirty years. The gown is unknown,
but when I ask I am handed the nearest garment to hand
from a broken chair. When I get up, a fireplace welcomes
me stocked with a proud pile of logs from an adjacent oak
wood and crowned by the housekeeper with many a pot.
The huntsman comes next, but one that you would like to
have with you in a secret grove. The smooth-skinned bailiff

gives my boys their rations and asks me to let him cut his
long hair. So it pleases me to live, so to die.

Withdrawal to Spain has made of the epigrammatist a confirmed
country-dweller (*rusticum*, 8; cf. 10.47.4), just as Epicurus, Lucretius,
Philodemus, and Horace recommend. Martial celebrates his idleness
(*pigri*, 10), marked by the oxymoronic "sweet toil" (*labore dulci*, 10; cf.
10.47.3) of visiting local villages. He finally enjoys the unbroken sleep
(indeed huge amounts of it, 13–14; cf. 10.47.11) promised the Epicurean
initiate. Nor does he wear the toga anymore (17; cf. 10.47.5) to transact
official business. Instead, he enjoys the warm hearth (19–20) he had
extolled in 10.48 (*focus perennis*, 4) and anticipated in 10.96 (7–8,
quoted above), on which the bailiff's wife cooks him dinner (21). The
huntsman who presumably supplies him with the famous local hares
(cf. 10.37.15–16) is himself worthy of this traditional love gift, "one
you'd like to have with you in a secret grove" (i.e., as a lover). Moreover,
his carefully selected bailiff sports the smooth skin and long hair (24–5)
of the *puer delicatus* (Greek ἐρώμενος), the sexually desirable adoles-
cent youth with soft skin and long hair (cf., e.g., 4.42, 9.17).[45] The final
line summarizes the closing wisdom of 10.47 (12–13) and asserts the
reasoned choices of Epicurean doctrine. If the epistolary preface to the
twelfth book as a whole, published some years later, asserts Martial's
very un-Epicurean reaction to his Spanish retirement, that is the story
of another book.[46]

UNIVERSITY OF TORONTO

WORKS CITED

Adamik, T. 1975. "Martial and the 'Vita Beatior.'" *Annales Universitatis
    Scientiarum Budapestensis, Sectio Classica* 3:55–64.
Annas, J. 1993. *The Morality of Happiness*. Oxford.

---

[45] Richlin (1992:34–44) discusses the male erotic ideal in Greek and Latin literature,
with a special focus on Martial (39–44).

[46] On Book 12, see Howell 1998. On Martial's representation of Spain, see Citroni 2002.

Armstrong, D. 1993. "The Addressees of the *Ars poetica*: Herculaneum, the Pisones, and Epicurean Protreptic." *MD* 31:185–230.

———. 2011. "Epicurean Virtues, Epicurean Friendship: Cicero vs. the Herculaneum Papyri." In Fish and Sanders 2011, 105–28.

———. 2014. "Horace's Epicurean Voice in the *Satires*." in *The Philosophizing Muse: The Influence of Greek Philosophy on Roman Poetry*, ed. M. Garani and D. Konstan, 91–127. Newcastle upon Tyne.

Bailey, C. 1922. *Lucreti. De Rerum Natura Libri Sex*. 2nd ed. Oxford.

Barwick, K. 1958. "Zyklen bei Martial und in den kleinen Gedichten des Catull." *Philologus* 102:284–318.

Buongiovanni, C. 2012. *Gli Epigrammata Longa del decimo libro di Marziale*. Pisa.

Citroni, M. 1975 *M. Valerii Martialis Epigrammaton liber primus. Introduzione, testo, apparato critico e commento*. Firenze.

———. 2002. "L'immagine della Spagna e l'autorappresentazione del poeta negli epigrammi di Marziale." In *Hispania terris omnibus felicior: Premesse ed esiti di un processo di integrazione, Atti del convegno internazionale, Cividale de Fruili, 27-29 settembre 2001*, ed. G. Urso, 281–301. Pisa.

Classen, C. J. 1978. "Horace—A Cook?" *CQ* 28:333–348.

Clay, D. 2004. "Vergil's Farewell to Education (*Catalepton* 5) and Epicurus' Letter to Pythocles." In *Vergil, Philodemus, and the Augustans*, ed. D. Armstrong, J. Fish, P. A. Johnston, and M. B. Skinner, 25–36. Austin, TX.

———. 2009. "The Athenian Garden." In Warren 2009, 9–28.

Coleman, K. M. 1990 (2000). "Latin Literature after AD 96: Change or Continuity?" *AJAH* 15(1):19–39.

Conte, G. B. 1992. "Proems in the Middle." *YCS* 29:147–159.

Damschen, G., and A. Heil. 2004. *Marcus Valerius Martialis. Epigrammaton liber decimus: Das zehnte Epigrammbuch*. Frankfurt am Main.

Dorandi, T., ed. 2013. *Diogenes Laertius. Lives of Eminent Philosophers*. Cambridge.

Fearnley, H. 2003. "Reading the Imperial Revolution: Martial, *Epigrams* 10." In *Flavian Rome*, ed. A. J. Boyle and W. J. Dominik, 613–635. Leiden.

Fedeli, P. 2004. "Marziale Catulliano." *Humanitas* 56:161–180

Ferguson, J. 1963. "Catullus and Martial." *Proceedings of the African Classical Association* 6:3–15.

Fish, J., and K. R Sanders, eds. 2011. *Epicurus and the Epicurean Tradition.* Cambridge.

Fitzgerald, W. 2007. *Martial: The World of the Epigram.* Chicago.

Fowler, D. 2002. *Lucretius on Atomic Motion: A Commentary on De Rerum Natura, Book Two, Lines 1-332.* Oxford.

Glad, C. E. 1996. "Frank Speech, Flattery, and Friendship in Philodemus." In *Friendship, Flattery, and Frankness of Speech: Studies on Friendship in the New Testament World,* ed. J. T. Fitzgerald, 21–59. Leiden.

Gordon, P. 2012. *The Invention and Gendering of Epicurus.* Ann Arbor, MI.

Grewing, F., ed. 1998. *Toto notus in orbe: Perspektiven der Martial-Interpretation.* Stuttgart.

Heilmann, W. 1984. "'Wenn ich frei sein könnte für ein wirkliches Leben ...,' Epikureisches bei Martial." *A&A* 30:47–61.

Hinds, S. 2007. "Martial's Ovid / Ovid's Martial," *JRS* 97:113-154.

Holzberg, N. 2002. *Martial und das antike Epigramm.* Darmstadt.

Howell, P., ed. 1995. *Martial. The Epigrams, Book V.* Warminster.

———. 1998. "Martial's Return to Spain." In Grewing 1998, 173–186.

Innocenti, P. 1972. "Per una storia dell'epicureismo nei primi secoli dell'era volgare: Temi e problemi." *RSF* 27:123–147.

Inwood, B., and L. P. Gerson, eds. 1994. *The Epicurus Reader: Selected Writings and Testimonia.* Indianapolis, IN.

Keith, A. 2008. *Propertius: Poet of Love and Leisure.* London.

———. 2019. "Epicurean Principle and Poetic Program in Martial, *Epigrams* 10.47–48." *Phoenix* 72(3–4):319–337.

Kleijwegt, M. 1998. "*Extra fortunam est quidquid donator amicis*: Martial on Friendship." In Grewing 1998, 256–277.

Kolosova, O. G. 2000. "*Callaicum mandas siquid ad Oceanum ...*: Zur Zeit und Ursache der Heimkehr Martials." *Gerión* 18:323–341.

Konstan, D. 1997. *Friendship in the Classical World.* Cambridge.

Konstan, D., D. Clay, C. E. Glad, J. C. Thom, and J. Ware, eds. 1998. *Philodemus. On Frank Criticism.* Atlanta.

Lindsay, W. M. 1929. *M. Val. Martialis. Epigrammata.* 2nd ed. Oxford.

Lorenz, S. 2002. *Erotik und Panegyrik: Martials epigrammatische Kaiser.* Tübingen.

Mayer, R., ed. 1994. *Horace. Epistles, Book I.* Cambridge.

Mendell, C. W. 1922. "Martial and the Satiric Epigram." *CP* 17 (1):1–20

Merli, E. 1993. "Ordinamento degli epigrammi e strategie cortigiane negli esordi dei libri I–XII di Marziale." *Maia* 45:229–56.

———. 1998. "Epigrammzyklen und 'serielle Lektüre' in den Büchern Martials: Überlegungen und Beispiele." In Grewing 1998, 139–156.

———. 2006. "Identity and Irony: Martial's Tenth Book, Horace, and the Tradition of Roman Satire." In *Flavian Poetry*, ed. R. R. Nauta, H. van Dam, and J. J. Smolenaars, 257–270. Leiden.

Neger, M. 2012. *Martials Dichtergedichte: Das Epigramm als Medium der poetischen Selbstreflexion.* Tübingen.

Nisbet, R. G. M., and M. Hubbard. 1970. *A Commentary on Horace, Odes, Book I.* Oxford.

Offermann, H. 1980. "Uno tibi sim minor Catullo." *Quaderni di Cultura e di Tradizione Classica* 34:107–139.

O'Keefe, T. 2010. *Epicureanism.* Berkeley, CA.

Pentzer, M. R. 2019. "Horace-ing Around with Martial Book 10." *CJ* 114(4):409–438.

Richlin, A. 1992. *The Garden of Priapus.* 2nd ed. Oxford.

Rimell, V. 2008. *Martial's Rome.* Cambridge.

Roman, L. 2001. "The Representation of Literary Materiality in Martial's Epigrams." *JRS* 91:113–145.

Roskam, G. 2007. *"Live Unnoticed" (Λάθε βιώσας): On the Vicissitudes of an Epicurean Doctrine.* Leiden.

Shackleton Bailey, D. R. 1993. *Martial. Epigrams.* 3 vols. Cambridge, MA.

Sider, D. 1997. *The Epigrams of Philodemos: Introduction, Text, and Commentary.* New York.

Smith, M. F. 2001. *Lucretius. On the Nature of Things.* Indianapolis, IN.

Spisak, A. L. 1998. "Gift-giving in Martial." In Grewing 1998, 243–255.

———. 2002. "The Pastoral Ideal in Martial, Book 10." *CW* 95(2):127–141.

———. 2007. *Martial: A Social Guide.* London.

Sullivan, J. P. 1991. *Martial, the Unexpected Classic: A Literary and Historical Study.* Cambridge.

Swann, B. W. 1994. *Martial's Catullus: The Reception of an Epigrammatic Rival.* Hildesheim.

———. 1998. "*Sic scribit Catullus*: The Importance of Catullus for Martial's Epigrams." In Grewing 1998, 48–58.

Szelest, H. 1963. "Martials satirisch Epigramme und Horaz." *Altertum* 9:27–37.

———. 1999. "Ovid und Martial." In *Ovid und Wirkung: Festgabe für Michael von Albrecht zum 65. Geburtstag*, ed. W. Schubert, 861-864. Frankfurt am Main.

Tait, J. I. M. 1941. *Philodemus' Influence on the Latin Poets*. Ph.D. Diss. Bryn Mawr University.

Tsouna, V., ed. 2012. *Philodemus. On Property Management*. Atlanta.

Usener, H., ed. 1887. *Epicurea*. Leipzig.

Vallat, D. 2008. *Onomastique, culture et société dans les* Épigrammes *de Martial*. Brussels.

Warren, J., ed. 2009. *The Cambridge Companion to Epicureanism*. Cambridge.

Watson, L., and P. Watson. 2003. *Martial. Select Epigrams*. Cambridge.

———. 2015. *Martial*. London.

Williams, C. A. 2002. "Ovid, Martial, and Poetic Immortality: Traces of *Amores* 1.15 in the *Epigrams*." *Arethusa* 35:417–433.

———. 2004. *Martial. Epigrams, Book Two*. Oxford.

Woolf, R. 2009. "Pleasure and Desire." In Warren 2009, 158–178.

Wray, D. 2001. *Catullus and the Poetics of Roman Manhood*. Cambridge.

Yona, S. 2018. *Epicurean Ethics in Horace: The Psychology of Satire*. Oxford.

EST ENIM DIFFICILIS CVRARVM RERVM ALIENARVM

TERENCE AND HIS CONTEMPORARY *ADVLESCENTES*

JEANNE NEUMANN

A FEW YEARS AGO, I started worrying about teaching Terence—not to students immersed in the language and culture of the ancient world, but exoterically. The self-selecting students reading Terence in Latin are willing to engage imaginatively as well as linguistically with the foreignness and the familiarity of ancient texts. Students encountering Terence in a course in literature in translation are likely to take exception to plays that include—even revolve around—misogyny, rape, poorly behaved adults, proto-frat boys. Learning cultural context is unlikely to be—nor should it be—mollifying.

Contextualizing the plays is an important—but not the only—goal. For an audience that might be tempted to throw away the book and go search out the modern equivalent of the tightrope walkers or gladiators who allegedly ruined the production of the *Hecyra*,[1] Terence offers an opportunity for conversation—lively, heated, uncomfortable, yes, but conversation still—about some of the hard realities of being human.

Terence's skillful character delineation and other-oriented perspective[2] have left us plays that explore the dynamics of power and marginalization, of talking without listening, of competing desires and interests. The opening scenes spark that engagement, presenting us with the viewpoints of both powerful and marginalized characters,

---

I am grateful to Cynthia Damon, Ann Merrill, and John O'Neill for their insightful readings of this paper.

[1] Ter. *Hec.* 4–5, 33–36.

[2] Copeland 2011:54: "In other-oriented perspective taking, a person represents the other's situation from the other person's point of view and attempts to simulate the target individual's experiences as though she were the target individual."

all swirling around fairly basic problems: obtaining or maintaining some status in the community (even if that status means only safety) and negotiating one's own wants around those of others. An audience that wants trigger warnings, that has become increasingly balkanized in their lives and their tolerance for others, perhaps provides us with precisely the audience that might find much to ponder and discuss in Terence's plays, despite the barriers of time, language, and medium.

Ancient spectators, both the highly literate and the illiterate, would have come to Roman comedy with shared assumptions about what a comic play means; they would have been familiar with the culture and conventions of the comic stage. They would have enjoyed an aural appreciation for the metrical sophistication and variation integral to performance. Readers, not spectators, now generally constitute our audience. Each approaches the plays not as action played out on a stage, but as "a reader of texts who is a member of an audience only by projection and imagination."[3] Our disadvantages as readers, however, are also advantages. Niall Slater recalls watching a performance of the *Hecyra* in which an actor "stopped the production, broke out of the illusionistic frame, and explained how he and his cast did not really approve of the actions of Pamphilus, the play's central figure—but, he continued, that character and his actions were simply part of the conventions of Roman comedy and so had to be endured."[4] As readers, we can move at will between illusion and evaluation.

Yet the plays are inherently disturbing. The plots of three or four[5] of Terence's six plays revolve around the social destabilization created by rape. All six involve prostitutes and/or prostitutes-in-training and underscore the limited options of women without access to the stable resources provided by male protectors. Even women with male protection are badly treated. The fathers themselves seem to have little idea of what they are doing. By and large, the action rests on the backs of slaves and assumes the normalcy of human trafficking.

---

[3] Sharrock 2009:18 (on the ideal reader of *Reading Roman Comedy*).

[4] Slater 1999:2–3.

[5] James (2013:187) and Paraskeviotis (2013:45) count as rape the seduction of Glycerium/Pasibula in the *Andria*.

The *fabulae palliatae* do not offer us the mythological distance of epic or tragedy. The outrages in ancient tragedies sadden us, make us think, and thereby perhaps also give us a heightened perspective on our own world. We are aware that we are watching the suffering of others. No one is asking us to laugh. And the "others" in epic and tragedy are really others: mythological kings, queens, and heroes. Quite unlike the *adulescentes* of comedy who, much like some of our students, are "too old to be considered children but not yet fully adult either," young people with "an interval of leisure ... before settling down to the responsibilities of adulthood."[6] Of course, the young men in Terence do not have to work, and an increasing number of college students do—but the general principle remains the same. The young women in Terence are either prostitutes, or invisible, or rape victims, or some combination of the three. The first category may not apply to our students,[7] but our women students know well the feeling of being silenced and/ or invisible, and a disturbing number have experienced the trauma of rape.[8] As more than one student has pointedly asked me: "*Why* are we reading this?"

Part of my response to that question is "What in this is unfamiliar?" Terence's representation of his social culture—revealed through his perceptive evocation of very real fictional characters—invites us to ask: What of this is truly foreign? What happens in these texts that, *mutatis mutandis*, does not happen still? Are the intrigues for retention of, or access to, resources any less ubiquitous or charged now than then? It is true that action centers on the wills and wants of (free) men, to the detriment of women and slaves, men either with their own resources

---

[6] Rosivach 1998:5.

[7] V. Pynchon and C. Aiken, "Coeds or Call Girls? Sugar Daddies Pay Tuition," *Forbes*, February 11, 2013, https://www.forbes.com/sites/shenegotiates/2013/02/11/coeds-or-call-girls-sugar-daddies-pay-tuition/#3f3adecd2c97. The rise in number of college students who work as escorts to help pay for their education, if the website SeekingArrangement.com's claim is accurate, suggests that "This feature of a poverty culture is gaining ground on college campuses throughout America."

[8] Thakur (2004:156n9) cites the Clery Act, its context, and the website for aggregated information (http://ope.ed.gov/security).

(the *senes*)[9] or with (albeit limited) access to them (the *adulescentes*)—
but, in fact, such a state of affairs is not so foreign either.

A second touchstone for a possible response comes from Cicero's
non-ironic commentary on Terence's ironic *homo sum: humani nil a me
alienum puto.*[10]

> Quando igitur duobus generibus iniustitiae propositis
> adiunximus causas utriusque generis easque res ante
> constituimus, quibus iustitia contineretur, facile quod
> cuiusque temporis officium sit poterimus, nisi nosmet
> ipsos valde amabimus, iudicare. Est enim difficilis cura
> rerum alienarum. Quamquam Terentianus ille Chremes
> 'humani nihil a se alienum putat'; sed tamen, quia magis
> ea percipimus atque sentimus quae nobis ipsis aut pros-
> pera aut adversa eveniunt quam illa quae ceteris, quae
> quasi longo intervallo interiecto videmus, aliter de illis
> ac de nobis iudicamus. Quocirca bene praecipiunt, qui
> vetant quicquam agere, quod dubites aequum sit an
> iniquum. Aequitas lucet ipsa per sese, dubitatio cogita-
> tionem significat iniuriae.

Cicero Off. I.29–30

> Since we have set out the two kinds of types of injustice,
> and added the causes of each, and since we established
> previously what are the things that constitute justice,
> we shall now be able to judge with ease what is our duty
> on each occasion—that is, if we do not love ourselves too
> much. For it is difficult to be concerned about another's
> affairs. Terence's Chremes, however, thinks that 'nothing
> that is human is another's affair'; yet in fact we do tend to
> notice and feel our own good and bad fortune more than
> that of others, which we see as if a great distance inter-
> venes; accordingly, we do not make the same judgements

---

[9] Nausistrata (the *uxor dotata* of the *Phormio*) both is and is not an exception. While
the resources are hers, her husband is managing the profits.

[10] Ter. *Haut.* 77.

about them and about ourselves. It is good advice therefore that prevents you from doing anything if you are unsure whether it is fair or unfair. For fairness shines out by itself, and hesitation signifies that one is contemplating injustice.

Trans. Griffin and Atkins

What Chremes effectively says here is, "Hey, I'm a person! I think no aspect of being a person is beyond the scope of my interest." But Cicero knows that, in fact, it is very hard to truly care about other people's advantage. We are obviously far more attuned to and affected by (*percipimus atque sentimus*) our own advantages (*prospera*) and disadvantages (*adversa*) than those of others, which, as Cicero says so well, we see only as if in a far-off distance (*quasi longo intervallo interiecto videmus*). We make different judgments, therefore, for ourselves than for others (*aliter de illis ac de nobis iudicamus*). Cicero goes on to give a proto-Kantian gloss to the whole problem, one that bids us step outside of ourselves and weigh a judgment in its larger context: do not do anything if you are uncertain about its fairness. Cicero is writing about the way he thinks folks *ought* to behave, Terence about the way they, in fact, *do*. Cicero claims doing the right thing is easy, unless we are just too fond of ourselves—which we are, as are the characters in Terence's dramas. The exploration of and the tension between the *honestum* and the *utile* can never get enough attention. Nor can the ability of self-interest to affect our perceptions about, and judgments on, those around us.

Reading the plays of Terence presents our students with the opportunity to evaluate these persistent tensions, to step outside themselves and assume the perspective of the characters as an exercise in seeing the world from different points of view, where the stakes are low (these are, after all, characters in plays two millennia old) but the struggles are still relevant. Slater envisioned moving the audience across the intellectual fourth wall to adopt a "worldview and set of assumptions not their own—or not necessarily their own—for the duration of the performance."[11] I advocate an audience participation that tries to

---

[11] Slater 1999:20.

understand the perspectives and assumptions of all the characters—not to agree with them or excuse behavior they might find inexcusable but rather to exercise their literary imagination in relation to a genre that might seem foreign, offensive, objectionable, not funny, and either irrelevant or, disturbingly, all too relevant.

Student reaction to the *fabulae* can range from cautious silence to passionate vehemence. We can encourage discussion while still buffering intensity by looking at language and interpretation. Close reading of scenes in different translations (both diachronically and synchronically) reveals much about the attitudes of individual translators (and offers a useful opportunity to talk about the Latin). Even the Latin-less reader benefits from reading the semantic range of key words, an exercise which illuminates the slippage between the ancient and modern language[12]—and also usefully prods students to think about the range of interpretation of their own words.

Introducing the *auctoritas* of someone else's interpretation facilitates conversation and gives students a "safe" opinion to consider. Scholarly arguments become members of the discussion *in absentia*. Mooting a variety of perspectives and writing about the texts ahead of time makes for more thoughtful discussion.[13] Especially challenging is to invite students to take a perspective that diverges from their own, or to craft *dissoi logoi*.[14]

Each of Terence's plays open with a problem, presented by a character who asks us to take a position or listen to her or (mostly) his position. Each of the dramas revolves around an issue created or exacerbated by the behavior of an *adulescens*, wanting what he wants which means coming up against others—mostly fathers, but also *meretrices*—who also want what they want.

Three plays open with the plights of fathers who want to keep both their positions of authority and their sons' affections. When it comes to raising their sons, they seem rather ill-equipped for, as Zola Packman

---

[12] Packman 1993, and 1997.

[13] Course management systems allow students to post their own thoughts and questions—and read their classmates'—before class discussion.

[14] Such an assignment is admittedly tricky; no student should be required to take a potentially traumatizing position.

has put it, "the successful navigation of the Scylla and Charybdis risks of financial ruin and filial alienation."[15] The dichotomy between Micio and Demea's parenting styles in the *Adelphoe* still resonates with students. Menedemus's anguish over his son Clinia (*Heauton Timoroumenos*) is no more our business than it is Chremes's, but it allows us to ponder the struggles of raising children and helps us appreciate that, even in antiquity, there were people like Chremes who thought unsolicited advice part of their human birthright (*Haut.* 75–78). We do not know what the *Andria*'s Sosia thinks of Simo's deception, but his status as *libertus* compels compliance with Sosia's demands of loyalty and silent cooperation (34).[16] Menedemus has his new friend Chremes (whether he wants him or not), and the brothers Micio and Demea have each other, but there is no one to stand up to Simo. Fathers ask us to listen to the worries of being a parent and to appreciate, perhaps, that even those who seem authoritative and powerful are mostly making it up as they go along, like Simo, or gilding their choices with the language of an ethical magnanimity, like Micio, or beating themselves up for not getting it right, like Menedemus.

Characters who are emphatically not in charge pull us into the other three plays: an *adulescens* in love (Phaedria, *Eunuchus*), *meretrices* (Thais, *Eunuchus*; Syra and Philotis, *Hecyra*) and *servi* (Davos and Geta, *Phormio*). On stage, protactic characters such as the slaves Geta and Davos and the prostitutes Syra and Philotis might pass by as information dispensers. But as readers, we go more slowly and give these opening characters our attention. It is up to us to give them voices and interpretation. We carry their perspectives forward as the developing plot introduces us to the viewpoints and goals of other characters with different, conflicting desires. And they remind us to consider the "protactic" people in our own world, those we value for their utility and support of our own goals or those outside the periphery of our notice.

---

[15] Packman 2013:202; cf. James 2013:108.

[16] McCarthy (2004:106) calls *Andria*'s Sosia a "genuine *prosopon protatikon*" but also points to Terence's deeper characterization: "What's distinctive about this scene and surprising in the context of ancient comedy is its invocation of a slave's life cycle outside of the bare necessities of a recognition scene, the only other place where we are likely to see slaves who remember anything further back than the day before."

The *Phormio* asks us to take the perspective of slaves. The protactic Davos's brief soliloquy shows us the reality of a slave's poverty and dependence. Davos worries about what a young master's marriage will mean for his fellow-slave Geta's already meager finances: wedding gifts, baby gifts, birthday gifts, special occasion gifts (*Phorm.* 7–15). Wedding gifts are the least of Geta's problems. The well-meaning but essentially powerless babysitter for his (absent) masters' sons, he makes the *adulescentes* happy by indulging their sexual escapades—and himself vulnerable to their fathers' wrath when they return. The opening asks us to think about the perspective of good low-status men trying to make the best of the bad situations that lie out of their control.[17]

Two prostitutes, the aged Syra and the young, naïve Philotis, introduce the *Hecyra*. Staged, the theatrical pomp of their retinue and costumes might distract us from the nuances of their conversation but not when the play is read as a text. Syra's age and experience have given her a practical view of the precarious economics of being a working woman. She encourages Philotis to make as much money as she can while she can. Philotis is young, desirable, apparently successful, and also apparently enjoying life as a professional party girl.[18] Her youthful lack of understanding is as affecting as it is naïve. Syra gives us a suggestion of Philotis's future[19] and the men who, as Syra knows, want to satisfy their desires at the smallest possible financial cost, paying instead with sweet words (*Hec.* 67–70). And that too, from their perspective, is understandable—people who have resources

---

[17] McCarthy 2004:109 (on this scene and the beginning of the *Andria*): "Both scenes show very clearly how integrated slaves and ex-slaves are into the workings of the household ... including the emotional circuits and the links of trust and knowledge. But they also show that the undeniable belonging of slaves to the *familia* is a belonging that is structured by hierarchy and complementarity."

[18] Strong (2106:45) includes her with Bacchis as a one of "two virtuous prostitutes in the *Hecyra*." Gilula (1980:151) thinks the controversy would have appealed to the audience, despite her assertion that all *meretrices* would have been seen as *malae*: "We praise Philotis since we ourselves do not advocate indiscriminate treatment of people, but we also understand the bitterness of Syra, since we know that experience has moulded her views and she has good reason to be bitter."

[19] *Pace* Rosivach (1998:3): "New Comedy is fixed on the present, with little thought of the future or of the consequences of the present actions."

want to hold on to them.[20] Syra asks us to contemplate women without ties to the community who have a limited amount of time to parlay their natural resources into financial security.

Philotis's opening exclamation, *"Per pol quam paucos reperias meretricibus / fidelis evenire amatores, Syra!"* (My god, Syra, how few lovers turn out to be faithful to their *meretrices!*, *Hec.* 58–59), presents an illustrative opportunity to talk about translation and interpretation. Serena Witzke rightly points out the problems in translating words for sex workers.[21] James Adams's evaluation of *meretrix* as somewhat "neutral and unemotive in tone"[22] might offer some support for the inadequate "working girl." Students reading this play in translation are likely to see "mistresses,"[23] "girls like me,"[24] "lovers,"[25] or "women of my class."[26] Elsewhere in the text, we find "mistress"[27] for *meretrix* but also "prostitute,"[28] "tart,"[29] and woman of my "class,"[30] "sort,"[31] "station,"[32] or "profession,"[33] or some variation that obscures the word.[34] These interpretations reinforce that translation *is* interpretation, encourage

---

[20] And fathers in Terence do not want their sons depleting the family resources, even though we hear from the fathers themselves that they behaved the same way in their youth, e.g. *Haut.* 216–221, 574–577.

[21] Witzke 2015. Strong (2016:10) offers "whore" to refer to the broad category of women identified in Roman sources by that label "to capture the sense of condemnation and insult attached to all women labeled as a *meretrix*, regardless of their profession."

[22] Adams 1983:325.

[23] Barsby 2001b:153; Ireland 1990:30; Brown 2009:63.

[24] Radice 1965:295.

[25] Carrier 1992:361.

[26] Sargeaunt 1912b:133.

[27] Barsby 2001b:lines 539, 689, 716, 789; Ireland 1990:lines 539, 689, 716, 776, 789; Brown 2009:lines 539; Sargeaunt 1912b:lines 539, 689; Radice 1965:lines 539; Carrier 1992:lines 539, 689.

[28] Brown 2009:lines 539, 776, 789, 834.

[29] Brown 2009:line 716.

[30] Sargeaunt 1912b:lines 58, 776, 843; Carrier 1992:line 834.

[31] Barsby 2001b:line 834; Ireland 1990:line 834; Radice 1965:line 834.

[32] Carrier 1992:line 776.

[33] Barsby 2001b:line 776; Ireland 1990:line 776; Radice 1965:line 776.

[34] Ireland (1990:line 716), Radice (1965:lines 689, 716) and Carrier (1992:line 716) have some version of "this/that/the woman." Sargeaunt (1912:line 789): "In the circumstances, we are natural enemies"; Carrier (1992:line 789): "We have a certain natural enmity."

students to consider the cultural ramifications of language, and ask them to confront *meretrix* in a more nuanced way.

The *Eunuchus* is the only play that begins with the *adulescens*, and at first it seems to offer us pure comedy: a young man in love and tormented by a woman who is toying with him. From Phaedria's first words, we expect to encounter the bad behavior characteristic of *meretrices* (*Eun.* 147–148). Right after we hear Phaedria's miserable complaints about his as-yet-unnamed lover, we meet the villainess. Yet Thais is not only a decent person,[35] but she also faces much more serious challenges than her hapless lover. As Thais tells Phaedria: "I'm alone; I have no one here, neither friend nor relative" (*Eun.* 147–148). All she wants is a few days to settle her free-born but currently enslaved foster sister Pamphila with her rightful family, thus creating for herself a protective bond of friendship in the community.[36]

But Phaedria sees the situation only from his standpoint (*Eun.* 152–153). From the beginning, the play asks us to evaluate the conflict between Phaedria's focus on his desire to possess Thais and her goal to secure her future social stability. By the end of the scene, Phaedria's generalizing about the bad behavior of *meretrices* appears for what it is: blanket condemnation of a whole group of women. Yet the family slave, Parmeno, knows Phaedria as a nice guy: "No one was less of an idiot, no one more serious or with more self-control."[37] He is not a jerk, then, but a decent person who is willing to believe that Thais is behaving as she behaves because she is a *meretrix* and all *meretrices* are, by definition, untrustworthy and bad.[38]

---

[35] Zeitlin 2005; *pace* Gilula 1980:162–163.

[36] Dutsch (2019:215): "This … insight, that prostitutes do not exist in a void, also informs Terence's *Andria*, *Eunuchus*, and *Hecyra*, which present *meretrices* as women who desperately want to be integrated into their respective communities."

[37] *Eun.* 226–227: *Hoc nemo fuit / minus ineptus, magis severus quisquam nec magis continens.*

[38] The *adulescens* Phaedria's assumptions about *meretrices* are shared by Chaerea (*Eun.* 382–387) and later the *servus* Parmeno (*Eun.* 929–940). That attitude expands its compass in the *Hecyra*, where the husbands (*senes*) assume the worst of their wives. Chremes believes Sostrata behaves as she does just because she is a woman, claiming that all women are part of a *coniuratio*, a conspiracy so universal that nary a female can be found whose character differs a jot from the rest (*Hec.* 198–204).

The opening scenes of the plays ask us to engage with a range of personalities, all struggling. Terence presents his world as problem-riddled and then only partially solves the problems. Yes, threatened hierarchies are safely reestablished, unruly young men more or less learn to grow up, and some young women get husbands from good families (although one wonders how they might have felt about that). Beleaguered wives keep their husbands. Some independent working women get ties of friendship with families of means. For the nameless music girls of *Phormio* and *Adelphoe*, however, there is no resolution.[39] Slaves are still powerless and unfree. Women at all levels of the society within the drama are, at the very least, trivialized and demeaned. Terence invites us to keep shifting perspectives, to keep asking questions.[40]

Perhaps most challenging to confront in Terence's plays is rape. Long before the #MeToo movement, we were teaching on campuses rife with sexual assaults—reported and unreported. Rape in ancient literature is, too, often minimized with variations on "different time, different culture,"[41] a justification that is both true and ... not. Alan Sommerstein observes, "Rape may have been, officially, a crime ... but the ability to perpetrate it was what made a man a real man."[42] One can easily find contemporary corroboration of this attitude.[43] Justifying the rape plot as cultural and dramatic necessity leads to the

---

[39] The character list at *Adelphoe* Act 2 generically names the *psaltria* Bacchis.

[40] To give two of many examples, whose version of Pamphilus and Bacchis's affair (*Hecyra*) do we believe? What was the relationship between Chremes and the woman on Lemnos (*Phormio*)?

[41] E.g., Fantham 1975:93: "Strange intrigues, these, for a comedy, but such tortuous, and in some ways, shocking, plots were necessitated by the romantic idea of a life sealed by marriage, in a society which all but excluded the combination of the two elements in everyday circumstances."

[42] Sommerstein 1998:109; James 1998:33: Young men who rape "show themselves prepared for the institution of Roman marriage."

[43] E. J. Carroll ("Corroborating E. Jean Carroll," interviewed by Meghan Twohey, *New York Times*, June 21, 2019) explains her silence during the 2016 elections about her allegation of rape against a presidential candidate: "Shocking as it sounds, I thought it would help him. And shocking as it sounds, I was correct ... Because it is a masculine, powerful, leader-like thing to do to take what you want, to have as many women for your own pleasure as you can take." See also Zuckerberg 2018.

inevitable—and equally justified—retort, "Right, and this is why we shouldn't read these texts."

The continued relevance—indeed, urgency—of grappling with themes of sexual violence is an excellent reason why we *should* read these texts, but we must also honor the request for trigger warnings from people who are suffering from posttraumatic stress—the violence in ancient literature is quite similar to the violence in their own lives.[44] We read in order to productively confront that violence, not to recapitulate or reenact it. We need to acknowledge the difficulty of (discussing) what we are reading while pushing past the impulse to capitulate to the desire of an unspeakable subject to not be spoken about.

We might choose to look at bad behavior as just bad behavior and allow these plays to enter into the conversation about what motivates people and how those around them interpret their words and actions. The challenge here for instructors is not, frankly, to make these characters resonate with contemporary readers but rather to talk about them neutrally—and to help students listen and talk to each other. The collection edited by Fiona McHardy and Nancy Sorkin Rabinowitz, especially the contributions of Sharon L James and Sanjaya Thakur,[45] provide starting points among the growing resources for classicists to address difficult topics, including rape, in the classroom.[46] Both offer wise examples of what one might say in class. Madeline Kahn's approach to teaching Ovid offers a mantra: "I was determined not to be baited by [the student], but to treat her every challenge as a legitimate intellectual inquiry."[47] Holding fast to a commitment to allow students to react to the plays entails not explaining away the discomfort or shutting down the conversation with our own ideological gloss.[48]

---

[44] See notes 45 and 46 below.

[45] McHardy and Rabinowitz 2014. While the value of trigger warnings remains disputed, James and Thakur strike a delicate balance of intellectual honesty and empathy.

[46] Thakur's (2014:170) exhortations are spot on: "We must begin by stating explicitly that it is not only acceptable for men to talk about these subjects, but that it should be standard practice for any teacher."

[47] Kahn 2004:446.

[48] T. Bien-Aime ("Prostitution as Financial Aid: Three College Students Speak Out," Huffington Post, April 5, 2017) cites a student's reaction to feeling ideologically pushed: "Professors ram down our throats the idea that 'sex work,' which is what they call

The *Eunuchus* is the only ancient comedy where the sexual attack occurs during the play. Abetted by the family slave Parmeno, Phaedria's younger brother Chaerea disguises himself as the eunuch that Phaedria had bought for his lover, Thais, so that he can gain access to Pamphila, Thais's free-born but currently enslaved foster sister, a gift to Thais from Phaedria's rival. Entrusted with the girl, he rapes her and escapes. He is eventually revealed as Pamphila's rapist, and she is revealed as free, allowing Chaerea to marry her.

Chaerea demands Parmeno get the girl by whatever means necessary (*Eun.* 319–320). As Thais's property, the girl should be off-limits. But Thais is a *meretrix* and does not count. Although we have already met this particular *meretrix* and understand some of the realities of both her character and her situation, Chaerea frames his behavior as a kind of vigilante justice against a whole class of women. If he behaved badly toward his father, everyone would blame him. But if he behaves badly toward Thais and *her* lot, everyone will agree that she had it coming (*Eun.* 382–87).

Chaerea's regard for women only as extensions of his own desires, is not, unfortunately, unfamiliar. I personally find him deeply repellent. Not everyone shares my opinion. I am grateful, therefore, to those who have read the play differently, whose arguments broaden the range of voices. They help me balance my own presentation in the interests of fostering dialogue. Packman, for example, cites H. J. Rose's judgment that the "perpetrator 'makes the most of his opportunities.'"[49] Readings that frame rape as an "opportunity" transcend the years since Rose wrote. James has argued that both Chaerea here and Pamphilus in the *Hecyra* "show a fully developed sense of masculine sexual privilege for Roman citizen men: they commit violent rape and abuse against the young women they claim to love, but feel pangs of guilt toward neither beloved nor father."[50]

---

prostitution, is empowering. Dissenting in the classroom is hard, particularly if a student has never thought about the issue. Even if there's a sense that something is amiss in the professor's reasoning, we don't always have the language, or the courage, to speak up."

[49] Packman 1993:47.

[50] James 2013:183; cf. James 1998b; Smith (1994) summarizes scholarly reactions to Chaerea.

After raping Pamphila, an exultant Chaerea appears on stage and brags about his prowess to his friend Antipho (*Eun.* 604–606). Is Antipho's blasé response to Chaerea ("Oh my god, you are totally right—but meanwhile, dinner? What's the deal with that?"[51]) a corrective?[52] Or, rather, does Antipho see the rape as "a trivial incident that has just delayed plans for dinner"?[53]

When Chaerea realizes he must face Thais, his reaction underscores his greater power: "What do I care? What will she do to me?" (*Eun.* 849).[54] How should we read his claim that he acted *amoris causa* (*Eun.* 878) and her reply, *neque ita inperita ut quid amor valeat nesciam* (*Eun.* 881). Lexica can be helpful here: the *Oxford Latin Dictionary* lists "sexual passion, love" first; but "love" needs much unpacking in any language. Translating *quid amor valeat* as "the power of love" points to that meaning,[55] but how do our students read "for love"[56] or because he was "in love,"[57] or even "for love of her" as a translation of *amoris causa*?[58]

Should we agree with scholars who accuse Thais of self-interest for her continued focus on a reliable relationship with an established citizen family (*Eun.* 871)?[59] Is self-interest in pursuit of security the same as that in the pursuit of pleasure? Is selfless altruism, like Caesar's *clementia*, a gift of those who are in a position to wield it? Thais accepts her powerlessness and moves on as best she can.[60]

---

[51] *Eun.* 607: *Sane hercle ut dicis. sed interim de symbolis. quid actumst?*

[52] Slater 1999:12: "Antipho does not point out that his friend is a rapist; but neither does he join in Chaerea's self-congratulatory posturing."

[53] Rosivach 1998:47; Norwood 1965:63; James 1998:39; for Gilula (2007:213) dissonance of words (rape) and costume (eunuch) combine for a "comical image."

[54] *Eun.* 849: *quid faciam? quid mea autem? quid faciet mihi?*

[55] Barsby 2012:417; Sargeaunt 1912a:326; Radice 1965:207.

[56] Barsby 2012:417; Sargeaunt 1912a:326; Parker 1992:210.

[57] Brown 2009:192; Brothers 2000:135 "because I love the girl."

[58] Radice 1965:207.

[59] Brothers 2000:32; Rosivach 1998:48. Gilula (1980:161–164) sees Thais as a *mala meretrix* because her primary goal is security. Goldberg 1986:118: "She is not entirely *mala*, but she is certainly a *meretrix*."

[60] Goldberg 1986:121; Smith (1994:29) points to her diminished autonomy by play's end.

The uncertainties continue. Pythias tells us that, after Chaerea raped Pamphila, he violently attacked her, tearing her dress and tearing her hair (*Eun.* 645–646). John Barsby notes that *if* this were true, it would be a "gratuitous act of violence," but Pythias's words are a "deliberate exaggeration" and should be heard in the context of her earlier suspicion that the Eunuch probably stole something as he ran away.[61] Is Pythias, talking to herself on stage, lying?[62] David Christensen, in contrast, suggests, "Since rape in New Comedy usually belongs to the play's prehistory, Terence's focus on the victim's trauma in the moment is striking."[63]

Barsby also suggests that it might "be relevant that the tearing of the girl's dress and hair is a standard feature of lover's quarrels in Latin love poetry."[64] That may be, and it is even possible that people in both the ancient and the modern audience would take that view. But it might also evoke a response questioning the nature of the "love" in Latin love poetry as well as in comedy[65]—both in ancient texts and in contemporary discourses, such as modern music. It might, as well, evoke a response to the kind of *adulescens* we wish did not roam our campuses, but does. Terence's depiction of Chaerea throws this kind of behavior into high relief.[66]

Chaerea's legal accountability is not clear.[67] But then, neither is the legal accountability of contemporary rapists (albeit for different

---

[61] Barsby 2012:209.

[62] Brothers (2000:190) points out that as Thais confirms that Pamphila's clothes are torn, and no one contradicts Pythia's assertions, "We have to accept Chaerea's actions, with all their unpleasant implications, as they stand." Since Pamphila remains mute to Pythias's repeated questions, we can, however, wonder why she is sure the violence continued *after* the rape.

[63] Christensen 2013:267; cf. Rosivach 1998:49 (also cited by Christensen): "[Terence] has created [Pythias] to make a point, from the victim's perspective rape is a terrible thing."

[64] Barsby 2012:209.

[65] James 2016:105.

[66] Christensen 2013:266: "Terence, through the unprecedented emphasis on the immediacy of Pamphila's rape, is provoking audience members, both male and female, to look at it from a fundamentally humane point of view."

[67] Harris 2006:303: "One cannot claim that drunkenness, youth, and passion were regarded as legitimate excuses in Athenian Law and society"; Scafuro 1997:218: "Judicious

reasons).[68] What about his moral accountability? According to Adele Scafuro, Chaerea's *contumelia* has "betrayed his own *dignitas*" as well as hers (865–866).[69] Packman and others have pointed nicely to the conundrum: if you acknowledge the rape, you have to condemn the rapist; if you want to like the young rapist, you have to downplay the rape.[70] You can, like David Konstan, call him "an engaging scamp."[71] You can reframe it as Donatus, and later Katerina Philippides, by pointing out elements of the marriage ritual woven into the play.[72] You can, as Victor Rosivach does, separate your own reaction from your assessment of what the play suggests.[73] It is clear, however, that "Terence has gone out of his way to foreground Pamphila's trauma to his audience."[74] The various characters' reactions (as well as the motivations behind those reactions) demand close reading, reasoning, and analysis. We do not, however, have to "solve" anything—nor are we likely to. But we may aim at doing better than Terence's characters in really listening and talking to, not at, each other.

It might seem that the plays do not care about their marginalized characters. But I do not think their perspective is quite as chilly—or chilling—as it might seem. That we know virtually nothing of Terence himself is a bonus: the ambiguity of Terence's social status, for example, presents "an opportunity to play out various scenarios about literature and status, which might in turn help to conceive new ways of thinking about this complex issue."[75] James argues that "Terence performs a skeptical autopsy of the Roman citizen family, beginning with its power

---

assessment of evidence suggests, then, that there were no laws that specifically concerned sexual offenses of or against women before the first century BC [in Rome]."

[68] See, for example, R. L. Dotsie, "She Didn't Act Like a Rape Victim," *New York Times*, July 21, 2019, https://www.nytimes.com/2019/07/22/opinion/armed-forces-rape.html.

[69] Scafuro 1997:226–228.

[70] Packman 1993:48.

[71] Konstan 1986:387.

[72] Philippides 1995.

[73] Rosivach 1998:169n133.

[74] Christensen 2013:267.

[75] McCarthy (2004:108) points to the ambiguity that arises from juxtaposing the opening scenes of *Andria* and *Phormio*: "The combination of the two confounds any simple alignment of Terence's viewpoint with or against the justification of the way masters make use of slaves' lives, skills and resources." See further p. 115.

center, the *paterfamilias*, who is repeatedly unjust, even cruel, to his wife, peremptory with his daughter, and often callous toward his children, particularly his son."[76] I would modify just one word of this astute statement: I am not convinced the autopsy is as much *skeptical* as it is *analytical*. The chances that Terence was criticizing the Roman status quo seem possible but rather unlikely to me. He seems rather to appreciate that each character had a story, a perspective, and a humanity worth listening to—even if the stories were marginal to the play or its milieu. In this way, Terence reminds me of Erasmus, and it is little surprise that Terence was one of Erasmus's favorite authors.[77] This empathetic perspective-taking[78] within a broad frame of hard-eyed realism brings us a framework for looking not only at Terence's world but also our own because the problems of Terence's plays are not just part of ancient culture but part of our culture as well.

The plays offer insight into why characters behave as they do, their motivations, goals, blind spots, and flawed humanity. We may not agree with the way the characters think—in fact, in many cases we are fairly likely not to—but we often get to listen to them tell us the "why" behind their behaviors. Knowing that Chaerea feels entitled to rape a woman *because* he thinks she is a slave and *because* she belongs to a *meretrix* will not redeem his character for many readers, but it is the kind of rationale for sexual violence that—again, make a few changes to allow for social context—still persists. The silence and silencing of the victims of sexual violence persist too, despite the recent catharsis of #MeToo. In a piece on sexual harassment, John Oliver explored the extent to which we have been here before.[79] Periodically we revisit the problems of sexual violence, emotional and physical, and systemic misogyny. We will no doubt be here again. Maybe now, at a time when no one wants to listen to each other, it is particularly helpful to engage

[76] James 2013:177.

[77] Grant 2017:10, 70. Terence ranks third (over 250 citations, 103 in the *Adagia* alone), after Plautus and Horace.

[78] Copeland 2011:43. "Empathy has three essential features: affective matching, other-oriented perspective taking, and clear self–other differentiation." Cf. Cuff et al. 2016:150.

[79] Oliver 2018.

imaginatively with scenes from a world both very different and yet somehow not so different from our own.

DAVIDSON COLLEGE

WORKS CITED

Adams, J. N. 1983. "Words for 'Prositute' in Latin." *Rheinisches Museum für Philologie*, n.s. 126:321–58.

Augoustakis, A., A. E. Traill, and J. E. Thornburn, eds. 2013. *A Companion to Terence*. Oxford.

Barsby, J. 2001a. *Terence. The Woman of Andros, The Self-Tormentor, The Eunuch*. Cambridge, MA.

———. 2001b. *Terence. Phormio, The Mother-In-Law, The Brothers*. Cambridge, MA.

———. 2012. *Terence. Eunuchus*. New York.

Brothers, A. J. 2000. *Terence. The Eunuch*. Warminster.

Brown, Peter. 2009. *Terence. The Comedies*. Oxford.

Butcher, S. H. 1902. *The Poetics of Aristotle*. New York.

Carrier, C. 1992. "Her Husband's Mother (*Hecyra*)." In *Terence. The Comedies*, ed. Palmer Bovie, 353–398. Baltimore.

Christensen, D. M. 2013. "*Eunuchus*." In Augoustakis, Traill, and Thornburn 2013, 262–280.

Copland, A. 2011. "Will the Real Empathy Please Stand Up? A Case for a Narrow Conceptualization." *Southern Journal of Philosophy* 49:40–65.

Cuff, B. M. P., S. J. Brown, L. Taylor, and D. J. Howat. 2016. "Empathy: A Review of the Concept." *Emotion Review* 8 (2):144–153.

Dinter, M. T., ed. 2019. *The Cambridge Companion to Roman Comedy*. Cambridge.

Dutsch, D. 2019. "Mothers and Whores." In Dinter 2019, 200–216.

Dutsch, D., S. L. James, and D. Konstan. 2015. *Women in Roman Comedy*. Madison.

Fantham, E. 1975. "Sex, Status, and Survival in Hellenistic Athens: A Study of Women in New Comedy." *Phoenix* 23:44–74.

Gilula, D. 1980. "The Concept of the *Bona Meretrix*: A Study of Terence's Courtesans." *RFIC* 108:142–165.

———. 2007. "Stage Business and Narrative: Plot Construction in Terence." In *Terentius Poeta*, ed. Peter Kruschwitz, Widu-Wolfgang Ehlers, and Fritz Felgentren, 207–216. Munich.

Goldberg, S. M. 1986. *Understanding Terence*. Princeton.

Grant, J. N. 2017. "Erasmus' Adages." In *Prolegomena to the Adages: Adagiorum Collectanea, Indexes to Erasmus' Adages*, ed. William Barker, trans. John Grant, 1–84. Toronto.

Griffin, M. T., and E. M. Atkins. 1991. *Cicero. On Duties*. Cambridge.

Harris, E. M. 2006. "Did Rape Exist in Classical Athens? Further Reflections on the Laws about Sexual Violence." In *Democracy and the Rule of Law in Classical Athens: Essays on Law, Society, and Politics*, 297–332. Cambridge.

Ireland, S. 1990. *Terence. The Mother-in-Law*. Warminster.

James, S. L. 1998. "From Boys to Men: Rape and Developing Masculinity in Terence's Hecyra and Eunuchus." *Helios* 25 (1):31–47.

———. 2008. "Feminist Pedagogy and Teaching Latin Literature." *Cloelia* 38:11–14.

———. 2013. "Gender and Sexuality in Terence." In Augoustakis, Traill, and Thornburn 2013, 175–194.

———. 2014. "Talking Rape in the Classics Classroom: Further Thoughts." In McHardy and Rabinowitz 2014, 171–186.

———. 2016. "*Fallite Fallentes*: Rape and Intertextuality in Terence's *Eunuchus* and Ovid's *Ars Amatoria*." *Eugesta: Revue sur le genre dans l'Antiquité* 6:87–111.

Kahn, M. 2004. "'Why Are We Reading a Handbook on Rape?' Young Women Transform a Classic." *Pedagogy* 4:438–459.

Knaur, R., and W. M. Lindsay. 1963. *P. Terenti Afri. Comoediae*. Oxford.

Konstan, D. 1986. "Love in Terence's Eunuch: The Origins of Erotic Subjectivity." *AJP* 107:369–393.

McCarthy, K. 2004. "The Joker in the Pack: Slaves in Terence." *Ramus* 33:100–119.

McHardy, F., and N. S. Rabinowitz, eds. 2014. *From Abortion to Pederasty: Addressing Difficult Topics in the Classics Classroom*. Columbus.

McHardy, F., and S. Deacy. 2015. "How to Teach Sensitive Subjects in the Classics Classroom." *Cloelia*, n.s. 5:1–6.

Norwood, G. 1965. *The Art of Terence.* New York.

Oliver, J. 2018. "Workplace Sexual Harassment." *Last Week Tonight*, July 29, 2018.

Packman, Z. M. 1993. "Call it Rape: A Motif in Roman Comedy and its Suppression in English-Speaking Publications." *Helios* 20:42–45.

Packman, Z. M. 1997. "*Adulescens* as *Virgo*: A Note on Terence's *Eunuch* 908." *Akroterion* 42:30–35.

———. 2013. "Family and Household in the Comedies of Terence." In Augoustakis, Traill, and Thornburn 2013, 195–210.

Paraskeviotis, G. C. 2013. "Place and Time in the Rape Scenes of Terence's Comedies." *Acta Antiqua Academiae Scientiarum Hungaricae* 53:49–59.

Parker, D. 1992. "The Eunuch (*Eunouchus*)." In *Terence. The Comedies*, ed. Palmer Bovie, 145–225. Baltimore.

Philippides, K. 1995. "Terence's *Eunuchus*: Elements of the Marriage Ritual in the Rape Scene." *Mnemosyne* 48:227–284.

Radice, Betty. 1965. *Terence. The Comedies.* Middlesex.

Rosivach, V. 1998. *When a Young Man Falls in Love: The Sexual Exploitation of Women in New Comedy.* London.

Sargeaunt, J. 1912a. *Terence. The Lady of Andros, The Self-Tormentor, The Eunuch.* London.

———. 1912b. *Terence. Phormio, The Mother-in-Law, The Brothers.* London.

Scafuro, A. 1997. *The Forensic Stage.* Cambridge.

Sharrock, A. 2009. *Reading Roman Comedy: Poetics and Playfulness in Plautus and Terence.* Cambridge.

Slater, N. W. 1999. "*Humani nil a me alienum puto*: The Ethics of Terentian Performance." *Syllecta Classica* 10:1–21.

Smith, L. P. 1994. "Audience Response to Rape: Chaerea in Terence's *Eunuchus*." *Helios* 21:21–38.

Sommerstein, A. H. 1998. "Rape and Young Manhood in Athenian Comedy." In *Thinking Men: Masculinity and its Self-Representation in the Classical Tradition*, ed. Lin Foxhall and John Salmon, 100–114. New York.

Strong, A. K. 2016. *Prostitutes and Matrons in the Roman World.* Cambridge.

Thakur, S. 2014. "Challenges in Teaching Sexual Violence and Rape: A Male Perspective." In McHardy and Rabinowitz 2014,152–170.

Winterbottom, M. 1994. *M. Tulli Ciceronis. De Officiis.* New York.

Witzke, S. S. 2015. "Harlots, Tarts, and Hussies? A Problem of Terminology for Sex Labor in Roman Comedy." *Helios* 42:7–27.

Zeitlin, A. 2005. "Plutarch, Menander, and Terence." In *Defining Genre and Gender in Latin Literature: Essays Presented to William S. Anderson on his Seventy-Fifth Birthday*, ed. William W. Batstone and Garth Tissol, 47–59. New York.

Zuckerberg, D. 2018. *Not All Dead White Men: Classics and Misogyny in the Digital Age.* Cambridge, MA.

PAVCA MEO STELLAE

LIFE CHOICE AND GENRE IN STATIUS *SILVAE* 1.2

Gianpiero Rosati

I. THE MARRIAGE OF AN ELEGIAC POET

STATIUS *SILVAE* 1.2 IS AN EPITHALAMIUM addressed to his friend Arruntius Stella, a fellow elegiac poet, in celebration of his marriage to Violentilla.[1] Neither the "dialogue" between the two poet-friends nor the epithalamium Statius composes for Stella's marriage have received the attention they deserve in scholarly literature, a gap which I seek to fill with this paper.

Several years ago, I proposed to read this text as a sort of allegory, a metapoetic discourse between Statius and his friend, the elegist Stella, on the history of Latin erotic elegy and its final trajectory.[2] Arruntius Stella was an elegiac poet,[3] but also an influential politician in Rome (a fact that belies the cliché of the elegist who rejects political life and its values). Statius's epithalamium commemorates his marriage to Violentilla, who is lauded with the Greek pseudonym *Asteris* in the manner of the Latin elegists. She is also referred to repeatedly as his *domina*, a Roman elegiac tag that occurs more than once (*Silv.* 1.2.23, 77, 211). As we know, marriage for an elegiac poet is a prospect outside the bounds of his *nequitia*; and yet Stella embraces the idea of the nuptials (and with a well-to-do woman, which contradicts yet another cliché,

---

[1] On Stella's prosopography, see Citroni 1975:40–43; Nauta 2002:58, 211–212.

[2] Rosati 1999.

[3] According to Martial 1.7, Stella published a poem titled *Columba*, evidently for the death of Violentilla's pet, which he does not hesitate to declare superior to Catullus's famous poem on Lesbia's *passer*. According to Nauta (2002:58, 156–157n40), this was not a single poem (as Citroni [1975] and others think) but "a collection of love-elegies."

that of the poor poet-lover). Thus, Stella legitimizes the formerly improper romantic relationship (verses 28–29) and brings a halt to his typically elegiac lifestyle (described in verses 26–37 and 195–199). In other words, with his decision to marry, Stella renounces the socially rebellious ideology underpinning elegiac poetry and adopts the traditional value system of Roman society. *Silv.* 1.2 is, in short, a discourse on the history of the elegy in Latin literature. The period of defiant, extremist elegy, as defined by Propertius and Tibullus, has by now ended; the time has come for a "return to order," a reconciliation with the Roman cultural and political establishment. What Statius presents, then, is an oxymoron: an epithalamium for an elegist and in hexameters, no less.

With this scenario in mind, I would like to take a look now at the literary models that are implicated in Statius's metapoetic discourse. Leaving aside for the purposes of this discussion his other major model, Ovid,[4] I linger on Statius's relationship with Vergil. Speaking as a poet to a friend who is also a poet, Statius closely replicates the model of what we might call the "dialogue on poetry and life between two poet-friends" that Vergil, in the tenth *Eclogue*, addresses to the elegiac poet Cornelius Gallus. Like Stella, Gallus was an eminent Roman politician as well as a love poet: he was in charge of administrative and military appointments along with Augustus, and he was the future prefect of Egypt. This famous text, the best-known case in Latin literature of a poet addressing a friend and fellow bard suffering because of unfulfilled love, taught us that when a poet addresses a work to another poet, we should expect it to contain some musings and a debate on the two colleagues' literary predilections. In Vergil's eclogue the bucolic poet invites his friend Cornelius Gallus—the founder of erotic elegy in Rome—to renounce a life tainted by the torments of unrequited passion, as well as the elegiac poetry that reflects this unhappy lifestyle. Instead, he should find refuge in a tranquil, pastoral world and in its associated literary genre, bucolic poetry.[5] That is, the debate

---

[4]   Rosati, forthcoming a.
[5]   I am thinking, of course, of the reading of this eclogue proposed by Conte (1986: 100–129). Cf. also Harrison 2007:34–74.

between the two poet-friends concerns not only their lifestyle but also the literary genre that reflects it and which they practice.[6]

Similarly, in *Silv.* 1.2 we have a poet, Statius, addressing his friend Stella, an elegiac poet and influential politician who is involved in an intense and agonizing love affair. In this epithalamium, Statius celebrates his friend's passage to a serene and satisfying lifestyle by means of this marriage, as well as his breaking out from the literary genre, elegy, which had been the expression of his tormented love. Statius's poem demands to be read against the background of Vergil's eclogue, and from this point of reference it draws much of its meaning.

The past suffering of the poet-lover Stella entails anguish and fear (*cedant curaeque metusque* [let cares and fears be gone], 26),[7] physical obstacles and social disapproval (*iam nusquam ianitor aut lex / aut pudor* [no more door-keeper, rule, or inhibition], 35–36), sleepless nights (*duras ... noctes*, 37) and frustrated desires (*pone o dulcis suspiria vates* [sigh no more, sweet poet], 33): Statius depicts—or rather, I would say, mimics—the typical lifestyle of elegy, with its pains and laments. Thanks to a persuasive plea from her son Cupid (65–102), Venus relents from her elegiac inexorability and shows herself unusually merciful to the poet-lover. She intervenes to bend the will of the *domina* Violentilla/*Asteris*, inducing her to acquiesce to Stella's entreaties:

> His mulcet dictis tacitaeque inspirat honorem
> conubii. Redeunt animo iam dona precesque
> et lacrimae vigilesque viri prope limina questus,
> Asteris et vatis totam cantata per urbem,
> Asteris ante dapes, nocte Asteris, Asteris ortu,
> quantum non clamatus Hylas. Iamque aspera coepit
> flectere corda libens et iam sibi dura videri.

Statius *Silv.* 1.2.194–200

---

[6] One of the earliest texts to take *Ecl.* 10 as a model for reflection on poetry and life is Ovid's *Epistula Sapphus*. In a forthcoming piece, I argue that the author of the *Lydia*, an anonymous poem included in the *Appendix Vergiliana*, is aware of the Ovidian parallel between Gallus and Sappho: Rosati, forthcoming b.

[7] Both text and translations (slightly modified) of Statius's poem are by Shackleton Bailey 2003.

With these words she beguiles the silent girl, inspiring love of wedlock. Now his gifts and prayers and wakeful plaints at the doorway return to her mind, and the poet's Asteris was sung through all the city—Asteris before dinner, Asteris by night, Asteris at dawn; never was Hylas so clamoured. Now she began to bend her stern heart, not loath, now to deem herself too hard.

Gifts, pleas, tears and *paraklausithyron* vigils—the entire repertoire of the elegiac poet-lover that Stella himself used to employ is evoked here, as well as his repeated but vain petitions to his beloved. His tribulations closely resemble those of Vergil's Gallus, the object of all of nature's pity:

> Illum etiam lauri, etiam flevere myricae,
> pinifer illum etiam sola sub rupe iacentem
> Maenalus et gelidi fleverunt saxa Lycaei
>
> Vergil *Ecl.* 10.13–15

> Even the laurels, even the tamarisks wept for him,
> even pine-clad Maenalus, and the rocks of cold Lycaeus
> wept as he lay beneath a lonely cliff.

But they also recall the elegiac lament of another of Vergil's great lovers, the poet-prophet Orpheus, at the loss of Eurydice:

> Ipse cava solans aegrum testudine amorem
> te, dulcis coniunx, te solo in litore secum,
> te veniente die, te decedente canebat.
>
> Vergil *Georg.* 4.464–466

> Orpheus, consoling love's anguish, with his hollow lyre,
> sang of you, sweet wife, you, alone on the empty shore,
> of you as day neared, of you as day departed.

In Stella's case, however, the elegiac life that had been a source of suffering has now finally been eclipsed: *Asteris*/Violentilla's capitulation to Stella's courtship leads to marriage and the acceptance of an alternative sort of eros that is no longer anticonformist and rebellious but institutional and civic. It is a mutual eros, appropriate for a peaceful and harmonious society under Domitian.

To convince Violentilla, who is reluctant to accept Stella's courtship, Venus employs a *suasoria* that hinges on three arguments:

> "Ergo age, iunge toros atque otia deme iuventae.
> Quas ego non gentes, quae non face corda iugali
> * * * * * * * * * ?
> Alituum pecudumque mihi durique ferarum
> non renuere greges; ipsum in conubia terrae
> aethera, cum pluviis rarescunt nubila, solvo.
> Sic rerum series mundique revertitur aetas.
> Vnde novum Troiae decus ardentumque deorum
> raptorem, Phrygio si non ego iuncta marito?
> Lydius unde meos iterasset Thybris Iulos?
> quis septemgeminae posuisset moenia Romae
> imperii Latiale caput, <ni> Dardana furto
> cepisset Martem, nec me prohibente, sacerdos?"

Statius Silv. 1.2.182–193

"Up then, join beds and away with youth's idleness! What races, what hearts has my nuptial torch ...? Neither birds nor cattle nor savage packs of wild beasts have said me nay. I melt the very heaven into marriage with earth when rains thin the clouds. So one thing succeeds another and the world's youth returns. Whence would have come Troy's new glory and the rescue of burning gods if I had not mated with a Phrygian spouse? Whence would Lydian Tiber have renewed my Iuli? Who could have founded the walls of sevenfold Rome, Latian imperial capital, if the Dardan princess had not taken Mars in secret dalliance— nor did I forbid."

Statius had already alluded to Lucretius earlier in the poem (line 11, *genetrix Aeneia* recalls Lucretius's *Aeneadum genetrix*). Now, Venus makes an appeal, in markedly Lucretian language (184–187),[8] to the law of nature, which regenerates itself through the universal energy of eros. Her second argument recalls the "Vergilian" history of Rome, whose founder, Aeneas, was born of Venus's own marriage to Anchises (188–190). The third focuses on the union between Rhea Silvia and Mars narrated in Ennius's patriotic poem, the *Annales* (191–193). The three literary models recalled by Venus suggest an ethical model as well. An "epic" eros is invoked, along an axis from Ennius to Vergil, whereby an institutional and mature form of love is proposed as an alternative to the elegiac eros (the *otia ... iuventae* [youth's idleness], 182). The latter is considered socially unproductive and a source of individual suffering. The shift from the limping, irregular cadence of the distich to the steady, constant one of the hexameter (7–15) is the formal counterpart to the lifestyle transition proposed by the epithalamium.[9] The model of Vergil inviting his friend Gallus to abandon elegy lies, then, behind Statius's "sermon" to Stella on repudiating elegy. Stella is Statius's Gallus, and *Silva* 1.2 is a metaliterary discourse on the obsolescence of erotic elegy in the Flavian age.

II. HOMAGES BETWEEN POETS AND COMPETITION WITH MODELS

The two poems, Vergil's eclogue and Statius's *Silva* 1.2, tell two parallel love stories of the two elegiac poets, Gallus and Stella. What in Vergil had been an attempt, even a failure, to convince his friend to get rid of the pains of love becomes, in the case of Statius's tribute to his friend, successful. In fact, it has already taken place: Stella has seen his dream come true, having obtained the hand of his *domina*, Violentilla. As master of ceremonies, Statius celebrates his friend's transition to a new life (*subiit leges et frena momordit / ille solutus amor* [that footloose love has bowed to rules and bitten the bridle], 28–29). But for Stella the end of his former elegiac life means also the end of elegy tout court. Indeed, Stella's case is shown to be paradigmatic within the history of the

---

[8]   Some indications in Pederzani 1995:112–113.
[9]   On this point, cf. Rosati 1999:160–161.

elegiac genre. As the last elegist of Graeco-Roman tradition, he represents the end of a genre and its connected lifestyle: it is no coincidence that the major exponents of the genre are summoned to attend his marriage (1.2.250–255). The socially rebellious elegy of the Augustan age is outdated and inadequate for the Flavian age, where there are no longer tensions or conflicts, and civic harmony apparently reigns.

As it is for every elegiac lover, Gallus's impossible dream of love is confirmed as unrealizable (*Ecl.* 10.52–69) and arouses his inconsolable pain. Stella, on the other hand, sees his dream come true. He expresses incredulous astonishment in response to Violentilla's acceptance (*Silv.* 1.2.31–34: *tu tamen attonitus, quamvis data copia tantae / noctis, adhuc optas permissaque numine dextro / vota paves. Pone o dulcis suspiria vates, / pone: tua est* [But you are nonplussed. Though such a great night is yours to enjoy, you are still yearning and fear the prayers that kindly deity has granted. Sigh no more, sweet poet, sigh no more: she is yours]). His words also recall the similar reaction of Ovid's Pygmalion, who cannot believe in the metamorphosis of his ivory woman into a real woman (*Met.* 10.281–289) who will be his bride (*Met.* 10.295). Both miracles are made possible by Venus, who participates in Pygmalion's marriage (*Met.* 10.295: *coniugio, quod fecit, adest dea* [the goddess graced the union she had made]) just as she attends Stella's wedding (*Silv.* 1.2.11–13: *ipsa manu nuptam genetrix Aeneia duxit / lumine demissam et dulci probitate rubentem, / ipsa toros et sacra parat* [Aeneas's mother with her own hand led the bride, whose eyes are downcast as she blushes sweetly chaste. She herself prepares the bed and the rites]).

If we return to our main thread of Vergilian allusion, a further explicit link between Vergil's eclogue and Statius's *Silva* consists in the name of Arethusa. Vergil had begun the eclogue by invoking this fountain nymph, symbol of Syracuse and thus of the home of his bucolic model Theocritus (*Ecl.* 10.1: *Extremum hunc, Arethusa, mihi concede laborem* [Arethusa, Sicilian Muse, allow me this last labour]). In exchange for her inspiration, he had wished to preserve the renowned purity of her water (*Ecl.* 10.4–5: *sic tibi, cum fluctus subterlabere Sicanos, / Doris amara suam non intermisceat undam* [If you'd not have briny Doris mix her stream with yours, when you glide beneath Sicilian waves, begin]). In Statius, too, there is a prominent reference to the myth of

Arethusa (*Silv*. 1.2.203–208), and in the *flumina ... intemerata* of 205 it seems possible to catch a pointed recall of Vergil's phrase *non intermisceat undam*. Without having any possible connection between Syracuse and the celebrated bridal couple, Statius nevertheless incorporates the myth of Arethusa into *Silv*. 1.2. He interprets it, however, in a way that is appropriate to the epithalamic context: that is, he makes Alpheus the husband of Arethusa and sees in his arrival in Syracuse the reunification of two legitimate spouses. In doing so, Statius rejects the erotic version attested by Ovid in the *Metamorphoses* (5.577–641),[10] in which the nymph avoids the river god's attempted rape by means of her submarine getaway to the Sicilian coast. Instead, he adopts in his epithalamium the version that presents a marital happy ending at the conclusion of Alpheus's harsh enterprise. The story of the river god who crosses the sea to rejoin his bride thus becomes the mythical model for Stella's experience: elegiac suffering crowned by marriage (*Silv*. 1.2.202–205: *durum permensus iter coeptique laboris / prendisti portus. Nitidae sic transfuga Pisae / amnis in externos longe flammatus amores / flumina demerso trahit intemerata canali ...* [you have traversed your hard way, the toils of your enterprise; you have gained harbour. So the renegade river of gleaming Pisa, on fire for a distant, alien love, draws on his inviolate stream in a sunken channel]).

Beyond these shared thematic elements, the two compositions are also located in striking relation to each other within their respective collections. Vergil's was the *extremus labor* of his bucolic collection. The proemial verses draw attention to this location, which is a position of undoubted prestige.[11] Statius instead assigns the initial position to the *silva* dedicated to Stella: the epithalamium is the first composition of the book, after the proemial one dedicated—as it had to be—to Domitian and his equestrian monument (in short *Silv*. 1.1 stands out from the rest of the sequence).[12] As such, it occupies the position of a prestigious tribute. It is not by chance that Stella is the dedicatee of

---

[10] On the different versions of the myth, see Rosati 2009:230.

[11] As was the final position that Vergil reserved for Gallus's praise in the last book of the *Georgics*, which according to Servius (*ad* Verg. *Ecl*. 10.6), the poet would have removed after the break of Gallus with Augustus.

[12] See Coleman 1988:54–56.

the first book, as the *praefatio* declares, a privilege that gives him a very special importance even compared to the other friends and patrons to whom the various books are dedicated. Moreover, with its 277 lines *Silv.* 1.2 will remain the longest of the entire collection. There is no doubt, therefore, about the significance that both compositions receive from their placement.

A further point of connection between Vergil and Statius lies in the possible relation between Statius's text and the poetic production of his addressee. We know from Servius that a section of Vergil's eclogue includes verses by Gallus himself (Servius *ad Ecl.* 10.46: *hi autem omnes versus Galli sunt, de ipsius translati carminibus* [all these are verses by Gallus, taken from his own poems]). Servius's claim has understandably fueled the hunt for the text of Gallus, of which we had just a pentameter until a few decades ago, and to which a dozen verses have been recently added.[13] It is impossible for us to ascertain precisely the section of Vergil's eclogue that includes Gallus's verses (likely they must come within his elegiac lament, the monologue of verses 31–69, perhaps starting at verse 46).[14] Much less are we in a position to understand the nature of this massive *translatio*—is it citation or, more likely, adaptation (which would be required to absorb the pentameter in the hexametric rhythm) or else more or less allusive recall? There is no reason to question the validity of Servius's information.[15] Now, if we postulate that Statius wanted to replicate with his friend-poet Stella the relationship between Vergil and Gallus, it is tempting to hypothesize that Statius too, as Vergil had done with Gallus, quoted, or allusively referred to, verses of Stella. If he did so, we can reasonably suppose that such verses were part of his elegies for the beloved *Asteris*. Obviously, such a suggestion, however intriguing, remains speculative.

Another aspect of the two compositions that invites comparison is the social dimension, namely the resonances that Gallus's and Stella's

[13] Bibliography in Rumpf 1996:10–11n3, and Cucchiarelli 2012:481–482.

[14] Just in the celebrated (and much imitated) line 69, the last line of Gallus's monologue, a distinctly elegiac flavor has been perceived (Grondona 1977:28–29; Conte 1986:124n27; Cucchiarelli 2012, ad loc.). Another passage of the eclogue where Gallus's presence has been strongly suggested is lines 22–23 (cf. again Cucchiarelli 2012, ad loc.).

[15] Cf. Cucchiarelli 2012:502.

love affairs have within their respective communities. In Vergil's eclogue the whole bucolic world rushed to participate in Gallus's inconsolable pain, his elegiac "defeat":

> Illum etiam lauri, etiam flevere myricae,
> pinifer illum etiam sola sub rupe iacentem
> Maenalus et gelidi fleverunt saxa Lycaei
>
> Vergil *Ecl.* 10.13–15

> Even the laurels, even the tamarisks wept for him,
> even pine-clad Maenalus, and the rocks of cold Lycaeus
> wept as he lay beneath a lonely cliff.

> Venit et upilio, tardi venere subulci,
> uvidus hiberna venit de glande Menalcas.
>
> Vergil *Ecl.* 10.19–20

> And the shepherd came, and the tardy swineherds,
> Menalcas came, wet from soaking the winter acorns.

> Venit et agresti capitis Silvanus honore,
> florentis ferulas et grandia lilia quassans.
> Pan deus Arcadiae venit ...
>
> Vergil *Ecl.* 10.24–26

> Silvanus came with rustic distinction on his head, waving his
>   flowering
> fennels and tall lilies. Pan, god of Arcadia, came ...

Conversely, the entire civic community of Rome, with its different social structures, participates in and contributes to the festive atmosphere of Stella's wedding, which represents the happy realization of his elegiac dream:

> Dum fervent agmine postes
> atriaque et multa pulsantur limina virga
>
> ...
>
> omnis honos, cuncti veniunt ad limina fasces,

omnis plebeio teritur praetexta tumultu;
hinc eques, hinc iuvenum coetu stola mixta laborat.

Statius *Silv.* 1.2.47–48, 233–235

While entrances and halls seethe with the throng and
doors are beaten with many a staff ... every office, all rods
come to that threshold, every gown of state is jostled in
commoners' turmoil. Knights mill on one side, on the
other the matron's robe mingles with a throng of youth.

Latin erotic elegy, as we know, is a place of ethical and literary
tensions and conflicts. Vergil shows it well, in representing Gallus's
impasse, and Statius demonstrates it no less clearly. In recounting
Stella's past elegiac life, he insists on the friction between alternative
ethical and cultural models: only Stella's adherence to the institution of
marriage enables the end of an improper romantic liaison and guaran-
tees the legitimacy of his relationship with Violentilla. Marriage represents a transition from an irregular bond, which was subject to social
censure (*Silv.* 1.2.27: *mendaces obliqui carminis astus* [a truce to lying
wiles of hinting buzz]), to full acceptance into the civic community
(*Silv.* 1.2.29–30: *consumpta est fabula vulgi / et narrata diu viderunt oscula
cives* [common tattle has run its course and the citizenry has seen kisses
so long retailed]). Unlike Vergil, who invited Gallus to reject elegy and
to get rid of his *solliciti amores* (*Ecl.* 10.6), Statius is pleased to see something that has already taken place, namely Stella's spontaneous exit
from elegy. Such an event was favored indeed by Venus (and prayed for,
in turn, by Cupid), a goddess who therefore must be far from the elegiac
one who, in the words of Catullus, "mixes sweet bitterness with cares"
(Cat. 68.18: *quae dulcem curis miscet amaritiem*). Now, she promotes civil
society and its values.

The road traced by Stella (and by Statius) as a happy alternative
to that of Vergil's Gallus is one which leads to individual happiness,
peace, and social success. Naturally, Statius's strategy, both literary and
political, should also be seen in the context of the latter's attempt to
promote himself as the Mantuan's poet successor—showing himself to
be the Vergil of the Flavian age. Making Stella into the Vergilian Gallus,

therefore, is a further way for Statius to assimilate himself to Vergil, of whom he considers himself to be the heir. Just as Vergil had been the singer of Augustan Rome and of its imperial destiny, Statius sees himself as the *poeta laureatus* of the Flavian regime and aspires to carry out the same cultural and political function that he attributes to his Augustan model.

This time, though, it will not be the bucolic world that represents the alternative to the elegiac one frequented by Gallus. Rather, the civic horizon of imperial Rome, which celebrates the splendour of Domitian, welcomes him as an exemplary citizen. In that role, he is no longer the object of malignant gossip but a Roman who can act as a model for the entire community (*Silv.* 1.2.233–235). And other *silvae* will offer themselves to the no longer elegiac Stella: not the bucolic *silvae* of Vergil (*Ecl.* 10.8) but the work of Statius, which is the mirror of Domitian's prosperous and peaceful Rome and which proposes itself to be the most effective literary tool for celebrating and authorizing political power. This is also a way of tracing a continuity with Vergil. Not only does Statius respond to Vergilian epic but also to his *minora*, in line with the principle enunciated in the prefatory epistle to the first book (*Silv.* 1.*Praef.*7–8: *et Culicem legimus et Batrachomachiam etiam agnoscimus* [we read *The Gnat* and even recognize *The Battle of the Frogs*]). One might see continuity, but perhaps we should also read Statius's attempt to surpass his great model. For Statius somehow succeeds, with Stella, where Vergil failed with Gallus. Such a reading confirms the ambivalence of Statius's position towards his poetic father and rival.[16] From this intergeneric confrontation and tension, then, stems much of the interest in this neglected poem, whose source of literary energy ultimately goes back to its author's competition with Vergil.

SCUOLA NORMALE SUPERIORE, PISA

WORKS CITED

Citroni, M. 1975. *M. Valerius Martialis. Epigrammaton liber I.* Florence

---

[16] Cf. Leigh 2006:218–225; Rosati 2008.

Coleman, K. M. 1988. *Statius. Silvae IV.* Oxford.

Conte, G. B. 1986. *The Rhetoric of Imitation: Genre and Poetic Memory in Vergil and Other Latin Poets.* Ithaca, NY.

Cucchiarelli, A. 2012. *Publio Vergilio Marone. Le bucoliche: Introduzione e commento.* Rome.

Grondona, M. 1977. "Gli epigrammi di Tibullo e il congedo delle elegie (su Properzio e Vergilio)." *Latomus* 36: 3–29.

Harrison, S. 2007. *Generic Enrichment in Vergil and Horace.* Oxford.

Leigh, M. 2006. "Statius and the Sublimity of Capaneus." In *Epic Interactions: Perspectives on Homer, Vergil, and the Epic Tradition Presented to Jasper Griffin by Former Pupils,* ed. M. J. Clarke, B. G. F. Currie, and R. O. A. M. Lyne, 217–241. Oxford.

Nauta, R. R. 2002. *Poetry for Patrons: Literary Communication in the Age of Domitian.* Leiden.

Pederzani, O. 1995. *Il talamo, l'albero e lo specchio: Saggio di commento a Stat. "Silv." I 2, II 3, III 4.* Bari.

Rosati, G. 1999. "La boiterie de Mademoiselle Élégie: Un pied volé et ensuite retrouvé (les aventures d'un genre littéraire entre les Augustéens et Stace)." In *Élégie et épopée dans la poésie ovidienne (Héroïdes et Amours): En hommage à Simone Viarre,* ed. J. Fabre-Serris and A. Deremetz, 147–163. Villeneuve d'Ascq.

———. 2005. "Elegy after the Elegists: From Opposition to Assent." *Papers of the Langford Latin Seminar* 12:133–510.

———. 2008. "Statius, Domitian, and Acknowledging Paternity: Rituals of Succession in the Thebaid." In *The Poetry of Statius,* ed. J. J. L. Smolenaars, H.-J. van Dam, and R. Nauta, 175–193. Leiden.

———. Forthcoming a. "An Authorized Desertion: Ovid's Model in Statius' *Silva* 1.2."

———. Forthcoming b. "Gallo in Vergilio e Saffo in Ovidio: Due metapoeti e la loro fortuna." *Dictynna* 17.

Rumpf, L. 1996. *Extremus labor: Vergils 10. Ekloge und die Poetik der Bucolica.* Göttingen.

Shackleton Bailey, D. R. 2003. *Statius. Silvae.* Loeb Classical Library 206. Cambridge, MA.

AX OF LOVE

CLYTEMNESTRA'S MOTIVATION FOR MURDER IN SENECA'S *AGAMEMNON*

Gareth David Williams

THIS PAPER PAYS TRIBUTE TO RICHARD TARRANT by exploring three aspects of the Senecan *Agamemnon* on which his celebrated 1976 commentary sheds important light and takes strong positions. First, what, in Seneca, is Clytemnestra's dominant motive for murdering Agamemnon upon his return from Troy? Second, what dramatic and literary function, or menu of functions, is served by the messenger Eurybates's extended account (421–578) of the storm that ravaged the Greek fleet on its return from Troy? Third, the fourth choral ode (808–866) separates the returning Agamemnon's entry into his palace at Argos from Cassandra's vision of his murder. This chorus amounts to an elaborate glorification of another Argive hero, Hercules, and it therefore perhaps reflects well on Agamemnon by Herculean association. But what might be the further or fuller function of this ode in the thematic economy of the drama?

I. THE BREAKING STORM

Given the storm's literal and figurative centrality to the *Agamemnon*, we begin with Eurybates's messenger speech before expanding outwards so as to encompass the two other concerns just outlined. From a

Text and translation follow Fitch 2018. The *Agamemnon* is plausibly one of Seneca's earliest plays (Fitch 1981), but uncertainty about the date does not affect my argument below. I thank the editors for their advice on a draft version of this chapter, which is offered as a humble gesture of gratitude to Richard Tarrant for the central role he has played in revitalizing the modern study of Senecan tragedy.

messenger so named,[1] we might expect a wide-ranging speech but perhaps not one of such vast and rhetorically charged dimensions. As Richard points out,[2] the Senecan storm scene owes little or nothing to its far briefer counterpart in the Aeschylean *Agamemnon*—a departure that typifies Seneca's more general distance from Aeschylus in this play.[3] As for Roman Republican drama, the Senecan voyage shows certain similarities in point of detail to Livius Andronicus's *Aegisthus* and Pacuvius's *Teucer*, albeit in the latter case Pacuvius's own indebtedness to the Sophoclean *Teucer* further complicates the chain of possible influence on Seneca;[4] Richard's own ruling in the matter is that "direct use by Seneca of either Sophocles or Pacuvius is less likely than imitation of an intermediate source, possibly Augustan."[5] More suggestive for present purposes is Lycophron's *Alexandra*: this is the earliest surviving work that contains (361–397) the complete series of events that Seneca describes in the three movements of Eurybates's speech, namely (i) the storm itself (421–527; cf. *Alex.* 373–383); then (ii) the death at sea of the Locrian Ajax at the hands of Athena and Neptune, in punishment for his rape of Cassandra in the temple of Athena during Troy's fall (528–556; cf. *Alex.* 387–395); and (iii) the destruction wrought when Nauplius lured the Greek ships on to the rocks off Cape Caphereus through his deceitful beacon light (557–578; cf. *Alex.* 384–386). Seneca's arrangement of these three parts in fact differs from Lycophron's, and other Hellenistic sources, especially Callimachus's *Aetia*, may have been more influential;[6] at the very least, Richard posits both for Seneca and for the cognate storm scene in Book 14 of Quintus of Smyrna's *Posthomerica*[7] a

---

[1] "Wide-ranging," "wide-striding," possibly "a generic name for a herald, since Agamemnon's herald in the *Iliad* is also so named" (1.320): Levaniouk 2011:156.

[2] Tarrant 1976a:19, 248.

[3] At one extreme Tarrant (1976a:10 and 1978a:215–216) finds no evidence of any direct knowledge of Aeschylus; more moderately for points of contact and response, see Marcucci 1996:11–47, Lavery 2004, and Degiovanni 2004.

[4] Further, Tarrant 1976a:13–14, 20–21; with Marcucci 1996:49–58 and Kugelmeier 2014:493 and n1.

[5] Tarrant 1976a:20n9.

[6] Tarrant 1976a:21. For the possible Callimachean dimension, see Harder 2012: vol. 2, 287–289 on *Aet.* fr. 1.35 (on the Locrian Ajax).

[7] The storm: 14.488–529, 590–610; Ajax: 14.530–589; Nauplius: 14.611–628.

major source that was unlikely to have been written later than the 3rd century BCE.[8]

Only limited light is shed on the Senecan storm scene, then, by relating it to its elusive matrix of possible influences; yet the scene is undoubtedly stamped with a distinctive Senecan personality, but only partly so because, as so often in his tragedies, chaos in nature macrocosmically reflects moral chaos at the human level.[9] This Senecan tragic storm is also distinctively epic in pedigree, with the swells of Virgilian and Ovidian storm scenes in particular washing over the text;[10] and for all his credentials as a textbook tragic messenger, Eurybates himself functions as an all-seeing, ubiquitous, and invulnerable epic narrator, who is careful for the most part to preserve his objectivity by describing the storm with a studied, third-person detachment.[11] True, his omniscience as he appears to capture every detail despite the darkness surely tests our credulity, a point to which we shall return;[12] but more important for now is the breakdown at this central dramatic moment within the *Agamemnon* of the linear model of epic teleology such as that offered by the *Aeneid*. "Once all of Pergamum fell to Dorian fire," Eurybates begins (421), announcing (as Alessandro Schiesaro puts it) "with Virgilian emphasis nothing short of a post-Homeric *Nostos*, complete with a retrospective narrative, albeit implicit, of the war's main events."[13] The crisis here, Schiesaro argues, lies not just in the devastation of the Greeks' homecoming; instead of reaching relentlessly towards its goal, Virgilian epic teleology is itself blocked and diverted, and ultimately recast into a cyclical phenomenon of tragic regression and return.[14] Hence, instead of moving beyond

---

[8]   Tarrant 1976a:22–23.

[9]   Cf. Shelton 1983:168 (Eurybates's account an actualization of Thyestes's *versa natura est retro*, 34); Schindler 2000:135; Tola 2009:3, 6–7.

[10]   See Tarrant 1976a:248; a more expansive overview in Schindler 2000.

[11]   For the epic dimension, see Baertschi 2010.

[12]   See p. 248 below; for a partial defense against the too-dark-to-see point, Baertschi 2000:254–256.

[13]   Schiesaro 2014:184.

[14]   Schiesaro 2014, esp. 184 ("Eurybates attempts to offer within the body of the tragedy an epic reading of the aftermath of the defeat of Troy which the rest of the play will call into question"); 188–189 ("Seneca shows the illusory nature of teleogy and its

Troy, the Greeks are mired in the consequences of their campaign; instead of winners and losers, there are only joint losers, as Trojans and Greeks are figuratively as well as literally in the same boat, both of them praying for deliverance from the storm (510–511). The dead Priam is now envied by Agamemnon, Menelaus envies Hector, Ulysses Ajax (512–514), and the confusion of all distinctions in nature as the storming elements rage against each other is matched by the merging of Greek and Trojan identities in shared catastrophe.[15]

To put this point about a recursive cycle differently: Eurybates duly describes the mixture of weary relief and pleasure with which the Greeks set sail for home after Troy's fall, but some 40 lines elapse (421–464) before the tempest finally erupts. Of course, his leisurely scene setting projects a calm that magnifies all the more the shock of the storm when it suddenly bursts forth; but a more interesting effect lies, I propose, in Seneca's evocation of a prior voyage that was itself significantly delayed and finally embarked upon with enthusiasm when the winds at last began to stir themselves. All is at first serene:

> Ad militares remus aptatur manus
> omnisque nimium longa properanti mora est.
> Signum recursus regia ut fulsit rate
> et clara laetum remigem monuit tuba,
> aurata primas prora designat uias
> aperitque cursus mille quos puppes secent.
>
> Sen. *Ag.* 425–430

Oars were fitted to the soldiers' hands; in their haste any delay seemed too long. When the signal for return shone forth from the king's ship, and the trumpet's clear notes alerted the joyful rowers, the gilded prow marked out the start of the voyage and opened the pathway to be cut by a thousand vessels.

---

poetic counterpart, poetic linearity"). Further, Tola 2009:9–12 ("La construcción cíclica de la historia") and Trinacty 2016, esp. 103–112.

[15] Hence for Agamemnon's murder as retribution for Priam's, and for Argos as a second Troy, see Lohikoski 1966, with Schiesaro 2014, esp. 182, and now Frangoulidis 2016.

Do we know at this point whether we are coming or going? While the Greeks make their return from Troy, the secondary *recursus* (cf. 427) implied here is our literary return to Aulis and to the Greek embarkation after Agamemnon's sacrifice of Iphigenia.[16] In Eurybates's account, a gentle breeze (*aura ... lenis*, 431) strengthens into an *aura ... fortior* (442) as the ships set forth (443); the waves subsequently swell up, roused by the mounting gusts (469), before the full-on *turbo* of the warring winds churns the sea (474–484). At least in the early stages of the storm's development from nothing, the evolution from *aura lenis* to *aura fortior* might remind us of the breeze at last coming to life at Aulis, to the effect that, with small amendment, the opening stretches of Eurybates's account might suitably characterize the voyage *to* Troy.[17] This double vision comes still more sharply into focus in light of Clytemnestra's words to her nurse in lines 138–144:

> Fluctibus uariis agor,
> ut, cum hinc profundum uentus, hinc aestus rapit,
> incerta dubitat unda cui cedat malo.
> Proinde omisi regimen e manibus meis:
> quocumque me ira, quo dolor, quo spes feret,
> hoc ire pergam; fluctibus dedimus ratem.
> Ubi animus errat, optimum est casum sequi.

I am driven by conflicting waves, as when wind and tide pull the sea each way, and the waters hesitate, uncertain which scourge to yield to. So I have dropped the rudder

---

[16] Cf. of reversion to a former state *OLD recurro* 2 and *recursus* 3. The case for detecting a sub-allusion to the outward voyage from Aulis is enhanced by Seneca's clear evocation of yet another departure here: as Caviglia (1986–1987:146–147) observes, Eurybates's account of the Greeks' happiness as they leave (435–436) echoes the Trojans' joy at the Greeks' apparent departure in Virgil (*Aen.* 2.27–28); that Greek departure is of course a ruse, with disastrous consequences for Troy. If that Virgilian subtext ominously qualifies Eurybates's focus on the Greeks' joy as they depart, the resonances of the voyage from Aulis function to the same ominous effect in advance of the punitive storm.

[17] So, e.g., if we momentarily imagine the transposition of lines 435–436 ("What a pleasure to see the empty shores of Troy, to see the lonely terrain of deserted Sigeum!") to a few lines yonder, it is surely not hard to reconceive 431–441 as a passable rendition of the outward journey.

> from my hands. Wherever anger, pain, hope carry me,
> there I shall proceed; I have given up the boat to the waves.
> When one's spirit is astray, it is best to follow chance.

Clytemnestra passively succumbs to her figurative storm, just as the Greek fleet succumbs to the real thing in Eurybates's speech; but in ceding to the storm, in raging tempestuously within herself, not least because of her anguish at Agamemnon's killing of Iphigenia, she also assumes a figurative deadliness of storm force that is later analogized in the full-blown *turbo* of the messenger speech. On this approach, the secondary, Aulis-centered reading that we explored above as the breezes rise in the early stages of Eurybates's report not only identifies a growth pattern and an Iphigenia factor in the winds of vengeance that finally descend on the Greek fleet; it also lends partial cause and build-up to the figurative storm that, in lines 138–144, has *already* engulfed and transported the vengeful Clytemnestra.[18]

The force of tragic repetition in the Pelopid dynasty is such that nothing can break the cycle of history replayed and of crime repaid by crime; hence it is no surprise that, in the midst of the tempest, and at the play's epicenter, all nautical experience, reason, and skill (*ratio*, *usus*, and *ars* in 507) count for nothing as the elemental forces run wild, albeit dispensing a form of higher justice to settle old scores. This judicial emphasis is showcased in the second movement of Eurybates's speech: the Locrian Ajax, after surviving Athena's onslaught with Jovian bolts (528–543), crows about his indestructability (544–552), only finally to be done to death by Neptune (552–556). Ajax thunders, *intonat* (544), in his fury, a verb used of Jupiter himself in Virgil and other contexts:[19] in stealing Jove's thunder, Ajax displays in yet another way the *hubris* that the scene as a whole punishes;[20] and another cycle of recurrence starts here, in that Ajax's arrogance prefigures the hubristic

---

[18] Cf. Tola 2009:7 on the chaos provoked by the storm as "una exteriorización" of Clytemnestra's inner condition.

[19] *OLD* 1b, adding (e.g.) Verg. *Aen.* 9.631, Ov. *Tr.* 5.14.27.

[20] See Baertschi 2010:265–266 with Schiesaro 2014:185–186 (the latter relating 544–546 to *Od.* 4.502–504).

signs displayed by Agamemnon just before he is cut down later in the drama.[21]

. For now, however, Eurybates's third movement, on Nauplius, warrants closer attention, and he perhaps gives us a special cue to that effect. After steadfastly observing third-person objectivity in his speech thus far, he suddenly reverts to the first-person in advancing to his new topic: *nos alia maior naufragos pestis uocat* (557: "Already wrecked, we were drawn by another, worse scourge"). True, Seneca may conceivably deploy the first-person *nos* here for simple variation, but to dig a little deeper: the language of deceit—*mendax* (558), *fallax* (560), *perfidus* (570)—condemns Nauplius's malevolence in using his beacon light to lure the Greek fleet on to the rocks of Cape Caphereus. What Eurybates fails to mention, however, is Nauplius's motivation for his actions. His son Palamedes, we remember, paid a heavy price for making an enemy of Odysseus: framed by Odysseus as a traitor to the Greek cause at Troy, Palamedes was put to death. Frustrated in his efforts to see justice done, Nauplius sought revenge against Agamemnon and his henchmen, and he took his opportunity through his beacon's false lure of safety when the storm struck. The saga of Palamedes's death and Nauplius's revenge was widely treated in 5th-century Greek tragedy and beyond,[22] but Eurybates offers no hint of any larger backstory in his judgmental condemnation of Nauplius's treachery. Nor does he show any inkling of the further revenge attested by Lykophron and Apollodorus,[23] to the effect that Nauplius caused the wives of three Greek leaders to be unfaithful; one of those wives was Clytemnestra, Aegisthus her lover.

In the fuller context of the Palamedes story, then, the deceptive shallows off Cape Caphereus are matched in a way by the misleading appearance of Eurybates's words, at least if they cause us to take against Nauplius without considering his motivation for such dastardly action. In this respect, Eurybates's reversion to the first-person *nos* at the start of this mini-episode suddenly takes on a fresh edge as soon as Nauplius's

---

[21] Schindler 2000:135–136; Harrison 2014:596 ("Ajax's hubris a metaphor" for Agamemnon's).

[22] See Hornblower 2015:202–203 on Lycoph. *Alex.* 384–386 and p. 390 on 1090–1098.

[23] Lycoph. *Alex.* 1093–1095, with Hornblower 2015:390 (on 1090–1098), 263 (on 611), and 434 (on 1214–1215); Apollod. *Epit.* 6.9.

revenge is seen to be intensely personal: after the resonances that we explored earlier of Iphigenia's sacrifice and the Greek departure from Aulis,[24] the Nauplius episode again points the finger at Agamemnon—a narrowing of the sphere of reference perhaps underscored by Eurybates's sudden turn of focus toward "us." But does Eurybates mean to invest his rhetoric with these disconcerting implications, as if a willfully unreliable narrator who exploits his role as the herald of privileged information to insert his own subtext and supra-message? Certainly, his all-seeing speech appears impossibly omniscient in reporting all that he allegedly witnessed in the pitch-black darkness of the storm,[25] and we might therefore suspect that hyperbole and projection may enhance certain aspects of his narrative; the reputation for villainy and deceit that had long been associated with the name Eurybates in the Greek tradition is also far from reassuring.[26] But even if we suspect him of a coded moral commentary on (and perhaps even implicit condemnation of) the Agamemnon-led Greeks, he can barely compete with Clytemnestra, that consummate controller of layered speech. Telling in this respect are her first words after Eurybates concludes his report:

> Utrumne doleam laeter an reducem uirum?
> Remeasse laetor, uulnus at regni graue
> lugere cogor.

Sen. *Ag.* 579–581

> Should I grieve or rejoice at my husband's return? I rejoice at his homecoming, and yet I must mourn the deep wound to our kingdom.

"There is a sense," observes Richard, "in which Clytem[n]estra may ask this question with propriety" (should she rejoice at Agamemnon's return or grieve at the storm that has blighted it?), but "a less innocent meaning is surely intended as well."[27] Any distress that Clytemnestra

---

[24] See pp. 244–245 above.

[25] See, on the question, Baertschi 2010:254–256, albeit she stresses "Seneca's efforts to enhance the authenticity and plausibility of Eurybates's speech" (256).

[26] See Levaniouk 2011:154–165.

[27] Tarrant 1976a:284 (on 579).

feels is offset by the joyful prospect of her husband's murder; but what, then, of her specific or primary motive—or perhaps her hierarchy of motives—for that murder?

II. DIARY OF A MURDERESS

"In contrast to Aeschylus," Richard asserts, "all three writers [Euripides in his *Electra*, Ovid in his *Ars amatoria*, and Seneca here] make Agamemnon's infidelities and not the sacrifice of Iphigenia the most important cause for Clytem[n]estra's resolve to kill her husband."[28] In challenging this position at least on the Senecan front, I argue that neither Agamemnon's infidelities nor Iphigenia's sacrifice is Clytemnestra's primary motive for murder, but that Seneca prioritizes a third, erotic cause—one importantly conditioned by the radical transformation that the literary typology of Clytemnestra undergoes in the time lapse between the *Oresteia* and the 1st century CE. As Edith Hall puts it, "Aeschylus's Clytemnestra is a daughter-avenging woman with a mind that deliberates like a man's, a female who slaughters two people, without help from her lover, before gloating, spattered with blood, over their corpses."[29] Through the broadening and softening processes that Hall traces in Clytemnestra's appearances through Republican Roman theatre,[30] the early imperial version of her that emerges is the "eviscerated form" of "the anodyne and sexy wife in book 2 of Ovid's *Ars Amatoria* [2.387–408] and the emotionally unstable adulteress of the Senecan *Agamemnon*."[31] Against this background, the dominant motive for her murder in Seneca is not her resentment at Agamemnon's infidelities, but her lust for Aegisthus; and she is an

---

[28] Tarrant 1976a:205 (on 162–202). For a useful listing of the motivations attributed to Clytemnestra in the major Greek accounts (Homer, Pindar, Aeschylus, Sophocles, Euripides), see Mader 1988:52–53.

[29] Hall 2005:54.

[30] Hall 2005:61–63.

[31] Hall 2005:56; cf. 62–63 (on Ovid's "most eviscerated of all ancient Clytemnestras") and 65–68 (on Seneca's "neurotic adulteress," "psychologically frail" and "self-confessedly amorous; her dominant motives, it is stressed, are sexual passion for Aegisthus and sexual jealousy of Cassandra"). Cf. also Mader 1988:53 (on Prop. 3.19.19–20; Clytemnestra "as an example of unrestrained feminine passion").

"eviscerated form" in Seneca because, try as she might to resist what she herself characterizes as her shameful desire (*cupido turpis*, 135), she cannot throw off what we shall see to be Aegisthus's irresistibly infatuating hold over her.

Critically important to this approach is Clytemnestra's mindset when she makes her first appearance in the drama:

> Quid, segnis anime, tuta consilia expetis?
> Quid fluctuaris? Clausa iam melior uia est.
> Licuit pudicos coniugis quondam toros
> et sceptra casta uidua tutari fide;
> periere mores ius decus pietas fides
> et qui redire cum perît nescit pudor.
> Da frena et omnem prona nequitiam incita:
> per scelera semper sceleribus tutum est iter.
> Tecum ipsa nunc euolue femineos dolos,
> quod ulla coniunx perfida atque impos sui
> amore caeco, quod nouercales manus
> ausae, quod ardens impia uirgo face
> Phasiaca fugiens regna Thessalica trabe:
> ferrum, uenena ... uel Mycenaeas domos
> coniuncta socio profuge furtiua rate.
> —Quid timida loqueris furta et exilium et fugas?
> Soror ista fecit: te decet maius nefas.

> Sen. *Ag.* 108–124

Oh sluggish spirit! Why look for safe strategies? Why vacillate? The better path is already closed. Once you had the option of safeguarding your husband's bed and his empty throne through chastity and loyalty. But integrity, right, honor, loyalty, faith are lost, and shame, which once lost cannot return. So loosen the reins, crouch forward, spur on each form of wickedness. For crimes the safest path is always through crimes. Unfurl now in your mind the tricks of womankind, all that any faithless wife, crazed with blind passion, all that stepmothers' hands have dared commit, or the girl blazing with disloyal lust as she fled her Phasian kingdom on a Thessalian ship: the steel, poison ... Or else take stealthy flight from Mycenae by boat with your partner. But why talk nervously of stealth and exile and escape? Your sister did such things; you are suited to some greater outrage.

Directly after this passage the nurse addresses Clytemnestra at the start of what becomes their extended dialogical exchanges until Aegisthus enters (226); but since the nurse begins by asking "Queen of the Danaans, ... why ponder *in silence?*" (125–126), Clytemnestra's opening words must surely amount, as Richard perceives, to "a quasi-aside, a representation of her inner thoughts which cannot be over-heard because it is not really put into speech."[32] To recast the point, however, this aside cannot be overheard because it is too revealing, too raw, too close to the bone: when she says that she had the option (*licuit*, 110) of safeguarding her husband's bed and throne through chaste loyalty, the force of *licuit* is to admit that she *chose* to reject the path of the virtues that she assembles in what looks like a *conge-ries* of self-rebuke in lines 112–113. As for the three models of female daring invoked in lines 117–120, who lurks behind this unnamed triad of *coniunx perfida*, *noverca*, and *virgo*? For the faithless wife, Richard canvasses Stheneboea but concedes the difficulty of "point[ing] to a prototypical *coniunx perfida* apart from Clytem[n]estra herself;"[33] could this be a moment of literary reflexivity akin to the Senecan Medea's flash of self-awareness about her own textual history when she famously declares *Medea nunc sum* (910)?[34] As for the *noverca*-type, she is "easily supplied in Phaedra;"[35] and the *virgo* must be Medea in flight with Jason from Colchis.[36] But the more general point to be stressed is that what connects the three women is blind love and destructive

[32] Tarrant 1976a:194.

[33] Tarrant 1976a :196.

[34] See Trinacty 2014:122 (line 910 makes good the promise of 171, "I shall become Medea").

[35] Tarrant 1976a:196.

[36] An identification underscored by the allusive signs of a wider "'medeic' presence" discerned in 108–124 by Battistella 2013.

intention or action out of love,[37] and that erotic charge is explicit when Clytemnestra looks to Helen's sisterly example of adultery in *soror ista fecit* (124). But what she intends when she subsequently says "you are suited to some greater outrage" is nothing short of murder, perhaps with a hint of sibling rivalry in her evil machinations: Helen may have left Menelaus for Paris, but Clytemnestra will leave Agamemnon for dead.

The formality of the nurse's opening words—"Queen of the Danaans, glorious child of Leda" (125)—well captures her larger bearing in the play as one whose loyalty is to protocol, restraint, and the disciplined official line. When Clytemnestra is drawn out of herself and into dialogue with the nurse, her erotic impulse remains irrepressible, but other elements now add to and intensify her emotional turmoil, perhaps allowing her to disguise or downplay the nakedness of the erotic motive:

> Maiora cruciant quam ut moras possim pati.
> Flammae medullas et cor exurunt meum;
> mixtus dolori subdidit stimulos timor;
> inuidia pulsat pectus, hinc animum iugo
> premit cupido turpis et uinci uetat;
> et inter istas mentis obsessae faces
> fessus quidem et deuictus et pessumdatus
> pudor rebellat.
>
> Sen. Ag. 131–138

My torments are too great for me to endure delays. Flames burn my heart and bones; mixed with my pain, fear goads me on; jealousy pounds in my breast, and again rank lust oppresses my spirit and will not be controlled. And amid these fires besetting my mind, though weary and defeated and ruined, shame fights back.

---

[37] *Pace* Mader 1988:54: "Less obvious is the relevance of the references to Phaedra ... and Medea ..., neither of whom were husband slayers."

Beyond her lust for Aegisthus (*cupido turpis*), the fear (*timor*, 133) that torments her is presumably of retribution if Agamemnon discovers her affair;[38] and her *invidia* (134) is presumably her jealousy of Cassandra. It is only after registering this concoction of lust, fear, and jealousy that she invokes Iphigenia's death as a cause of her murderous resentment against Agamemnon (cf. 158–159, 162–173), and even then her outrage at the killing appears mingled with outrage at the slight to her dignity. After all, she, that self-styled noble "Tyndarid, child of heaven" (162), bore a child who was offered up in deceitful circumstances as a victim in a *lustratio classis* performed to gain divine favor for the Trojan expedition:[39] given that "human sacrifice for such purposes was seen as ... exceptional or as barbaric,"[40] Clytemnestra's outrage appears generated in part by the circumstances, and not just by the terrible fact, of Iphigenia's death. The nurse urges restraint by appeal to "the holy name of marriage" (155), to the Realpolitik point that Iphigenia's sacrifice enabled the Greek fleet to set sail (160–161),[41] and to the "official" version of Agamemnon's record as "victor over fierce Asia, avenger of Europe" (205). Clytemnestra resists by stressing the other side of the story, arguing that his stewardship of the Trojan campaign was flawed because of his amorous designs first on Chryseis and then on Achilles's Briseis (174–188)—a pattern of behavior that continues, she insists, in his passion for Cassandra (188–191). But then an extraordinary development: despite Clytemnestra's lust; despite the further motivation supplied by her *timor* and *invidia*; and despite her outrage at Iphigenia's death, the nurse's restraining hand is apparently not without effect. When Aegisthus suddenly enters, Clytemnestra appears wholly converted to the path of purity, showing no trace of her earlier emotions and now asserting instead that "married love

---

[38] The fear resurfaces/is addressed in 147, 284–287.

[39] See Tarrant 1976a:205 (on 163).

[40] Tarrant 1976a:205 (on 163).

[41] Albeit, in contrast to the Aeschylean *Agamemnon*'s yoke of necessity (cf. 205–221), Seneca gives no explicit indication of absolute *compulsion* to go to Troy (see Shelton 1983:165); hence the implication that Iphigenia might have been spared (cf. 169–173 for Clytemnestra's denial of any divine agency in the fleet's departure from Aulis).

overcomes me and turns me back" (239). What are we to make of this remarkable change of attitude?[42]

An important clue is offered by Aegisthus's first exchanges with Clytemnestra in lines 234–243:

> [Ae.] Tu nos pericli socia, tu, Leda sata,
> comitare tantum: sanguinem reddet tibi
> ignauus iste ductor ac fortis pater.
> Sed quid trementes circuit pallor genas
> iacensque uultu languido obtutus stupet?
> [Cl.] Amor iugalis uincit ac flectit retro:
> referimur illuc, unde non decuit prius
> abire. Sed nunc casta repetatur fides,
> nam sera numquam est ad bonos mores uia:
> quem paenitet peccasse paene est innocens.

> [Ae.] Partner of my danger, seed of Leda: if *you* will only keep me company, then that cowardly and brave father will pay you in blood. But why are your cheeks pale and trembling, your eyes downcast and listless and dazed-looking? [Cl.] Married love overcomes me and turns me back. I am reverting to the place I should never have left. At least *now* I should recover loyalty and chastity, for the path to goodness is never too late. One who repents of wrongdoing is virtually innocent.

When Clytemnestra replies that "married love overcomes me and turns me back" (239), it is as if she seeks to escape her emotional vortex by turning time backwards or by canceling reality so as to achieve again a stable union with Agamemnon. But Aegisthus is quick to expose the fragility of her attempt at self-persuasion that begins in lines 239–243, and he does so with an eye for the nasty pragmatics of life that perhaps reflects his own difficult origins; he was, after all, incestuously

---

[42] On this "conversion," see Fitch 2018:121–122; with Mader 1988:63 and 69n57 (for bibliography on how to explain it). In that note Mader resists the simulation thesis of Croisille 1964; my own developing argument is equally incompatible with the dissimulation hypothesis of Aygon 2014.

conceived for the sole purpose of exacting revenge for what Atreus did to his father, Thyestes.[43] He immediately cuts to the chase:[44] arrogant before, Agamemnon will return to Argos as a still more arrogant *tyrannus*, and Cassandra will hardly tolerate spousal competition from Clytemnestra (244–259). The latter nevertheless persists in her vision of reconciliation with Agamemnon (260–267, 288–289), and their exchanges become more heated; but the sly Aegisthus knows all too well how to manipulate her. "Begone at once," she cries, "remove from my sight this disgrace to our house" (300–301), an outburst to which Aegisthus immediately responds with (calculated?)[45] melodrama by speaking of exile, even his suicide if she wishes it (302–305). She seemingly toys with that notion (306)[46] but fleetingly so; for her position suddenly collapses, her effort at reconciliation with Agamemnon now giving way to her renewed complicity with her lover. "But she who sins with another owes loyalty even to her offense," she now declares (307), in effect stating her allegiance to her partner in crime;[47] and so the scene does indeed end on a note of reconciliation, but her reconciliation with Aegisthus, and certainly not with Agamemnon.

Why this sudden collapse, this time in Aegisthus's favor? In a key development, after Aegisthus insists that Cassandra will never tolerate competition from Clytemnestra (253–259), the latter cries out:

> Aegisthe, quid me rursus in praeceps agis
> iramque flammis iam residentem incitas?

> Sen. *Ag.* 260–261

---

[43] Cf. Apollod. *Epit.* 2.14, Hyg. *Fab.* 87, 88; schol. ad Eur. *Or.* 14 (Schwartz 1887:98.25; cf. ad *Or.* 16 Schwartz 99.6 in app.); Gantz 1993:551.

[44] With evident schooling in the negative characterization of hope as illusory from Hesiod onwards: see Mader 1988:63.

[45] On his keen and manipulative psychological insight here, Mader 1988:64.

[46] *Siquidem hoc cruenta Tyndaris fieri sinam!*: for Reinhardt (2010), not a wish (*pace* Tarrant 1976a:230) but a rejoinder ("Yes, if ..."), and spoken not necessarily in soliloquy but ambiguously blending controlled bite with concession if Aegisthus hears (p. 35): "If indeed I could let this [sc. Aegisthus' suicide] happen as a Tyndarid who is to be bloodstained when she kills her husband."

[47] For this shift of direction as implying her recognition of "an ethical claim upon her loyalty," Wray 2009:254.

Aegisthus, why drive me toward the abyss once more, and
inflame my anger as it dies down?

Compare now Cassandra as the chorus finds her in lines 710–725, silent
and pallid, trembling and pent up, her gaze unsteady and drooping.[48]
Raising her head aloft, she makes ready to unseal her lips but her
mouth resists (716–718), only then to try in vain to hold in the words
that struggle for release (718–719); for hers is a gradual, maenad-
like surrender to Apollo (719). Goaded by the spur of fresh madness
(*furoris ... novi*, 720), she yet resists:

> Recede, Phoebe, iam non sum tua;
> extingue flammas pectori infixas meo.
>
> Sen. *Ag.* 722–723

Leave me Phoebus: I am not yours any longer. Smother the
flames you have planted in my breast.

But speak out she must in her frenzy, and her infatuation takes its
course as she foresees Agamemnon's murder (726–740). Her gradual
submission to Apollo is essential to the dramatic coherence of the
Agamemnon because of the critical analogy it facilitates: in her reluctant rise to infatuation, Cassandra is to Apollo as Clytemnestra is to
Aegisthus. In both cases, pallor, trembling, and the languid look of an
unfocused eye mark the subdued phase before fresh infatuation strikes
again as Aegisthus fans the flames that Clytemnestra decries in lines
260–261 ("Why drive me toward the abyss once more ...?") and Apollo
fans the flames that Cassandra decries in line 723 ("Smother the
flames ..."). This link between Aegisthus and Apollo is explicitly spelt
out when, in response to a jibe from Clytemnestra about his origins,
Aegisthus asserts that he "was born at Phoebus' instigation" (*auctore
Phoebo gignor*, 294); he was conceived, that is, at the command of an
oracle for the sole purpose of revenge against Atreus.[49] Of course,
Aegisthus's claim to association with Apollo is evidently contrived
and self-serving in his confrontation with Clytemnestra, as he tries to

---

[48] See, on Seneca's Cassandra, Littlewood 2004:215–225 and now Pillinger 2019:195–225.
[49] See pp. 254–255 above and note 43 for references.

ennoble the circumstances of his birth after she has scorned his origins (292–294); but for present purposes his appeal to the god seals a vital correlation between Phoebus as inspirer and Aegisthus as infatuator.

In her subdued phase, before being re-infatuated through fresh ignition from Aegisthus, Clytemnestra contemplates reconciliation with Agamemnon. So too, when Cassandra cries "Leave me, Phoebus: I am not yours any longer" (722), she means—however reluctantly and resignedly—that she is now Agamemnon's. Re-infatuation in both cases, through Aegisthus and Apollo respectively, results in a strange form of rapprochement between Cassandra and Clytemnestra, in that each is distanced from Agamemnon, even in a sense abducted, by her given inspirer. In turn, this dyadic relation of Cassandra and Clytemnestra as complementary opposites in the play, the one a truthteller unbelieved, the other a deceiver who effortlessly beguiles Agamemnon after his homecoming, has important consequences for assessing Clytemnestra's hierarchy of motives for murder. The affair with Aegisthus supplies the decisive cause:[50] other obvious factors (Iphigenia's sacrifice, Agamemnon's love for Cassandra) may certainly support her motivation or enable her to disguise her truest motive,[51] but without that primary lust and without her resulting vulnerability to her lover's infatuating coaxings, she will not be induced to become Aegisthus's convenient assassin. This last point—Aegisthus as too weak-willed to carry out the murder singlehandedly[52] and hence his reliance on Clytemnestra to complete the act—crucially distinguishes Seneca's treatment of the story, at least in comparison with other extant versions of it. Hence our focus now turns to Aegisthus's devilish cunning in co-opting Clytemnestra as his *de facto* murder weapon.

---

[50] So Antoniadis 2015:63: "Seneca's principal interest seems to lie not in a character study of the queen of Argos but *in the adultery itself as a motivating factor of the passions and actions in play*" (my emphasis).

[51] Hence rightly Mader 1988:53: "In the complexity of her motivation, Seneca's Clytem[n]estra surpasses all the Greek prototypes."

[52] On "the reversal of Aegisthus' gender identity," see Philippides 2013:122–123; on his characterization more generally in the *Agamemnon*, see Schenkeveld 1976.

III. THE USE AND ABUSE OF CLYTEMNESTRA

In the fourth choral ode (808–866), the chorus offers an elaborate celebration of Hercules as Argive hero:[53] if the memory lingers of the ghostly Thyestes's allusion in the prologue to the sun reversing itself at the sight of the Thyestean cannibalistic feast (36; cf. 295–297), the fourth choral ode announces a happier prolongation of night for the mighty Jovian task of conceiving Hercules in the first place (814–818).[54] Then, after briskly cataloguing Hercules's 12 labors (829–862), the ode ends with a flourish that connects Hercules's attack on Laomedon's Troy with Agamemnon's own recent Trojan conquest: Agamemnon is thus indirectly extolled as a victor in the Herculean vein, albeit the ode concludes by hailing Hercules's conquest of Troy in but ten days, not ten years (865–866).[55] What, then, are we to make of this unexpected detour into Hercules's familiar story?

Despite its attractive alignment of Hercules and Agamemnon, Richard characterizes the ode as "apparently, a mere interlude separating Agamemnon's entry into the palace from Cassandra's report of his death."[56] Certain verbal and thematic links relating the ode to its context help to challenge this view.[57] But far more relevant for now is

[53] Hercules was linked to Argos through his grandfather Electryon. Cf. Eurip. *Arch.* fr. 228a.13–15 (Collard and Cropp 2008:238–239): "Alcmene's father Electryon, who held the city of Mycene in the Argolid," albeit the referent of the "who ..." clause (Electryon or Sthenelus, his brother?) has been contested; see, on the problem, Harder 1985:197–199 (on 13–14).

[54] On this exception to the play's many negative time disorders, see Philippides 2013:125–126.

[55] Hence, despite the happy *prima facie* implication of "Herculean" Agamemnon, perhaps the shadow of a "demeaning comparison" (Philippides 2013:127) looms over 865–866, complicating the question of who sings the fourth ode, a chorus of loyal Mycenaean maidens or of captive Trojans. The majority view favors the former (bibliography in Philippides 2013:127n16), but see now the intriguing intervention of Kohn 2013:52–53 ("It is most sensible to think ... that there is only one Chorus, which portrays citizens of Mycenae when it first appears, and which later exits to return as captive Trojan women and remains in that persona for the rest of the play").

[56] Tarrant 1976a:323.

[57] See esp. Philippides (2013:120), stressing as a major connecting mechanism "the juxtaposition of Hercules and Aegisthus"; see also Davis 1993:116–118 (Hercules and Agamemnon already conjoined in the third ode, 611–614).

Cassandra's vision of how Clytemnestra persuades Agamemnon to don the mantle that she has woven for him:

> Detrahere cultus uxor hostiles iubet,
> induere potius coniugis fidae manu
> textos amictus. Horreo atque animo tremo!
> Regemne perimet exul et adulter uirum?
> Venere fata: sanguinem extremae dapes
> domini uidebunt, et cruor Baccho incidet.
> Mortifera uinctum perfidae tradit neci
> induta uestis: exitum manibus negant
> caputque laxi et inuii claudunt sinus.

Sen. Ag. 881–889[58]

His wife bids him take off this enemy attire [sc. Priam's robes; cf. 880], and put on instead a mantle woven by her hand, his faithful spouse. I shudder and tremble in spirit! Shall the king be murdered by an exile, the husband by an adulterer? The hour of fate has come. The feast's last course will see the master's blood—yes, blood will drop into the wine. The deadly garment he has put on binds him and delivers him to death by treachery. Its loose, impenetrable folds imprison his head and give his hands no way out.

The Hercules ode may be neatly self-contained in one sense, but it proves to be proleptic in another, readying us as it does for the Herculean connotations of Agamemnon's murder. Hercules had sacked a city, Oechalia, and returned home with Iole as his prize: according to the familiar Sophoclean storyline as treated in Ovid's *Heroides* 9 and

---

[58] On Seneca's fusion here of two versions of Agamemnon's death, see Degiovanni 2004:380–381: murder at a *banquet* (as in Homer, Sophocles, and probably Livius Andronicus), but Seneca maintains the textile associated with Agamemnon's murder in his *bath* (Aeschylus, Euripides). Further and more important, it may be that Seneca was following an established tradition in portraying the infamous *uestis* as made by Clytemnestra's own hand (Degiovanni 382–384, citing schol. ad Eur. *Or.* 25 [Schwartz 1887:100.5–7]); but Seneca exploits that strand for a very particular reason, I suggest, to facilitate the Clytemnestra-Deianira parallel adduced below (pp. 260–262).

Metamorphoses 9 or in the pseudo-Senecan *Hercules Oetaeus*, Deianira
is no stranger to Hercules's straying; but the new development of
Iole's presence brings fresh humiliation as the latter is paraded before
Deianira's very eyes.[59] Her last hope is to regalvanize Hercules's
attention through what, she thinks, is the love charm that the dying
Nessus had vouchsafed her in his gore; the robe she sends to Hercules
is smeared with that gore, only for him of course to die an agonizing
death when he dons the garment and Nessus's poison takes effect. In
Sophocles's *Trachiniae*, Deianira asks Lichas to deliver to her husband
the robe that she has made by her own hand (τῆς ἐμῆς χερός, 603);[60]
if with *mortifera vestis* (887–888) Seneca directly echoes Sophocles's
θανάσιμον πέπλον (758) of the robe,[61] then Clytemnestra's insistence
that she wove the mantle for Agamemnon by her own hand (882–883) is
a further Sophoclean touch.

These various insights are keenly perceived in Silvia Marcucci's
demonstration of the vital role that the fourth choral ode plays in
introducing Hercules within the drama just before the Herculean
analogy turns deadly;[62] but in one respect, I contend, Marcucci's position can be taken significantly further. Deianira had no intention of
killing Hercules, as she stresses in the *Hercules Oetaeus*:

> Inuicte coniunx, innocens animus mihi,
> scelesta manus est. pro nimis mens credula,
> pro Nesse fallax atque semiferi doli!
>
> Sen. *Herc. Oet.* 964–966[63]

---

[59] Cf. esp. Ov. *Her.* 9.119–136, *Met.* 9.134–151, [Sen.] *Herc. Oet.* 233–253, 278–282,
discussed alongside *Ag.* 174–191 and 252–259 (Agamemnon as a straying Hercules,
Clytemnestra as a Deianira, Cassandra as an Iole) by Marcucci (1995):192–197 and
(1996):66–68.

[60] Cf. Easterling (1982):148 on 603: "i.e. woven by D. herself, but the audience may also
think of her subsequent 'treatment' of the robe [cf. 580] with the charm."

[61] On these Sophoclean traces, Marcucci (1995):199–200 and (1996):69–70. For
Clytemnestra as a negation of the faithful Penelope in her weaving, Philippides
(2013):123n9.

[62] (1995):202–203 and (1996):70–71.

[63] Cf. 938–941, 1464–1471, her innocence in keeping with the Sophoclean Deianira (cf.
Soph. *Trach.* 841–850, 932–935); but for possible complications to this Senecan vision of
innocence see n64 below.

O invincible husband, my spirit is innocent, but my hand
bears the crime. Oh for my credulous mind, oh for Nessus'
deceit and half-bestial guile!

On one level, the evocations of Hercules's death in the *Agamemnon*
merely intensify the horror of Clytemnestra's premeditated murder
through contrast with the innocence of Deianira's deadly actions. Or
does Seneca aim for a rather more nuanced effect? Here Aegisthus's
role becomes pivotal once more, and the infatuated Clytemnestra's
erotic motive for the murder crucial: the full force of the Herculean
analogy lies, I propose, not just in correlating the two victims who
don the fatal robes, and not just in contrasting cruel Clytemnestra and
woebegone Deianira, but also in comparing the sinister male hands
who are behind both killings. Nessus deceived Deianira, and Aegisthus
too exerts a controlling influence over Clytemnestra. Certainly,
Clytemnestra has other (sub-)motives for the killing, and it is striking
that after Aegisthus has the first ineffectual stab, she is left to drive
the action and to deliver the mortal blow with the ax (897–903). She
means business, and is not put up to the task solely through her lover's
mesmerizing influence; but so much of the force that goes into that
blow has nevertheless been generated by the psychological (even path-
ological) hold that Aegisthus has over her.

The Hercules-Agamemnon analogy in the death scene is
complicated yet further, then, by the stress placed in this study on
Clytemnestra's love affair as her primary motive for murder: Nessus
avenged himself on Hercules by tricking Deianira, and Seneca's
Aegisthus avenges his father partly by inflaming—even *cynically
inducing?*—the infatuated Clytemnestra to murder Agamemnon.[64] In
effect, is Clytemnestra Aegisthus's instrumental agent for a killing

---

[64] But for traces of a very different, pre-Sophoclean Deianira, killing Hercules either
vindictively or through reckless delusion, see Carawan 2000, esp. 194–195 (on the
Hesiodic *Catalogue of Women* fr. 25.17–23 M-W [cf. p. 195 for Deianira "not an innocent
victim of Nessus' deception before the fifth century"]). This point may conceivably have
significant implications for the view taken above of Seneca's Clytemnestra as duped
like Deianira: could it be that Seneca adds yet another layer of complexity by invoking
a Deianira whose actions he knew to be ambiguously portrayed/interpreted in the
received tradition? On this line of inquiry, doubt about Deianira's "true" motivation in

that, as the play itself repeatedly reminds us, he can barely summon the nerve to accomplish on his own? And then, perhaps, the final sting in the tail: has Aegisthus used her all along, and is one branch of the tragedy here that Clytemnestra, while far from innocent in so many other ways and motivations, is nonetheless a victim of Nessus-like deception? It is clearly hazardous to speculate when so little survives of Greco-Roman tragedy: but we are left to ponder if a major Senecan innovation in his *Agamemnon*, or at least an idiosyncratic point of Senecan emphasis in his treatment of the well-worn storyline, was to portray Clytemnestra as horribly used by her ruthlessly exploitative partner(-in-crime).[65] In effect, for the dastardly Aegisthus, was Clytemnestra more a lever than a lover, less the sincere object of his passion than the unwitting subject/agent of his prewritten revenge script? A despicable scenario, certainly, but a plotline that was by no means too otherworldly, perhaps, for as knowing an aficionado of 1st-century imperial intrigue as Seneca.

COLUMBIA UNIVERSITY

WORKS CITED

Antoniadis, T. 2015. "*Scelus Femineum*: Adultery and Revenge in Valerius Flaccus' *Argonautica* Book 2 (98–241) and Seneca's *Agamemnon*." *Symbolae Osloenses* 89(1):60–80.

Aygon, J.-P. 2014. "Les tragédies de Sénèque: cohérence dramaturgique, mise en scène et interprétation 'stoïcienne.'" *Pallas* 95:13–32.

Baertschi, A. M. 2010. "Drama and Epic Narrative: The Test Case of the Messenger Speech in Seneca's *Agamemnon*." In *Beyond the Fifth Century: Interactions with Greek Tragedy from the Fourth Century BCE to the Middle Ages*, ed. I. Gildenhard and M. Revermann, 249–268. Berlin.

---

sending the poisoned cloak to Hercules would potentially obscure yet further the cloud of uncertainty surrounding the hierarchy of Clytemnestra's own murder-motive(s).

[65] Cf. *Herc. Oet.* 715–719 for Deianira's "vague fear" (*nescioquid animus timuit*, 717) of treachery on Nessus' part (so already Soph. *Trach.* 705–722). Seneca's Clytemnestra in the *Agamemnon* shows no such fear, suspicion, or prevarication at all: bleak evidence to reinforce the thought that Aegisthus has ruthlessly duped her?

Battistella, C. 2013. "Clytemestra's Deception and Glory (Seneca, *Agamemnon* 108–124)." *Museum Helveticum* 70(2):199–205.

Carawan, E. 2000. "Deianira's Guilt." *TAPA* 130:189–237.

Caviglia, F. 1986–1987. "Elementi di tradizione epica nell'*Agamemnon* di Seneca." *Quaderni di Cultura e di Tradizione Classica* 4–5:145–165.

Collard, C., and M. Cropp, eds. 2008. *Euripides. Fragments, Aegeus-Meleager.* Vol 7. Loeb Classical Library 504. Cambridge, MA.

Croisille, J. M. 1964. "Le personage de Clytemnestre dans l'*Agamemnon* de Sénèque." *Latomus* 23:464–472.

Damschen, G., and A. Heil, eds. 2014. *Brill's Companion to Seneca: Philosopher and Dramatist.* Leiden.

Davis, P. J. 1993. *Shifting Song: The Chorus in Seneca's Tragedies.* Hildesheim.

Degiovanni L. 2004. "Sui modelli nell'*Agamemnon* di Seneca: Tre note testuali e interpretative." *Studi Classici e Orientali* 50:373–395.

Easterling, P., ed. 1982. *Sophocles. Trachiniae.* Cambridge Greek and Latin Classics. Cambridge.

Fitch, J. G. 1981. "Sense-Pauses and Relative Dating in Seneca, Sophocles, and Shakespeare." *AJP* 102(3):289–307.

———, ed. 2018. *Seneca. Oedipus, Agamemnon, Thyestes; [Seneca]. Hercules on Oeta, Octavia.* Loeb Classical Library 78. Orig. pub. 2004, revised 2018. Cambridge, MA.

Frangoulidis, S. 2016. "Seneca's *Agamemnon*: Mycenaean Becoming Trojan." In *Roman Drama and Its Contexts*, ed. S. Frangoulidis, S. J. Harrison, and G. Manuwald, 395–409. Berlin.

Gantz, T. 1993. *Early Greek Myth: A Guide to Literary and Artistic Sources.* Baltimore.

Hall, E. 2005. "Aeschylus' Clytemnestra Versus Her Senecan Tradition." In *Agamemnon in Performance, 458 BC to AD 2004*, ed. F. Macintosh, P. Michelakis, E. Hall, and O. Taplin, 53–75. Oxford.

Harder, A. 1985. *Euripides. Kresphontes and Archelaos: Introduction, Text, and Commentary.* Leiden.

———. 2012. *Callimachus. Aetia.* 2 vols. Oxford.

Harrison, G. W. M. 2014. "Characters." In Damschen and Heil 2014, 593–613.

Hornblower, S. 2015. *Lykophron. Alexandra.* Oxford.

Kohn, T. 2013. *The Dramaturgy of Senecan Tragedy.* Ann Arbor, MI.

Kugelmeier, C. 2014. "Agamemnon." In Damschen and Heil 2014, 493–500.

Lavery, J. 2004. "Some Aeschylean Influences on Seneca's *Agamemnon*." *Materiali e Discussioni per l'Analisi dei Testi Classici* 53:183–194.

Levaniouk, O. 2011. *Eve of the Festival: Making Myth in Odyssey 19*. Hellenic Studies Series 46. Cambridge, MA.

Littlewood, C. J. 2004. *Self-Representation and Illusion in Senecan Tragedy*. Oxford.

Lohikoski, K. K. 1966. "Der Parallelismus Mykene-Troja in Senecas *Agamemnon*." *Arctos* 4:63–70.

Mader, G. 1988. "*Fluctibus Variis Agor*: An Aspect of Seneca's Clytemestra Portrait." *Acta Classica* 31:51–70.

Marcucci, S. 1995. "Per una interpretazione della morte di Agamennone in Seneca." *Studi Classici e Orientali* 44:191–203.

———. 1996. *Modelli "tragici" e modelli "epici" nell'*Agamemnon *di L. A. Seneca*. Milan.

Philippides, K. 2013. "On the Fourth Choral Song of Seneca's *Agamemnon*." *Logeion* 3:120–131.

Pillinger, E. 2019. *Cassandra and the Poetics of Prophecy in Greek and Latin Literature*. Cambridge.

Reinhardt, T. 2010. "The Moods of Clytemestra (Sen. *Ag.* 306)." *Millennium Jahrbuch* 7:29–36.

Schenkeveld, D. M. 1976. "Aegisthus in Seneca's *Agamemnon*." In *Miscellanea Tragica in Honorem J. C. Kamerbeek*, ed. J. M. Bremer, S. L. Radt and C. J. Ruijgh, 397–403. Amsterdam.

Schiesaro, A. 2014. "Seneca's *Agamemnon*: The Entropy of Tragedy." *Pallas* 95:179–191.

Schindler, C. 2000. "Dramatisches Unwetter: Der Seesturm in Senecas *Agamemnon* (vv. 421–578)." In *Skenika: Beiträge zum antiken Theater und seiner Rezeption*, ed. S. Gödde and T. Heinze, 135–149. Darmstadt.

Schwartz, E., ed. 1887. *Scholia in Euripidem*. Vol. 1, *Scholia in Hecubam Orestem Phoenissas*. Berlin.

Shelton, J.-A. 1983. "Revenge or Resignation: Seneca's *Agamemnon*." *Ramus* 12:159–183.

Tarrant, R. J., ed. 1976a. *Seneca. Agamemnon*. Edited with a commentary. Cambridge Classical Texts and Commentaries 18. Cambridge.

———. "Senecan Drama and its Antecedents." *HSCP* 82:213–263.

Tola, E. 2009. "Una lectura del *Agamemnon* de Séneca: *Nefas* trágico e imaginario poético." *Auster* 14:85–99.

Trinacty, C. V. 2014. *Senecan Tragedy and the Reception of Augustan Poetry.* Cambridge.

———. 2016. "Catastrophe in Dialogue: *Aeneid* 2 and Seneca's *Agamemnon.*" *Vergilius* 62:99–114.

Wray, D. 2009. "Seneca and Tragedy's Reason." In *Seneca and the Self*, ed. S. Bartsch and D. Wray, 237–254. Cambridge.

PART THREE

MUSIC

AUGUSTAN POETRY AND THE AGE OF RUST

MUSIC AND METAPHOR IN ANAÏS MITCHELL'S *HADESTOWN*

Thomas E. Jenkins

ANAÏS MITCHELL'S *HADESTOWN*, a musical version of the story of Orpheus and Eurydice as narrated by Virgil in the fourth book of the *Georgics* (*G.* 4.453–527), has witnessed a particularly circuitous route to the Broadway stage. Indeed, it began with a 2010 concept album that responded, through classical reception, to two contemporary events in the American landscape: the continuing American occupation of Iraq (through 2006 and beyond) and the financial crisis of 2008, the so-called Great Recession.[1] Composed in an American folk-rock idiom—with echoes of Dixieland jazz, country, Woodie Guthrie, and Bob Dylan—*Hadestown*'s initial album nabbed a number of critical accolades, including a rave from the *Times*' Dan Cairns: "a multi-layered, sensationally good and endlessly absorbing 'folk opera.'"[2] While a few critics caviled that plot was not the album's especial virtue—"There's clearly a narrative, even if it isn't easy to follow," observed the BBC's John Lusk, correctly—there was the germ here of a more ambitious project.[3] Eventually, Rachel Chavkin—the breakout director of the innovative Tolstoy adaptation *Natasha, Pierre, & The Great Comet of 1812*— signed on to help shape the concept album into a full-length evening of theater. The successful Off-Broadway production, at New York

---

[1] B. Hallenbeck, "*Hadestown* 2016: Anaïs Mitchell's *Hadestown* Reborn Off-Broadway," *Burlington Free Press*, April 16, 2019, https://eu.burlingtonfreepress.com/story/news/2019/04/16/anais-mitchells-hadestown-reborn-off-broadway/84198858/.

[2] D. Cairns, "Anaïs Mitchell Hadestown," *Times*, April 25, 2010, https://www.thetimes.co.uk/article/anais-mitchell-hadestown-0wzwl5q9d6p.

[3] J. Lusk, Review of *Hadestown*, by Anaïs Mitchell, BBC, https://www.bbc.co.uk/music/reviews/rqcg/.

Theater Workshop in 2017, received a full recording in album format; subsequent reworkings of the show premiered in Edmonton, Alberta, Canada, and at the National Theatre in London ahead of a Broadway premiere in the spring of 2019. In June 2019, *Hadestown* won a slew of Tony Awards, including Best Musical, Score, Set Design, and Direction. (André de Shields won a Tony for his role as the narrator, Hermes; of the principal cast, Eva Noblezada, Patrick Page, and Amber Gray were all nominated.)

This essay proposes to examine *Hadestown* as an act of extraordinary literary translation, from classical Latin to contemporary *American*. And so by translation, I do not mean simply a word-for-word translation but rather one in the sense that theorists of reception employ: a process of linking culturally relevant signifiers from the source language to the new.[4] There are (literal) Orphic themes and images on the stage, of course, but there is also a metaphorical translation to a distinctly American mise-en-scène. As Mitchell observes in a lengthy blogpost: "When I play *Hadestown* songs in my own shows, I usually introduce [*Hadestown*] as quick as I can saying, 'It's based on the Orpheus myth, and set in a post-apocalyptic American Depression era ...'"[5] It is worth pulling apart the interwoven strands of Mitchell's own interpretation of *Hadestown* as a reception: it is both strictly temporal (the Great Depression) *and* economic/political (dystopian plutocracy). The first strand—the classics and the Great Depression—has surprisingly generated its own spatial field in artistic reception, and so Mitchell continues a tradition of "thinking through" the American Great Depression while (counterintuitively?) thinking through Latin poetry.

As a comparable example of the use of the Depression as the basis for an eco-critical classical reception, there is the powerful version by Tom Biby and Jonathan Fetter-Vorm (fig. 1). These illustrators

[4] For an illuminating guide to categories within classical reception, see Hardwick (2003:9–10), who distinguishes between translation, adaptation, and refiguration, while noting the semantic slippages between the three. For Hardwick, translation can be used metaphorically—such as "translation to the stage" (10)—and it is in that sense that Mitchell has translated Virgil (and to some extent, Ovid).

[5] A. Mitchell, "The Long-Winded Story of Hadestown," in "Anaïs Mitchell—Hadestown," Basement Rug, March 3, 2010, http://basementrug.com/3424.

translate the drought of Lucretius's *De Rerum Natura* to America's Dust Bowl and conclude with an evocative image of a tired farmer pausing from his pointless exertions on the parched heartland landscape. As the artists note, "Here is Lucretius' tale of the earth overtaxed and of lands too choked to bear fruit, retold with a twist: from the perspective of American farmers during the Great Depression."[6] Book 2's devastating drought—illustrated by billowing clouds of dust—illuminates the *American* consequences of Nature's fickleness: in Lucretius's golden age, "Nature itself gave forth its sweet fruits and happy crops—which scarcely now swell even with the application of our toil (*labor*) ... But now the fruits are drying up and serve only to increase our toil (*labor*)" (Lucr. 2.1161–1163). This development is terrible enough; but then Lucretius—and Biby/Fetter-Vorm—transfer the desolation of the landscape to the desolation of the *landscaper*: as the caption in figure 1 reads, "Now see the ancient ploughman shake his head and sigh again that the work (= *labores*) of his tired hands has come to naught ..." (= Lucr. 2.1164–1165).[7] I have emphasized the repetition of *labor* in the Latin text to underscore the link in the Roman poetic imagination between landscape and labor, a link emphasized by Biby/Fetter-Vorm and (as we shall see) by both Virgil and Mitchell. For all these artists, the essence of existence may be ceaseless, and at times literally fruitless, *labor*.[8]

But the Depression was, of course, an economic as well as natural disaster. In his surprising and endlessly inventive version of Ovid's Erysichthon episode from the *Metamorphoses*, poet James Lasdun hits upon a similar translation of ecological disaster—but ties it even more firmly to American capitalistic greed.[9] In Ovid's version—adapted from Callimachus's *Hymn to Demeter*—Erysichthon's felling of Demeter's sacred tree is accomplished for the sheer and unadulterated *joy* of it: the king spurns the divinity of the gods (*Met.* 8.739–740) and chops

---

[6]   Kick 2012:140.

[7]   "The Ancient Plowman," © Tom Biby and Jonathan Fetter-Vorm, 2007; Kick 2012:147.

[8]   For a passionate, Marxist-tinged investigation of *labor* in the *Georgics*, see Geue 2018; Geue argues that *labor* is central to the poem both in its presence but also (crucially) in its *elision*—the labor of agricultural slaves that is necessary but literally unsung.

[9]   Lasdun 1994. Further citations in the essay are to page numbers.

Figure 1. "The Ancient Plowman," © Tom Biby and Jonathan Fetter-Vorm, 2007.

down the tree to prove his power. The king's terrible comeuppance—he is so hungry, he eats himself—is the delicious finale to this morality tale: autophagy as lesson for us all. Lasdun's modern-day version preserves the moralistic tone of Ovid's myth but appends to it a *different* moral: here, Erysichthon's vendetta against trees is part of a real-estate mogul's entrepreneurial ambitions, as he deforests large swathes of (apparently) upstate New York, traditionally sacred to the Iroquois tribes. In an invocation to the goddesses, Lasdun makes explicit the translation between ancient and modern divinities: "Demeter, Ishtar, Ceres, / Papothewke ..." (205), and it is with distressingly modern technology—a roaring chainsaw—that Ceres's dogwood comes crashing down. But it is the central episode that most firmly ties this text to Biby/Fetter-Vorm's image (fig. 1). An acolyte of Ceres is sent to fetch the goddess Hunger: in Ovid's original poem, Fames appropriately inhabits a barren tundra on the outermost rim of Scythia (*Met.* 8.788).[10] In Lasdun's version, however, Ceres's messenger must pass through a Depression Era evocation of America's blighted heartland: "[She followed] a thin / ooze of mud-coloured sludge / that crawled across a desolate moonlike plain / of exhausted farmland; barren / skeletal orchards, rusting silos, / Dry irritation pipes crisscrossing meadows / of dust ..." (206–207). But this is not *just* an environmental wasteland but a man-made one, with "strip-mines, foundries, factories" adding oil and pesticides to the water and *creating* this depressed landscape, one directly linked to the avarice of Erysichthon (and his ilk). Scarcity and plutocracy go hand-in-hazmat-glove.

The genius of *Hadestown*, as classical reception, is that it combines *all* of these themes: it tackles the Great Depression, climate change, plutocracy, *and* the tragedy of wasted labor, including love's labors lost. And it does so with the most infectious score since Cole Porter: including a toe-tapping number by the Fates and a brilliant mosaic of arias for its main characters. In addition, *Hadestown* not only juggles the wasted labor of Orpheus but the blighted dreams of Persephone, here

---

[10] This episode is a terrific example of the pathetic fallacy in Ovid, in which landscape mirrors the ethical or aesthetic character of its denizens. For a monograph-length treatment of this trope, see Segal 1969.

trapped in a difficult marriage to the King of the Dead. It thus combines a tale dripping with political implications—the iron rule of Hades over a polluting factory town—with the timeless and perhaps even senti-mental overtones of Roman love elegy.[11] Ultimately *Hadestown*'s hipster sensibility shines through: Hades might be a ruthless corporate over-lord, but even he is not immune to the charms, and the power, of a downtown, West Village Virgil.

The interpretative heart of Mitchell's show—what makes it tick as *art*—are the competing visions of Hadestown as a semiotic space. In Ovid and Virgil, the underworld is a place of unalloyed terror, the unknowable made frightful: *loca plena timoris* (*Met.* 10.29), as Ovid evocatively terms it. (Virgil's "infernal maws," *Taenarias fauces* [*G.* 467], sound equally unin-viting.) Mitchell's choral Fates, however, sing a different tune:

> Everybody dresses in clothes so fine
> Everybody's pockets are weighted down
> Everybody sipping ambrosia wine
> It's a goldmine in Hadestown
>
> From "Way Down Hadestown"

There is much to note here. The ancient conflation of *Ploutos* (Πλοῦτος; wealth) with Pluto is in full force.[12] Hadestown—at least on the Fates' Pollyanna view—is a place replete with riches: sartorial, numismatic, culinary, and economic. It is a *literal* goldmine: a descent not to hell but to a helluva lifestyle. Hades, as leader and company foreman, has

---

[11] The subjectivity of Persephone in Augustan Latin texts is mostly occluded: Ovid treats the etiological aspects of her assault twice (once at *Fast.* 4.417–620 and again at *Met.* 5.341–661), while Propertius and Tibullus focus on her numinous powers of mercy (Prop. 2.28.47 and Tib. 3.5.6). In her rewriting of Persephone into a modern and desperate housewife, Mitchell seems to be creating a revisionist, "realist" version of the Augustan *scripta puella*, an elegiac trope famously analyzed by Wyke 1987. (On Wyke's reading, many modern critics are seduced by the notion that they are reading of a *real*, "flesh and blood" elegiac mistress [47]; in a sense, Mitchell makes that illusion "real" by creating a fleshed-out Persephone—though she is assuredly a wife, not a mistress per se.)

[12] See especially Oosterhuis 2013:113–116, with a survey of the ancient conflation. Oosterhuis concludes (based on Mitchell's concept album): "*Hadestown* benefits from that conflation as it allows Hades to take an even greater metaphorical role. He is wealth, commerce, and cold, unfeeling capitalism" (116). That symbolism became even more pronounced in the piece's productions following the inauguration of Donald Trump.

managed (through the "mass media" of the Fates) to broadcast to the upper world a vision of his town as an upper-class utopia, where all needs are met (particularly shelter and food), and everybody is blessed. But it is the bohemian Orpheus—toiling in a day job as a barista—who offers a gimlet-eyed version of the great down below: "Everybody hungry, everybody tired / Everybody slaves by the sweat of his brow / The wage is nothing, and the work is hard / It's a graveyard in Hadestown." This is a clever bit of imagery: the verse first disputes the metaphors employed by the Fates—not ambrosia but hunger; not finery but sweat; not a goldmine but a graveyard. The last metaphor is particularly pointed: the *classical* Hades is a literal graveyard, filled with souls; the American Hadestown is a metaphorical graveyard, filled with the walking, proletariat dead. Critic Adam Feldman lauds the "intensity of [*Hadestown*'s] eco-Marxist vision of solidarity and the liberating potential of art"—a verdict that also glances at *Hadestown*'s reflections on aesthetics.[13]

Here, too, we have the first inkling that Mitchell combines capitalistic and environmental critiques in her examination of Hades, both place and king. In the Latin texts, it is striking how many images of regency and monarchy cluster around Hades and Persephone, including *regem* (*G.* 4.469), *tyranni* (4.492), *ipsae domus* (the "court," 4.481), and the breathless run of royal terminology in the *Metamorphoses* (10.15–16; 10.30; 10.35; 10.46; 10.47, all featuring the root of *reg-*, "to rule"). Clearly, Hades, as a politician, is not particularly amenable to alternative forms of netherworld governance. But who rules—*regit*—in America? Mitchell's answer: the CEO. Indeed, *Hadestown*'s Hades lords over his dominion as if a 1920's company town, such as Pullman, Illinois, or Hastings, Maine.[14] In fact, nearly every aspect of *Hadestown*'s lyrics works on three intertwined levels: the political, the economic, and the

[13] A. Feldman, Review of *Hadestown*, by Anaïs Mitchell, *TimeOut New York*, April 17, 2019, https://www.timeout.com/newyork/theater/hadestown-review-broadway.

[14] On the expansive social engineering of Pullman and his company town, see Reiff 2000: "For almost as long [as its defenders praised Pullman], its critics had excoriated the town as representing the worst excesses of a capitalist society where one man and his company could dominate every aspect of a worker's life in their dual roles as landlord and employer" (8).

environmental. Thus Orpheus's perceptive reframing of the rumors of underworld wealth, with my own backward-facing translation (translating "back" into Latin) in parentheses:

> King [*rex*] of silver
> King [*rex*] of gold
> And everything glittering
> under the ground
>
> Hades is king [*rex*]
> of oil and coal ...
> King [*rex*] of mortar
> King [*rex*] of bricks
> The River Styx is a river of stones
> and Hades lays them high and thick
> with a million hands that are not his own
> With a million hands, he builds a wall
>
> From "Epic II"

Here, Mitchell preserves the emphasis on kingship already found in Ovid and Virgil but ties this power explicitly to *labor:* Hades is a king not of subjects but of laborers, a million hands. (It is also a nifty synecdoche, as in the term *farmhand.*) In the next song ("Chant"), we meet these dispossessed "hands": the wretched "workers" who "keep [their] head low" as they toil to convert Hades's geological property into material wealth and prosperity. Michael Krass's costume design of the London and Broadway productions (fig. 2) makes clear the proletariat aspect of these workers' existences with safety goggles, tool belts, blacksmith aprons, and other necessary implements.

But while the workers drone on (ah, *le mot juste*), Hades boasts of the source of his considerable power in a misguided bid for his wife Persephone's continued affections:

> I built a foundry
> in the ground beneath your feet
> and there I fashioned things of steel
> oil drums and automobiles

And then I kept that furnace fed
with the fossils of the dead

From "Chant"

If much of *Hadestown* seems lyrical and atemporal, this particular lyric comes across, contrariwise, as prosaic and pointed: an indictment of 20th- (and now 21st-) century industrialization. In its evocation of steel, cars, and oil, it is reminiscent of the hellscape of Lasdun's *Erysichthon*, a geography destined for blight and hunger. But for Hades, this hunger is not human but mechanical, as he feeds the living machines with the remnants—the fossils—of the dead. The evocation of fossil fuel must be intentional as well: human labor as interchangeable with coal. And Hades's link to the specter of climate change is made explicit, as Persephone remarks that "up above / the harvest dies and people starve / Oceans rise and overflow / it ain't right and it ain't natural."

Figure 2. HADESTOWN by Anaïs Mitchell. Workers in Hades: Shaq Taylor, Beth Hinton-Lever; Sharif Afifl; Alesha Pease; Seyi Omooba. Directed by Chavkin; set designed by Hauck; costumes designed by Krass; lighting designed by King; choreographed by Neumann; at the National Theatre, London, UK, 1 November 2018. Credit Helen Maybanks/ArenaPAL.

Hades's great aria—"Why We Build the Wall"—shares in common with Mary Zimmerman's *Metamorphoses* an extraordinary shift in *meaning* engendered by monumental events. In 2001, Zimmerman's play—her stage version of Ovid's epic—was preparing for its off-Broadway premiere after a successful run in Chicago. The attack on New York's Twin Towers occurred during rehearsals, and suddenly the meaning of a classical reception *changed*—more properly, metamorphosed—instantly and irrevocably. As Zimmerman recounts in a 2002 interview with Bill Moyers, "There are at least two stories in the play where someone goes away, off to work basically, and is suddenly taken from the earth—just destroyed. And I remember on our first public performance, which was the 18th [of September], just sort of shaking and trembling off stage about showing this and dragging the audience through this story, including the dying prayer of a man saying, 'I only pray my body is found. Just let my body be found.'"[15] Most powerfully, the myth of Ceyx and Alcyone is now read as a metaphor for the missing dead in the rubble of the Twin Towers. What had been a more general rumination on loss now possesses a specific, American referent: the terror attacks on 9/11. In the same way, it is hard, in 2020, to imagine "Why We Build the Wall" as referring to anything *other* than American President Donald Trump's repeated exhortation to build a border wall between Mexico and the United States. The London and Broadway production design even features a tattoo of a wall on Hades's muscular forearm (fig. 3), a gesture that transparently connects America's physical might to its most prominent political symbol.

Let us now look at the song's lyrics (ruthlessly excerpted) through two sets of interpretative lenses, pre- and post-Trump:

> Why do we build the wall?
> My children, my children
> We build the wall to keep us free
>
> How does the wall keep us free?
> The wall keeps out the enemy

---

[15] M. Zimmerman, interviewed by Bill Moyer, *Now PBS*, March 22, 2002, https://www.pbs.org/now/transcript/transcript_zimmerman.html.

Who do we call the enemy?
The enemy is poverty
And the wall keeps out the enemy
And we build the wall to keep us free

Because we have and they have not
My children, my children
Because they want what we have got

What do we have that they should want?
We have a wall to work upon
We have work and they have none
And our work is never done

Let us first interpret this song *post*-Trump (which is how many critics of the Broadway premiere took it). In a Trumpian worldview, the enemy

Figure 3. HADESTOWN by Anaïs Mitchell. Patrick Page as Hades. Directed by Chavkin; set designed by Hauck; costumes designed by Krass; lighting designed by King; choreographed by Neumann; at the National Theatre, London, UK, 1 November 2018. Credit Helen Maybanks/ArenaPAL.

are foreigners (of any ilk) but particularly Mexicans, whom Trump infamously smeared on the campaign trail in 2015 as drug runners and rapists.[16] Trump's notorious solution—an "artistically-designed" 2000-mile long border wall—even inspired his *Game of Thrones*-themed tweet, "The Wall is Coming," of January 5, 2019.[17] In "Why We Build The Wall," the song's endless invocation of "freedom"—long a conservative rallying cry—would (on a Trumpian reading) signify the preservation of American economic liberty against the encroachment of Latin American societal ills, including crime, narcotics, and even welfare. A wall is then necessary to preserve the integrity of the American experiment, which rewards hard work and self-reliance (or self-*labor*). It is easy to read the penultimate stanza as Mexicans wanting (and thus *stealing*) what we Americans have got.

But this song was composed pre-Trump, and it is worth pondering in that light as well: after all, we shall all eventually be post-Trump. (Even Trump will be post-Trump.) The last stanza points us in a new interpretative direction: after all, it is not a Trumpian ideal—at least notionally—that we will *always* be building a wall. In theory, we could (and should) *finish* the wall. Rather, it is *Hades's* fantasy (and ideological position) that labor is its own reward: labor/*labor* and life are indivisible. Through working and building, we maintain the division between the haves and the have-nots: labor determines status, which determines the worth of a life.

So the climax of *Hadestown* features a fascinating sociopolitical twist: how might a song of Orpheus persuade a Libertarian Hades to bend his economic principles? It has long been observed that Virgil's and Ovid's versions of Orpheus's song are inverted negatives of each other: Virgil is long on affect, short on content, while Ovid is the other way around.[18] So in Virgil, the shades are moved by Orpheus's song (*G.*

---

[16] B. LoGiurato, "The Long, Wild Ride to Iowa: How Donald Trump Set the Presidential Campaign on Fire," *Business Insider*, February 1, 2016, https://www.businessinsider.com/donald-trump-presidential-campaign-iowa-caucus-polls-2016-1?IR=T.

[17] D. Trump, Twitter post, January 5, 2019, https://twitter.com/realDonaldTrump/status/1081735898679701505.

[18] For instance, Otis argues that Ovid intentionally avoids the *ethos* and *pathos* of the Virgilian version and investigates the genres of parody and comedy instead of tragedy:

4.471 *cantu commotae*), first stupefied by its beauty (*G.* 4.481 *stupuere*) and then sliding into immobility; even the hellhound Cerberus holds its tongue(s). Orpheus ascends, victorious, and this affect *substitutes* for the song, its charm (and efficacy) proven by the audience, not the song itself. Ovid, contrariwise, info-dumps a surprisingly prolix song of Orpheus, beginning with a rolling invocation to the masters of the Dead (*Met.* 10.17 *o positi sub terra numina mundi*) and next following the contours of a Ciceronian court case. (He even bluntly declares: *causa viae est coniunx* [*Met.* 10.23] to seal the generic reference.) But then an interesting twist: not only does Orpheus tout the power and efficacy of *Amor*—which we might expect—but he ties it specifically to the *amor* between Persephone and Hades, which we might not. In vatic vein, Orpheus contends that unless the story of Persephone's rape is fake news (*Met.* 10.28 *fama mentita*), Amor joined Persephone and Hades together as well: *vos quoque iunxit Amor* (*Met.* 10.28–29).[19] Thus Orpheus relies on identification and empathy as a tool of persuasion: the song works not because it is universal, but because it is *specific* to its audience of a loving (or at least love-possible) royal couple.

Given these different emphases in its two primary ancient Roman versions, the song of Orpheus presents a challenge for Mitchell as a reception artist. She has figured Hades as a proto-Trump and Orpheus as a proletariat laborer, and so neither ancient "solution" to the shape or content of the song seems quite right. Virgil reveals the *effect* of the song, not the song itself, but that solution would be anticlimactic in a contemporary Broadway musical where the power of performed song is paramount. Ovid transforms the song into a brilliant forensic display piece, but that choice does not fit Mitchell's characterization of her millennial protagonist—her Orpheus may be many oh-so-American things, but Clarence Darrow is not one of them. Instead, Mitchell turns

---

"Orpheus' long speech to Pluto and Prosperina (X, 17–39) is the king of amusing *suasoria* that Ovid thoroughly enjoyed" (1970:184). Lively expands on that interpretation, with a list of inversions and subversions that signal how "Ovid seems to challenge every detail of Virgil's famous version" (2011:100).

[19] See especially Guestella (2017:167–184) on the depictions of *Fama*, "rumor," in Virgil and Ovid; Guestella argues that Ovid, in particular, emphasizes the *unknowability* of rumor's origins: false because unsourced (183).

to poetic *imagery* as an agonal tactic: having constructed Hades/Trump at the center of a constellation of eco-Marxist images (including the exploitation of fossil fuel, climate change / global warming, barrier walls and concrete, and a literal sweatshop), Mitchell's Orpheus fights fire with water: he employs a different *style* (a countertenor lullaby as opposed to Hades's *basso profundo* rumblings) as well as an entirely different tonal world, with images drawn from pastorals, from love elegy, even from Sappho. (Roses and flowers—which featured prominently in the musical's staging—might well be drawn from Sappho's *Fragment 2*, with its apple-boughs and roses). In *Epic 3*—Orpheus's famous "song"—Orpheus conjures a world of imagery *first* ("King of shadows / king of shades"), thereby laying the groundwork for his competing imagistic world, of what a world *could* be. In a meta-theatrical twist, Hades is surprised by this song ("Oh, it's about me?")—this is a new reception, more Hades-centric than even Ovid's. Orpheus continues: "[H]e fell in love with a beautiful lady / Who walked up above / In her mother's green field / He fell in love with Persephone / Who was gathering flowers in the light of the sun." This insertion is clearly Mitchell's intertextual allusion to the *Homeric Hymn to Demeter*, in which Persephone gathers roses, crocuses, violets, iris blossoms, and hyacinths (*ll.* 6–7)—but Orpheus (or Mitchell) cannily elides the subsequent detail: that the narcissus was used a lure by Gaia to allow for Hades's ambush and assault (*ll.* 8–20).[20] Instead, Orpheus employs *empathy*, drawing a comparison across difference: "And I know how it was because / He was like me / A man in love with a woman."

There is a germ of Ovid's version but here made more pointed—and perhaps uncomfortably alluding to a fraternity of men desiring women. But at this point, Mitchell springs a surprise: Orpheus launches into a vocalize of, in effect, pure music: "La la la la la la la." The tune is set in a high register, childlike and whimsical, and in a semiotic vacuum: there are no longer flowers, sunlight, shadows. Simply *la la la la la la*. And then the audience experiences a redoubled surprise with Hades's response:

---

[20] Given the Augustan subtext of *Hadestown*, this detail might even be more specifically a reference to Ovid's version of the rape of Persephone starting at *Fast.* 4.419, particularly the flower-picking sequence of 429–444.

"Where'd you get that melody?" Hades clearly *knows* that melody; and we will learn he once *sang* that melody (he may even have been the first). Orpheus then is a type of *Hades redivivus*, or more accurately, a Hades rejuvenated. When he first met Persephone, Hades conflated epistemology and desire: "It was like she was someone you'd always known / It was like you were holding the world when you held her"—words that exactly echo *Eurydice's* song of love to Orpheus earlier in the musical ("All I've ever known is how to hold my own / but now I wanna hold you."). So Orpheus not only draws connections between himself and Hades but (surprisingly) between Eurydice and Hades, refiguring Hades as a lovestruck (and tongue-tied) singer: "So you opened your mouth and you started to sing: La la la la la la la."

Having established what a pre-Libertarian Hades might have sounded (and felt) like, Orpheus then attends to the climax of his song, which both acknowledges and undercuts Hades's metaphor world, a world so carefully established throughout the architecture of the musical. Orpheus wonders where Hades's "heart" has gone—a heart Hades possessed while a man but abandoned "now that the man is king." Orpheus then cleverly paints the material rewards of Hadestown as curses instead: "[T]he more he has ... the greater the weight of the world ... / see how he <u>labors</u> beneath that load ... / So he keeps his head low, he keeps his back bending / He's grown so afraid that he'll lose what he owns / but what he doesn't know is that what he's defending / is already gone ..." The gold and diamonds of Hadestown are figured as weight, and it is *Hades*, now, who is the true sufferer of *labor*: the song of Orpheus even harkens back to the workers' "Chant" ("Low, keep your head, keep your head low"), with its evident evocation of American prison chain gangs. Riches did not bring happiness: when penniless, Hades possessed pleasure, youth, and a metaphorical "treasure inside of [the] chest": a heart. The young Hades reaching out for Persephone had—in both material and emotional senses—"nothing to lose."

Having torpedoed Hades's free-enterprise-based metaphor world with a sly combination of historically-grounded argument and song, Orpheus simply waits for the results. At which point, Hades muses, "la la la la la." Orpheus responds, "la la la la la." And *Persephone*, affected by this lyrical evocation of her shared past, chimes in, "la la la la la la."

Orpheus's song—or, more accurately, Mitchell's song—has rolled back time to simpler days without *labor*, without riches, without loss, without even words. We are back, as in a golden age, to a time when *amor* (love) need not compete with *labor* because *labor* simply does not exist. (In this, Orpheus's song obliquely alludes to Virgil's all-giving earth (*G.* 1.127-128)—before *labor improbus* makes its late and unlamented appearance).

At the performance I attended in May of 2019, the final moments of *Hadestown* drew gasps from the audience, partly because of the effective staging of the dénouement and partly because Americans, weaned on television such as *America's Got Talent*, could not process that a winning song might nonetheless culminate in tragedy. It is worth pondering why Mitchell preserves this classical ending when she might—as in Gluck's famous operatic version—tack on the happiest of conclusions instead. (In that work, the goddess *Amore* takes pity on Orpheus after he loses Eurydice *again*; she resurrects Eurydice to great fanfare, if not to particularly great sense.)[21] But having firmly tied Orpheus's tale to a capitalist and eco-critical framework, Mitchell *could not* alter the ending: the forces of capitalism and climate change are not arcing towards a happy ending in American *reality* and so cannot be honestly portrayed as such in art. Thus, for Orpheus, "Doubt Comes In" reflects a diffidence in himself as refracted both though Eurydice ("Who am I to think that she would follow me into the cold and dark again?") as well as Hades ("Who am I to think that he wouldn't deceive me just to make me leave alone?"); he thus falls into Hades's trap, set in the song "His Kiss, the Riot." Hades correctly intuits that this millennial Orpheus can only thrive as part of a corporate body (of laborers, of artists, of millennials) and that divorced from "the safety of a crowd," Orpheus will buckle to doubt. Indeed, Orpheus loses confidence in his own powers of prognostication and even perception ("I used to see the way the world

---

[21] The reception history of Orpheus in music is vast: for a good starting place on the enlightenment and post-enlightenment refiguring of Orpheus in Western music, see Agnew 2008. On Gluck's transformation of a "gloomy" myth into other affective modes (including high-spiritedness), see especially Agnew 2008:121–122. On the reception history of Orpheus in opera as well as film (including *Rabbit Hole* and *Slumdog Millionaire*), see Solomon 2019.

could be / But now the way it is is all I see and ...”). To ascertain reality, Orpheus turns around.

The rest, as they say, is history. Or rather, tragedy. The narrator, Hermes—something of an emotional wreck himself—recognizes the weirdness of singing, and *re*-singing, “a tragedy”: “’Cause here’s the thing / To know how it ends / And still begin to sing it again / As if it might turn out this time / I learned that from a friend of mine.” And then Hermes’s singing falters, as the god simply speaks: “[Orpheus] could make you see how the world could be.” Yes, it is a sentimental conclusion to the evening, made even more so by the surprise toast to Orpheus during the curtain call: “We Raise Our Cups.” And, yes, Mitchell might be accused of promoting an oversize veneration of the misunderstood artist, a bohemian stance that would not be out of place in, say, fin de siècle Paris. But what saves (and elevates) *Hadestown* is its razorsharp evisceration of contemporary pillars of conservative economic thought, including competition, efficiency, fossil-fuel reliance, and nativism. By weaving together these strands as a *system*, Mitchell has, intentionally or otherwise, created a spectacularly political piece of art, one that stresses the tragedy of the solitary artist, or the solitary person, fighting the system—and losing. It is the transplantation of heartless tragedy into the depressed American heartland. And the only succor, then as now, is *carmen* (song) (*G*. 4.514).

This volume is dedicated to Richard Tarrant, whose teaching and wisdom have touched so many of us. Many years ago, in a lecture on Virgil’s *Aeneid* delivered to Trinity University undergraduates, Richard observed—and I quote this from memory—“In my lifetime, the greatest change in the field of classics has been the shift of *modern* perspective: from the classical authors as ‘masters’ to the classical authors as peers.” In other words, for many aspects of human inquiry—particularly in ethics and the humanities—we have reconsidered the notion (and even the desirability) of an answer flowing ineluctably from classical texts. Rather, we have an apprehension of Virgil and Ovid as colleagues in inquiry, who observe, describe, and critique the worlds and even underworlds around us. A happy corollary to this observation is that our fellow artists—rarely fearless in transforming antiquity—have taken the spirit of classical observation to realms of inquiry unheard of, including those of climate change and income inequality.

In *Hadestown*, the god Hermes has the last word, but for this chapter on *Hadestown*, it seems only fitting that Richard should. So from an email of October, 2019, here are Richard's *ipsissima verba*, penned after watching the musical *Hadestown*: "By the end I was hooked. (I even got a little moist in the eye when Hades and Persephone did their little dance.)" And so we raise our cup to Orpheus *and* Richard Tarrant: heroes, both.

Trinity University

WORKS CITED

Agnew, V. 2008. *Enlightenment Orpheus: The Power of Music in Other Worlds.* Oxford.

Geue, T. 2018. "Soft Hands, Hard Power: Sponging Off the Empire of Leisure (Virgil, *Georgics* 4)." *Journal of Roman Studies* 108:115–140.

Guastella, G. 2017. *Word of Mouth: Fama and Its Personifications in Art and Literature from Ancient Rome to the Middle Ages.* New York.

Hardwick, L. 2003. *Reception Studies.* Greece & Rome: New Surveys in the Classics 33. Oxford.

Kick, R. 2012. *The Graphic Canon.* Vol. 1. New York.

Lasdun, J. 1994. "Erysichthon." In *After Ovid: New Metametamorphoses*, ed. Michael Hoffman and James Lasdun, 198–212. New York.

Lively, G. 2011. *Ovid's Metamorphoses: A Reader's Guide.* London.

Mitchell, A. 2019. *Hadestown.* Original Broadway cast album. Sing It Again Records.

Oosterhuis, D. 2013. "Orpheus, the Original Penniless Poet: Plutus/Pluto in Anaïs Mitchell's Hadestown." *Syllecta Classica* 23:103–126.

Otis, B. 1970. *Ovid as an Epic Poetic.* 2nd ed. Cambridge.

Reiff, J. 2000. "Rethinking Pullman: Urban Space and Working-Class Activism." *Social Science History* 24 (1):7–32.

Segal, C. 1969. *Landscape in Ovid's Metamorphoses: A Study in the Transformations of a Literary Symbol.* Wiesbaden.

Solomon, J. 2019. "Cinematic Signatures of Orpheus and Operatic Evocations." *Illinois Classical Studies* 44 (1):111–136.

Wyke, M. 1987. "Written Women: Propertius' *scripta puella*." *JRS* 77:47–61.

ROMAN CIVIL WAR IN VERDI'S *TROVATORE*

MICHÈLE LOWRIE

MANY OF VERDI'S TRAGIC OPERAS end on a note of redemption. Aïda and Rhadames sing a hymn to death in each other's arms while the sky opens to receive them into heaven ("Si sciud' il ciel"). In *La Traviata*, Violetta, already ill, gives the ultimate sacrifice of her love for Alfredo at the request of his father, Germont; all renew love and find forgiveness as she dies in her beloved's embrace. King Gustavo/Riccardo had decided to renounce his adulterous passion for Amelia, when her husband, Anckarström/Renato, stabs him in *Ballo in Maschera*; he grants the conspirators clemency with his final breath. Love conquers all even in the face of death. In *Il trovatore* (1853), however, the last words are Azucena's "Sei vendicata, o madre!" (You are avenged, mother!) and the Count di Luna's "E vivo ancor" (And I live on).[1] Vengeance prevails. A mother witnesses the death of her beloved adopted son. Brother kills brother. The survivor must live with heartbreak and guilt. Why the anomaly? Extensive civil war tropes, a Roman tradition,[2] challenge the Christian overtones of Leonora's self-sacrifice and Manrico's pardon of his rival and enemy. Instead of ending with love and mercy, the opera's climax shocks all the more for its rapidity.[3] As in Vergil's *Aeneid*, vengeance overwhelms clemency in an abrupt ending that lacks resolution.[4]

---

[1] Stambler's 1963 text and translation, the latter adapted for literal fidelity to the Italian. Latin and French translations are my own. In my references, the first number refers to the act, the second to the scene.

[2] On civil war as a Roman inheritance in the Western political imaginary, see Armitage 2017a.

[3] The tragedy belongs as much to Azucena and the Count as to Manrico and Leonora, *pace* Chusid 1997:215.

[4] Quint (2018) argues for a deeper, figurative basis for civil war in the *Aeneid*'s ending than even the darkest earlier readings. The vast scholarship on this topic can be accessed through his bibliography.

The genre and modality of *Trovatore*, however, are far from Vergilian. Where the verbal texture of the Latin epic is emotionally unsettling, but its teleological plot is clear,[5] Verdi's melodramatic romance inverts the strategy. Despite an incoherent story and mostly flat characterization, the music conveys overt, if conflicted, emotions and compels with its expressive power.[6] *Trovatore* exemplifies opera as medium of the "absolute present," of the "reality of inner life."[7] Instead of coalescing into a cogent story or fusing chronological layers—Rome, the medieval plot, and the 1948 revolutions of contemporary context—, disconnected civil-war tropes bear no narrative burden. Rather, they bolster with their intensity the passion conveyed.[8]

Trovatore's civil war, as generic as its characters, makes no reference or allusion to Rome. It was first performed, however, in the eternal city despite various pragmatic inconveniences and the obstacle of papal censorship,[9] which prohibited reference to outlaws or partisans, as well as suicide.[10] Verdi found ingenious ways around censorship: the troubadour could be a rebel, provided he was not called one; Leonora could just die for love without being seen taking poison. Verdi tended anyway to address political issues indirectly, through personal and familial themes.[11] The original venue, however, speaks to the longevity of thinking of civil war in Roman terms even when Rome goes absent. Its traces are more apparent, as I will show, among contemporary Romantics and are revealed in the opera's reception history.

For all the conflict, the characters express moral certainty in distinct structures through clear and uplifting song.[12] The catastrophic ending challenges no basic sense of meaning, ethical, hermeneutic,

---

[5] Johnson 1976.

[6] Parker 1982:155–156; Budden 1992: vol. 2, 112.

[7] A libretto, verbally more economical than other literary works, unfolds through the arrangement of static elements, whose mythic function surpasses causality and the linear passage of time; see Gier 1998:6–9, with *Trovatore* as his example.

[8] Clément (1988:45) stresses opera's "brutality," particularly against women.

[9] On composition history and first performance, see Chusid 2012:9–34.

[10] Kimbell 1981:287.

[11] Smart 2004:31–33, 39.

[12] Originality and unity dwell in the music's "maximum functionality" and "simplicity, clarity and elementariness," Petrobelli 1982:130–131.

or aesthetic.[13] Love and art, embodied in the troubadour and his lady, may not prevail in the world on stage, but vengeance rebounds onto the avengers, and the lovers are confident in their mystic union in heaven.[14] Trovatore's robust melodic drive counters the forces of destruction. The music's vigor elevates and reassures. With a wealth of memorable tunes, Trovatore remains popular and a performance favorite. Its tropes of civil war enhance the horror only to build up an even greater obstacle for art to overcome. In Romanticism's classic gesture, the opera affirms art and love through its own artistic power.

I. CIVIL GUERRA

As early as the second scene, "civil guerra" (civil war, 1.2) names the political context. The opera's dramatic setting and Verdi's life experience were both tumultuous. As a child in northern Italy, Verdi saw Napoleon's rise and fall up close, and in the 1830s, he became entangled in local contestation between pro-Austrian Reds and anti-Austrian Blacks. He witnessed the 1848 revolutions in Paris and Milan.[15] A republican supporter of Italian unity who made the necessary compromises, he was elected Deputy to the Parliament of Borgo San Donnino during the Risorgimento.[16] In Trovatore's medieval setting, the Count received the County di Luna, hence his name, for withdrawing his claim to the throne at the death of King Martí of Catalonia-Aragon (1410) and for pledging his support to Fernando, Martí's nephew and eventual successor. Manrico backs the rebel, Jaume II di Urgell.[17]

Trovatore's sympathy lies with the rebels, but the opera affirms valor, art, and love while it condemns vengeance and discord rather

---

[13] Berlin (1980:1–3) makes Verdi "naïve" and Vergil "sentimental" in Schiller's sense: the former lack any sense of the cleft between life and art that tortures the latter.

[14] Martin 1980:30, 41: Verdi's sense that life is "hopeless but magnificent" and of death's unimportance before "some nobler principle" is the "quintessence of the Risorgimento."

[15] Gosset 2012:277–278. Smart (2004) shows how the myth of Verdi as a nationalist hero grew in retrospect, but Gosset documents his lifelong republican sentiments and their censorship.

[16] For overviews of his life, see Martin 1980; Phillips-Matz 2004:3, 5, 12.

[17] Hillgarth 1978:229–238; Earenfight 2005:99.

than supporting one side in a war of succession.[18] Civil war is not a matter of historical events. Neither pretender to the throne appears in the opera and, although the champions' fates mirror their princes,' three of the principal characters—Manrico, the troubadour; Leonora, his noble lover; and Azucena, his gypsy mother—are fictitious. Love, construed as universal, occupies the foreground; the political background makes the rivals enemies without otherwise affecting details of the plot. Civil war surpasses any referential function and rather unites the opera's imagery figuratively, through a set of traditional tropes whose contribution has received insufficient recognition.[19] Musicologists have examined links between tones and themes that reveal character and structure the plot. A representative example is how Manrico bridges the keys associated with aristocrats and gypsies respectively.[20] Civil war has no musical signature per se. Rather, the verbal tonality of its tropes intensifies the catastrophe as it unfolds.

Civil war stands out in *Trovatore* all the more against the political register of Gutiérrez's play, principally concerned with class, legitimacy, and the "abuse of authority,"[21] rather than civil war per se, which never receives mention. Such concerns correspond to Spanish preoccupations leading up to the play's first performance in 1836. Ferdinand VII, the son of the king deposed by Napoleon, was generally regarded as a tyrant. He took the throne when the monarchy was restored upon Napoleon's fall, and liberals fled Spain for Italy, Germany, France, and England. Returning after his death in 1833, they brought Romanticism with them.[22] Gutiérrez, who had been unable to leave, arrived in Madrid that year and took advantage of the new political and aesthetic

[18] Gosset 2012:281: upon election, Verdi affirmed his commitment to work for the "unification of our Country, so long under attack and divided by foreign forces and civil discord"; Verdi hated "oppression, inequality, fanaticism, and human degradation" and embraced the Italian struggle for "unity and freedom." Berlin (1980:5) states, however, that politics is "not at the center of Verdi's art."

[19] Parker 1982:163–164: that the Count and Manrico are brothers is nothing more than a "gesture within the intricate plot mechanism."

[20] For "tonal-dramatic association," see Chusid 1997:221; and for extensive analysis, see Chusid 2012:40–68.

[21] Whiston 2004:i.

[22] Trimble 2004:xii and xvi.

openings with his writing. A Romantic valorization of the underdog pervades the play. The troubadour Manrique's low social status irritates his rival, the Count (1.5) and causes him dismay (3.1). Even Leonor cares about class (4.8). Honor and nobility of spirit in the end align with social status when the troubadour is revealed as the Count's older brother. Legitimacy plays out in the play's politics as well as its social structures. His opponents characterize Manrique as a rebel and traitor (e.g., 5.1); inversely, he calls the king, whom the Count serves, a usurper (4.6). The Count plays the tyrant and is repeatedly called such: he equates himself with the law when the king appoints him Chief Justice of Aragon and commits summary justice (2.1–2; 5.2–3). The play nods to civil war late and through metaphor: the military conflict is a "fratricido combate" (fratricidal battle, 4.8). But it is left to the reader to connect the battle with the fraternal conflict.

In the opera, by contrast, the declaration of civil war toward the start announces a consistent register that augments the horror of a story about personal relations. *Trovatore* does not allude to any specific work in Latin, despite close links, nor does it refer to the Roman civil wars. Rather, it participates in a tradition, deriving from Latin literature, that puts a precise set of tropes addressing social collapse under the rubric of *bellum civile*.[23] Some of these, such as fratricide and suicide, figure civil war, while others, including degeneration, the violation of love and marriage, and feminine abjection, hover at its margins. Verdi and his librettists assume their audience's familiarity with the Western canon. Vergil and Homer, like Tasso, Ariosto, and Shakespeare, were "touchstones" for "an Italian man of letters" of his generation.[24]

Trovatore's dominant affiliation with romance would seem to preclude strong influence from a tradition where epic took the lead. The tropes of civil war in Latin literature, however, occur in many genres, including lyric, love elegy, and tragedy beyond epic. Verdi's affirmation of Shakespeare as a model for creative eclecticism sits fully within Romantic commitments to mixing high and low, sublime and

---

[23] Lowrie and Vinken (forthcoming) trace this tradition with a focus on French literature.

[24] Weiss 1982:139.

grotesque.[25] Civil war tropes underwrite the opera's fantastic elements, derived from romance, with a high-style grandeur that sustains the music's expression of strong emotion. It is the power of the music that lets audiences suspend disbelief. What mother would ever throw her own child onto a pyre by mistake? The trope of filicide captures the strength of Azucena's passion beyond realism.

Fratricide is the most obvious among *Trovatore*'s civil-war tropes. Vergil refers to such when "discord" drives "brothers" in the *Georgics* (*discordia fratres*, 2.496). Azucena's final revelation doubly slams the Count: he has violated family and the political order alike by executing his brother. Civil war comes as a fratricide's ancestral curse back to Romulus and Remus at Horace, *Epodes* 7. Azucena and the Count each obeys an ancestral imperative, laid on them by their mother and father, respectively. The Count attempts to find his brother and meet his father's demand for vengeance by reenacting his original vengeful act, burning a witch on a pyre. Timeless repetition prevents history from moving forward. As in the Roman civil wars, history repeats itself in a bloodbath within the family. Azucena first kills one son, then loses the other. Civil war's logic operates behind the characters' backs. The figurations stand despite her not intending to kill her son nor the Count his brother.

Performance may deploy another conventional civil-war trope: fighting within one side. In Latin literature, Vergil's Trojans, disguising themselves in spoils taken from Androgeos's slaughtered men, suffer friendly fire when their comrades fail to recognize them beneath enemy armor (*Aeneid* 2.391–393, 410–412). The fall of Troy thereby resonates with civil war. Romans who kill each other to escape death at fellow citizens' hands paradoxically reenact the civil war they would escape. Lucan's commentary on the Vulteius episode, *totumque in partibus unis / bellorum fecere nefas* (and they enacted the whole evil of the wars within one party, 4.548–549), articulates the structure. These figures stand for civil war without hostility between characters. The 2018 staging of *Trovatore* at the Lyric Opera in Chicago lent this trope

---

[25] Weiss (1982:138) cites a letter to Antonio Somma (April 22, 1853) in which Verdi declares, "I prefer Shakespeare to all other dramatists."

to each side. As background to the anvil chorus, gypsies honed their swordsmanship against each other, until play fighting turned real (2.1). Besieging Manrico in Castellor, the Count's men, flirting with some ladies, came to blows among each other. The *militia amoris* inverts: the soldiers take their captain Ferrando's news they will attack the castle at dawn as an invitation to dance ("Tu c'inviti a danza," 3.1).

Civil war separates lovers physically at the same time as erasing the friend/enemy distinction notionally, with betrayal as the logical result. Twinning (Romulus and Remus) and indistinction, here between brothers, marks civil war as a fight of same with same. An unknown warrior, who appeared mysteriously to win a tournament—and Leonora's love—disappears from her sight precisely at the outbreak of civil war: "civil guerra intanto arse—nol vidi più!" (1.2). When Manrico returns to serenade her, he is indistinguishable from his brother and rival, both in shadow. Manrico's outburst at her mistake, their first meeting in the opera, "infida!" (faithless, 1.2), announces their love as a question of faith and presages his accusations at the end. Civil war threatens to separate the lovers in actuality, when Manrico answers its call, and figuratively, through his fundamental sameness to his brother. Their second meeting in darkness restores the difference between friend and foe as it reunites the lovers: Manrico saves her from the Count, who lurks nearby, intending to abduct her. By saving each other in turn, Manrico and Leonora attempt to overcome the logic of civil war with their love—until the Count's final and deadly intervention.

A number of topoi have strong ties to Latin literature. In Horace's sixth Roman Ode, the perversion of love and duty is symptomatic of social collapse in civil war.[26] When Rome is *occupatam seditionibus* (occupied by sedition, 3.6.13), marital prostitution degrades the foundations of society. A broad statement of degeneration concludes the poem:

> Aetas parentum, peior avis, tulit
> nos nequiores, mox daturos
> progeniem vitiosiorem.

Hor. Carm. 3.6.46–48

---

[26] Lowrie 2018.

The age of our fathers, worse than our grandfathers, bore
us, more vile, soon to give birth to progeny more corrupt.

For Azucena, the Count instantiates such decadence: "D'iniquo geni-
tore / Empio figliuol peggiore" (Impious son, worse than his wicked
father, 3.1).

Some topoi recall Vergil's *Aeneid*. Manrico refers to the book of fate:
"se nella pagina / De' miei destini è scritto" (if in the page of my fates
it is written, 3.2). This metaphor underlies Jupiter's prophecy to Venus
about Rome's future, when he reassures her by "unrolling the secrets of
the fates" (*volvens fatorum arcana*, 1.262), and is expanded by Ovid (*Met.*
15.810–815). The Latin epics predict Roman history, a story of repeated
civil war ended finally under Augustus. In *Trovatore*, salvation shifts
from the political to the personal. If the Count's degeneracy promises
ever more violence, the celestial love of Manrico and Leonora will make
earthly violence indifferent, no matter what is written in the book of
fate.

Although battles fought in the field by opposing male Roman
generals dominate historical narratives of civil war, the story told in
literature accords a special role to feminine forces of disorder.[27] Women
are less cause than symptom. Their desires and struggles capture raw
emotion and broaden civil war's scope from politics and the military
to pose an existential challenge. In the *Aeneid*, Dido, Juno, Allecto, and
Cleopatra represent the dangerous power of feminine passion as an
obstacle to Rome's foundation and hence to the eventual establishment
of the *pax Augusta* in the wake of civil war. In *Trovatore*, Azucena is the
voice and heir of chthonic, maternal vengeance, even at the price of
love. An orientalized outsider like Cleopatra, the gypsy witch affords an
external screen on which to project the abjection of internal conflict.
Young Caesar's declaration of war on Egypt masks the civil war against
Antony at Actium with foreign conflict against Cleopatra. She appears
as the dominant enemy in Latin literature and distracts attention from

---

[27] Women loom large in Roman conspiracy narratives; see Pagán 2004. Owens (2017)
provides a feminist critique to the masculinist history told by Armitage (2017a, to which
he accedes in Armitage 2017b). For marriage's perversion as a trope for civil war in Lucan,
see Lowrie and Vinken 2019.

the unwelcome fact that Romans were fighting Romans.[28] The sudden appearance of Azucena's mother, allegedly casting a spell over the Old Count's baby son, is itself unmotivated: that is just what witches do in folktale. But the punishment taken against her and the ensuing twists of plot provide a logical and external cause to a primordial conflict: brothers simply fight brothers. The civil war context is contingent. It frames without causing the actual rivalry between Manrico and the Count. In both the *Aeneid* and *Trovatore*, the figurations of civil war work independent of causation.

The figure of the witch conjures up civil war's horror through a fantastic and disturbing side show. Although the singular witch is a minor character in Vergil's *Aeneid*, others—Canidia in Horace, Erichtho in Lucan—have strong civil war associations.[29] Azucena's mother is marked with attributes of the witches found in the *Aeneid*. Dido's description of the hag, who allegedly helps her with an antidote to love, and her own playacting, in the guise of magic practitioner, put exoticized women on display as deadly theater. Dido is single-sandaled and *recincta* (unbelted, *Aeneid* 4.483–491, 518). The gypsy mother, no real witch, is figured as such when dragged to the pyre "barefoot, unbelted" ("scalza, discincta," 2.1). A funeral pyre—"pira"/*pyra* and "rogo"/*rogus* in both works—burns Dido in self-inflicted violence, the gypsy as retribution for sorcery, both as a spectacle visible from afar. Fire is a consistent image: Dido's passion is a wound and a flame; Azucena sings "strida la vampa," Manrico "Di quella pira," the Count burns for Leonora, and poison burns her.[30] These horrific deaths, meant to end suffering, only perpetuate more violence in a dramatic display. Dido's love, which could have joined Carthaginians and Trojans into one harmonious people, transforms into a hateful curse: an avenger against the Romans will rise from her bones (4.622–629). From the perspective of the failed union, the Punic Wars result from an intimate conflict, with Hannibal as Dido's vengeful substitute child. Azucena pursues her

---

[28] Gurval 1995; Lowrie 1997:138–164; 2015; Lange 2016:122–123, 125–153.

[29] Canidia figures the dissolution of sense-making categories in civil war; see Oliensis 1998:64–101; Erichtho is Western literature's "first recognizably modern witch" (Johnson 1987:19); she mixes generic registers in civil war's discordant machine (19–33).

[30] Parker 1982:157.

mother's call to vengeance (2.1) and the old Count's sons press their rivalry into fratricide, civil war's central figuration. Accessory to civil war's unfolding, the witches heighten its horror.

The climactic scene of the *Aeneid*, where Aeneas hesitates before choosing vengeance over clemency, instantiates the double bind of the recently ended civil wars. Either choice fails a moral imperative, but the choice of vengeance sets Roman history on a course of perpetual conflict that, from a Christian perspective, cannot be resolved through politics. *Trovatore* elevates clemency, a merely political virtue, to mercy, a quality of soul in accord with God's grace. The drive to mercy or to vengeance becomes an innate spiritual orientation that transcends politics.

II. VENGEANCE VERSUS MERCY

Trovatore's ending, where vengeance appears simultaneously glorious and horrific, at first appears parallel to the shocking end of the *Aeneid*. The opera's abruptness is by design. *Trovatore*'s larger message of transcendent art and love, however, aims to overcome Roman politics with Christian values and secular aesthetics. Verdi intervened strongly in shaping the libretto, based on Antonio Garcia Gutiérrez's play *El trovador* (1836).[31] He corresponded actively with Salvatore Cammarano and, after the latter's untimely death, gave clear direction to his new librettist, Leone Emanuele Bardare. His chief concerns include developing the relationship between Azucena and Manrico and increasing Leonora's prominence, especially when taking the veil.[32] Verdi's revisions reinforce the structuring antitheses of the plot, which the opera outlines more clearly than Gutiérrez's play.

For Verdi's first concern, love between mother and adopted son heightens the atrocity of Manrico's death, all the more chilling because the Count's victory over his rival simultaneously answers Azucena's consuming desire. She has been obsessed with vengeance since the

---

[31] Gossett (2008:364–406) stresses the complex interconnection between word and music.

[32] For the libretto's composition, see Weaver 1980:121, 126; Kimbell 1981:283–293; Budden 1992: vol. 2, 59–70; Chusid 2012:9–34.

Count's father burned her mother at the stake, allegedly for bewitching his other son. By executing Manrico, the Count unwittingly kills his own brother, a trope of civil war. For the second, the convent scene defines Leonora's love in Christian terms. She is the perfect match for Manrico, who obeys a heavenly voice forbidding him to strike the Count. His clemency also comes in a Christian register as "pietà" (2.1). The conflict, between pagan and Christian, vengeance and mercy, relations determined by power or by love, gains in crispness with his revisions.

These constitutive contrasts balance the principal characters in matched pairs.[33] Leonora and Manrico risk their lives for love and mercy in a register of secularized Christian values.[34] In the Spanish original, Leonor feels continual ambivalence about betraying her vow to Christ for an earthly love (3.4; 4.5–6); the opera shows no scruples about her violation of religion's higher calling. Christian spirituality in *Trovatore* is entirely sublimated into erotic love. Leonora's self-sacrifice is a secular *imitatio Christi*. Her failed attempt to exchange her death for Manrico's life comes with no suggestion of misdirected love, but rather enhances pathos.[35] The poison operates too fast; the Count discovers her ruse to give herself to him only as a corpse; Manrico's manly valor forbids him from abondoning her. Manrico himself obeys the divine call to mercy and always fulfils duty defined by love. Maternal love takes priority, so he rushes to save his mother from the pyre and leaves Leonora suffering at his departure in a Christian-colored, erotic "martyrdom" ("martir"). Salvific language exalts their attempts to rescue those they love: Manrico says, "Madre infelice, corro a salvarti" (Unhappy mother, I run to save you, 3.2), and Leonora exclaims, "Vengo a salvarti" (I come to save you, 4.2). Manrico's anger at Leonora for selling herself to his rival melts when he realizes she has poisoned

---

[33] The pairings parallel the symmetrical structure, four acts each divided in two, and "internal symmetries" in the music; Parker 1982:157, 162. On the generally "static contrastive structure of opera," see Gier 1998:9.

[34] Verdi, no believer, had strong anticlerical views; Martin 1980:38–39; Phillips-Matz 2004:5, 13.

[35] Kerman classifies Leonora's action as a "virtuous betrayal," one of several rubrics governing operatic women's demise for their sexuality (2006:23).

herself, an act of secular self-sacrifice, to circumvent the ultimate price. His malediction converts to blessing: "quest'angelo" (this angel, 4.2).

Religious musical themes consecrate the lovers in an aesthetic uniting the setting's medieval romance with Verdi's 19th-century Romanticism. Erotic love resounds in Christian strains. Manrico sings a serenade in "versi di prece ed umile, / qual d'uom che prega Iddio" (verses of prayer and humility / as of a man who prays to God, 1.2). A chorus of nuns welcomes Leonora to their refuge—she joins the convent to escape from the Count under the mistaken apprehension her beloved is dead. The nuns' promise, "il cielo / si schiuderà per te!" (heaven will open for you), is realized on earth. Once Manrico, miraculously returned from a false death and saves Leonora from the Count's attempted abduction, the distinction dissolves between divine savior and earthly lover: "Sei tu dal ciel disceso, / o in ciel son io con te?" (Have you come from the sky or am I in the sky with you?, 2.2). Even the nuns support secular love: the heaven she trusted has had mercy, "piedade," on her. Organ music graces the duet of reunited lovers as a mystic union (3.2).[36]

> L'onda de' suoni mistici
> Pura discenda al cor!
> Vieni, ci schiude il tempio
> Gioje de casto amor!
>
> Let a wave of mystic sounds descend pure into our heart!
> Come, the temple opens for us the joys of a holy love!

With perfect gender balance, a chorus of monks matches the nuns. Their thematic and structural necessity overrides the lack of logical motivation.[37] Their prayers waft in from a chapel offstage as they invoke "bontà divina" (divine goodness) to pity the captives held in the Count's palace. These now include Manrico, captured with Azucena while saving her from the pyre. The peal of church bells announces

---

[36] Budden 1992: vol. 2, 97.
[37] Budden 1992: vol. 2, 99.

Leonora's *imitatio Christi*. She determines to overcome death itself with her love, or to unite with Manrico in the grave: "amore in terra / mai del mio non fu più forte ... vincerà la stessa morte ... o con te per sempre unita / nella tomba scenderò" (No love on earth was ever stronger than mine ... it will overcome death itself ... or united with you forever, I will descend into the tomb, 4.1). It is no blasphemy in this opera to suggest that earthly love could do Christ's work in overcoming death. Rather, the divine parallel spiritualizes her erotic passion.

Against such perfect love, elevated in Christian tones, the destructive faithlessness of Azucena and the Count stands as equally well-matched foil. Blasphemers in *Trovatore*'s moral universe, they pursue vengeance, driven by no transcendent desire for justice, but by an ancestral inheritance. By fulfilling a parent's dying wish, they each kill their nearest and dearest in a classic trope of civil war. Loyal to a pagan spirituality and radical freedom without integration, the gypsy's roof is the sky, her fatherland the whole world (3.1). She obeys no divine voice, but her mother's horrific call for vengeance. Her vengeance commutes into self-punishment: she unwittingly commits filicide by hurling into the fire not the elder Count's stolen son but her very own child. She blasphemes doubly in asking Manrico, "Compi, o figlio, qual d'un Dio, compi allor il cenno mio!" (to fulfil her command as if it were the word of a God, 2.1). She fails to recognize the one God of Christianity, equates her word with that of any pagan god, and urges Manrico to reject the divine voice he obeyed and not spare the Count again. She pays for her impiety with the loss of yet another son, when Manrico falls to the Count's mercy. Her triumphant vengeance comes with heartbreak.

The Count, plotting to abduct Leonora before she enters the nunnery, matches Azucena in blasphemy. His exultation turns not Manrico but God himself into his rival (2.2):

> Invanno un Dio rivale
> s'oppone al amor mio,
> non può nemmeno un Dio,
> donna, rapirti a me!

> In vain a rival God sets himself against my love. Not even a god, woman, can snatch you from me!

His violent love transgresses heavenly and erotic love alike. His witch-burning, a reenactment of his father's, comes not as divine retribution, but infernal vengeance ("Le vampe dell'inferno / A te fian rogo eterno," 3.1). His punishment of his human rival results in a fratricide that makes his life unlivable.

Azucena's repeated call for vengeance builds anticipation. Given the systematic contrast between sacrilege and reverent love, however, vengeance's closing triumph surprises all the more. In a letter to De Sanctis, who preferred Cammarano's original, longer ending, Verdi defends shifting Azucena's final line from "tarda vendetta! ... ma quanto fiera avesti o madre" (Yours is late vengeance, ... but how proud you had been, o mother!") to the concise "sei vendicata, o madre" (You are avenged, o mother!).[38] He sticks closely to Gutiérrez's "Ya estas vengada" and insists that one word—"vengeance!"—sums up everything. As in the *Aeneid*, the shocking ending speaks to the heartbreak of civil war.

Aeschylus's *Oresteia* establishes the classical paradigm for ending internal conflict in family and city by the establishment of a court. The Atreids' perpetual cycle of vengeance yields finally to the rule of law. In the *Aeneid*, Rome's expansion into empire does not so much end civil war as externalize violence in an ever-expanding political extension. Verdi's *Trovatore* turns its back on law and politics altogether in favor of love and art. If the cycle of vengeance cannot end on earth, the opera at least makes available an alternative mode of being.

III. *ET OMNIA CEDENDA ARTI*

The two principal characters who offer a new paradigm for human existence, Manrico and Leonora, die respectively from fratricide and suicide, two of civil war's basic tropes.[39] By contrast, the characters on a course of vengeance live to achieve their destructive goal, only to recoil at their success. The plot yields no hope of overcoming abject violence in this world. Leonora and Manrico, however, have faith they will

---

[38] Kimbell 1981:292–293; Budden 1992: vol. 2, 65.
[39] On suicide, see Ahl 1976:320–325, including triumph in defeat; Bartsch 1997:24–25.

realize perfect, transcendent love after death. As outlined above, their erotic love for each other secularizes Christian love, marked by touches of church music, which graces the pair in turn. But the achievement of perfect union is deferred beyond this world. A force for good on earth, however, dwells in *Trovatore*, namely art.

Transcendent art is a central tenet of Romanticism, with music occupying first position.[40] Verdi's particular brand owes much to Victor Hugo, whose name became synonymous with the movement. The Italian composer lived in the French capital for two years spanning the 1848 Revolution, where he fell under the "spell of grandiose Parisian spectacle" shortly before composing *Trovatore* (1853).[41] He adapted to opera two of Hugo's plays, both banned, before composing *Trovatore*: *Hernani* (1830; *Ernani* 1844) and *Le roi s'amuse* (1832) as *Rigoletto* (1851).[42] Both cited Shakespeare as a formative influence, although Verdi relied on translation for *Macbeth*, *Otello*, and *Falstaff*. Both looked to the English bard as precedent for loosening the strict chains of classicism and verisimilitude.[43] Hugo's Romantic manifesto, the preface to his play *Cromwell* (1827), repeatedly cites Shakespeare and argues for mixing comedy and tragedy, the sublime and the grotesque, to achieve a new, postclassical art for a Christian modernity.[44] Hugo consistently secularizes Christian values by translating them into love and, further, into a new, redemptive politics of loving fraternity. From self-imposed exile, he could permit himself the freedom to make explicitly republican ideological claims the Italian composer eschewed, whether from preference or to escape censorship. *Trovatore* secularizes Christianity with a different mix of genres and styles but in a similar spirit: romance with its hopeful celebration of love counters the gruesome civil-war tropes of the Roman classical tradition.

---

[40] Smart 2004:43–44.

[41] Weiss 1982:145; Giger 2004.

[42] Kimbell (1981:460–484) analyzes the good fit between Hugo's dramatic art and the libretto through the example of *Ernani*.

[43] Weiss 1982:138–139; Giger 2004:111–112.

[44] Hugo 1968:68–69; Kimbell 1981:462.

Hugo repudiates the classical tradition without, however, discarding it, and Italian Romanticism was loathe to reject classicism.[45] Both Verdi and Hugo transform this heritage into a new Romantic guise. The repertory of Roman civil-war tropes that circulates in Western literature exemplifies the persistence of traditions transformed. But whereas this tradition's Roman origins are occluded in *Trovatore*, they become evident in Hugo. His *Quatrevingt-treize* (1874), responding to the slaughter of the *Commune*, yet further civil war, cites Lucan in a chapter title, *plus quam civilia bella* (wars more than civil, 3.2.1), that looks to the first line of *De bello civili*. Hugo also sets the conflict during the post–Revolutionary Terror between a great-uncle (Lantenac) and great-nephew (Gauvain).[46] Their relation evokes Augustus's to Julius Caesar. The novel's ending shares many elements with *Trovatore*: suicide, self-sacrifice, a chthonic maternal figure, and a man executed by the authority of family. An adoptive father figure (Cimourdain) casts the final vote that condemns his beloved son (Gauvain) of treason. Vengeful law perversely triumphs over secular clemency. Cimourdain commits suicide as the guillotine beheads Gauvain, but the young man's *imitatio Christi* transfigures the civil-war tropes into salvific, Romantic redemption.

Trovatore and *Quatrevingt-treize* use types instead of well-developed characters.[47] Flaubert commented with exasperation on the novel: "Quels bonhommes en pains d'épice, que ces bonhommes! Tous parlent comme des acteurs" (What fellows in gingerbread are these fellows! They all talk like actors, *Letter to Mme Roger des Genettes*, May 1, 1874). Hugo's interest lay not "in the psychology of his wooden or stone characters" but in their "symbolic value."[48] Scholarship consistently assesses *Trovatore*'s characters as types, with Azucena as the

---

[45] Smart 2004:30.

[46] Lowrie and Vinken 2018, and forthcoming.

[47] Balthazar 2004:237; Kerman 2006:23. Gier (1998:7, 9–10) compares dramatically static elements in arias, which capture a soul's condition, and in Hugo's monologues, where speech's communicative function yields to exuberant tirades. Gossett (2008:375) lists Hugo among other Romantics as parallels for Risorgimento verbal style.

[48] Eco 2006:291.

Shakespearean exception.[49] The civil-war tropes in the opera harmonize with its use of emblems. The two techniques convey significance simply and transparently. The figures of romance represent political and aesthetic stances: the Count stands for tyranny; the troubadour for love, art, and freedom; Leonora for transcendent love. Fratricide, filicide, doomed love all signify social dissolution under the banner of civil war.

Trovatore's more direct reception in opera also reveals Rome as the ur-site of civil war. Puccini's *Tosca* was based on Victorien Sardou's play, which took inspiration from Verdi's opera.[50] The aging composer trembled with emotion at a reading of Giuseppe Illica's libretto and himself read aloud Cavaradossi's intended aria, "Farewell to Life and Art." A heroine again sacrifices herself for her lover in a ruse, although Tosca learns from Leonora's fate to murder her oppressor—but to no avail. She similarly fails to thwart the tyrant: both she and Cavaradossi die, he by execution, she by suicide. *Tosca*'s setting is Napoleonic-era Rome, once again embroiled in civil conflict, now between republicans and royalists. The hoped-for passage to freedom leads ironically through Città Vecchia—the ancient city's blood-soaked heritage dooms the imagined foundation of a new life in love and art.

In the struggle between world views, *Quatrevingt-treize* tilts toward redemption, and *Tosca* toward recurrent civil war. What about *Trovatore*? Despite the accumulation of civil-war tropes throughout and although, in the end, horrifically triumphant vengeance defers love's potency to heaven, it is not the plot's conclusion that determines the opera's predominant effect. A contemporary review of its first run at Rome attests that "the public was only saddened somewhat by the distressing finale."[51] The powerful emotions of the preceding so-called *Miserere* scene, "the most remarkable and successful number in the opera,"[52] subsume into song the final failure of love and politics

---

[49] For Verdi's stress on her ambivalence between *amor filiale* and *amor materno*, see Petrobelli 1982:132–133.

[50] Chusid 2012:112–114.

[51] Chusid 2012:88.

[52] Chusid 2012:69. The musicological details below derive from his chapter on the scene (69–86).

to prevent death, so that the lasting impression is one of a strong, Romantic affirmation of art despite civil war, despite death, despite vengeance.

Three separate kinds of stage music—music even if the opera were a play—inform the scene in a musical *mise en abyme*. All underscore the upcoming deaths. A church bell, labeled in the score and libretto a "campana dei morti" (bell of the dead), peals in E flat, a pitch with strong associations with death. The monks intone "miserere," a prayer for death. Manrico, the artist figure in the opera, sings what Cammarano called a "death farewell," accompanying himself on the lute. Dissonance and prosodic irregularity heighten the tense anticipation of death as the emotive background to Leonora's determination to sacrifice herself for life and for love. She fails. But Verdi's music does not. The layering of death onto death through one and another form of song and sound paradoxically sustains art's power to immortalize love and to move the living to pity. As the opera is performed again and again, we the audience are elevated. Moved by the music, we become the life-affirming vehicle for clemency, for mercy, for *pietà*.

UNIVERSITY OF CHICAGO

WORKS CITED

Ahl, F. 1976. *Lucan: An Introduction*. Ithaca, NY.

Armitage, D. 2017a. *Civil Wars: A History in Ideas*. New York.

———. 2017b. "On the Genealogy of Quarrels." *Critical Analysis of Law* 4(2):178–189.

Balthazar, S. E., ed. 2004a. *The Cambridge Companion to Verdi*. Cambridge.

———. 2004b. "Desdemona's Alienation and Otello's Fall." In Balthazar 2004a, 227–254.

Bartsch, S. 1997. *Ideology in Cold Blood: A Reading of Lucan's Civil War*. Cambridge, MA.

Berlin, I. 1980. "The Naiveté of Verdi." In Weaver and Chusid 1980, 1–12.

Budden, J. 1992. *The Operas of Verdi*. Oxford.

Chusid, M. 1997. "A New Source for *El trovador*." In *Verdi's Middle Period, 1849 to 1859*, ed. M. Chusid, 214–225. Chicago.

———. 2012. *Verdi's Il trovatore: The Quintessential Italian Melodrama.* Rochester.

Clément, C. 1988. *Opera, or the Undoing of Women.* Minneapolis.

Earenfight, T. 2005. *Queenship and Political Power in Medieval and Early Modern Spain.* Aldershot.

Eco, U. 2006. "Excess and History in Hugo's *Ninety-three.*" In *Forms and Themes*, vol. 2 of *The Novel*, ed. F. Moretti, 274–294. Princeton.

Gier, A. 1998. *Das Libretto: Theorie und Geschichte einer musikoliterarischen Gattung.* Darmstadt.

———. 2004. "French Influences." In Balthazar 2004a, 111–138.

Gossett, P. 2008. *Divas and Scholars: Performing Italian Opera.* Chicago.

———. 2012. "Giuseppe Verdi and the Italian Risorgimento (Jayne Lecture, 2010)." *Proceedings of the American Philosophical Society* 156 (3):271–282.

Gurval, R. A. 1995. *Actium and Augustus: The Politics and Emotions of Civil War.* Ann Arbor, MI.

Vaughen, H. H., and M. A. De Vitis. 1930. *A. G. Gutiérrez. El Trovador.* Boston.

Johnson, W. R. 1976. *Darkness Visible: A Study of Vergil's Aeneid.* Berkeley, CA.

———. 1987. *Momentary Monsters: Lucan and His Heroes.* Ithaca, NY.

Hillgarth, J. N. 1978. *The Spanish Kingdoms, 1250–1516.* 2 vols. Oxford.

Hugo, V. 1968. *Cromwell.* Ed. A. Ubersfeld. Paris.

Kerman, J. 2006. "Verdi and the Undoing of Women." *Cambridge Opera Journal* 18 (1):21–31.

Kimbell, D. R. B. 1981. *Verdi in the Age of Italian Romanticism.* Cambridge.

Lange, C. H. 2016. *Triumphs in the Age of Civil War: The Late Republic and the Adaptability of Triumphal Tradition.* London.

Lowrie, M. 1997. *Horace's Narrative Odes.* Oxford.

———. 2015. "The Egyptian Within: A Roman Trope for Civil War." In *Translatio Babylonis: Unsere Orientale Moderne*, ed. B. Vinken, 13–28. Paderborn.

———. 2018. "Figures of Discord and the Roman Addressee in Horace, *Odes* 3.6." In *Intratextuality and Latin Literature*, ed. S. J. Harrison, S. Frangoulides, and T. D. Papanghelis, 211–225. Berlin.

Lowrie, M., and B. Vinken. 2018. "Correcting Rome with Rome: Victor Hugo's *Quatrevingt-treize*." In *Roman Error: Classical Reception and the Problem of Rome's Flaws*, ed. B. Dufallo, 179–190. Oxford.

———. 2019. "Married to Civil War: A Roman Trope in Lucan's Poetics of History." In *The Historiography of Late Republican Civil War*, ed. C. H. Lange and F. J. Vervaet, 263–291. Leiden.

———. Forthcoming. *Civil War and the Collapse of the Social Bond: The Roman Tradition at the Heart of the Modern*.

Martin, G. 1980. "Verdi and the Risorgimento." In Weaver and Chusid 1980, 123–141.

Oliensis, E. 1998. *Horace and the Rhetoric of Authority*. Cambridge.

Owens, P. 2017. "Decolonizing Civil War." *Critical Analysis of Law* 4 (2):160–169.

Pagán, V. 2004. *Conspiracy Narratives in Roman History*. Austin.

Parker, R. 1982. "The Dramatic Structure of *Il trovatore*." *Music Analysis* 1 (2):155–167.

Petrobelli, P. 1982. "Towards an Explanation of the Dramatic Structure of *Il trovatore*." *Music Analysis* 1 (2):129–141.

Phillips-Matz, M. J. 2004. "Verdi's Life: A Thematic Biography." In Balthazar 2004a, 3–14.

Quint, D. 2018. *Virgil's Double Cross: Design and Meaning in the Aeneid*. Princeton.

Roller, M. B. 2018. *Models from the Past in Roman Culture: A World of Exempla*. Baltimore.

Stambler, B. 1963. *Il trovatore, music by Giuseppe Verdi, libretto by Salvatore Cammarano*. New York.

Smart, M. A. 2004. "Verdi, Italian Romanticism, and the Risorgimento." In Balthazar 2004a, 29–45.

Trimble, R. G. 2004. *A Translation of Antonio García Gutiérrez's El Trovador (The Troubadour)*. Lewiston, NY.

Weaver, W. 1980. "Verdi and His Librettists." In Weaver and Chusid, 121–143.

Weaver, W., and M. Chusid, eds. 1980. *The Verdi Companion*. London.

Weiss, P. 1982. "Verdi and the Fusion of Genres." *Journal of the American Musicological Society* 35 (1):138–156.

Whiston, J. 2004. "Preface." In Trimble 2004, i–vi.

BOB DYLAN AND THE ART OF THE CITHARODE

RICHARD F. THOMAS

In a distant past, all poetry was sung or tunefully recited, poets were rhapsodes, bards, troubadours; "lyrics" comes from "lyre."

—Horace Engdahl, Nobel Prize presentation speech for laureate Bob Dylan, December 10, 2016

IN *WHY BOB DYLAN MATTERS*, I explored the ways singer-songwriter Bob Dylan has, from early on in his career, been engaging with the culture of the classical, particularly the Roman, worlds.[1] I traced this connection back to his exposure to Latin: his membership in the Latin Club in his sophomore year of high school, 1956–57, in Hibbing, Minnesota; and his viewing of Hollywood movies focused on Rome and antiquity that proliferated in the 1950s and 1960s. In his later years, starting in 1978, as evidenced particularly on his three albums of the 21st century, Dylan's songs essentially formed a chapter in the domain of classical reception through his creative reuse of lines from Virgil's *Aeneid*, the exile poems of Ovid, and the *Odyssey*. As the Swedish Academy recognized when it awarded him the 2016 Nobel Prize for Literature, Dylan's music is a link to a "distant past, when all poetry was sung, or tunefully recited." This essay will explore Dylan's engagement—conscious and subconscious—with the ancient performance

---

I gladly offer this contribution to the current volume in honor of the research, teaching, and mentorship of Richard Tarrant, friend and colleague of almost 40 years. I hope this offering will please Richard, with whom I share an interest in Virgil, Horace, and the other Augustans, as well as in the connection between lyric poetry and music. To those who might point to a difference in the register of Richard's and my preferred modes, I would say, first, that all music is popular before it becomes classical and, second, that I remember, as will he, a late night in 1982 when he, I, and one or two other revelers knowledgeably and enthusiastically sang along to the music of Bob Dylan.

[1] Thomas 2017:42–94, 161–192, 227–266; see also Thomas 2007.

traditions of musical storytelling from which we get some of our earliest literary texts.

I. DYLAN AND THE CITHARODE

Long before he began engaging these texts, however, Dylan created art that belonged to one of the oldest musical and literary traditions of the Greek and Roman worlds: solo singers who accompanied themselves on string instruments. The ancient Greek citharode played and sang solo to the lyre (*cithara*). In the definitive work on this topic, *The Culture of Kitharôidia*, Tim Power describes the art of this shadowy figure, comparing it to other, more civic modes of performance:

> It was solo song accompanied by a stringed instrument ... It was generally performed out of doors, before the scrutiny of a large festival audience, and often in competitive setting ... It was more secular than religious, more a demonstration of personal skill, charisma, and the individual performer's body than of corporate solidarity and the "body politic," more Panhellenic [international] than epichoric [local], less an expression *of* the community than entertainment and edification *for* it.[2]

As Power notes, the citharode was more than a musician. Citharodic performances were also about physical movement, charisma, and performative persona. Quintilian discusses the topic of whether speakers can be trained to deliver their speeches, use gestures, and carry out appropriate movement of the body. He takes as an analogy the art of the citharode, showing clear admiration for the player's ability to sing, play, and tap his feet to the music:

> An uero citharoedi non simul et memoriae et sono uocis et plurimis flexibus seruiunt, cum interim alios neruos dextra percurrunt, alios laeua trahunt continent

---

[2] Power 2010, preface.

praebent, ne pes quidem otiosus certam legem temporum
seruat—et haec pariter omnia.

Quintilian *Inst.* 1.12.3

Singers to the lyre simultaneously attend to their memory
and to the sound and various inflections of the voice, all
the time strumming certain strings with their right hand,
while plucking, damping or releasing others with the left.
Even the foot is kept busy in beating time. And they do
this all at the same time.

Trans. Russell, with modifications

Elsewhere Power cites an anonymous poem also from the Roman
empire, showing the harmony between singer and lyre:

> Musica contingens subtili stamina pulsu
>   ingreditur, uulgi auribus ut placeat.
> Stat tactu cantuque potens, cui bracchia linguae
>   concordant sensu conciliata pari.
> Namque ita <ab> aequali ambo moderamine librat
>   atque ori socias temperat arte manus
> ut dubium tibi sit gemina dulcedine capto
>   uox utrumne canat an lyra sola sonet.

Anthologia Latina 102 Kay = 113 Riese

He goes on stage to please the ears of the crowd. He
stands there, supremely capable in both his touch and his
song; his hands harmonize with his tongue, united with it
in equal expression. For he deploys both with equivalent
expertise in balanced proportion and mingles his hands as
allies with the art of his mouth in such a way that, capti-
vated by the twin delight, you are unsure whether it is his
voice singing or the lyre sounding by itself.

In the contemporary world, a big part of the deep attraction of guitar-
playing singers of the caliber of Dylan resides precisely in the appreciation of the words, instrumental accompaniment, vocal modulation,

and the way the singer's movements, gestures, facial expressions, and handling of the instrument harmonize with the song's lyrics and melody. That was true in antiquity as it is now.

Dylan has not been regularly playing the guitar in concert for some years now, and when, for whatever reasons, he stopped playing, there was a general yearning for him to take it up again. Something both visual and aural had been lost, even though the lack was, to some extent, compensated by the guitars and other instruments of his band, particularly the lead guitar of Charlie Sexton, with whom Dylan had played intermittently for the last two decades. He has found other ways to combine his instrumental self with his voice and appearance, often playing the piano or the harmonica, which has been an essential part of his art almost from the beginning. There was something special, therefore, about the moment when the 75-year-old took up the guitar in a concert in Las Vegas on October 13, 2016, the day of the Nobel Prize award, as he sang the second half of the 1975 song "Simple Twist of Fate."[3] This response had to do with the audience's association of the presence of the guitar with the singer, as was clearly the case with the cithara and the citharode, and a longing for Dylan's earlier citharodic persona. In performances now, Dylan has almost entirely replaced the guitar with the piano, which works well enough. But still there is a yearning for what came before. Dylan surely knows this, and in his fall 2019 U.S. tour (October 11–December 8), he accompanied himself with the guitar for the first song of each show, as well as the first song of the encore performances.

In July of 64 CE, Rome burned. Nero probably did not fiddle during the actual fire; by all accounts, however, he was an expert citharode[4]— who also played the water-organ[5]—so he certainly did fiddle either earlier that year or in 65 CE.[6] There is no reason to doubt the essentials of Suetonius's account at *Ner.* 20.1:

---

[3] Recreate Magazine, 2016, https://www.youtube.com/watch?v=c8PD3TfB7As.

[4] See Gyles 1962; Griffin 1984:160–163.

[5] Suet. *Ner.* 41.2.

[6] See Bolton (1948:84–87) for inconsistencies between Suetonius and Tacitus, along with attempts to reconcile accounts of the *Neronia* festival; see also Bradley 1978:129–131.

inter ceteras disciplinas pueritiae tempore imbutus et musica, statim ut imperium adeptus est, Terpnum citharoedum uigentem tunc praeter alios arcessiit diebusque continuis post cenam canenti in multam noctem assidens paulatim et ipse meditari exercerique coepit neque eorum quicquam omittere, quae generis eius artifices uel conseruandae uocis causa uel augendae factitarent.

Suetonius Ner. 20.1

Among the other subjects he studied as a boy, he was instructed in music, and as soon as he became emperor, he summoned Terpnus, the most eminent of the citharodes of that time. He listened to him singing late into the night after dinner for many successive days, he gradually began to study and practice himself, and to neglect none of the activities which artists are accustomed to repeat over and over again either to preserve their voice or to strengthen it.

The conservative Roman elites, suspicious of what they saw as Greek decadence and traditionally averse to the sight of Roman elites taking to the stage, were not appreciative of their emperor's lyre-playing and singing. Nero, therefore, according to the senatorial Tacitus, chose to perform in Naples:

C. Laecanio M. Licinio consulibus acriore in dies cupidine adigebatur Nero promiscas scaenas frequentandi. nam adhuc per domum aut hortos cecinerat Iuuenalibus ludis, quos ut parum celebres et tantae uoci angustos spernebat. non tamen Romae incipere ausus Neapolim quasi Graecam urbem delegit.

Tacitus Ann. 15.33

In the consulate of C. Laecanius and Marcus Licinius [64 CE] Nero was driven by a desire that grew sharper by the day of appearing on the public stage. To this point he had only sung in his palace or gardens at the Juvenile Games,

which he held in contempt for its small crowds and space
too cramped for a voice such as his. However, not daring
to debut at Rome, he chose Naples as being more or less a
Greek city.

Suetonius (*Ner.* 20.2–3) and Tacitus (*Ann.* 15.33.2–34.1) independently
give accounts of Nero's debut in Naples, where he sang frequently over
the course of some days. In the account of Tacitus (*Ann.* 15.34.1), he
even finished a concert as an earthquake, which miraculously harmed
no one, shook the theater—presumably an apocryphal detail.[7]

From what survives, we can see similarities between the styles and
effects of Nero's and Dylan's performances and audience receptions:
it is reasonable to conclude that the art of the citharode and that of
musical performers like Dylan show little difference in terms of the
complete aesthetics of performance. Suetonius reports that, speaking
in Greek instead of Latin, Nero promised the crowd that after having
something to drink, he would "ring out something really loud" (*aliquid
se sufferti tinniturum*).[8] Suetonius also recounts that the crowd, including
Greek sailors visiting from Alexandria, applauded rhythmically, as did
five thousand young Romans recruited to form a noisy crowd. The

---

[7]   See, again, Bolton (1948:84–87) for the possibility that the two treatments refer to
different occasions.

[8]   This line may also be translated as "something wild," if one reads *sufferi*, just as rare
as *sufferti* (alternative to *sufferciti*, p. part. of *suffercio*). The use of *sufferri* of some manuscripts makes no sense. Whatever Nero promised the crowd in Greek (*Graeco sermone*)
would have been striking, thus something strongly worded would be appropriate. This
detail is reminiscent of the evening of May 17, 1966, at a Dylan concert at the Free Trade
Hall, Manchester, England, in the course of a tumultuous European spring tour. Dylan had
been following the first acoustic half of each concert with an electric second half, backed
up by The Hawks (who became The Band in 1968). These second halves of the shows were
getting mixed reception from fans, many of whom had not followed Dylan's development since the Newport Folk Festival of the previous year, when he "went electric." They
yearned for a continuation of the previous year's solo, acoustic act. As may be seen from
footage of the concert on Martin Scorsese's 2005 documentary *No Direction Home*, right
before the final song, "Like a Rolling Stone," a fan shouts "Judas!" Dylan pauses, visibly
shaken, perhaps by the explicit antisemitism, perhaps because of the association of the
name. He replies, "I don't believe you ... you're a liar," before turning to guitarist Robbie
Robertson and commanding, "Play fucking loud!" The band proceeds to do so. Nero
would have like that moment.

Romans were taught these Alexandrian styles, enigmatically referred to as "buzzings," "rooftiles," and "bricks" (*Ner.* 20.3 *bombos et imbrices et testas*). Citharoedia may not have found approval with Roman elites, which may be paralleled—in the modern world to the way those of conservative musical tastes or political outlooks criticize the music, lifestyles, assumed moral outlooks of rock and pop musicians. But citharoedia was certainly the most popular and the most lucrative art form.[9] Entire cities all across the Mediterranean, for over the course of hundreds of years, would turn out to attend a citharode show.

Then there was the *appearance* of the citharode, which was as meticulous and as much part of the performance as his playing and singing. In the Metropolitan Museum of Art in New York, there is an exquisite masterpiece of Greek vase painting, an amphora from around 490 BCE attributed to the Berlin Painter, that depicts a young man playing a seven-stringed *kithara* (fig. 1).[10] He is dressed in an ornate cloak that flows down to his feet. His left hand is positioned behind the strings, poised to mute any of them as the tune required; his right holds the plectrum with which he would have struck the strings. He appears alone, his head is back, his mouth is open to show he is singing, and his gaze is turned upward to suggest intensity and even inspiration. From the lyre hangs a floor-length embroidered or patterned cloth, which would sway to the music, as would the floor-length cloak the musician wears. The contours of the cloth and the position of his feet suggest that he, too, is swaying to the music. On his head is a gold crown, indicating his victory in the song competition. This is the citharode, who took his art on the road, traveling around Greece from festival to festival, his appearance and performance transporting his audience. The entirety of his costume and instrument is known as his *skeuê* (complete outfit). As Power states:

---

[9] See Power 2010:1.3.1: "Citharodes far out-earned fellow musicians as well; winning citharists won a crown worth only 300 drachmas and a 200-drachma cash prize, while first-place winners in *aulos* singing, *aulôidia*, went home with a crown worth 300 drachmas, the same as the last-place citharode."

[10] Berlin Painter, attrib., terracotta amphora (jar), ca. 490 BCE, Metropolitan Museum of Art, New York, http://www.metmuseum.org/art/collection/search/254896.

Figure 1. Terracotta amphora, Greek, Attic, Red-figure, ca. 490 BCE, attributed to the Berlin Painter, Metropolitan Museum of Art, New York. Gift of Fletcher Fund, 56.171.38. Photograph © The Metropolitan Museum of Art.

The *skeuê* vividly marks the ritualized assumption of this larger-than-life persona in the moment of performance, symbolically mediating the transformation of the performer's identity from ordinary musician to extraordinary *kitharode*. Like the modern-day superhero who must change into costume in order to assume his powers, when the citharode put on his *skeuê* he became "another man," the musical magician capable of wonders.[11]

Similarly, while Dylan is not quite an actor, he embraced early on, in part because of his outfit and appearance, the self-identification of the nineteenth-century symbolist poet Arthur Rimbaud, "I is an other."[12] He assumes the character of Bob Dylan when he wants to or when he needs to: chiefly when he steps out on stage in performance. Any number of photographs show parallels with the transported citharode (fig. 2). One of the ways that this "other" establishes itself in concerts is by way of the costumes worn by Dylan and his band. Dylan's garb is always distinct from the others: a stripe of satin down the outer seam of his pants; cowboy boots of black, gold, or silver; polka-dotted shirts; turquoise bolero ties; myriad hats and jackets that do not quite belong in this world. His dress helps transport viewers into the timeless world of his songs. The world to which his clothes belong could be that of the 1930s Bluesman or 19th-century Vaudeville. Some even suggest the attire of a Civil War general. This last association finds powerful resonance in the video of the song "'Cross the Green Mountain" for the television show *Gods and Generals*. Here Dylan appears on horseback, attended by his band, reviewing the dead and dying of the war that was central to his exploration of America and American history.

The website of Dylan expert and collector Bill Pagel (www.boblinks.com) includes concert reviews posted by random members of the audience. These comments give us a record of audience response to the appearance of our modern-day citharode and his immaculate outfits. A sampling from Dylan's tour in late 2016 reveals the sense of visual

---

[11] Power 2010:1.3.3.
[12] Thomas 2017:151–152.

Figure 2. Bob Dylan, Portland, Maine, October 23, 2003. With thanks to Duncan Hume. Copyright © Duncan Hume.

wonder that Dylan, then 75-years-old, created, which recalls the specificity of antique textual and visual depictions of musicians:

> He's a slight fellow, sort of hunched over, in a black suit with gold trim down the arms and legs. He stands with his legs spread wide at the microphone, as though he's sitting on a fat, invisible horse. He plays with his hair some. (October 18)

> He had a hat, a grey suit, black shirt, silver bolo tie, and what appeared to be some snazzy two-tone wing tips. Half the show he donned his hat, but it was hats off when he tickled the ivories. (November 10)

> He was wearing a black suit, with wavy decorations on the legs and sleeves, a dark grey hat, a scarf, and black and white boots. I was in the cheap seats, so that's the best I can do. Hat came off only when Bob was seated at the piano. (November 12)

> He was wearing the gray suit with black piping and white hat. (November 22)[13]

The regularity of these impressions, along with the slight variation in detail, show that the entire effect of the outfit is a vital part of the performance, as it was for Nero in Naples or for the citharodes of Athens six hundred years earlier. We can imagine similar post-concert discussions among the Greek audiences of the visual aspects of their favorite citharodes.

There are more than ninety depictions of lyre-playing singers that survive from Greek art, mostly from the years following the production of the Berlin Painter's amphora.[14] This number far exceeds depictions of musicians with any other instruments from the period. That fact alone shows that what citharodes did mattered in fundamental ways to the broad musical, cultural, and social life of Athens and other Greek

---

[13] For the assembled reviews by date, see http://boblinks.com/dates34c.html.
[14] See the plates in Power 2010.

cities two and a half millennia ago. They sang to large audiences and in competitive festivals. Next to no lyrics survive, but we can get a sense of what they sang. One ancient source tells us they emulated the epic verse of Homer and the tunes of Orpheus. And their appeal was ultimately sexual in nature. Power, too, makes a connection between the worlds of instrumental soloists then and now:

> Beyond any divine and heroic resonances potentially evoked by his stage persona, the citharode, decked out in his stunning concert regalia, exudes a worldly sexual charisma—a powerful amalgam of visual glamour, the projection of technical wizardry, and the promise of overwhelming sensual mastery—which foreshadows that of the modern instrumental virtuoso, concert tenor, or pop star. Standing on the stage, with the eyes of thousands of festival-goers fixed on him, he is an object of wonder and desire, the larger-than-life embodiment of popular acclaim, of wealth and success, of awesome artistic accomplishment. It seems safe to say that no other type of musical or verbal performer in Greek or Roman antiquity ... had exerted such consistently powerful sway over the mass libidinal imagination.[15]

Among modern-day citharodes, one could include solo Bluesmen, starting with Robert Johnson (1911–1938), originator of the Delta Blues. He would be dead at age 27, but his guitar-playing, songwriting, and performances would be inspirational for Dylan, as they were for Keith Richards and Eric Clapton. Many contemporary musicians discovered the now-legendary Johnson after Columbia Records' 1961 release of *King of the Delta Blues Singers*, a profoundly influential collection of his recordings. Dylan, Richards, and Clapton all learned much about the electric blues from Johnson, which is a central component of their art.

Dylan's engagement with the citharodic tradition may well have been unconscious during the early years of his career. Recently, however, he has begun to use citharodic symbolism deliberately. The

---

[15] Power 2010:1.6–7.

god of the citharode was Apollo, himself the divine lyre player. In Athens Apollo was joined by Pallas Athena, patron goddess of that city and of the arts in general. In the Museum of Fine Arts in Boston, a Greek amphora of the 5th century BC depicts Apollo playing the lyre, attended by Athena holding a spear. This scene recalls the musical performance at the Panathenaic Festival. Dylan seems to have made the connection. The cover of his 2012 album *Tempest* depicts a river goddess from the statue group of the Pallas Athena/Minerva fountain outside the Parliament Building in Vienna—a placement meant to suggest a connection between the Austrian and Athenian democracies. The river goddess and, by association, Minerva herself have also become part of the staging for Dylan's concert. He added what appears to be a bust of the self-same river goddess, now generally referred to by fans as Minerva, to the Oscar statuette (for the song "Things Have Changed" from *Wonder Boys*) that is welded to his amplifier. Athena is also, of course, the patron goddess of the hero Odysseus, whose words, in Robert Fagles's translation, Dylan has appropriated for a number of the songs on the 2012 album.[16] So, for the last few years, our modern citharode, who has, through the intertextuality of his songwriting, become Odysseus, has been performing in the presence of a cult statue of his and Odysseus's patron, Minerva. Time to turn to Homer and the rhapsodes.

II. DYLAN AND THE RHAPSODE

The surviving images of citharodes, along with ancient texts that describe their performances, are enough to show that such performers, with their singing and playing stringed instruments, brought pleasures worth remembering. What was recorded on the Metropolitan vase—the open mouth of the singer, his stance, his elaborate dress, and not least his instrument—gives a glimmer of this pleasure. But what did the citharodes sing? Probably a variety of themes and a rich range of Homer that they likely put into their own melodic form. If so, they would have been in the company of rhapsodes (song-stitchers), another

---

[16] See Thomas 2017:254–265, for the chapter "Dylan Becomes Odysseus."

distinct group of performers, who, also in competitive settings, played a large role in the survival of the Homeric epics.

These rhapsodes performed throughout Greece from the 6th or 5th century BCE and for the centuries that followed. They too had an identifiable *skeuê*—showy, sometimes including the lyre, and later with a staff and cloak—when they came to recite episodes from Homer. They performed at various festivals, most importantly at the great Panathenaic Festival. Indeed, these recitals may even have been part of the process by which the *Iliad* and *Odyssey*, as we have them today, came to be set down in writing.[17] M. L. West notes the rhapsode was "evidently less of a musician than the citharode," and on the evidence of Plato's *Ion* was "noted for histrionic rather than musicianly qualities."[18]

Whether he realized it or not at first, Dylan and his art belong to a tradition of musical storytelling that is as old as anything we have. From the oral song and storytelling traditions that, once they were written down, gave the world its foundational texts—the *Iliad* and *Odyssey* of Homer and the lyric poems of Sappho and her contemporaries—we see that song is part of the fabric of storytelling, and storytelling is what song is. Poetry grows out of song and always has.

What Dylan did know from the beginning was the ballad, the closest song gets to epic. In October 1962, at the Gaslight Café, he sang a pure and melodious eight-minute version of "Barbara Allen," a song mentioned in the diary of Samuel Pepys on January 2, 1666, and much older in the oral tradition. By then he had already written his own ballads, "Ballad of Donald White" and "The Death of Emmet Till" (1962). "Ballad of Hollis Brown" (1962) would soon follow, and the ballad has been with him ever since, with a number of the songs from *Tempest* (2012) qualifying for that classification, including the title song on the sinking of the Titanic and especially "Tin Angel" and "Scarlet Town," two of the darker songs of the album. Some versions of "Barbara Allen," like the song on *Tempest*, begin "In Scarlet Town ..."—though at the Gaslight he began "In Charlotte town ..." Well before *Tempest* Dylan

---

[17] See Nagy 2008.
[18] West 1981:114.

had been writing his own ballads, with fragments of the old traditional forms, but with his own songwriting creating new versions.

Bob Dylan indeed seems to have recognized the connections between his own techniques and Homeric storytelling some years before he started introducing the words of Fagles's translation of the *Odyssey* into his song lyrics. In an interview with Paul Zollo for the magazine *Song Talk* in November 1991, Dylan was asked about his new song "Joey," the 11-minute song on the life and violent death of mafioso Joseph "Crazy Joe" Gallo (1929–1972):

> It's in its infant stages, as a performance thing. Of course, it's a long song. But to me, not to blow my own horn, but to me the song is like a Homer ballad ... to me, "Joey" has a Homeric quality that you don't hear every day. Especially in popular music.[19]

By then, Dylan had performed the song in concert over 40 times. It is notable that he himself saw this song, which heroizes the mobster quite outrageously, as having a "Homeric quality." In the popular imagination, citharodes and rhapsodes perpetuated tales of heroism so as to occupy a similar space. As solo musicians they work in similar traditions and can therefore, like Bob Dylan, be associated with ballads and storytelling in ways that at the heart of how heroic deeds are passed on through the ages.

III. DYLAN AND HOMER

Song and singing, and what loosely qualify as proto-ballads, are even embedded into the narrative of Homer. Sometimes we find extended song, as in the central books of the *Odyssey*. Elsewhere we just get a glimpse of song, more or less titles, for instance in the ninth book of Homer's *Iliad*. Achilles has withdrawn from the battle after the quarrel with Agamemnon. When the embassy visits him, he is in his tent, nursing his anger, singing and playing the lyre, which he learned as a boy from his tutor, Chiron the Centaur. In the Naples Archaeological

---

[19] Dylan 1991.

Museum, a wall painting of the two of them shows Achilles holding his lyre like any citharode, as he stands beside his hybrid teacher. In *Iliad* 9 we see the fruits of that training:

> Μυρμιδόνων δ' ἐπί τε κλισίας καὶ νῆας ἱκέσθην,
> τὸν δ' εὗρον φρένα τερπόμενον φόρμιγγι λιγείῃ
> καλῇ δαιδαλέῃ, ἐπὶ δ' ἀργύρεον ζυγὸν ἦεν,
> τὴν ἄρετ' ἐξ ἐνάρων πόλιν Ἠετίωνος ὀλέσσας·
> τῇ ὅ γε θυμὸν ἔτερπεν, ἄειδε δ' ἄρα κλέα ἀνδρῶν.
> Πάτροκλος δέ οἱ οἶος ἐναντίος ἧστο σιωπῇ,
> δέγμενος Αἰακίδην ὁπότε λήξειεν ἀείδων

Homer *Iliad* 9.185–191

And so they came to the shelters and ships of the Myrmidons
and found him delighting his heart in a pure-toned lyre,
exquisitely wrought, with a bridge of silver upon it,
which he won from spoils when he laid waste the city of Eëtion.
With this he was delighting his spirit and singing of the glorious
    deeds of men.
Patroclus by himself was sitting opposite in silence,
watchfully awaiting Achilles, for when he would break off his
    singing.

Achilles, the greatest of the Greek warriors at Troy, was also a musician, and here he uses music to soothe his anger. Achilles's instrument is "exquisitely wrought" (καλῇ δαιδαλέῃ) and has a strong effect on the singer: he "delights his heart" (φρένα τερπόμενον) in the "pure-toned" lyre (φόρμιγγι λιγείῃ) and "delighted his spirit" (θυμὸν ἔτερπεν) in the song. He keeps the riveted attention of his audience of one, Patroclus, who "sits opposite in silence" (ἐναντίος ἧστο σιωπῇ). The delight that song brings and the appearance of the lyre are as much part of the culture of Achilles the cithara-singer as of the later citharodes we have seen and of Dylan, the singer and guitar-player.

It is clear from the Homeric pages that Patroclus and Achilles have a long and intimate relationship centered, in part, on shared song. With its focus on the role of music and song in creating shared human experience, friendship, and memory, Homer's depiction of the men's friendship is not so different from the room recreated in "Bob Dylan's Dream," a song Dylan wrote at the age of 21, remembering school friends from a few utterly transforming years before:

> With half-damp eyes I stared to the room
> where my friends and I spent many an afternoon
> where we together weathered many a storm
> laughin' and singin' in the early hours of the morn.
>
> By the old wooden stove where our hats was hung
> Our words were told, our songs were sung ...

Dylan gives a compelling account of the sort of friendship through song that he found when he left Hibbing for the University of Minnesota in the summer of 1959. After trading in his electric guitar for an acoustic, he began to frequent the Beat coffee houses of Dinkytown, where he played and sang with various like-minded musicians:

> I was looking for players with kindred pursuits. The first guy I met in Minneapolis like me was sitting around in there. It was John Koerner and he also had an acoustic guitar with him. Koerner was tall and thin with a look of perpetual amusement on his face. We hit it off right away.[20]

The memory constructed in "Bob Dylan's Dream" is part reality, part traditional song. He wrote it in London in 1962, having heard English folksinger Martin Carthy sing a version of the traditional "Lady Franklin's Lament." Clinton Heylin is surely right to connect the lyrics of the song to the "nostalgia Dylan was feeling for the North Country, 5000 miles away."[21]

The song Achilles sings to his friend is "of the glorious deeds of men," itself an *Iliad* in miniature. The song was no laughing matter but had deadly connections to the broader context of the poem. Glory is what Achilles chooses in this poem, staying in the battle and so sealing his

---

[20] Dylan 2004:237–238.
[21] Heylin 2009:124.

fate, doomed to die young with unfading glory rather than leaving the battle and returning home to a peaceful old age, without glory. Almost inevitably, song about glory is song that commemorates death in battle. The embassy of Greeks fails and eventually Patroclus puts on the armor of his friend, with consequences that take up the rest of the poem. Did the song to which he silently listened in Achilles's tent inspire him to a course of action that would end his life? Is that what such music does?

All Homer gives us is the title of Achilles' song, "The Glorious Deeds of Men." We do not have to look far for those in the folk tradition. Fast forward to another ballad, "The Ballad of the Green Berets," by Marine Staff Sergeant Barry Sadler, a 1966 song valorizing the elite special forces of the U.S. Army. The ballad is written to the tune of "The Butcher Boy," the English folk song in the voice of a girl who hangs herself after being seduced by the butcher's boy. Regardless of the message, the tune was very singable and was #1 on the Billboard Hot 100 for five weeks. The ballad was meant to do what the song of Achilles did, in this case promote fighting in Vietnam. The last request in Sadler's song is addressed by the dead warrior to his war-widow: "Put silver wings on my son's chest / Make him one of America's best / He'll be a man they'll test some day / Make him win the Green Beret." Ultimately Sadler's song belongs in a long tradition of ballads, many collected in volume 3 of Francis James Child's *The English and Scottish Popular Ballads* (1888–1889), with titles like "Durham Field," "Flodden Field," "Musselburgh Field," and "The Rising in the North." Whatever Achilles sang in his tent, it belongs in this tradition. As Dylan said of another aspect of his artistic style, "It's an old thing—it's part of a tradition. It goes way back."[22]

IV. A TALE OF TWO ADULTERIES:
"ARES AND APHRODITE," AND "TIN ANGEL"

In a section of *Why Bob Dylan Matters*, I traced the ways in which the narrator of a number of songs on the album *Tempest*, through precise appropriation of the words of Odysseus from Fagles's translation of the *Odyssey*, essentially *becomes* Odysseus, a process which Dylan allusively

---

[22] Gilmore 2012.

confirmed in his Nobel Prize lecture of 2016. In a section of the lecture detailing the travails of Odysseus in the *Odyssey*, Dylan makes a transition from the experiences of the epic hero to those of an unspecified "you," a figure who is obviously Dylan himself:

> He's been gone twenty years. He was carried off somewhere and left there. Drugs have been dropped into his wine. It's been a hard road to travel. In a lot of ways, some of these same things have happened to you. You too have had drugs dropped into your wine. You too have shared a bed with the wrong woman.[23]

In *Odyssey* 8–9, between the Greek hero's speech to the Phaeacian princes and his taunt of the Cyclops (Dylan lifts from both),— Demodocus sings another song that Dylan assimilated into his own ballad. In the translation of Fagles that Dylan had been reading as he wrote the songs on the 2012 album, the episode is titled, "The Love of Ares and Aphrodite Crowned with Flowers" (*Od.* 8.267).[24] The song is in effect an ancient version of a ballad, a tale of adultery between the god of war and goddess of love, "how the two first made love in Hephaestus' mansion" (303) while the lame, misshaped husband, Hephaestus, was away. The sun god reveals the affair to Hephaestus, who goes to his workshop and, through his skill as fire god and master of metalworking, devises a fine set of chains designed to trap the adulterous pair the next time they cheat on him. Hephaestus pretends to go off on a trip to the island of Lemnos, at which point Ares enters the "famous god of fire's mansion" (326) and professes his love. The pair proceed to make love, at which point down around them come "those cunning chains of the god of fire." Hephaestus arrives, bewails the situation, complains to Zeus, and the other gods come to observe the spectacle. The ballad now turns humorous, in effect becoming a comedy, with Apollo and Hermes (Mercury) cracking salty jokes, Poseidon pledging to stand surety for the fine Ares is to pay, and Ares and Aphrodite going off with some embarrassment to their separate cult places in Thrace and Cyprus respectively.

[23] Dylan 2017.
[24] All translations are from Fagles 1996.

The song of Demodocus clocks in at 110 lines in Fagles's translation. Dylan allots 112 lines to his dark adultery ballad "Tin Angel," the
song that follows "Early Roman Kings," one of the most Odyssean songs
on *Tempest*. "Tin Angel" begins with the same opening line as Woody
Guthrie's "Gypsy Davy"—"It was late last night when the boss came
home"—a song about a lady who runs off with guitar-playing Gypsy
Davy, of which Dylan did a version in the folk covers album of 1992, *Good
As I Been to You*. But the second line of "Tin Angel" parts company with
the folk song with the words, "to a deserted mansion," which may send
us more in the direction of Hephaestus's "mansion." There is only one
substantial phrasal "theft" from the song, where Odysseus's "You're
a reckless fool—I see *that*" (*Od.* 8.192) is rhythmically and metrically
capped by the wife's opening address to the boss: "You're a reckless
fool, I can see it in your eyes." This is one of many thefts from Fagles on
the album.

The early verses of Dylan's song build up in sinister ways, as the
cuckolded boss, "with all the nobility of an ancient race," catches
sight of the adulterous couple: "Peered through the darkness, caught
a glimpse of the two / It was hard to tell for certain who was who."
The moment is similar to when, in the *Odyssey*, Helios the sun god tells
Hephaestus that he "spied the couple / lost in each other's arms and
making love" (*Od.* 8.307–308). While Hephaestus is away, Ares "strode
right in / and grasped her hand" (329–330), while the seducer of
Dylan's song, Henry Lee, "came riding through the woods and took her
by the hand." Just as chains were central to the Homeric passage ("and
down around then came those cunning chains," *Od.* 8.337), so they are
in "Tin Angel" but now put to different use by the boss as he discovers
the two: "He lowered himself down on a golden chain." The lovers in
the song become "one single unit inseparably linked," an updated
version of Hephaestus's complaint that Ares and his wife are "locked in
each other's arms," although they will soon held by other links: "then
my cunning chains will bind them fast." For Hephaestus, the pledge
of the adulterer Ares is of no value: "A pledge for a worthless man is a
worthless pledge indeed" (*Od.* 8.394). The statement finds an echo in
the words of the wronged husband in Dylan's song: "He's a gutless ape
with worthless mind." This last phrase is also a conflation of *Od.* 8.205,

when Odysseus refers to one of the contestants who insulted him: "but the mind inside is worthless."[25]

As in Homer, so in "Tin Angel," narrative is succeeded by dialogue, but tone, action, and outcome are switched from Homeric comedy to tragedy in Dylan's song. In the last third of the ballad, over nine verses, lover shoots husband, wife stabs lover, and then stabs herself, with the Shakespearean ending as dark as it gets: "All three lovers together in a heap / Thrown in the grave forever to sleep."[26] Nothing could be further from the final sunlit vision of Aphrodite, bathed and anointed by the Graces.

In "Tin Angel" Dylan pursues a type of intertextuality somewhat different from that found in other songs on this and his other recent albums. The "Love of Ares and Aphrodite" ballad sung by Demodocus is a digression from the action of *Odyssey* 8, in which Odysseus obviously plays no role. The song is loosely and thematically connected to the Homeric lines: the model is visible but does not intrude itself into a song that blends the Homeric and the Shakespearean and is rooted, as always, in the folk tradition that is evoked by its opening line. Those are the various literary ingredients that go into the composition of the song.

In closing I return to Rome, the city that has most fired the imagination of Dylan across the decades, ever since he took Latin in school and joined the Latin Club of Hibbing High School, helping it pay tribute to the Ides of March of 1957. He responded not so much to the decadent Rome of the citharode Nero but rather to the century before, when a cultural revolution was coinciding with the breakup of the republic. As he himself sang in an unpublished, unrecorded song in early 1963, written during his first visit to Rome and now available on the bootleg "Banjo Tape": "I'm going back to Rome / That's where I was born." So he was, in his artistic imagination, although he took his first breaths on the Mesabi Iron Range of northern Minnesota. Across the years the Eternal City would stay with him and enter a number of his songs.

[25] Thomas 2017:259.

[26] For the Shakespearean aspects of this story (including echoes of the woman and her two lovers/husbands in *Romeo and Juliet* and *Hamlet*), see Daniel 2017:68–69; Muir 2019:287, 289–290.

Then, Virgil in 2001 and Ovid in 2006, two of the poets who have been so well served by the scholarship of our honorand, became intertexts of the songs that Dylan has been creating in the 21st century.[27]

But the origins of Dylan's art and his craft belong most squarely in archaic Greece in the figure of the citharode. In becoming Odysseus, it is to Greece that he returned in his penultimate album, *Tempest*, and he has stayed there in the new 2020 album, *Rough and Rowdy Ways*. Citharodes and rhapsodes, blind bards and Bob Dylan, are all part of a song tradition whose connections lie beneath the surface in oral and folk traditions at some times and emerge explicitly at others. Dylan did not realize it in the very beginning, when, like the rhapsode, he mostly sang the songs of others in the folk tradition. "I can't say when it occurred to me to write my own songs," he wrote in *Chronicles*.[28] As a modern-day citharode or guitar-singer, he started to write and sing his own songs. When he did so, Dylan transformed a genre and an art as radically as did the transcribers of the Homeric epics. But, as radical as Dylan is, his music is also tied inextricably to the oldest literary traditions we have—not just through lyric allusions to Greek epic and Roman history but through the very form of his ancient craft.

HARVARD UNIVERSITY

WORKS CITED

Bolton. J. D. P. 1948. "Was the Neronia a Freak Festival?" *CQ* 42: 82–90.
Bradley, K. R. 1978. *Suetonius' Life of Nero: An Historical Commentary*. Collection Latomus 157. Brussels.
Child, F. J. 1889. *The English and Scottish Popular Ballads*. Vol. 3. Boston.
Daniel, A. M. 2017. "*Tempest*, Bob Dylan, and the Bardic Arts." In *Tearing the World Apart: Bob Dylan and the Twenty-First Century*, ed. N. Goss and E. Hoffman, 63–72. Jackson.
Dylan, B. 1991. Interview by Paul Zollo. *Song Talk*. November 1991.
———. 2004. *Chronicles*. Vol. 1. New York.
———. 2017. *The Nobel Lecture*. New York.

---

[27] For an account of this process, see Thomas 2017, esp. chapters 3, 7, 8.
[28] Dylan 2004: vol. 1, 51.

———. "Bob Dylan's Dream." Copyright © 1963, 1964, Warner Bros. Inc.; renewed 1991, 1992, Special Rider Music.

———. "Tin Angel." Copyright © 2012, Special Rider Music.

Fagles, R., trans. 1996. *Homer. The Odyssey.* New York.

Gilmore, M. 2012. "Dylan Unleashed." *Rolling Stone.* September 27, 2012. http://www.rollingstone.com/music/news/bob-dylan-unleashed-a-wild-ride-on-his-new-lp-and-striking-back-at-critics-20120927.

Griffin, M. 1984. *Nero: The End of a Dynasty.* London.

Gyles, M. F. 1962. "Nero: Qualis Artifex?" *CJ* 57:193–200.

Heylin, C. 2009. *Revolution in the Air: The Songs of Bob Dylan, 1957–1973.* Chicago.

Kay, N. M., ed. 2006. *Epigrams from the Anthologia Latina: Text, Translation, and Commentary.* London.

Muir, A. 2019. *Bob Dylan and William Shakespeare: The True Performing Of It.* Penryn, Cornwall.

Nagy, G. 2008. *Homer the Classic.* Hellenic Studies Series 36. Washington, DC.

Recreate Magazine. 2016. "Bob Dylan—Simple Twist of Fate, Las Vegas 10–13–16." YouTube video, 2:44, October 15, 2016. https://www.youtube.com/watch?v=c8PD3TfB7As.

Riese, A., F. Buecheler, and E. Lommatzsch, eds. 1869–1926. *Anthologia Latina.* Leipzig.

Russell, D. A., trans. 2002. *Quintilian. The Orator's Education.* Vol. 1, Books 1–2. Loeb Classical Library 124. Cambridge, MA.

Pagel, B. "Bob Dylan 2016 Tour Guide." Bob Links. www.boblinks.com.

Power, T. 2010. *The Culture of Kitharôidia.* Hellenic Studies Series 15. Washington, DC. http://nrs.harvard.edu/urn-3:hul.ebook:CHS_Power.The_Culture_of_Kitharoidia.2010. (References in text are to section numbers of the online book.)

Thomas, R. F. 2007. "The Streets of Rome: The Classical Dylan." In *The Performance Artistry of Bob Dylan, Oral Tradition,* ed. C. Mason and R. F. Thomas. Project Muse. *Center for Studies in Oral Tradition* 22(1): 30–56. http://muse.jhu.edu/article/224286/pdf.

———. 2017. *Why Bob Dylan Matters.* New York.

West, M. L. 1981. "The Singing of Homer and the Modes of Early Greek Music." *JHS* 81:113–129.

CONTRIBUTORS

Rebecca R. Benefiel (Ph.D. Harvard) is Professor of Classics at Washington & Lee University, where she teaches Latin literature and Roman archaeology. She has published numerous articles focusing on Latin epigraphy and Roman social history and has been interviewed on NPR and National Geographic, and in *Smithsonian Magazine, Forbes,* and *The Atlantic.* She co-edited the volume *Inscriptions in the Private Sphere in the Roman World* (Brill 2016) and is Director of the Ancient Graffiti Project (http://ancientgraffiti.org). She is currently President of the American Society of Greek and Latin Epigraphy.

Kathleen M. Coleman is the James Loeb Professor of the Classics at Harvard University. Her major works comprise editions, with translation and commentary, of Statius, *Siluae* IV and Martial, *Liber spectaculorum,* both for Oxford University Press, and an extensive series of articles on Roman spectacle and punishment.

Frank T. Coulson is Arts and Humanities Distinguished Professor of Classics at the Ohio State University where he serves as Director of Palaeography for its Center for Epigraphical and Palaeographical Studies. He is co-editor of the volume *Ovid in the Middle Ages* (Cambridge, 2011). His edition of Books 1–5 of the Vulgate Commentary on the *Metamorphoses* (co-authored with Pierandrea Martina) is forthcoming from Garnier.

Lauren Curtis is Associate Professor of Classics at Bard College. She works on Roman poetry, especially its relationship with ancient musical and literary culture. She is the author of *Imagining the Chorus in Augustan Poetry* (CUP, 2017) and is currently working on a commentary of Ovid, *Tristia* 3 for Cambridge Greek and Latin Classics.

Cynthia Damon is a Professor of Classical Studies at the University of Pennsylvania. She is the author of *The Mask of the Parasite: A Pathology of Roman Patronage* (1997), a commentary on Tacitus, *Histories* 1 (2003), a translation of Tacitus' *Annals* in the Penguin series (2013), and, with William Batstone, *Caesar's Civil War* (2006). She recently published an OCT of Caesar's *Bellum civile*, a companion volume on the text of the *Bellum civile* (2015), a new Loeb edition of Caesar's *Civil War* (2016), and a variorum commentary on Tacitus' *Agricola* (2017: http://dcc.dickinson.edu/tacitus-agricola/preface). She is currently preparing a pilot edition of the *Bellum Alexandrinum* for the Library of Digital Latin Texts, a new Loeb edition of Caesar's *Gallic War*, and a how-to book on the Elder Pliny entitled *How to Wonder*.

Thomas E. Jenkins is Professor of Classical Studies at Trinity University in San Antonio, TX, and the Director of its Collaborative for Learning and Teaching. He is the author most recently of *Antiquity Now: The Classical World in the Contemporary American Imagination* (Cambridge, 2015) and "The Reception of Hesiod in the 20th and 21st Centuries," in the *Oxford Handbook of Hesiod* (Oxford, 2018, ed. Loney and Scully). He is also an occasional theater critic for the *San Antonio Current*.

Stephen Heyworth is Professor of Latin at the University of Oxford, Bowra Fellow and Tutor in Classics at Wadham College. He works on Latin poetry from Catullus to Seneca, and the transmission and editing of ancient texts. He produced the Oxford Classical Text of Propertius, together with a companion volume *Cynthia* (both OUP 2007), and has published commentaries on Propertius 3 (OUP 2011), Vergil *Aeneid* 3 (OUP 2017), both with James Morwood, and Ovid *Fasti* 3 (CUP 2019). His current major project is an OCT of the whole of Ovid's *Fasti*.

Alison Keith is Professor of Classics and Director of the Jackman Humanities Institute at the University of Toronto. She has published widely on gender and genre in Latin literature and Roman society, and is the author most recently of a volume on *Virgil* in the Understanding Classics series published by Bloomsbury Academic.

James Ker is Associate Professor of Classical Studies at the University of Pennsylvania. He has published books and articles on Latin literature and Roman cultural history, including *The Deaths of Seneca* (2009).

Michèle Lowrie, Andrew W. Mellon Distinguished Service Professor of Classics and the College, University of Chicago. Author of *Horace's Narrative Odes* (Oxford 1997), *Writing, Performance, and Authority in Augustan Rome* (Oxford 2009), *Oxford Studies: Readings in Horace's Odes and Epodes* (Oxford 2009), "Roman Law and Latin Literature" in the *Oxford Handbook of Roman Law and Society* (2016), and "Political Thought" in the forthcoming *Cambridge Critical Guide to Latin Literature.*

Jeanne Neumann is Professor of Classics at Davidson College. She is a leading expert in Latin pedagogy for which work she has received the Hunter-Hamilton Teaching Award (2005), the CAMWS Award for Excellence in College Teaching (2018), and the SCS's Award for Excellence in Teaching of the Classics at the College Level (2019). She is the author of *Lingua Latina: A Companion to Familia Romana* (2008, 2nd edition 2016) and *Lingua Latina: A Companion to Roma Aeterna* (2017).

Irene Peirano Garrison is Professor of Classics at Yale University. She works on Roman poetry and its relation to rhetoric and literary criticism, both ancient and modern. She is the author of *The Rhetoric of the Roman Fake: Latin Pseudepigrapha in Context* (CUP, 2012) and *Persuasion, Rhetoric and Roman Poetry* (CUP, 2019).

Michael Reeve, F. B. A. since 1984 and a foreign member of academies in Germany and Italy, is an emeritus fellow of Exeter College Oxford, where he was a tutorial fellow and university lecturer from 1966 to 1984, and of Pembroke College Cambridge, where he was a professorial fellow from 1984 to 2007 by virtue of holding the Kennedy Chair of Latin. A bibliography up to 2015 can be found in Richard Hunter and S. P. Oakley, eds, *Latin Literature and Its Transmission* (Cambridge 2016), 322–338.

Gianpiero Rosati is Professor of Latin Literature at the Scuola Normale Superiore (Pisa), where he is currently Dean of the Faculty of Humanities. He has worked on Augustan poetry, in particular on Ovid (with essays, editions and commentaries), the literature of the Neronian and Flavian ages (Seneca, Statius, Martial), and Latin narrative (Petronius, Apuleius). He is currently working on a project on the interaction between poetry, material culture and visual arts in the Flavian age.

Richard F. Thomas is George Martin Lane Professor of the Classics at Harvard University. His teaching and research interests are focused on Hellenistic Greek and Roman literature, intertextuality, translation, the reception of classical literature, and the lyrics of Bob Dylan. Publications include: *Lands and Peoples in Roman Poetry* (1982), *Reading Virgil and his Texts. Studies in Intertextuality* (1999), *Virgil and the Augustan Reception* (2001); commentaries on Virgil, *Georgics* (1988) and Horace, *Odes* 4 and *Carmen Saeculare* (2011); the co-edited *Classics and the Uses of Reception*(2006), *Bob Dylan's Performance Artistry* (2007), and the *Virgil Encyclopedia* (2014), and *Why Dylan Matters* (2017).

Gareth D. Williams is Professor of Classics at Columbia University and has published books on Ovid and Seneca and, most recently, *Pietro Bembo on Etna: The Ascent of a Venetian Humanist* (Oxford University Press 2017).